Innovation and the Future of Rural Development in Europe

Dominique Barjolle · Paweł Chmieliński ·
David Miller
Editors

Innovation and the Future of Rural Development in Europe

Understanding the Science-Society-Policy Interface from a Local and Regional Perspective

palgrave
macmillan

Editors
Dominique Barjolle
Institut Für Agrarwissenschaften
ETH Zürich
Zürich, Switzerland

Paweł Chmieliński
Institute of Rural and Agricultural Development, Polish Academy of Sciences
Warsaw, Poland

David Miller
James Hutton Institute
Aberdeen, Scotland, UK

ISBN 978-3-032-22569-6 ISBN 978-3-032-22570-2 (eBook)
https://doi.org/10.1007/978-3-032-22570-2

This Palgrave Macmillan imprint is published by the registered company Springer Nature Switzerland AG
The registered company address is: Gewerbestrasse 11, 6330 Cham, Switzerland

Contents

List of Contributors

Tarek Allali Department of Agriculture, Food and Environment, University of Pisa, Pisa, Italy

Dominique Barjolle Institut Für Agrarwissenschaften, ETH Zürich, Zürich, Switzerland

Tristan Berchoux TETIS, University of Montpellier, Montpellier, France;
Mediterranean Agronomic Institute of Montpellier (CIHEAM-IAMM), Montpellier, France

Ioan-Sebastian Brumă Institute of Agricultural Economics—Romanian Academy, Bucharest, Romania;
Gheorghe Zane Institute for Economic and Social Research, Romanian Academy, Iasi Branch, Iaşi, Romania

Gianluca Brunori Department of Agriculture, Food and Environment, University of Pisa, Pisa, Italy

Fabienne Buchmann Institute of Natural Resource Sciences, Zurich University of Applied Sciences, Zurich, Switzerland

Lorena Florentina Chiţea Institute of Agricultural Economics—Romanian Academy, Bucharest, Romania

Mihai Alexandru Chiţea Institute of Agricultural Economics—Romanian Academy, Bucharest, Romania

Paweł Chmieliński Institute of Rural and Agricultural Development, Polish Academy of Sciences, and European Rural Development Network, Warsaw, Poland

Manola Colabianchi Department of Agriculture, Food and Environment, University of Pisa, Pisa, Italy

Emil Erjavec Biotechnical Faculty, University of Ljubljana, Ljubljana, Slovenia

Catarina Esgalhado Mediterranean Institute for Agriculture, Évora, Portugal

Francesco Felici Department of Agriculture, Food and Environment, University of Pisa, Pisa, Italy

Samuel Féret Institute for Climate Economics (I4CE), Paris, France

María Amparo Ferreira-Golpe University of Santiago de Compostela, Escola Politécnica Superior, Lugo, Spain

Carmen Forrer ZHAW, Lausanne, Switzerland

Ana Isabel García-Arias University of Santiago de Compostela, CISPAC, Escola Politécnica Superior, Lugo, Spain

Živilė Gedminaitė-Raudonė Lithuanian Centre for Social Sciences, Institute of Economics and Rural Development, Vilnius, Lithuania

Katarzyna Gizińska Institute of Economics and Rural Development, Lithuanian Centre for Social Sciences, Vilnius, Lithuania, and European Rural Development Network, Warsaw, Poland

Roman Grüter Institute of Natural Resource Sciences, Zurich University of Applied Sciences, Zurich, Switzerland

Beatriz Guimarey-Fernández University of Santiago de Compostela, Escola Politécnica Superior, Lugo, Spain

Isabel Jaisli Institute of Natural Resource Sciences, Zurich University of Applied Sciences, Zurich, Switzerland

Aurélie Kirsch Mediterranean Agronomic Institute of Montpellier (CIHEAM-IAMM), Montpellier, France

Idan Kopler European Wing Unit, MIGAL Galilee Research Institute, Kiryat Shmona, Israel

Agnieszka Kurdyś-Kujawska Faculty of Economics, Koszalin University of Technology, Koszalin, Poland, and European Rural Development Network, Warsaw, Poland

Rita Lankauskienė Lithuanian Centre for Social Sciences, Institute of Economics and Rural Development, Vilnius, Lithuania

Edelmiro López-Iglesias University of Santiago de Compostela, Facultade de Ciencias Económicas e Empresariais, Santiago de Compostela, Spain

Uri Marchaim European Wing Unit, MIGAL Galilee Research Institute, Kiryat Shmona, Israel

Chiara Mignani Department of Agriculture, Food and Environment, University of Pisa, Pisa, Italy

David Miller The James Hutton Institute, Aberdeen, Scotland, UK

Olivier Mora INRAe, Paris, France

Michele Moretti Department of Agriculture, Food and Environment, University of Pisa, Pisa, Italy;
Department of Engineering Management, University of Antwerp, Antwerp, Belgium

Claudiu Cătălin Munteanu Institute of Agricultural Economics—Romanian Academy, Bucharest, Romania

Marie Noëlle Ottavi INRAe, Paris, France

Emilia Pellegrini Department of Agriculture and Food Sciences, University of Bologna, Bologna, Italy

Mar Pérez-Fra Institute for Research in Global Health and Sustainable Development, iTERRA, University of Santiago de Compostela, Campus Terra, Lugo, Spain

Eugenia Petropolou Department of Sociology, University of Crete, Greece, Greece

Teresa Pinto-Correia MED–Mediterranean Institute for Agriculture, Environment and Development CHANGE–Global Change and

Sustainability Institute Departamento de Paisagem Ambiente e Ordenamento, Escola de Ciências e Tecnologia, Universidade de Évora, Évora, Portugal

Cristian Gheorghe Popescu Institute of Agricultural Economics—Romanian Academy, Bucharest, Romania;
National University of Science and Technology Politehnica, Bucharest, Romania;
Pitești University Centre, Pitești, Romania

Ilona Rac Biotechnical Faculty, University of Ljubljana, Ljubljana, Slovenia

Meri Raggi Department of Statistical Sciences, University of Bologna, Bologna, Italy

Elisabeta Ștefania Roșu Institute of Agricultural Economics—Romanian Academy, Bucharest, Romania

Emilia Schmitt ZHAW, Lausanne, Switzerland

Jean-Michel Sorba INRAe, Corsica, France

Loredana Sorg Biovision, Zürich, Switzerland

Borut Stojilković Ministry of Higher Education, Science and Innovation, Ljubljana, Slovenia

Lucian Tanasă Institute of Agricultural Economics—Romanian Academy, Bucharest, Romania;
Gheorghe Zane Institute for Economic and Social Research, Romanian Academy, Iasi Branch, Iași, Romania

Stefano Targetti Department of Agriculture and Food Sciences, University of Bologna, Bologna, Italy

Sabrina Tomasi Department of Agriculture, Food and Environment, University of Pisa, Pisa, Italy

Sofia Triliva Department of Psychology, University of Crete, Greece, Greece

Monica Mihaela Tudor Institute of Agricultural Economics—Romanian Academy, Bucharest, Romania;

Research Institute for Agricultural Economics and Rural Development, Bucharest, Romania

Davide Viaggi Department of Agriculture and Food Sciences, University of Bologna, Bologna, Italy

Andreas Vavvos Department of Psychology, University of Crete and Department of Social Anthropology, University of Saint Andrews, St Andrews, Great Britain

Barbara Wieliczko Institute of Rural and Agricultural Development, Polish Academy of Sciences, and European Rural Development Network, Warsaw, Poland

List of Figures

Chapter 5

Chapter 6

Chapter 7

Chapter 8

Chapter 9

Chapter 10

Chapter 11

Chapter 12

Chapter 13

List of Tables

Chapter 13

CHAPTER 1

Introduction

Paweł Chmieliński, Dominique Barjolle, and David Miller

The volume *Innovation and the Future of Rural Development* in Europe brings together a collection of interdisciplinary analyses rooted in European rural territories that are navigating profound economic, environmental, technological and social transformations. Innovation—whether technological, organizational or social—has become central to both European rural policy and contemporary rural scholarship (Bock, 2012; Neumeier, 2017; Richter, 2019). In a context marked by climate change, demographic decline, the digital transition and new types of territorial

P. Chmieliński (✉)
Institute of Rural and Agricultural Development, Polish Academy of Sciences, Warsaw, Poland
e-mail: pchmielinski@irwirpan.waw.pl

D. Barjolle
Institut Für Agrarwissenschaften, ETH Zürich, Zürich, Switzerland
e-mail: barjolle@ethz.ch

D. Miller
The James Hutton Institute, Aberdeen, Scotland, UK
e-mail: david.miller@hutton.ac.uk

D. Barjolle et al. (eds.), *Innovation and the Future of Rural Development in Europe*,
https://doi.org/10.1007/978-3-032-22570-2_1

inequalities, rural futures increasingly depend on the ability of institutions, communities and economic actors to adapt, reorganize and co-create new vitalization pathways (Dax & Fischer, 2018; Soriano et al., 2023). The contributions assembled in this book respond to this transformative moment by examining on-going rural development at multiple scales: the macro-level of European visions and systemic transitions, the meso-level of regional trajectories and cross-territorial comparisons, and the micro-level of sectoral innovations and grassroots experimentation. By weaving together these perspectives, the volume positions rural innovation as a socio-economic mechanism and as a process anchored in socio-ecological systems shaping the long-term sustainability and resilience of Europe's rural areas (Berkes & Ross, 2013; Meuwissen et al., 2019).

European rural areas are at a decisive turning point, characterized by both profound vulnerabilities and untapped potential, against a backdrop to economic challenges linked to geopolitical instability. Far from being mere 'problem areas', these territories are presented as living laboratories for socio-ecological innovation, participatory governance and experimentation with local policies. The authors of the chapters explore how participation through multi-stakeholder platforms, dialogue-based foresight exercises, and interfaces between science, society and politics can bridge the gap between local realities and European ambitions, with a view to serving as examples for the EU's long-term vision for rural areas (LTVRA). This volume is the result of collaborative research carried out within the framework of Horizon 2020 projects such as MOVING,[1] SHERPA[2] and POLIRURAL,[3]which brought together stakeholders from

[1] MOVING (Mountain Valorization through Interconnectedness and Green Growth) has received funding from the European Union's Horizon 2020 research and innovation programme under grant agreement No. 862739. MOVING aimed to build capacities and co-develop policy frameworks, screen and assess value chains across European mountain regions, and enhance the resilience and sustainability of mountain areas in the face of climate change. https://doi.org/10.3030/862739

[2] SHERPA (Sustainable Hub to Engage into Rural Policies with Actors) has received funding from the European Union's Horizon 2020 research and innovation programme under grant agreement No. 862448. SHERPA aimed to strengthen evidence-based rural policy by creating science–society–policy interfaces, mobilising research and local knowledge, and engaging stakeholders across Europe to develop policy recommendations and future research agendas. https://doi.org/10.3030/862448

[3] POLIRURAL (Future Oriented Collaborative Policy Development for Rural Areas and People) has received funding from the European Union's Horizon 2020 research and innovation programme under grant agreement No. 818496. POLIRURAL aimed to equip

the Mediterranean, Alps, Central Europe and Baltic states to co-produce knowledge on the future of rural areas.[4] Through case studies in Italy, Switzerland, Portugal, Romania, Slovenia, Poland, Spain, Israel, Greece, France and Lithuania, the contributions reveal common challenges such as depopulation, land abandonment, climate-induced disruptions. Further, interesting alternative trajectories are presented which are shaped by the diversity of values that permeate socio-ecology, integrating natural and cultivated biodiversity, unique heritage landscapes, and traditional food that satisfies both local consumers and tourists.

Section I "Frameworks for Understanding Rural Futures" addresses innovation from a systemic and strategic standpoint, focusing on the profound transformations reshaping Europe's rural landscapes. This section explores how long-term visions, policy narratives and structural transitions, such as reduction of emissions, climate neutrality and the reconfiguration of food systems, inform new paradigms of rural development (EC, 2019; OECD, 2016). Current debates increasingly emphasize the need to integrate multi-level governance, participatory foresight and the co-creation of rural futures, reflecting a shift away from top-down approaches toward inclusive forms of territorial policy design (Chmieliński et al., 2025). Scholarship on rural resilience and system change highlights that preparing for the future requires technological innovation, institutional learning and narrative reframing (Copus & de Lima, 2015). In line with these debates, the chapters in Section I investigate the drivers of rural transformation at the European scale and examine how policies structure the strategic orientation of rural development pathways.

Section II "Territorial Dynamics and Regional Pathways" provides examples at the meso-level, analyzing how rural communities experience and interpret change through their specific economic, institutional and socio-ecological contexts. Comparative territorial studies have demonstrated that rural development trajectories diverge significantly across European regions, shaped by history and culture, governance arrangements and natural resource stewardship. Mountain regions, Mediterranean territories and Central and Eastern European rural areas face

policymakers with advanced analytical tools, comparative insights, and multi-stakeholder frameworks to better understand regional challenges and enhance the attractiveness and livability of rural areas. https://doi.org/10.3030/818496

[4] This publication and all chapters reflect only the author's view and the Commission is not responsible for any use that may be made of the information it contains.

distinct constellations of challenges and opportunities, from demographic shrinkage and socio-economic restructuring to ecological pressures and changing land-use regimes (ESPON, 2020; Eurostat, 2023). This section brings together analyses that emphasize regional capacity building, multi-actor governance and the construction of shared regional futures, resonating with ongoing research on participatory rural governance and collaborative territorial development (Maglietti et al, 2025; Schmitt et al., 2025). By foregrounding the diversity of European rural territories, in this section, authors highlight how regional structures mediate innovation processes and shape the institutional conditions in which rural futures are negotiated.

Section III "Sectoral Innovations and Transformative Approaches" focuses on the micro level, examining how specific agricultural sectors, technological developments and localized governance models drive rural transformation "from below." Literature on agricultural innovation and rural digitalization shows that shifts in production systems, technological adoption and new forms of local coordination can significantly accelerate sustainable transitions. Emerging evidence further suggests that grassroots initiatives and sector-specific experiments (such as organic farming, diversification strategies or novel crop systems) play an increasingly important role in redefining rural resilience and sustainability. These themes resonate with longstanding contributions emphasizing the role of entrepreneurship, knowledge exchange and local institutional arrangements in driving multifunctional rural development. Thus, Section III illustrates how micro-level innovations, grounded in community action, sectoral shifts and new technological regimes, contribute to the broader evolution of Europe's rural futures.

A comprehensive overview of this volume is provided by an analysis of the diverse approaches presented by teams of authors who combine unique knowledge with an open and inquisitive view of specific, often local, development conditions, without losing sight of the macro-regional context. This is clearly evident when reading the individual chapters.

In the chapter 2, the authors examine participatory processes mobilised around the EU's Long-Term Vision for Rural Areas, drawing on evidence from multiple European regions. They analyse how multi-actor platforms, stakeholder dialogues and co-creation processes have been used to articulate rural futures, paying particular attention to whose voices are represented and how knowledge is integrated. Anchored in debates on neo-endogenous development and social innovation, the chapter demonstrates that participatory foresight can generate more context-sensitive policy priorities, but only when supported by robust facilitation, adequate resources and clear links to decision-making. In doing so, it speaks directly to the book's central concern with innovation as both a technological process and a transformation in governance and policy design.

Chapter 3 offers a critical reflection on the symbolic and functional roles ascribed to rural areas within contemporary European policy discourses. The authors interrogate whether the growing rhetorical emphasis on vibrant, innovative and climate-resilient rural territories is matched by substantive policy change, or whether it risks producing "Potemkin villages" – attractive narratives that conceal persistent structural weaknesses. Drawing on the Slovenian case and wider European evidence, they analyse demographic ageing, service provision, social policy frameworks and regional planning instruments. Their argument highlights tensions between cohesion rhetoric and reality, as well as uneven investment patterns, whilst providing examples of social innovation and local initiative that challenge the notion of rural passivity. This critique is central to the volume's effort to move beyond celebratory accounts of innovation towards a more realistic assessment of constraints and contradictions in rural futures.

The authors of chapter four investigate how policy cycle innovation, operationalised through multi-actor platforms (MAPs) and science–society–policy interfaces, can reshape the design and implementation of the EU's rural agenda, focusing on the Lithuanian experience within the SHERPA project. They trace how iterative dialogue, Delphi-based methods and multi-level governance mechanisms have been used to articulate a national rural vision to 2040 and feed it into EU processes. The chapter provides empirical insights into stakeholder satisfaction, perceived added value, and the translation of bottom-up perspectives into European-level visions for Europe's rural areas. By conceptualising these processes as policy cycle innovation, the authors demonstrate how rural futures can be co-produced in ways that challenge traditional hierarchical policy-making, thereby offering a methodological and institutional innovation directly aligned with the book's overarching theme.

Chapter 5 focuses on the challenge of steering specialised agricultural systems towards carbon neutrality, with an emphasis on regions where intensive production and market integration are deeply entrenched. Drawing on case studies and modelling exercises, the authors analyse how technological innovation, management change and policy incentives can combine to reduce greenhouse gas emissions while sustaining farm incomes. The chapter highlights trade-offs between productivity, mitigation and adaptation, and emphasises the role of advisory services, knowledge networks and supply-chain actors in enabling transitions. This contribution aligns closely with ongoing work on climate-change mitigation in rural Europe and situates agricultural innovation at the heart of future-oriented rural development strategies.

Chapter 6 undertakes a comparative analysis of three Mediterranean mountain regions, exploring how diverse territorial trajectories emerge from the interaction of environmental constraints, demographic trends, and policy frameworks. Using scenario-building and stakeholder engagement, they contrast pathways characterised by continued marginalisation with more optimistic futures built on tourism, quality agri-food products and ecosystem services. The comparison underscores the importance of place-based strategies for mountain regions and demonstrates how futures thinking can inform more differentiated, territorially sensitive rural policies across Europe. By foregrounding the specificity of Mediterranean mountain systems, the chapter enriches the broader debate on European rural futures with a nuanced regional lens.

Chapter 7 reflects on the contemporary rural development trajectories in Poland, with particular emphasis on regional disparities, multifunctional rural economies and the evolving role of EU and national policies. Building on previous works on rural entrepreneurship and multifunctional development, the authors analyse how different Polish regions combine agricultural restructuring, non-farm employment, environmental initiatives and infrastructural investment. They highlight both persistent challenges, such as depopulation, limited access to services and uneven labour-market opportunities, and emerging opportunities associated with social innovation, LEADER-type initiatives and place-based strategies. The chapter illustrates how a large Central and Eastern Europe European Union member state contributes to, and is shaped by, the broader debate on resilient and innovative rural futures.

The chapter eight focuses on Galicia in north-west Spain and analyses the contribution of a regional science-society-policy platform to the formulation of a long-term vision for rural areas. Using a Delphi-based methodology embedded in the SHERPA framework, the authors document how a multi-actor platform identified key trends, challenges and opportunities, and translated them into a shared vision for 2040. They show how issues such as depopulation, land-use change, service provision and fire risk intersect with opportunities in sustainable food production, local industry development, ecosystem services and digital connectivity. The chapter exemplifies how participatory science-policy interfaces can generate territorially nuanced futures and concrete policy proposals, reinforcing the volume's argument that innovation in rural development is as much institutional and procedural as it is technological.

The authors of chapter 9 provide a wide-ranging assessment of European mountain areas, interrogating the structural challenges and emergent opportunities that shape their future trajectories. They examine demographic decline, ageing, service withdrawal and land abandonment alongside the potential offered by tourism, renewable energy, ecosystem services and niche agri-food products. Drawing on comparative evidence from different mountain areas, the chapter shows that mountain territories are potential pioneers of innovative development models that integrate environmental stewardship and economic diversification (Dax & Fischer, 2018), rather than merely "problem regions". By framing mountain futures in terms of resilience, multi-functionality and territorial justice, the chapter reinforces the volume's broader message that rural innovation must be tailored to the specificities of different types of territory.

In Chapter 10, the authors examine the governance of agri-food systems in Romania through the lens of participation and multi-actor engagement. They explore how diverse stakeholders – including farmers, cooperatives, civil-society organisations, researchers and public authorities – interact within emerging governance arrangements and policy platforms. By identifying barriers to effective participation, such as power asymmetries, limited organisational capacities and fragmented institutional frameworks, the chapter provides a nuanced picture of the challenges facing participatory governance in a post-socialist context. It also documents innovative practices and institutional experiments that point towards more inclusive and responsive models of agri-food governance. In doing so, the chapter connects national-scale transformations to European debates on food system transitions, rural democracy and multi-level governance.

The contribution in Chapter 11 addresses digitalisation as a pivotal driver of contemporary rural change in Europe. The authors analyse the opportunities and risks associated with digital infrastructure, platforms and services in rural territories, considering domains ranging from precision agriculture and e-commerce to teleworking and digital public services. Drawing upon empirical material and policy analysis, they show how digitalisation can either exacerbate existing divides or help to bridge gaps in accessibility and opportunity, depending on the quality of connectivity, skills and institutional support. By situating digital transformations within broader dynamics of labour markets, entrepreneurship and territorial cohesion, the chapter directly engages with the book's central question of how innovation can underpin more inclusive, future-oriented rural development.

In Chapter 12, the authors investigate the diffusion of organic agriculture as a form of socio-technical and socio-institutional innovation within European rural regions. Combining statistical analysis with case-based evidence, they explore the drivers and barriers that shape farmers' adoption of organic practices, including market incentives, policy support, value-chain dynamics, advisory systems and local cultural norms. The chapter explains how organic agriculture can contribute to environmental sustainability, product differentiation and diversification of rural incomes, and highlights tensions related to certification costs, market volatility and uneven access to knowledge. By framing organic farming as part of broader innovation trajectories in agri-food systems, the authors demonstrate how alternative production models can influence the future of rural development in Europe, particularly when linked to territorial quality schemes, local food networks and remuneration for ecosystem-services.

In the final chapter, authors investigate the potential of mountain crops as alternatives to, or complements to, livestock production in Swiss mountain agriculture. They analyse how shifts towards crop-based systems might contribute to climate mitigation, biodiversity conservation, dietary change and new value chains, whilst also considering implications for farm viability, labour requirements and cultural landscapes. Through scenario analysis and stakeholder engagement, the chapter illustrates the complex trade-offs involved in reconfiguring long-established pastoral systems and highlights the types of institutional, market and knowledge innovations needed to support such transitions. As a forward-looking contribution, it encapsulates the overarching ambition of this book: to critically explore how innovation, in practice, policy, governance, can shape more sustainable and resilient futures for rural Europe.

Together, three sections and twelve chapters form a coherent architecture of the book, reflecting the multilevel nature of innovation in rural development. From strategic European visions to regional trajectories and sectoral transformations, the volume provides a comprehensive, cross-scalar account of rural areas. The interplay between macro-, meso-, and micro-levels deep dives into layered, interactive and place-dependent dynamics. This integrated approach reflects contemporary rural scholarship's increasing emphasis on territorial complexity, multi-actor governance and the co-construction of sustainable futures (Bock, 2012). It positions the book within current academic debates on resilience, sustainability transitions and socio-ecological innovation.

References

Berkes, F., & Ross, H. (2013). Community resilience: Toward an integrated approach. *Society & Natural Resources, 26*(1), 5–20. https://doi.org/10.1080/08941920.2012.736605

Bock, B. B. (2012). Social innovation and sustainability: How to disentangle the buzzword and its application in the field of agriculture and rural development. *Studies in Agricultural Economics, 114*(2), 57–63. https://doi.org/10.7896/j.1209

European Commission. (2019). *The European Green Deal.* Brussels: European Commission. https://ec.europa.eu/info/sites/default/files/european-green-deal-communication_en.pdf

Chmieliński, P., Collins, A., Cox, A., & Torrisi, G. (2025). Overlapping payoffs and policy synergies: The case of CAP and EU cohesiveness. *Global Challenges & Regional Science, 2*, 100012. https://doi.org/10.1016/j.gcrs.2025.100012

Copus, A. K., & de Lima, P. (2015). *Territorial cohesion in rural Europe. The Relational Turn in Rural Development.* Routledge.

Dax, T., & Fischer, M. (2018). An alternative policy approach to rural development in regions facing population decline. *European Planning Studies*, *26*(2), 297–315. ISBN: 978–2–919795–70–3

ESPON (2020). *Shrinking rural regions in Europe: Challenges, patterns and potentials.* ESPON. https://www.espon.eu/rural-regions

Eurostat. (2023). *Regional gross domestic product (PPS per inhabitant) by NUTS 2 regions.* https://ec.europa.eu/eurostat/databrowser/view/TGS00005/default/table

Maglietti Smith I., Schmitt E., Casabianca F., & Barjolle, D. (2025). Envisioning the future of mountain regions: A participatory foresight approach. *Journal of Regional Environmental Change*, Springer Nature. https://doi.org/10.1007/s10113-025-02454-1

Meuwissen, M. P. M., Feindt, P. H., Midmore, P., et al. (2019). A framework to assess the resilience of farming systems. *Agricultural Systems, 176*, Article 102656. https://doi.org/10.1016/j.agsy.2019.102656
Neumeier, S. (2017). Social innovation in rural development: Identifying the key factors of success. *The Geographical Journal, 183*(1), 34–46. https://doi.org/ https://doi.org/10.1111/geoj.12180
OECD. (2016). Innovation, agricultural productivity and sustainability in the Netherlands. *OECD Publishing*. https://doi.org/10.1787/9789264238473-en
Richter, R. (2019). Rural social enterprises as embedded intermediaries: The innovative power of connecting rural communities with supra-regional networks. *Journal of Rural Studies, 70*, 179–187. https://doi.org/ https://doi.org/10.1016/j.jrurstud.2017.12.005
Schmitt E., Barjolle D., et al. (2025). Understanding innovation in European mountain product value chains: Empirical. typology, patterns of co-occurence and policy implications. *Journal of Mountain Research and Development Mountain Research and Development, 45*(3), R9-R20. https://doi.org/10.1659/mrd.2024.00042
Soriano, B., Garrido, A., Bertolozzi-Caredio, D., Accatino, F., Antonioli, F., Krupin, V., Meuwissen, M. M. P., Ollendorf, F., Rommel, J., Spiegel, A., Tudor, M., Urquhart, J., Vigani, M., & Bardají, I. (2023). Actors and their roles for improving resilience of farming systems in Europe. *Journal of Rural Studies, 98*, 134–146. https://doi.org/10.1016/j.jrurstud.2023.02.003

PART I

Frameworks for Understanding Rural Futures

CHAPTER 2

Beyond the Long-Term Vision for Rural Areas: Policy Anchoring, Strategic Alignment With the CAP Strategic Plans and Funding Mechanisms Towards a Modern Rural Policy in The EU

Tristan Berchoux, Aurélie Kirsch, and Samuel Féret

1 Introduction

The European Union's Common Agricultural Policy (CAP) stands as a pivotal policy framework for the development of rural areas in the EU with a multifaceted approach aimed at achieving diverse objectives (Pagnon et al., 2023). This intervention has evolved into a strategic

T. Berchoux
TETIS, University of Montpellier, Montpellier, France

T. Berchoux (✉) · A. Kirsch
Mediterranean Agronomic Institute of Montpellier (CIHEAM-IAMM), Montpellier, France
e-mail: berchoux@iamm.fr

A. Kirsch
e-mail: kirsch@iamm.fr

D. Barjolle et al. (eds.), *Innovation and the Future of Rural Development in Europe*,
https://doi.org/10.1007/978-3-032-22570-2_2

landscape, with Member States intricately weaving their plans through pluri-annual national frameworks, overseen by a performance matrix governed by target values and indicators set by the European Commission (EC) (European Commission, 2021). At the forefront of these strategic plans is a request from the EC to align them with the ambitions and strategies outlined in the EU Green Deal (EUGD), notably embodied in the Farm-to-Fork strategy and the biodiversity strategy (European Commission, 2021). Simultaneously, the EC has issued a new strategy for rural areas: A long-term vision for rural areas (LTVRA): towards stronger, connected, prosperous, and resilient rural areas by 2040 (European Commission, 2021).

The present chapter capitalises on the two policy developments for rural areas: the 28 CAP strategic plans (CSPs) and the LTVRA communication. We reviewed the 28 CAP strategic plans submitted by Member States and analysed how the specific objectives outlined in these plans relate to the socio-economic fabric of rural areas. The goal was twofold: first, to unravel the unique contributions of each Member State in shaping their rural areas, and second, to assess the alignment of these objectives with the broader vision articulated in the LTVRA. The analysis sheds light on the interplay between national and European-level strategies and highlights the potential synergies and challenges that emerge in steering the course towards stronger, connected, prosperous, and resilient rural areas by 2040.

Through Multi-Actor Platforms (MAPs) in 41 rural territories, we gathered evidence from across Europe, at multiple levels through the project Chapter 1 SHERPA. MAPs identified opportunities and challenges that could be encountered in their territories, and priorities for policy, practice and research. Those deliberations are provided in the 41 Position Papers of the MAPs We use the knowledge of those papers and from other EU rural networks to analyse the alignment of CSPs to local needs, which advocate for systemic policy development pathways that firmly anchors the LTVRA within sectoral policies.

Our analysis revealed intriguing, often complex, nuances. Multiple CAP strategic plans showed alignment with the LTVRA, with indications

S. Féret
Institute for Climate Economics (I4CE), Paris, France
e-mail: samuel.feret@i4ce.org

highlighting possibilities for stronger coordination. Yet, despite these inroads, there was a pervasive sense of untapped potential. We identified fundamental disconnects and missed opportunities for synchrony between the vision of the LTVRA and the strategic objectives laid out by the CAP. The most significant among these was the disconnect in timelines, the LTVRA aimed at 2040 and the CAP at 2027, revealing a fundamental lack of alignment in the policy formulation process.

(i). The Common Agricultural Policy (CAP): Background and Role

In conjunction with the cohesion policy, the Common Agricultural Policy (CAP) serves as the primary framework for supporting rural areas (Pagnon et al., 2023). While the cohesion policy operates within the European Structural and Investment Funds (ESIF), the rural development component of the CAP underwent restructuring in the new 2021–2027 programming period. From 1999 until 2022, the EU governed and consistently updated a rural development policy, employing the EAFRD (European Agricultural Fund for Rural Development) dedicated fund for national and multi-annual rural development programs. Starting in 2021, previous sectoral, direct payment, and rural development regulations were amalgamated into a strategic plan regulation, retaining distinct envelopes for the European Agricultural Guarantee Fund (EAGF) and the EAFRD. Despite the absence of a specific rural development regulation, the EAFRD continues to operate, co-financing interventions under "Pillar 2." Since 2020, Member States have been tasked with devising national strategic plans to address the ten specific objectives of the CAP, including two explicitly related to the socio-economic fabric of rural areas: generational renewal (specific objective G) and vibrant rural areas (specific objective H). Each specific objective necessitates a logical intervention strategy, outlining specific needs, interventions, result and impact indicators, along with targets and allocated funding. As part of the Common Evaluation and Monitoring Framework, primary impact indicators for assessing policy delivery concerning the socio-economic fabric of rural areas include: the number of new and young farmers by gender, GDP per capita, poverty rate, employment rate by gender, and internet broadband coverage (European Commission, 2022).

The CAP undergoes regular reforms, with its most recent iteration initially intended to cover the period from 2021 to 2027. However, due to prolonged negotiations between the co-legislators, the current policy period effectively commenced on January 1, 2023, spanning five years. As in previous policy periods, the CAP comprises direct payments and sectoral support funded annually from the European Agricultural Guarantee Fund (EAGF), alongside rural development interventions financed by the European Agricultural Fund for Rural Development (EAFRD) and co-financed by Member States. While the funding objectives of the CAP remain consistent, each reform of the CAP results in the formulation of more tailored objectives that address the pertinent issues facing the agricultural sector and rural development within the European Union. The CAP strategic plans must therefore be built around the following nine specific objectives:

- SO1: Support viable farm income and resilience across the Union to enhance food security;
- SO2: Enhance market orientation and increase competitiveness;
- SO3: Improve the farmers' position in the value chain;
- SO4: Contribute to climate change mitigation and adaptation, as well as sustainable energy;
- SO5: Foster sustainable development and efficient management of natural resources such as water, soil and air;
- SO6: Contribution to the protection of biodiversity, enhance ecosystem services and preserve habitats and landscapes;
- SO7: Attract young farmers and facilitate business development in rural areas;
- SO8: Promote employment, growth, social inclusion and local development in rural areas, including bio-economy and sustainable forestry;
- SO9: Improve the response of EU agriculture to societal demands on food and health, including safe, nutritious and sustainable food, as well as animal welfare;
- CCO: Additional, cross-cutting objective aims at fostering knowledge, innovation and digitalisation in agriculture.

The European Commission also provides recommendations to Member States to ensure the attainment of the ten specific objectives of the CAP, as well as to ensure the alignment of CAP strategic plans with the EU Green Deal, notably the Farm-to-Fork strategy and the Biodiversity strategy.

(ii). The Long-Term Vision for Rural Areas (LTVRA): Emergence and Alignment

The European Commission's communication, "A Strong Social Europe for Just Transitions" (2020a, 202b), outlined key factors necessitating a re-evaluation of rural considerations in the new decade. First, demographic shifts have led to declining populations in many rural areas, exacerbated by an ageing EU population, particularly pronounced in rural regions due to a more negative demographic balance compared to urban areas. This communication highlighted the need to recognize that the green, digital, and demographic transitions impact different segments of society differently. It announced plans for a long-term vision for rural areas in 2021, aiming to address their unique challenges, including ageing, depopulation, connectivity, poverty, and limited access to services. The COVID-19 pandemic further underscored the importance of enhancing rural quality of life, achieving balanced territorial development, and fostering economic growth in rural areas.

In response to these challenges, the LTVRA communication of June 2021 focuses on addressing issues such as ageing, depopulation, access to basic services, poverty risks, and enhancing digital connectivity in rural areas. Aligned with the EU Green Deal commitments and mindful of demographic changes, the LTVRA serves as a roadmap for ensuring a just transition in rural areas by 2040, with a commitment to leaving no one or no place behind. The LTVRA also presents a new framework for rural development, building upon the evolution of EU rural policies since 1988, including initiatives such as the Cork declarations (1996, 2016), the OECD's new rural paradigm (2006), and the Rural Policy 3.0 framework (2018). These efforts prioritize the well-being of rural communities, forming a comprehensive strategy for rural development.

The LTVRA is accompanied by both an Action Plan and a Rural Pact, which encompass a broader scope than the CAP due to their comprehensive, territorial, and spatial approaches. In contrast, the CAP has historical objectives outlined in the Treaty on the Functioning of the EU and is now tasked with achieving performance goals through strategic plans devised by Member States. The LTVRA signifies the European Commission's intent to revitalize the EU's rural policy framework, while the CAP strategic plans represent 28 national strategies aimed at addressing rural needs in line with regulatory guidelines.

The LTVRA highlights four areas for action towards stronger, connected, resilient and prosperous rural areas by 2040 (Fig. 1). The Vision highlights four specific strands under which action will be taken, supported by flagship initiatives (Miller et al., 2022):

- **Stronger:** Rural areas should be home to empowered and vibrant local communities, involving a broad range of stakeholders and networks as well as all levels of governance, is key to developing tailor-made, place-based and integrated policy solutions and investments;
- **Connected:** Maintaining or improving public transport services and connections, as well as deepening digital infrastructures, are essential to ensure better-connected EU rural areas;
- **Resilient:** Preserving natural resources, restoration of landscapes (including cultural), greening of farming activities and shortening supply chains to make rural areas more resilient to climate change, natural hazards and economic crises;
- **Prosperous:** Diversifying economic activities to new sectors with positive effects on employment, and improving the value added of farming and agri-food activities.

We aligned CAP-specific objectives with the areas for action outlined in the LTVRA to identify commonalities and potential synergies (Table 1). Each area for action identified in the LTVRA corresponds to at least one CAP-specific objective. For instance, in terms of strengthening the socio-economic fabric of rural areas, the CAP aligns with the LTVRA through its objectives on generational renewal and vibrant rural areas. Sustainable food production, a key aspect of one LTVRA strand, is also covered extensively by another EU initiative, the Farm-to-Fork strategy. Additionally, the cross-cutting CAP objective for knowledge and innovation directly corresponds with four areas outlined in the LTVRA.

According to the approved versions, a total of EUR 264 billion in European resources will be allocated through 28 CAP strategic plans to primarily support farmers' income and transition to sustainability. Out of this amount, EUR 7.23 billion is earmarked for the generational renewal objective, specifically for the establishment of young farmers, and EUR 5.06 billion for vibrant rural areas through the LEADER program. Similar to the former EAFRD regulation, the CSP regulation mandates Member

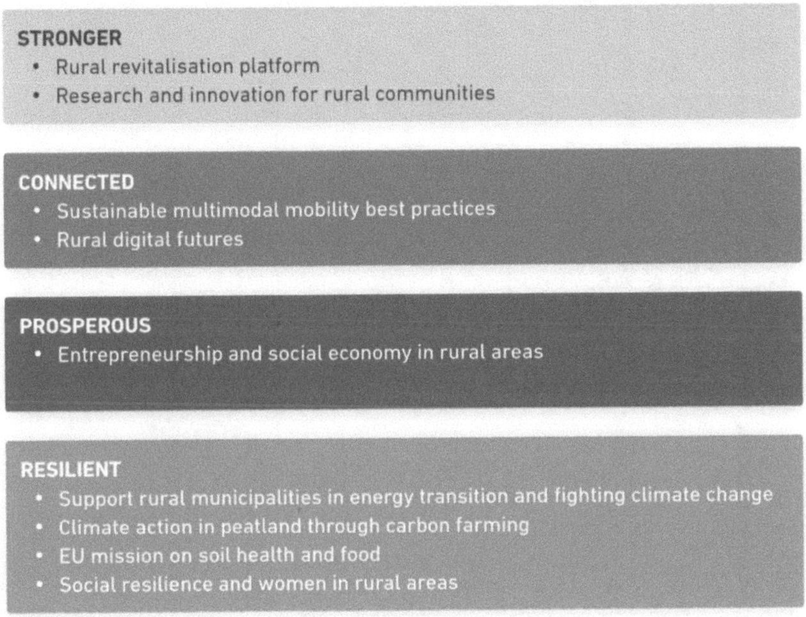

Fig. 1 Rural Action Plan flagship initiatives, European Commission, 2021

States to allocate at least 5% of EAFRD funds to the LEADER program (Article 92; summary in Fig. 3 and detailed breakdown per country in Table 3). In proportion, the intervention strategies and measures under SO7 and SO8 are projected to spend EUR 11.85 billion between 2023 and 2027. This amount represents approximately 4.49% of all interventions across all specific objectives outlined in the 28 CAP strategic plans.

Specific Objective 7 (SO7: Generational Renewal) supports young farmers and new farmer entry through business start-up investments and advisory services, with complementary income support provided through direct payments (Pillar 1). Specific Objective 8 (SO8: Vibrant Rural Areas) supports broader rural development through LEADER local development strategies, rural enterprise support, and infrastructure investments. Together, these objectives address the socio-economic fabric of rural areas, though as shown in our analysis, with varying emphasis across Member States.

Table 1 Aligning CAP specific objectives with the LTVRA areas for action

Beyond the long-term vision	*Beyond the long-term vision*			*Beyond the long-term vision*		*Beyond the long-term vision*		*Beyond the long-term vision*		
Beyond the long-term vision	*Beyond the long-term vision*	*Beyond the long-term vision*	*Beyond the long-term vision*	*Beyond the long-term vision*	*Beyond the long-term vision*	*Beyond the long-term vision*	*Beyond the long-term vision*	*Beyond the long-term vision*	*Beyond the long-term vision*	*Beyond the long-term vision*
Fair income (SO1)						x	x			
Competitiveness (SO2)						x				
Food value chain (SO3)							x			
Climate change (SO4)							x	x		
Environmental care (SO5)							x		x	
Landscapes (SO6)								x	x	
Generation renewal (SO7)	x					x	x			x
Rural areas (SO8)	x	x	x	x	x	x	x	x	x	x
Food and health (SO9)							x	x	x	
Knowledge and innovation (SO10)	x		x	x		x				

2 Methodology

The intervention logic approach employed in our analysis draws from evaluation frameworks established by the European Commission (2022/1475) and aligns with recent EU rural policy scholarship emphasizing the need for systematic policy coherence assessment (Hennessy & Rehman, 2007; European Court of Auditors, 2021). This methodology allows for transparent examination of how strategic visions translate—or fail to translate—into concrete policy interventions (Fig. 2). We referred to key evaluation elements and recommended success factors outlined in the EC implementing regulation for CAP strategic plans (European Commission, 2022) before proceeding. Within this framework, the specific objective of strengthening the socio-economic fabric of rural areas is examined across three primary dimensions: rural sustainable economy, local development, as well as gender equality and social inclusion. Rural sustainable economy encompasses aspects such as economic growth, narrowing the urban-rural gap, improving employment rates, promoting bio-economy businesses, and enhancing sustainable forestry practices. Local development focuses on enhancing the provision of local services and infrastructure. Gender equality and social inclusion entail increasing women's employment and participation in farming, ensuring fair distribution of CAP supports, and reducing rural poverty.

For each of the 28 CAP strategic plans, we analysed sections related to Specific Objectives 7 (SO7) and Specific Objectives 8 (SO8). We restricted analysis to SO7 and SO8 because these are the two specific objectives explicitly designed to address the socio-economic fabric of rural areas, as distinct from sectoral objectives such as SO1 (farm income) or environmental objectives (SO4–SO6). This focus reflects the LTVRA's holistic rural development approach rather than sectoral interventions. Key interventions for these objectives were identified based on the strategic plan regulation and the content of the 28 CAP strategic plans (Table 2). All relevant information was consolidated into a simplified intervention logic matrix. This involved examining the description of needs and intervention strategies outlined in the plans to achieve specific goals under SO7 and SO8. For some countries, we delved into their rural ambitions expressed through target values for result indicators. The category labelled "EC observations" pertains to observation letters sent by the European Commission to Member States after analysing the

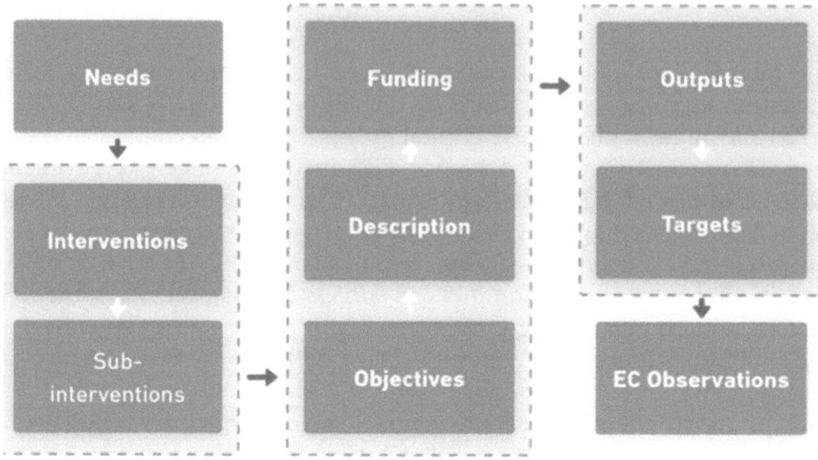

Fig. 2 Simplified intervention logic matrix adapted from EC (2022)/1475) for evaluating CAP strategic plan design. *Note* The components represent the mandatory structure Member States must follow: identification of rural development Needs (left), translation into specific policy Interventions (center-left), establishment of measurable Results through indicators (center-right), and quantified. Targets for these indicators across 2023–2027 (right)

submitted versions. These letters may have requested clarification and/or improvements.

While aligned with the intervention logic prescribed to Member States for designing their strategic plans, we acknowledge certain methodological limitations inherent in our approach. Focusing solely on aligning SO7 and SO8 with the objectives of the Long-Term Vision for Rural Areas provides a simplified perspective. While both SO7 and SO8 pertain to the socio-economic fabric of rural areas, it is important to note that almost all CAP interventions can contribute to rural development in some capacity. Therefore, this analysis does not cover the contributions from SO4, SO5, SO6, and the horizontal specific objectives (AKIS). Additionally, regarding SO7, it is essential to clarify that we do not address the complementary income support provided to young farmers under Pillar 1, which contributes to SO7 but primarily relates to SO1 (fair income).

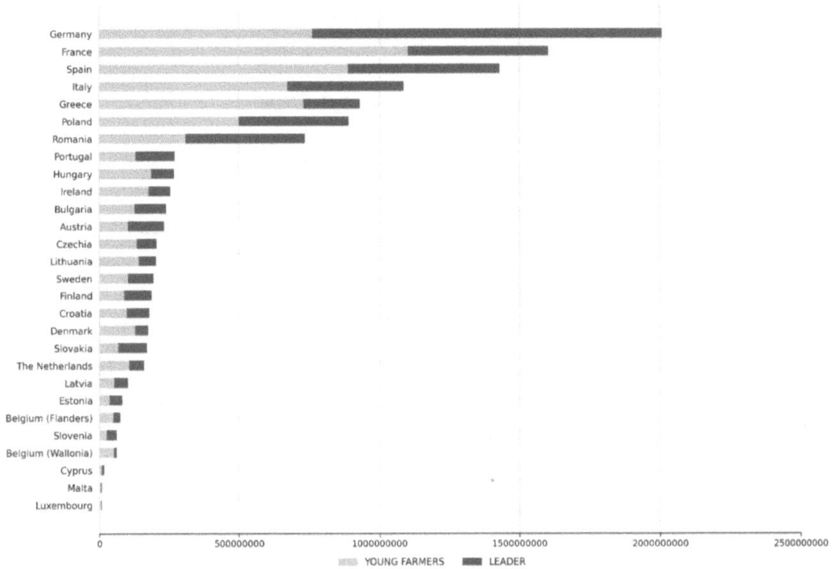

Fig. 3 Financial provisions for young farmers and LEADER in CSPs (2023–2027)

Table 2. Main interventions for SO7 and SO8 in the CAP strategic plans

	SO7: Generational renewal	*SO8: Vibrant rural areas*
Interventions	Investments (art. 73)	Investments (art. 73)
	Setting-up young farmers (art. 75)	Setting-up of rural business start-up (art. 75)
	Setting-up of rural business start-up (art. 75)	LEADER (art. 77)
	Setting-up new farmers (art. 75)	Other cooperation projects (art. 77)
	Cooperation for generational renewal (art. 77)	Outside the CAP: national policies and strategies
	Outside the CAP: access to land, training through national, regional and local supports	

Table 3 Financial provisions for young farmers and LEADER under EAFRD in the 28 CAP Strategic Plans 20,232–2027

	Generational renewal (SO7)	*Vibrant Rural Areas (SO8)*	
Strategic plan	*Young farmers (EAFRD)*[1]	*% Eafrd for leader*	*Leader*
Belgium (Flanders)	49,291,775,00	7.4	25,278,700,00 €
Belgium (Wallonia)	51,494,000,00	5.0	9,937,440,00 €
Bulgaria	127,593,295,00	8.1	113,865,060,00 €
Czechia	136,082,097,00	5.0	70,532,348,00 €
Denmark	129,360,000,00	7.1	46,262,400,00 €
Germany	761,129,891,00	15.1	1,246,106,364,47 €
Estonia	35,158,587,00	10.8	47,589,703,20 €
Ireland	177,942,300,00	5.0	77,940,000,00 €
Greece	730,000,000,00	5.5	200,000,000,00 €
Spain	887,233,201,00	10.0	542,154,229,09 €
France	1,102,218,802,00	5.0	502,089,706,20 €
Croatia	98,653,495,00	5.7	82,338,579,00 €
Italy	672,734,347,00	5.7	413,611,479,83 €
Cyprus	7,230,000,00	8.1	9,600,000,00 €
Latvia	53,757,114,00	7.2	49,724,133,00 €
Lithuania	142,579,625,00	6.4	62,912,950,00 €
Luxembourg	5,263,000,00	5.2	3,175,000,00 €
Hungary	186,892,301,00	5.0	81,757,330,30 €
Malta	4,983,840,00	5.3	4,196,124,00 €
The Netherlands	107,654,800,00	5.0	54,150,012,00 €
Austria	103,407,083,00	5.0	130,200,000,00 €
Poland	500,424,381,00	8.3	389,680,000,00 €
Portugal	131,578,125,00	6.2	140,240,181,90 €
Romania	309,621,824,00	8.4	424,750,000,00 €
Slovenia	25,895,588,00	6.5	35,542,556,00 €

(continued)

[1] Complementary income support for young farmers is not included in these figures as it primarily pertains to Specific Objective 1 (SO1).

Table 3 (continued)

	Generational renewal (SO7)	*Vibrant Rural Areas (SO8)*	
Strategic plan	*Young farmers (EAFRD)*	*% Eafrd for leader*	*Leader*
Slovakia	67,198,142,00	8.0	105,291,866,00 €
Finland	88,720,000,00	6.6	99,459,000,00 €
Sweden	103,357,244,00	8.7	92,204,301,00 €
Total	6,797,454,857,00 €		5,060,589,463,99 €

In the section "Needs" of the CAP strategic plans, which outlines objectives such as establishing new rural enterprises, supporting rural employment, and addressing gender disparities, we evaluated whether the following topics were addressed across the 28 intervention strategies: ageing, agroecology, biodiversity, bioeconomy, broadband access, depopulation, gender equality, poverty alleviation, quality of life improvement, rural inclusion, short supply chains, smart villages, transportation, support for vulnerable groups, youth engagement, and water management. Additionally, we examined any references to the Long-Term Vision for Rural Areas and national strategies related to rural development. Furthermore, we looked for any specific mentions of rural areas that might have emerged from the mandatory national public debate. Lastly, we reviewed all approved versions of the 28 strategic plans to assess the extent to which Member States made revisions to address observations from the European Commission regarding Specific Objectives 7 and 8, examining how the plans referenced the Long-Term Vision for Rural Areas and any rural action plans.

3 Interview Design and Implementation

Following a call to the 41 SHERPA Multi-Actor Platforms (MAPs), we conducted bilateral interviews with national experts holding responsibility for rural components of CAP strategic plans. Six Member States were selected for interview: Finland, France, Italy, Poland, Slovenia, and Portugal. This selection was based on geographic diversity, variation in funding levels for SO7 and SO8, and availability of contact persons with direct involvement in CSP drafting processes.

Table 4 Rural intervention strategy target values of the top-three contributing CSPs (based on EAFRD funding for SO7 and SO8)

SO	*Result indicators*	*Target value France*	*Target value Germany*	*Target value Spain*
7–8	Advisory, training and knowledge exchange—Number of beneficiaries receiving CAP support for advisory, training, knowledge exchange or EIP-related cooperation project (R01)	131,457	–	–
8	Less favoured areas- % of additional support per hectare in areas having upper needs compared to the average (R07)	112.2%	–	–
7	On-farm investments—% of young farmers receiving CAP support for on-farm investments (R09)	16.2%	–	–
8	Better organization of the supply chain - % of farms participating in producer groups, producer organizations, local markets, short distribution circuits and quality schemes supported by the CAP (R10)	–	–	13.6%
8	Renewable energy from agriculture and forestry and other renewable sources—Investments in renewable energy production capacity, including those of biological origin supported by the CAP in MW (R15)	–	–	251 MW
8	Investment support in forest sector—Total investments to increase forest sector performance (R18)	M€476	M€140	M€283

(continued)

Table 4 (continued)

SO	*Result indicators*	*Target value France*	*Target value Germany*	*Target value Spain*
8	Results linked to the environment or climate thanks to knowledgeź– Number of people receiving advisory, training and knowledge exchange or EIP-related cooperation project in relation to agrienvironmental and climate results (R28)	–	–	208,518
7	Generational renewal—Number of young farmers who set-up with CAP support (R36)	27,235	20,100	16,639
7–8	Growth and employment in rural areas—New jobs in supported CAP projects (R37)	30,544	20,800	17,347
8	LEADER coverage - % of rural population covered by a local development strategy (R38)	57.6%	60.0%	55.2%
7–8	Rural development economy—Number of rural businesses, incl. Bioeconomy businesses, developed with CAP support (R39)	5445	40,000	58,699
8	Smart transition of the rural economy—Number of smart villages strategies supported by the CAP (R40)	–	–	16

(continued)

Table 4 (continued)

SO	*Result indicators*	*Target value France*	*Target value Germany*	*Target value Spain*
8	Rural connectivity in Europe - % of rural population having better access to services and infrastructure as a result of CAP support (R41)	2.1%	11.1%	8.3%
7–8	Promote social inclusion—Number of people covered by social inclusion projects supported by the CAP (R42)	–	–	0

Table 5 Common items between LTVRA and CSPs

CSP	*LTVRA items to which CSPs refer*
AT	Social services
CZ	Basic services
FR	Rural agenda / Quality of life
GR	Healthy food
HR	Demographic declinc
IE	Smart villages
IT	Coherence of the CSP with the LTVRA
SI	Employment / Quality of life / Smart villages
SP	Demographic decline

Interview design: We developed a semi-structured interview guide containing 12 core questions addressing: (1) the rationale for SO7 and SO8 intervention strategies; (2) integration of LTVRA principles into CSP design; (3) consultation with multi-actor platforms; (4) challenges in policy alignment; and (5) recommendations for future policy coherence. Questions were informed by our initial document analysis and designed to elicit qualitative insight into decision-making processes not evident in official documents.

Sampling and interviews: Interviews were conducted between March and June 2022 via video call (15 interviews total; 2–3 per country).

Participants included regional agriculture ministry officials, rural development program managers, and policy advisors. Average interview duration was 45 minutes. All interviews were conducted in English or translated via simultaneous interpretation.

Budget analysis: Financial provisions for SO7 and SO8 were extracted from approved CSP documents using standardized data sheets. All figures are drawn directly from official EC summaries and approved national strategic plans. When CSPs presented information in regional rather than national totals, figures were aggregated to permit cross-country comparison.

4 Results

(i). Overview of EAFRD financial provisions under SO7 and SO8

Among the two specific objectives addressing the socio-economic fabric of rural areas, SO7 —focusing on generational renewal— receives the most attention and provisions in almost all CSPs, with a total allocation of EUR 6.79 billion from the European Agricultural Fund for Rural Development (EAFRD). This emphasis on SO7 underscores the importance of rejuvenating farm holders to address the significant ageing within the farming population. The top three countries allocating the most EAFRD funds for young farmers and LEADER interventions are Germany, France, and Spain, collectively mobilizing 42% of the EU-28 funds for both interventions. Moreover, the top five countries dedicating the most EAFRD funds for generational renewal are France, Spain, Germany, Italy, and Poland, accounting for 57% of the EU-28 funds allocated to support generational renewal through interventions for young farmers.

Despite the requirement for a minimum 5% spending within the EAFRD envelope on LEADER interventions (Article 92), nearly all CSPs prioritize the LEADER program as the primary delivery mechanism for SO8, with an average allocation of 7.7% of EAFRD funds. In fact, under the general objective of enhancing the socio-economic fabric of rural areas, nine CSPs plan to allocate more EAFRD funds to the LEADER program than to interventions for young farmers. The German CSP stands out with 16.8% of the total EU EAFRD funds allocated to young farmers and LEADER, followed by the French (13.5%)

and Spanish (11.9%) CSPs. Remarkably, almost a quarter of the total EU EAFRD funds dedicated to LEADER is concentrated within the German CSP (24.62%). The German CSP provides detailed insights into current regional strategies for rural areas under SO8, including initiatives for entrepreneurship, small and medium-sized enterprises (SMEs), innovation, tourism, digitalization, and capacity building.

Finally, it is noteworthy that among the needs identified for CAP intervention strategies (Specific Objective 7: Generational Renewal, and Specific Objective 8: Vibrant Rural Areas), cross-cutting priorities such as gender equality, social inclusion, rural youth development (excluding young farmer support programs), support for elderly rural populations, and representation of minority groups are seldom prioritized in the intervention logic. This pattern emerges across both SO7 interventions (which focus primarily on farm-level entrepreneurship for young farmers) and SO8 interventions (which emphasize LEADER local development strategies). The relative absence of these vulnerable groups from explicit policy targeting suggests potential gaps between LTVRA action area commitments and actual programmatic focus.

(ii). Ambition and targeted goals for SO7 and SO8 in the CSPs with the highest EAFRD expenditures

Germany, France, and Spain lead in allocating the highest percentage of their EAFRD budget to interventions under SO7 and SO8. We unpacked the target values established by each CSP, using result indicators to reveal their rural aspirations outlined for SO7 and SO8. Our aim was to uncover any territorial or regional strategies for rural areas and communities emphasized in their CSPs. Table 4 presents the target values set by these three CSPs alongside their respective result indicators.

For SO7, France outlines target values that also incorporate Pillar 1 interventions for young farmers (complementary payments to young farmers) and sets target values for on-farm investments (R09), which Germany and Spain do not. The number of young farmers to be established during the 2023–2027 period appears significant across all three countries. Regarding SO8, the percentage of the rural population covered by a local development strategy ranges between 55% and almost 60% in the three countries. Target values for the number of rural businesses developed with CAP support vary, with France setting it at 5445, while

Germany and Spain set theirs much higher at 40,000 and 58,699, respectively. Similarly, there is a divergence in the percentage of the rural population expected to have improved access to services and infrastructure as a result of CAP support, with France at 2.07% compared to Germany at 11.07% and Spain at 8.25%. Spain stands out by mentioning a target value for implementing 16 smart village strategies through the CAP. Under this specific objective, France justifies the use of less-favoured area payments to reduce the income gap among regions and towards the most vulnerable agricultural territories.

(iii). Ambition and targeted goals for SO7 and SO8 in the CSPs with the highest EAFRD

Following our results from the alignment of CAP specific objectives with the LTVRA strands, we conducted a review of the 28 approved CSPs to triangulate Member States' perspectives using a topic-driven approach. Table 5 outlines the elements referenced in the CSPs related to the LTVRA. Interestingly, we observed that prior to their approval, only one CSP made reference to the LTVRA, with the remaining nine doing so after approval, likely influenced by observation letters from the EC.

Among the approved CSPs, nine (Czech Republic, France, Greece, Croatia, Ireland, Italy, Slovenia, Spain) explicitly refer to the LTVRA, citing various aspects. However, the reasons behind these references are generally scantily explained and are not explicitly linked to SO7 and SO8. Instead, they indicate a general inclination to align with the LTVRA and often mention national cross-cutting strategies for rural areas.

While demographic decline, quality of life, and smart villages are commonly referenced in three CSPs, only one properly aligns with the shared features between CAP specific objectives and LTVRA strands, particularly regarding sustainable food production and healthy food (Greece).

Overall, the CSPs referring to the LTVRA do not position it as a comprehensive strategic framework for rural development. The choices of interventions and financial provisions in these plans are not necessarily integrated into this new holistic approach to rural policy.

5 Discussion

(i). An inadequate integration of the LTVRA in CSPs

From the perspective of national managing authorities, there is often confusion regarding the division of responsibilities between DG Agri and DG Regio. Initially, rural issues were expected to be addressed through the lens of democracy and demographics, including concerns about ageing and geographic disparities. However, in practice, the CAP ends up encompassing most aspects of the Long-Term Vision for Rural Areas. This transition has caused confusion, especially since the European Agricultural Fund for Rural Development (EAFRD) has been removed from partnership agreements, resulting in the loss of multi-fund local development strategies (France, Portugal).

Many public administrations in Member States still perceive the LTVRA as too closely linked to agriculture. There is a sense that the European Commission did not sufficiently promote the LTVRA at the national level. Moreover, experts agree that the LTVRA came too late for the 2023–2027 programming period. While the LTVRA promotes a positive vision of rural areas, management authorities often view rural areas solely as agricultural or underdeveloped regions (Portugal).

Some CAP strategic plans primarily focus on the farming sector and may lack a comprehensive rural policy approach. In such cases, the cohesion policy could complement rural development efforts, particularly in low-density areas, as these regions receive more funding from the cohesion policy than from the CAP. Regarding SO8, the total financial provision seems low compared to SO7. However, many countries plan to support rural areas using other EU funds, notably from the cohesion policy and the Recovery and Resilience Fund (Poland, Slovenia).

The LTVRA was seen as an invitation to develop more territorial policies using EU funds and to integrate the regional level. However, this vision is not prevalent in the majority of CAP strategic plans. Conversely, designing integrated rural policies poses a significant challenge, requiring increased capacity building at the managing authority level (Italy).

This temporal and institutional misalignment is not merely procedural; it fundamentally undermines policy effectiveness. Research on EU rural development demonstrates that integrated, place-based approaches require sustained institutional coordination (Bosworth et al., 2016). When strategic visions arrive mid-cycle, without corresponding regulatory or funding modifications, they function as rhetorical frameworks rather than operational drivers. Our evidence suggests this was the case with LTVRA in the 2023–2027 CSP cycle.

(ii). Farming remains central to the vitality of rural areas in many CSPs

In many CAP Strategic Plans, there is a prevailing assumption that bolstering the farming economy will foster local development in rural areas. This is particularly evident under the two specific objectives addressing the socio-economic fabric of rural areas, a key dimension of the CAP. Notably, the ambitions and funding allocated to SO7 far exceed those of SO8, despite fewer interventions and result target values. Promoting generational renewal through robust support for young farmers is a common trend across most CSPs. However, financial provisions for rural start-ups are relatively modest under SO7.

Additional funding from the Recovery and Resilience Facility (RRF) would enable Member States to support agrifood industries and remote or underserved areas lacking adequate infrastructure. Although the RRF is not exclusively designated for rural areas, investments in mobility infrastructure and broadband internet would enhance the standard of living in rural communities, while also bolstering agricultural research. The smart village intervention, often aligned with LEADER, offers support for rural municipalities, including for sewage systems. During the strategic planning process, the primary focus was on agriculture and addressing energy challenges. Developing the food sector is seen as highly beneficial for rural areas (Poland).

Many CSPs suggest that the European Agricultural Fund for Rural Development's (EAFRD) intervention for young farmers is insufficient to support generational renewal. Generational renewal is also facilitated by other interventions, such as cooperation, advisory services, knowledge transfer, and LEADER. Additionally, triggering Pillar 1 interventions with complementary payments for young farmers is considered essential (France, Finland).

Agriculture is deemed a vital component of the economy in many CSPs. The economic status of the agricultural sector forms the backdrop of strategic planning efforts, with farmer income prioritized in strategic objectives. The overarching goal for designing the CSPs was to maintain existing support for farmers while introducing new instruments to further this objective (Poland).

To better operationalize LTVRA principles, future CAP reforms should establish more balanced financial provisions between SO7 and SO8. Current allocations suggest an implicit assumption that rural vitality flows automatically from agricultural viability. However, research on rural regeneration demonstrates that economic diversification, social infrastructure investment, and community-level decision-making processes are at least equally important (Steiner & Atterton, 2015). A rebalancing toward 60% SO7 / 40% SO8 allocations would better reflect integrated rural development priorities.

(iii). LEADER and Smart Villages' approaches are widely recognized as the primary interventions to implement the LTVRA in CSPs

Although the Long-Term Vision for Rural Areas has not been directly translated into programmatic requirements for CAP Strategic Plans, the LEADER program has been perceived as the primary means to operationalise it, particularly through SO8. LEADER is seen as embodying the LTVRA approach within the CAP, despite its long-standing implementation and limited expansion at the EU level beyond the mandatory 5% earmark in the European Agricultural Fund for Rural Development (EAFRD) (France).

While LEADER and smart villages share interactions, smart villages encompass broader initiatives than LEADER alone. Regional authorities can utilize this instrument to promote small-scale cooperation among municipalities through public and private partnerships. As a novel approach, 10 regions plan to activate the smart village intervention independently of LEADER (Italy).

Many interventions under SO7 and SO8 of the CAP would contribute to the implementation of the EU rural action plan. These include funding for broadband, smart villages, generational renewal, support for rural businesses, knowledge transfer, cooperation, and investment in improving the rural socio-economic structure. However, it is noted that these interventions would likely have been implemented even without the explicit influence of the LTVRA (Finland).

6 Conclusion

In this Chapter, we assessed the 28 CAP strategic plans through a rural lens aimed to investigate references to the LTVRA, issued by the European Commission in 2021.

Despite the LTVRA's positive strategic framing, our analysis reveals a fundamental disconnect between this vision and its operationalization through CAP strategic plans. This disconnect reflects not policy failure but rather a systemic challenge in EU governance: translating cross-sectoral strategic visions into coordinated regulatory and funding mechanisms. The temporal misalignment alone—LTVRA arriving mid-cycle and lacking operational requirements—undermined its potential impact. However, our analysis also reveals that many Member States and regional authorities recognize the LTVRA's value and are seeking integration mechanisms. The gap between strategic aspiration and operational reality is thus not inevitable but addressable through deliberate institutional reform.

The LTVRA strategy received positive reception from national experts we interviewed, including representatives from public research and regional authorities involved in drafting CSPs. However, due to a disjointed policy timeline with the CAP reform process initiated during the previous European Commission mandate, the LTVRA arrived too late in the EU policy process to influence the design of CSPs with specific directives or requirements. Unlike the Farm-to-Fork and Biodiversity strategies, which set mandatory targets under the EU Green Deal, the LTVRA did not introduce any innovative approach to CSP design through a more integrated rural policy perspective. Consequently, we observed a lack of alignment between the expected contribution of the CAP to supporting LTVRA action areas and the relatively modest financial allocation of the 28 CSPs for the socio-economic fabric of rural areas, as outlined in Specific Objectives 7 and 8.

In the post-Covid-19 era, the Recovery and Resilience Fund may have provided significant momentum for rural development, encompassing various policy interventions such as agrifood chains, infrastructure, irrigation, cultural heritage, and water treatment in rural areas. Through analysis of the CSPs and interviews, it became evident that the LTVRA holds potential to influence future policy developments, although its impact remains uncertain. One key challenge lies in the lack of integration of the LTVRA with existing EU policy frameworks and implementation, possibly due in part to insufficient information and awareness about the LTVRA among Member States, managing authorities, and stakeholders in rural policy.

Future policy developments must prioritize temporal alignment between major strategic initiatives. We recommend that any new EU rural strategy be developed simultaneously with, rather than parallel to, sectoral policy reforms such as the CAP. This synchronized approach would ensure that high-level visions translate into concrete programmatic requirements, not post-hoc alignments.

At the European Union level, we recommend:

1. **Regulatory anchoring of LTVRA principles:** Incorporate LTVRA action areas (stronger, connected, prosperous, resilient) into the regulatory framework for the next generation of CAP strategic plans (post-2027), establishing explicit requirements for CSP alignment with LTVRA objectives. Unlike the current voluntary approach, LTVRA alignment should be mandatory and subject to European Commission performance review.
2. **Synchronized policy development:** Ensure that major EU rural and agricultural strategies are developed and enacted simultaneously, not sequentially. This requires institutional reform at the European Commission to coordinate DG Agri, DG Regio, and DG Connect in joint strategy development.
3. **Expanded LEADER and rural development funding:** Increase the mandatory LEADER earmark from 5% to 10% of EAFRD allocations, and create an additional dedicated funding line within CSPs specifically for LTVRA cross-cutting priorities (gender equality, rural youth, social inclusion, broadband access, healthcare, education). Current SO8 allocations (~3% of total CAP funds) are insufficient to operationalize an integrated rural development vision.
4. **RRF coordination mechanisms:** Develop formal links between Recovery and Resilience Facility allocations and CSP rural provisions, ensuring that national RRF plans complement rather than duplicate or contradict rural investments financed through CAP.
5. **LTVRA monitoring and accountability:** Establish specific result indicators tied to LTVRA action areas (quality of rural life, rural inclusion, demographic stability, broadband coverage) and integrate these into the CAP Common Evaluation and Monitoring Framework alongside traditional agricultural output metrics.

At the regional and local level, we recommend:

1. **Multi-level governance structures:** Member States should establish formal inter-ministerial bodies (agriculture, regional development, transport, digital, social affairs) with explicit mandate to coordinate rural policy implementation across CSP and other funding sources. This requires overcoming historical siloes between agricultural and regional development authorities.
2. **Integrated rural development strategies:** Regional authorities should develop multi-year rural strategies that explicitly operationalize LTVRA principles and map out how different EU funding sources (CAP, cohesion policy, RRF, sectoral programs) will be coordinated toward common territorial objectives. These should identify specific place-based outcomes (not just activity targets) for each LTVRA action area.
3. **LEADER expansion and evolution:** LEADER programs should move beyond their traditional focus on preserving rural character and cultural heritage to actively support economic diversification, digital infrastructure, and social inclusion. This requires enhanced capacity building for local action groups and alignment with regional digital and entrepreneurship strategies.
4. **Community engagement in policy design:** Future rural policy cycles should include mandatory engagement with Multi-Actor Platforms and rural communities in CSP development, not just consultation on draft plans. This participatory approach, core to LTVRA philosophy and demonstrated through SHERPA processes, should be operationalized as a standard practice rather than project-specific initiative.
5. **Gender and social inclusion integration:** Specific targets and dedicated funding should be established for women's participation in agricultural and rural business development, youth engagement in place-based strategies, and inclusion of vulnerable populations in rural policy design and benefits.

This analysis of LTVRA-CSP alignment offers a case study in EU policy coherence challenges that extend beyond rural development. As the EU faces interconnected challenges (climate change, demographic decline, digital transformation, pandemic resilience) requiring cross-sectoral coordination, the LTVRA experience demonstrates both the necessity and difficulty of integrating sectoral policies toward common territorial goals. Future EU policy cycles should systematize mechanisms for policy coordination from the outset of strategy development, not as post-hoc alignment efforts. The recommendations above, if implemented, could transform the next CAP reform cycle into a more genuinely integrated rural development framework, with implications for broader EU governance approaches.

References

Bosworth, G., Annibal, I., Carroll, T., Price, L., Sellick, J., & Shepherd, J. (2016). Empowering local action through neo-endogenous development: The case of LEADER in England. *Sociologia Ruralis, 56*(3), 427–449. https://doi.org/10.1111/soru.12089

European Commission. (1988). The Future of Rural Society. Commission communication transmitted to the Council and to the European Parliament on 29 July 1988. *COM, 88*(501).

European Commission. (2020a). *Communication to the European Parliament, the Council, the European Economic Social Committee and to the Committee of the Regions, The European Green Deal*. https://eur-lex.europa.eu/legal-content/EN/TXT/?qid=15761%2050542719&uri=COM%3A2019%3A640%3AFIN

European Commission. (2020b). Proposal for a regulation of the European Parliament and of the Council establishing the Just Transition Fund. Brussels. *COM 2242*. https://eur-lex.europa.eu/legal-content/EN/TXT/?uri=CELEX%3A52020PC0022

European Commission. (2021). *Communication to the European Parliament, the Council, the European Economic Social Committee and to the Committee of the Regions, Recommendations to the Member States as regards their strategic plan for the Common Agricultural Policy*. https://eur-lex.europa.eu/legal-content/EN/TXT/?uri=CELEX%3A52020DC0846

European Commission. (2022/1475). *Commission implementing regulation laying down detailed rules for implementation of regulation (EU) 2021/2115 of the European Parliament and of the Council as regards the evaluation of the CAP strategic plans and the provision of information for monitoring and evaluation*. https://eur-lex.europa.eu/legal-content/EN/TXT/?uri=CELEX:32022R1475

European Commission. (2023). *Approved 28 CAP strategic plans (2023–2027), Summary overview for 27 Member States, Facts and figures*. https://agriculture.ec.europa.eu/system/files/2023-04/approved-28-cap-strategic-plans-2023-27.pdf#page88

European Commission (COM). (2021). *Communication to the European Parliament, the Council, the European Economic Social Committee and to the Committee of the Regions, A long-term Vision for EU's rural areas: Toward stronger, connected, prosperous and resilient rural areas by 2040.*

Féret, S., Berchoux, T., Requier, M., Abdelhakim, T., Slätmo, E., Chartier, O., Nieto, E., & Miller, D. (2020). *Framework providing definitions, operational typology and review of EU strategies for rural areas*. https://zenodo.org/records/5337099

Hennessy, T. C., & Rehman, T. (2007). An investigation into factors affecting theźOccupational choices of nominated farm heirs in Ireland. *Journal of Agricultural Economics, 58*, 61–75. https://doi.org/10.1111/j.1477-9552.2007.00078.x

Miller D., Chartier O., Salle E., Zomer B., Irvine K., Schwartz G. (2022). *First set of recommendations for the development of future rural policies*. https://rural-interfaces.eu/wp-content/uploads/2022/04/SHERPA_D7.3_Recommendations-future-rural-policies_set1.pdf

OECD. (2006). *Rural 3.0. a framework for rural development.*

Official Journal, Regulation (EU). (2021). *2021/2115 of the European Parliament and of the Council of 2 December 2021 establishing rules on support for strategic plans to be drawn up by Member States under the common agricultural policy (CAP Strategic Plans) and financed by the European Agricultural Guarantee Fund (EAGF) and by the European Agricultural Fund for Rural Development (EAFRD) and repealing Regulations (EU) No 1305/2013 and (EU) No 1307/2013*. https://eur-lex.europa.eu/eli/reg/2021/2115/oj

Pagnon J., Springer K., Hiller N., & Féret S. (2023). *Timetable of EU negotiations and policy developments: An overview of the rural policy framework post-2020 (2023 update)*. https://rural-interfaces.eu/wp-content/uploads/2023/04/SHERPA-Deliverable-3.1-final.pdf.

Pertoldi, M., Fioretti, C., Guzzo, F., Testori, G., De Bruijn, M., Ferry, M., Kah, S., Servillo, L.A., & Windisch, S. (2022). *Handbook of territorial and local development strategies*. In M. Pertold, C. Fioretti, F. Guzzo & Testori, G. (Eds.), *EUR 31263 EN*. Publications Office of the European Union. https://doi.org/10.2760/133519,JRC130788

Steiner, A., & Atterton, J. (2015). Exploring the contribution of rural enterprises to local resilience. *Journal of Rural Studies, 40*, 30–45. https://doi.org/10.1016/j.jrurstud.2015.05.004

CHAPTER 3

Potemkin's Villages: The (Weak) Institutional Framework for Rurality and Rural Policy in Slovenia?

Ilona Rac, Borut Stojilković, and Emil Erjavec

1 Introduction

In June 2021, the EU Commission published *The Long-term Vision on Rural Areas*, (LTVRA, 2021) which outlines the EU's vision of rural areas in 2040, and the means for achieving this vision. The strategy reads as an optimistic, ambitious document with a common pan-European direction for holistic and balanced rural development. However, assessing

I. Rac (✉) · E. Erjavec
Biotechnical Faculty, University of Ljubljana, Ljubljana, Slovenia
e-mail: ilona.rac@bf.uni-lj.si

E. Erjavec
e-mail: emil.erjavec@bf.uni-lj.si

B. Stojilković
Ministry of Higher Education, Science and Innovation, Ljubljana, Slovenia
e-mail: borut.stojilkovic@gmail.com

D. Barjolle et al. (eds.), *Innovation and the Future of Rural Development in Europe*,
https://doi.org/10.1007/978-3-032-22570-2_3

the extent to which such ambitions may be fulfilled requires a critical reflection on the degree to which different Member States' (rural) policy institutional environments and implementation even allow for such a holistic consideration of rural areas as promoted by the LTVRA. Can the strategy materialize into something more tangible than a well-intentioned wish list?

Notions on what constitutes an 'ideal' rural policy differ; generally, the principles seem to converge around ideas of bottom-up, place-based, inclusive formulation with attention to territorial diversity (cf. e.g. Asai et al., 2023). For example, the OECD's *Rural Policy 3.0* (OECD, 2016), building on the New Rural Paradigm, which promoted a shift from sectoral (agricultural) support to holistic support for rural areas, emphasised improving well-being for rural dwellers, understanding the economic characteristics of low-density economies, employing a variety of policy instruments in an inclusive, multi-sectoral approach, and attention to specificities of rural areas, their needs, circumstances, opportunities and challenges.

The LTVRA is somewhat less explicit about the goals for rural policy, though it mentions certain specific policy goals for both the Common Agricultural Policy (e.g. "balanced, fair, green and innovative development of rural areas«, »a smart, resilient and diversified agricultural sector, bolstering environmental care and climate action and by strengthening the socio-economic fabric of rural areas«) and Cohesion policy (e.g. »promoting and supporting the harmonious overall development of Member States, regions and territories«, with »tailor made strategies to the needs of each territory«, »integrated territorial development with multi-level governance« and»place based solutions developed in and by rural areas«). In addition, it provides a vision for rural areas with four strands (Stronger, Connected, Resilient and Prosperous), and proposes a *Rural Action Plan* to achieve them. The Commission also announced the introduction of a mechanism for rural proofing of policies, which is to draw on territorial impact assessment and improved monitoring of rural areas. At the moment, however, this is still a vision, not a binding policy.

In addition to discussions on optimal rural policy, the literature on what even constitutes 'rurality' is voluminous and disparate, and includes numerous attempts at defining the rural, using different criteria and typologies. A problem often plaguing rural policies thus stems from a high level of variability in defining and describing the 'rural', which is also dependent on geographical and historical context (Asai et al.,

2023). Attempts to define rurality range from purely technical attempts at selecting the 'right' indicators for distinguishing different types of areas (e.g. the UN's DEGURBA; see Féret et al., 2020) to critical assessments of the concept as a tool for imposing a unified conceptualisation of EU spatial policy and EU integration (Richardson, 2000). The present contribution leans towards the latter, adopting the position that, significant funding for RD notwithstanding, rurality may at present be little more than a vague discourse in a significant part of the European Union, especially in countries acceding more recently. Our aim is therefore not to provide another typology or categorization, but to build on the idea that the notion of rurality, as promoted by the EU and OECD since at least the 1990s, largely remains part of a non-institutionalised discourse in at least some if not most of the EU's member states (MS).

A literature review reveals that the observation that 'rurality' is not quite equally internalised by all European policymakers is not particularly new. It was already suggested by, for example, Hubbard et al. (2007), that rural development policy was 'imported' by new MS (especially those from Central and Eastern European Countries, CEEC) before and after their accession in 2004 to accommodate EU demands to be eligible for rural development funding, and that even in old MS, traditional agricultural and newer rural models of development were often in conflict. Maintaining that this is largely still the case due to different historical and current conditions across European countries and regions (Faludi, 2000; Dax, 2002), including institutional capacity and the institutional subordination of 'rural' to 'agricultural', we argue that such differences are still present. We aim to illustrate this assertion using a post-transitional EU MS, Slovenia, as an example.

Particularly, we investigate the hypothesis that, except for parts of agricultural policy, rural areas are not addressed specifically and comprehensively enough in CEEC as exemplified by Slovenia; indeed, the different developmental policies only address them in a fragmented fashion, which is not sufficiently sensitive to differences and specificities between and within rural areas. Furthermore, we posit that Rural development policy, the CAP's second pillar, only addresses rural areas nominally and in a very limited way – subordinate to the needs of agriculture and with only very limited funding. Institutionally, the situation is similar, with the rural development department being only a small sector of the agricultural ministry, regional development a policy in name more than in substance, and cohesion policy largely blind to the specificities of rural areas. Given this fragmented and uncoordinated policy environment, we argue that achieving balanced rural development as envisaged by the EU Commission and its LTVRA will be exceedingly difficult, as it does not take into account that the notion of rurality may not yet be internalised in New Member states.

Our analysis is largely based on a literature review and overview of policies relevant to rural areas. This information is complemented with insights gathered in the Horizon 2020 SHERPA project, where different contextual and institutional issues regarding rural policies were discussed with rural stakeholders. They gathered as multi-actor platforms (MAPs), formed specifically to provide policy recommendations on contentious issues (see Chapter 2 in this volume). Within each round of discussions, a research team was tasked with analysing the current state of the art on specific issues. The resulting discussion papers were then adapted to local conditions, discussed among the actors of the MAPs, complemented with additional research (interviews and/or surveys) if necessary, and finally synthesised into position papers through group discussion (see e.g. Rac et al., 2022). In this contribution, we mainly lean on the round of discussions on 'Social dimension in rural areas' (ibid.), during which literature review and focus groups discussions were complemented with semi-structured in-depth interviews with representatives of the Association of Farmer Women of Slovenia, the Association of Slovenian Rural Youth, the Slovenian Rural Development Network and Karitas. We also build on insights from the formulation of the Slovenian contribution to the LTVRA (Rac & Erjavec, 2020), where expert knowledge was complemented by a widely disseminated survey.

In the chapter, we first provide an overview of Slovenian rural areas, with some illustrations of specific developmental needs. In this way, we answer the question of whether there is an actual need for a separate policy for rural development. This is followed by an evaluation of the extent to which these issues are addressed by current public policies in Slovenia. We provide an overview of the main policies aimed at addressing rural areas, notably agricultural and cohesion policy, with some discussion on (the absence of) implementing the territorial approach. Finally, we synthesise findings and provide some recommendations for the national and EU levels.

2 Trends in rural development in Slovenia

The Slovenian administrative system operates on two levels: national and local. National institutions, based mainly in Ljubljana, include the Government, ministries, government offices, agencies, and public institutes. Services are extended through 58 local administrative units (local state administrative offices), offering access to various functions such as internal affairs, transportation, construction, agriculture, and denationalization. Local matters, by contrast, fall under the jurisdiction of 212 municipalities, which vary significantly in size and capacity. The absence of an intermediate regional level creates challenges in handling certain tasks of regional importance, impacting areas like public transport, spatial planning, waste management, and natural disasters. Smaller municipalities face difficulties in executing demanding tasks due to limited resources and influence compared to the national level (Nared et al., 2020).

Existing research on rural development shows that various endogenous and exogenous factors affect key developmental processes in Slovenian rural areas (Potočnik Slavič, 2010). While rural economies are diversifying beyond traditional agriculture by promoting rural tourism and supporting rural entrepreneurship (Potočnik Slavič et al., 2022), the agricultural sector is also modernising (often as a result of subsidies and EU funding) towards the usage of modern technologies and improving infrastructure (Cigale & Lampič, 2023). Due to the vast complexity of diverse developmental factors, Slovenia has not developed a comprehensive strategy for rural development – yet; however, many communities have been developing due to internal social capital (Potočnik Slavič, 2009) and the active role of enthusiastic individuals, their associations (Logar, 2019), or youth engagement (Kotnik, 2022).

Slovenian rural areas are diverse and face specific needs. Their development has been affected by historical factors, placement of motorway corridors (having the greatest developmental pressure), and dependency on internal initiatives (Klemenčič et al., 2008). The key questions on rural development as well as the need for public and policy support depend in Slovenia heavily on urban–rural settlement distribution and centralisation of workplaces in urban areas, which are also the causes of major demographic issues in more remote and deprived areas. Other aspects affecting rural inequalities are related to the distance and under-maintained transportation infrastructure and affect both youth and the elderly by limiting access to education (Ostrožnik, 2020) and healthcare services. Young and working-age populations in rural areas are often affected by a lack of proper digital infrastructure as well as well-paid employment opportunities, often resulting in income disparities and population decline (as seen in Table 1). The social assistance service is the worst developed in the most peripheral (and rural) NUTS 3 statistical regions (i.e. Mura and Carinthia) (Kovač & Petrič, 2023).

While Mura, Sava, and Carinthia statistical regions face population decline in total, all of the Slovenian statistical regions except Central Slovenia have at least some municipalities that face population decline. Such municipalities are positioned further away from the motorway junction and major employment centres (Nared et al., 2023). Demographic settlement types of municipalities (Table 1) in Slovenia can be classified into four groups (Ibid.), two of them rural:

- Rural municipalities with a rising number of inhabitants, which cover 19.4% of the country, gaining in population due to immigration, which results in an aging index below average.
- Rural municipalities with a declining number of inhabitants, the largest group among the four by area; these municipalities face daunting conditions: they are characterized by sparse settlement, declining population (–5% over the last decade) due to emigration and negative natural population growth, prevailing number of people with only primary education or without it, weak municipal economy and lack of access to centres and motorways due to their remoteness.

The other two, urban, types of municipalities, also fall into two categories (with population either rising or falling), but are not addressed here in further detail.

As can be seen from Fig. 1 and Table 1, the categorisation of rural municipalities into those with increasing populations and those with decreasing ones, albeit crude, already demonstrates some striking differences, with perhaps the most obvious being the vicinity of the motorway network as a determinant of demographic trends. Rural municipalities with decreasing populations exhibit both a higher percentage of farmers and lower wages, as well as a lower number of enterprises per inhabitant, than those with rising numbers; hence, it can be said that their potential for development or even long-term viability is much lower. Furthermore, there is also a deeper historical, cultural and political rift between rural

Table 1 Selected indicators showing socio-economic and environmental differences among demographic settlement types (Nared et al., 2023)

	Urban municipalities with a rising number of inhabitants	*Urban municipalities with a declining number of inhabitants*	*Rural municipalities with a rising number of inhabitants*	*Rural municipalities with a declining number of inhabitants*	Slovenia
Area (%)	23.35	27.97	19.53	29.18	*100*
Inhabitants (%)	43.07	30.36	14.02	12.56	*100*
Population density (people/km^2)	187,92	110,73	73,15	43.85	*101.90*
Natural increase per 1000 inhabitants	1.30	–8.37	0.65	–1.38	*–0.10*
Migration increase per 1000 inhabitants (2016)	1.06	–1.84	5.70	–1.50	*–0.13*
Population growth index (2008–2017)	105.85	97.13	107.91	95.55	*101.98*
Average monthly wage index	104.80	95.30	92.80	87.70	*100*
Number of enterprises per 1000 inhabitants (2016)	112.10	102.70	82.40	70.60	*95.00*
Share of self-employed persons – farmers, of total active population by municipality of residence (%, 2016)	1.10	1.78	2.99	5.16	*2.06*

(continued)

Table 1 (continued)

	Urban municipalities with a rising number of inhabitants	*Urban municipalities with a declining number of inhabitants*	*Rural municipalities with a rising number of inhabitants*	*Rural municipalities with a declining number of inhabitants*	Slovenia
Share of unoccupied dwellings (%, 2015)	18.94	18.45	22.71	26.06	*20.22*
Share of Natura 2000 (%, 2016)	30.59	35.60	31.58	49.61	*37.74*
Road network density (km/km^2)	1.73	1.56	1.61	1.54	*1.59*

Source Nared et al. (2023), p. 28; Note: data are for 2017 unless otherwise indicated

and urban areas, one that still strongly characterises the Slovenian political space and is perhaps less linked to the physical and demographic characteristics of different areas (Tiran, 2015).

As indicated above, a particular issue faced by rural areas is access to basic services, such as healthcare and education. For example, many Slovenian rural municipalities face either a low fertility rate due to population aging, immigration, or a combination of both, leading to a declining number of pupils in many rural primary schools and subsequent closing of smaller schools. Slovenia has a long tradition of schools being one of the central pillars of rural communities (Jelen, 2010), even if they are only branch elementary schools, i.e. schools that belong to bigger or more central primary schools (Organisation and Financing…, 2023). Branch schools are financed by municipalities, which are also their founders (and in the end "closers") (Organisation and Financing…, 2023). Being a core of rural communities (Jelen, 2010), such institutions help their communities thrive, and when they are shut down, they often cause the local community to decline at an even greater pace (Ostrožnik, 2020). Their existence also depends on parents' decision as to where to enrol their children, which often depends on their workplace, but the decision mainly remains in the hands of local mayors and their councils, which results in a decline in the number of such institutions even if the trend of pupils

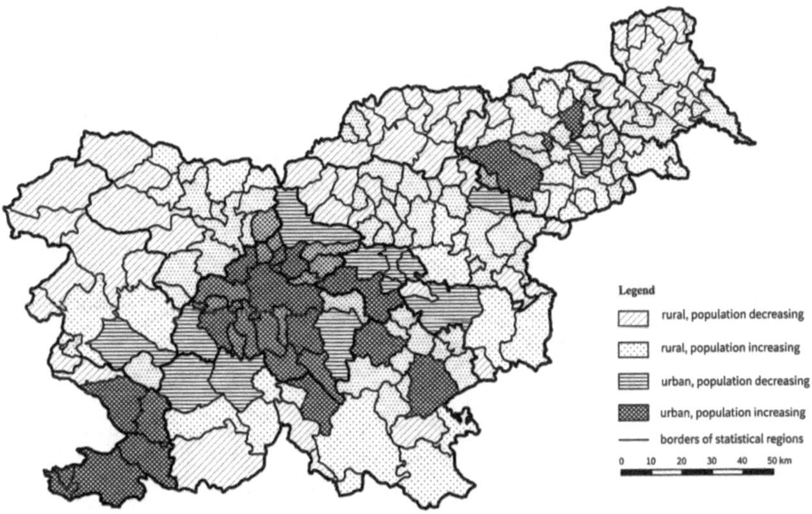

Fig. 1 Classification of Slovenian municipalities, Nared et al. (2019a, 2019b)

attending them has been positive in recent years. Due to their importance for the vitality of rural communities, it would be crucial to evaluate the significance of such institutions for rural areas at the national level and to base decisions on whether or not to close them on cost–benefit analyses. However, no such national strategic assessments have been carried out yet. This example illustrates the situation in a variety of sectors.

Spatial processes in Slovenian rural areas are also significantly affected by spatial plans, natural resources exploitation and protected areas. As interests concerning the use of space expand, so does the array of interested stakeholders in rural areas grow beyond farmers to include local and national authorities, investors, entrepreneurs, environmentalists and others, and conflicts of interest have arisen in Slovenian rural areas accordingly (Guštin & Potočnik Slavič, 2015). To avoid such conflicts, a comprehensive multi-layered policy should be introduced, expanding from the current one, which in Slovenia is mainly limited to agricultural policy (discussed below), and introducing monetary transfers for those areas. In terms of knowledge and data availability to support such a policy, while certain issues are relatively well explored, reviews and interviews conducted under SHERPA (Rac et al., 2022) revealed that many are not, especially social issues. Thus, there are significant data gaps in the field of rural poverty, access to services, quality of life and social inclusion; data are often too coarse or partial. This points to a need to address knowledge gaps and rural developmental issues more comprehensively to cover not only agriculture but also developmental potentials in other sectors, infrastructural issues, employment opportunities, etc.

3 Public Policies Addressing Rural Development in Slovenia and Their Success

Spatial and Regional Development Policies

Even though Slovenia is not yet administratively regionalized, it does have regional policy; it is administered through developmental regions, the borders of which coincide (in principle) with NUTS3 borders, while cohesion regions for the implementation of cohesion policy coincide with NUTS2 (ZSRR-2, 2011). Slovenia is divided into two cohesion regions, the Eastern Slovenia (si. *Vzhodna Slovenija*) cohesion region and the Western Slovenia (si. *Zahodna Slovenija*) cohesion region, currently classified as less developed and developed, respectively. Based on a uniform EU methodology, in the financial period 2015–2022 European Regional Development Fund (ERDF) and European Social Fund (ESF) funds were allocated so that the Eastern region received 60.6% of the available funds, while the Western received 39.4% of the available funds (SVRK, 2021) (76,1% and 23,9% in the current period; SVRK, n.d.). However, this division is much too crude to reflect the actual diversity found across Slovenian municipalities (Fig. 2). Therefore, territorial development is monitored at the level of statistical regions (Partnership Agreement, 2014).

From a developmental perspective, Slovenian areas are covered by several national strategies, the first being the overarching Slovenian Development Strategy 2030 (SVRK, 2017), which strives to achieve quality of life for all through balanced economic, social and environmental development. This strategy only mentions rural areas once explicitly when highlighting their developmental deficit; other than stating that certain areas are disadvantaged or at risk of demographic decline, the strategy is not spatially differentiated.

The Strategy on Slovenian Spatial Development 2050 (DZ, 2023), on the other hand, being the key national strategic spatial development

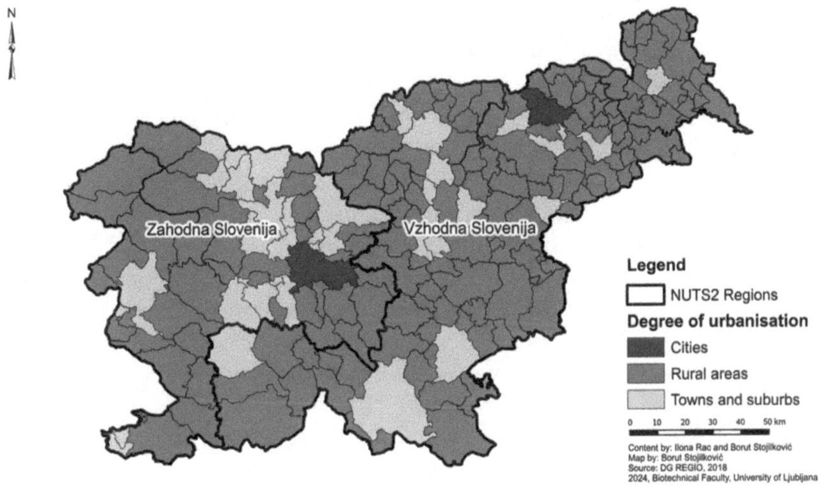

Fig. 2 Division of Slovenia into Cohesion (NUTS2) regions and municipalities as classified according to the Degree of Urbanisation methodology (*Source* DG REGIO, 2016)

act based on the Slovenian Spatial Management Act (ZUreP-3), is much more detailed and also more explicit in addressing rural areas. It promotes polycentric spatial development (in line with the European spatial development perspective and Territorial agenda 2030), with a vision to achieve territorial (spatial) cohesion and ensure a high quality of life for all people, including through equitable access to general services and infrastructure. The strategy defines rural areas as areas with similar natural, economic, and social characteristics, distinctive spatial identity and resources. They are characterized by smaller settlements and lower population density, and the predominant features in the landscape are agricultural and forest land use. Furthermore, rural settlements are those with 500–2,000 inhabitants, a proportion of agricultural households greater than 7%, lower population density and a predominant share of agricultural and forest land use. Three kinds of rural areas are recognized: central rural areas (developmentally 'vital'), hinterland of urban areas and remote rural areas.

The vision of spatial development sees ideal future rural areas as areas that keep their landscape character despite modernization, with an important role of agriculture and forestry, and further development of the service economy and local entrepreneurship. Important emphasis is placed on local production, national food self-sufficiency, short supply chains and maintaining landscape features, as well as a traditional settlement pattern. Furthermore, settlement in areas most vulnerable to flooding and avalanches is to be abandoned.

While the Strategy is to be followed up by a detailed action programme to implement it, including measures, funding and competent institutions, there are also other national strategies not based on ZUreP-3 that affect spatial planning, notably the Programme for implementing European cohesion policy and the Rural development programme (subsumed under the CAP strategic plan after 2023), and sectoral policies influencing spatial planning such as transport, housing, energy and climate, and efforts in the field of land policy (Bizjak et al., 2021).

While regional development has no official sectoral strategy (Pečar, 2020), it is governed by its own law (Promotion of Balanced Regional Development Act, ZSRR-2, 2011), and the Ministry of Economy and Technology prepared a document in 2019 that outlined the goals and guidelines of regional policy in the period 2021–2027 (MGRT, 2019). In this period, regional policy thus has four general objectives aimed at strengthening the development capacities of regions based on endogenous developmental potentials and global opportunities: (i) improving the quality of life in all regions, (ii) catching up in development with European regions, (iii) reducing regional development disparities, and (iv) fostering international interregional connectivity and cooperation (Pečar, 2020). The third goal acknowledges developmental disparities between regions and addresses maintaining settlement and developmental vitality of problem areas but does not specifically address rural areas.

Regional policy is implemented through regional development plans, which outline priority developmental projects, their value and sources of funding. In principle, they must be adopted at the same time or after regional spatial plans. In its analysis of the success in achieving regional policy goals, UMAR (2020) notes that the Regional developmental risk index shows improvement, though with notable regional differences and even bigger differences at low territorial levels, with Border-adjacent problem areas a particular cause of concern. These areas have been the subject of decades-long efforts to improve the situation and are the first priority area of regional and developmental policy, but continue to decline due to unfavourable demographic trends, peripheral location and poor access to general services. By contrast, regional policy pays no special attention to rural areas. On the whole, the policy is not considered to be holistically implemented, nor are its effects consistently monitored (ibid.). Furthermore, it is currently still decoupled from regional spatial planning, a situation that an amendment of the *Spatial Planning Act* (ZUreP-2, 2011) tried to remedy by tying the adoption of regional development plans to the simultaneous adoption of regional spatial plans (Nared et al., 2019b). However, it is unlikely that the legislative demand to adopt spatial plans before developmental plans will be met in the period 2021–2027 (Bizjak et al., 2021).

In 2020, the Slovenian Court of Auditors issued a scathing report on regional development policy in Slovenia between 2014 and 2017 (CoA, 2020). It reviewed the efficiency of the operations of the Slovenian Government, Ministry of Economic Development and Technology (responsible for regional policy at the time), and 6 municipalities, and found that the Government and Ministry were only partially effective in managing regional development. Criticism of both the Government and the Ministry pertained to a lack of definition of clear objectives for regional development, guidance for preparing regional development programmes, criteria for selecting programmes, a deficient monitoring system, and lack of usage of data in the programming and monitoring process. This demonstrates that the institutional system for implementing the policy is still a work in progress.

The two policy areas that are most closely related to rural areas and have comprehensive financing, namely agricultural and cohesion policy, are covered in more detail in the following sections. In addition to these policies, there is emerging potential for covering developmental gaps in rural areas through certain sources such as the Recovery and Resilience Facility (RRF), InvestEU, other EU programmes, and European Investment Bank funding (LTVRA, 2021). Furthermore, Slovenia has a nationally funded Public Fund for Regional and Rural Development, which offers financial products aimed at balanced regional development and has approximately 130 million EUR at its disposal (SRRS, 2023).

Rural Development Policy in Slovenian Agricultural Policy

The public policy that most explicitly addresses rural development issues in Slovenia is agricultural policy, specifically the second (rural development) pillar, financed by the EAFRD and national co-financing. In this section, we discuss how rural development policy has been implemented in terms of objectives, instruments and resources in the period since Slovenia's accession to the EU (2009–2022). In particular, we are interested in the extent to which this policy reflects the priorities that go beyond agricultural issues and their productive, economic and environmental dimensions.

Before accession to the EU, the objectives of Slovenian agricultural policy were introduced in the Strategy for the Development of Slovenian Agriculture (1993), modified in the *Agriculture Act* (2008) and further built upon in two agricultural policy resolutions adopted by the National Assembly in 2010 and 2020. The latter two documents were adopted when Slovenia was already embedded in the legal framework, priorities and support mechanisms established by the European Union's Common Agricultural Policy (CAP). In these documents, the countryside is viewed predominantly from an agricultural perspective; objectives that go beyond agriculture are in the minority and are formulated in rather general terms. They appear in the form of 'Ensuring coherent and socially sustainable rural development (in cooperation with other policies)' (National Assembly, 2010). The last document in this succession reflects the structure of the general and specific objectives of the CAP and identifies the general objective: 'Improving the quality of life and strengthening economic activity in rural areas' (National Assembly, 2020). More detailed specific objectives that go beyond the agricultural framework somewhat are "Strengthening local initiatives and inter-industry cooperation and strengthening the link between tourism and quality locally produced food"; "Developing the bio-economy"; "Social inclusion, rural women and care for vulnerable groups"; "Reducing the gap in accessibility and quality of services in urban and rural areas". These objectives also formed the basis for the priorities for the Rural Development Policy (RDP) programming documents (MAFF, 2015, 2023a, 2023b, 2023c) and the CAP Strategic Plan (MAFF, 2023b). The wording of the objectives has been slightly modified but reflects the wording of the objectives as contained in the CAP strategic documents from this period (European Commission, 2010, 2017).

The generality of the objectives gives the first impression that Slovenian decision-makers are intensively engaged in holistic aspects of rural development that go beyond agriculture, but a more in-depth analysis of the content of measures, and especially their financial allocations (Fig. 3), suggests otherwise.

Analysing the measures over the whole period is complex, as the form of measures changes and acquires new emphasis and financial weight. We have therefore used the classification of agricultural policy measures used by the Agricultural Institute of Slovenia in its systematic monitoring of agricultural policy (Bedrač et al., 2023). Each year, they examine individual measures and classify them (Table 2), which makes it possible to compare trends in funding and identify priorities for agricultural policy.

In the classification in Table 2, only the group *Measures in support of the rural economy and population* contains interventions that are not linked to agriculture, indicating that broader aspects of rural development are not a strong priority of agricultural policy. This is further underlined by the analysis of budgetary transfers for each group of measures in the classification (Fig. 3) for the period 2009–2022. We have tried to identify how much of the funds was spent on measures related to broader aspects of rural development and how much on agriculture. We have further divided the latter into the environmental dimension of agriculture and everything else (i.e. other).

This rather rough comparison clearly shows that the general aspects of rural development are a weak priority of Slovenian agricultural policy. Over the observed period, the share of these funds varied minimally between 4,32% and 6,14%, so there was no significant change in the share (Bedrač et al., 2014; Bedrač et al., 2020; Bedrač et al., 2023).

It can be concluded that there is a strong orientation of agricultural policy towards agriculture and its developmental issues in Slovenia. Broader rural development measures are of secondary importance, a kind of "obligatory element", seemingly stemming more from European legislation and obligations than from an actual decision to address the rural development territorial issues of Slovenia.

Cohesion Policy

Similarly to agricultural policy, cohesion policy stems from the EU level. In the current programming period, it is funded through the ERDF, the Cohesion Fund (CF) and the European Social Fund Plus (ESF +). The basis for acquiring funds from these funds in each multiannual financial period (MFF) period is a Partnership agreement between the Member state and the European Commission, which covers the Cohesion funds, as well as the EAFRD and the European Maritime and Fisheries funds (EMFF); in the period 2021–2027, Slovenia is entitled to about 3,3 EUR

Table 2 Classification of agricultural budget support by group of measures (taken and adapted from Bedrač et al., 2023, p. 52)

Market measures and direct support to producers	*Rural development and agricultural structural policy*	*General services in support of agricultural development*
Market support measures • Market measures • Export support	**Measures to strengthen the competitiveness of the agri-food sector** • modernisation and restructuring of agricultural holdings • improving agricultural infrastructure • organisation, processing, marketing and promotion of the agri-food sector	**Research, development, advisory and professional services** • Research and development • advisory and public services • agricultural education and infrastructure • professional tasks
Direct support to agricultural producers • Direct payments and cost reduction measures • direct payments to producers • cost reduction measures	**Measures to ensure environmental and other social benefits** • payments to farmers in areas with natural and other constraints • payments to farmers for agri-environmental services and animal welfare	**Safety and quality control** • veterinary measures • phytosanitary tasks and measures and plant protection • food and feed quality measures
Compensatory or other exceptional payments • exceptional aid on specific markets • other compensation and refunds • compensatory payments for production reductions	**Measures in support of the rural economy and population** • development of non-agricultural activities in rural areas • rural infrastructure, basic services and village renewal • Strengthening local development initiatives (Leader)	**Other general services** • support to non-governmental organizations • technical assistance • other

billion (SRRS); in the previous period (2014–2022), it was 3,068 billion (3,3 with the funds added by React-EU) (MKRR, 2023). In the programming period 2014–2020, Cohesion Policy investments were divided into eleven Thematic Objectives (TOs; determined for all ESI funds in Regulation 1303/2013; European Union, 2013); in the current period, they centre around five policy objectives (Regulation 2021/1060; European

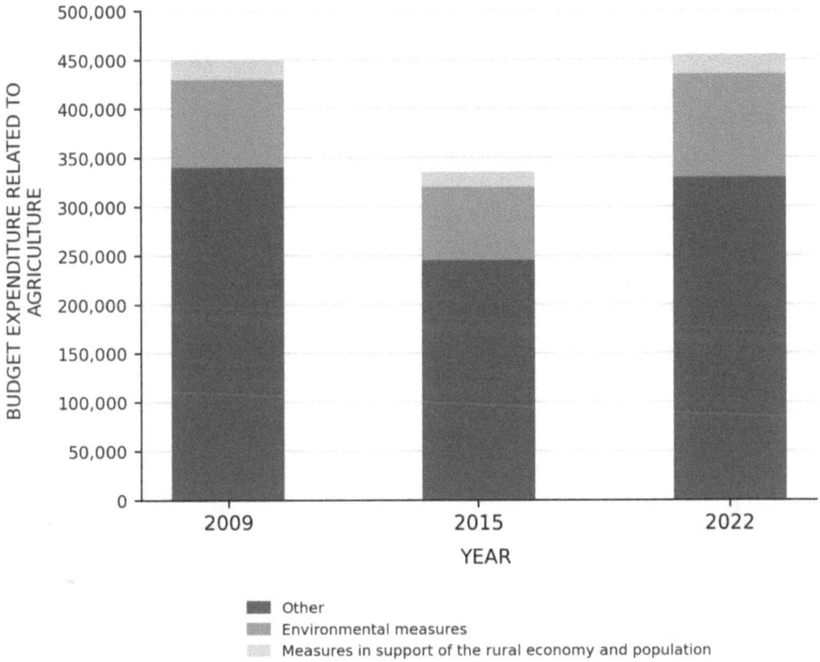

Fig. 3 Breakdown of budget expenditure related to agriculture by group of measures (EUR 000). *Data sources* Bedrač et al. (2014), Bedrač et al. (2020), Bedrač et al. (2023)

Union, 2021a, 2021b), of which the last is to be achieved exclusively through so-called territorial tools (European Commission, n.d.), a novelty under the policy.

Already at the EU level, there is no specific territorial focus on rural areas; rather, the policy differentiates between less-developed, transition and more-developed regions (EU Monitor, 2018). Rural areas are mentioned in the ERDF and CF regulation (2021/1058; European Union, 2021b), however, which states that "the ERDF shall pay special attention to addressing the challenges of disadvantaged regions and areas, in particular rural areas and areas which suffer from severe and permanent natural or demographic handicaps" (Art. 10). The ESF regulation does not refer to rural areas.

In the period 2014–2020, the *Operational programme for implementing Cohesion policy* adopted all 11 TOs as Priority Axes. The main areas addressed (nominally) directly related to rural areas in the *Partnership Agreement* (Partnership Agreement, 2014) were: broadband infrastructure under TO2; "competitiveness of rural areas, in particular agriculture", under TO3; "development of non-agricultural activities in rural areas (subsidiary on-farm activities and in micro-enterprises) that will create conditions for the creation of green jobs and an additional source of income on farms" under TO8; and "attaining the EUSDR objectives of improving the competitiveness of rural areas, especially agriculture, by promoting entrepreneurship in rural areas, supporting innovation and cooperation in agriculture, and supporting economic diversity in rural areas", under TOs 9 and 10. LEADER was also highlighted as a way of promoting social inclusion (TO9).

The Agreement highlighted five substantive and one horizontal intervention area for the EAFRD, of which only one ("green jobs and coherent and sustainable development of rural areas based on the development of the endogenous potential of the local environment") was not agriculture- or forestry-oriented. For the structural funds (ERDF, ESF, CF), rural areas were not addressed specifically, but were mentioned in the sections justifying investment in broadband infrastructure and enhancing employment, although the ESF was explicitly excluded from supporting job creation and developing social capacities in rural areas – these areas were left to the EAFRD. Rural areas were mentioned as relevant for the European Maritime and Fisheries Fund (EMFF), as well, as a possible beneficiary of more developed aquaculture. In its discussion of territorial development, the text itself highlighted the fact that Slovenia is predominantly rural, differences between rural areas themselves, and the underexploited potential of regional development. Similarly, the Operational Programme (Operational Programme, 2023) mainly deals with rural areas in relation to access to broadband and improving employment opportunities.

When discussing financing, this lack of differentiation per type of territory at the programming level means that it is difficult to assess the amount of funding allocated to rural areas. This includes the Community-led local development (CLLD) approach, which was applied in three funds, i.e. EAFRD, EMFF and ERDF (with the notable exclusion of the ESF), in the period 2014–2020 (PA, 2014). As per the agreement, EUR 41.8 million of the EAFRD were earmarked for the implementation of the CLLD approach, supplemented with resources from the EMFF and ERDF: EUR 5 million and EUR 30 million, respectively. However, it is not possible to assert that all this funding was allocated to rural areas, as the approach is also applied to non-rural areas.

The lack of differentiation and targeted funding is reflected in the European Commission's description of the allocation of funding (Table 3), in which only 4% of Cohesion funding for Slovenia is allocated to rural (i.e., thinly populated) areas, while 58% is categorised as 'not applicable' territorially; at the EU level, this percentage is as high as 61% (DG REGIO, 2019).

In the current programming period (2021–2027), there is also no special emphasis placed on rural areas in the Partnership agreement (SVRK, 2022), other than stating that "in parallel with regional disparities, consideration should be given to the specific characteristics of different forms of settlement" and that "Urban and rural areas face different challenges in development that affect quality of life". Again, the main areas of concern for rural areas are digital connectivity and sustainable mobility, the latter to promote balanced regional development. Similarly, under Objective 5, the PA aims to promote territorial approaches in interlinking rural and urban areas as complementary functional areas. CLLD, also classified under Objective 5, is intended to improve the general quality of life, and only funding under the LEADER approach (under the EAFRD) is specific to rural areas (or rather, settlements with fewer than 10,000 inhabitants). Similarly, the Operational

Table 3 Planned Cohesion policy investment by territory type, 2014–2020

Territory type	*EU amount (€)*	*% of total*
Not applicable	1,950,344,103	58
Cooperation across national or regional programme areas ...	556,860,379	17
Large Urban areas (densely populated > 50 000 population)	294,044,080	9
Macro regional cooperation area	284,389,163	9
Small Urban areas (intermediate density > 5 000 population)	132,601,015	4
Rural areas (thinly populated)	118,632,395	4

Source DGREGIO (2019)

programme (Program…, 2022) is mainly concerned with digital connectivity in rural areas and an occasional mention of the lack of teachers; it is left to CLLD to address quality of life and access to services.

In the period 2021–2027, CLLD will still be implemented through the EAFRD and ERDF, again without the ESF, and will receive EUR 84,55 million (MAFF, 2023c), of which 44,4 million through LEADER under the CAP strategic plan (MAFF, 2023b). Neither the Operational programme nor the Commission webpage (DG REGIO, 2022) differentiates funding by type of area in terms of 'rurality', only in terms of more- and less-developed regions.

Institutionally, even Cohesion policy in the narrower sense (ignoring the EAFRD, which has its own Managing authority) is implemented in Slovenia in a highly complex setting. Since its beginnings, it has been burdened by an implementation system involving many bodies at different levels (including restructuring and changes in management accompanying changes in government), frequent changes of responsible persons and a changing structure of the system and implementation procedures, a complex and an unharmonised regulatory environment (numerous Slovenian regulations applying to the implementation, both general for the state budget funds and specific for European funds) and lack of coordination between different governmental offices and ministries (CoA, 2012; SVRK, 2021; MKRR, n.d.). Furthermore, it has been pointed out that not enough attention was paid to quality conditions and criteria in public tenders to ensure the selection of the best projects, nor were critical assessments of needs ex ante or performance ex post carried out (CoA, 2012). The attention to the percentage of EU funds absorbed still seems to take precedence over the quality of their spending.

These implementation issues indicate that the current institutional set-up is still developing and struggling to adapt to implementing these complex policies. Since the quality of implementation is secondary to acquiring EU funding, these policies, while useful to some extent, still suffer from insufficiently strategic, comprehensive, coordinated and targeted implementation necessary to address the complex developmental needs of rural areas.

4 Discussion and Conclusions: Weak Policy Concept and Necessary Steps in Formulating Rural Development Policy

Slovenia and its rural areas are characterized by significant developmental disparities. Despite efforts to promote regional development, these disparities persist, with differences within regions often greater than between them. In the absence of regional administrations, one notable factor exacerbating this divide is the small size of Slovenian municipalities, which often operate independently or even compete rather than cooperate (Nared, 2020). In this setting, which merits nuanced and more locally tailored intervention-setting (Penko Seidl et al., 2017), policies intended to address disparities seem ill-equipped to do so, marked by a lack of coherent and targeted measures. A key issue lies in the lack of policy coherence and acknowledgment of regional specificities. This is evident in the disjointed implementation of EU funds, such as the exclusion of the European Social Fund from CLLD initiatives. Moreover, the separation of regional and spatial planning (RRA GIZ, 2023a, 2023b; Nared et al., 2019b), compounded by short-term regional planning approaches (Nared et al., 2019b), further exacerbates the disconnect between policy objectives and realities on the ground.

While there seems to be some shift, at least nominally, towards 'territoriality' at both the EU and national level, especially through the CLLD approach, this shift still relates to a rather small fraction of funding. It seems that the majority of funds are still allocated through broad-brushed approaches, either through the agricultural silo or through silos under the Cohesion policy, which appears characterised by increasing rather than decreasing complexity in implementation. At the administrative level, the absence of a dedicated regional planning authority hampers the creation of cohesive regional development strategies; thus, spatial planning is left to municipalities, disconnected from developmental planning done at the regional level (Nared et al., 2019b). While regional development agencies exist, their limited budgets and competencies hinder effective coordination. Furthermore, the current NUTS2 level of differentiation within cohesion policy fails to capture the nuanced needs of local communities, rendering existing policies insufficiently tailored to address specific developmental deficits. Certainly, the lack of consistent definitions of rural areas based on criteria beyond population density is not helpful, although admittedly this issue also plagues 'rural' policy at the EU level, not only in Slovenia or New Member States (see e.g. Féret et al., 2020).

Slovenia, as an example of a CEEC, thus has a weak rural policy. The question arises, should this be understood as a consequence of national policy choices, given that Slovenia does not fully reflect the collectively agreed strategies of the EU? Or is it rather the EU institutions that do not sufficiently take into account the fact that in CEEC, rural areas are of secondary importance, overshadowed by regional development? At any rate, this mismatch might indicate a deeper EU problem.

Legislative complexity and inconsistency further obstruct effective rural planning efforts. Frequent changes in legislation across various sectors (Nared et al., 2019b), coupled with dispersed policy implementation (e.g. MKRR, n.d.) and insufficient communication across multiple institutions (see e.g. CoA, 2012), create administrative inefficiencies and hinder long-term strategic planning. Additionally, the focus on acquiring EU funding often takes precedence over ensuring its efficient utilization, undermining the effectiveness of rural development initiatives. It is therefore necessary to ensure a more appropriate regulation of processes and organization of regional development until the establishment of administrative regions, as well as strengthen the financial and personnel capacity of regional agencies and place more emphasis on long term strategic and professionally-led approaches, as well as bottom-up collaboration and decision-making (RRA GIZ, 2023b). Moreover, there is a need to strengthen the coordination and cooperation between different line ministries (Nared, 2019b).

Under the umbrella of the CAP, Rural development policy (RDP, pillar 2) in Slovenia continues to prioritize agriculture rather than addressing rural areas in a holistic manner, and the policy, particularly the first pillar, has even been judged to work against broader territorial cohesion objectives at the EU level due to the uneven distribution of support (ESPON, 2003; Kull et al., 2014; Matthews, 2006). The critique of RDP as essentially agricultural is hardly new or specific to Slovenia: it has been voiced by researchers since its beginnings (e.g. Dwyer et al., 2003; Kull et al., 2014; Papadopoulos et al., 2015). Thus, as Kull et al., (2014) assert, "*Most member states chose to tackle socio-economic and environmental challenges in rural areas by improving the situation in the agricultural sector*« - and we maintain that this largely remains the same to this day, at least in CEECs. In other words, the policy rhetoric of territoriality, and even more of rurality, largely remains a rhetoric – mainly at the EU level, and only in traces at the national level. This reflects still-ongoing power struggles at a number of levels – between different national and EU institutions, interest groups, and policy areas (cf. Richardson, 2000).

To conclude, it is clear that, despite the lack of detailed analyses, there is a need to formulate a real specialized rural development policy, as indicated by various documents. Currently, rural development is not comprehensively addressed; therefore, we propose several solutions for Slovenia, which can be transposed to other CEECs: to establish a specialised national rural council comprising policy, science and society representatives, provide a clear definition of rural areas, and fill the all too numerous data gaps. For policymakers, the solution to the issues outlined above seems quite straightforward: they must prioritize the development of more coherent and targeted policies that integrate regional planning, streamline administrative processes, and ensure efficient allocation of resources; this also includes establishing administrative regions. However, it is likely that the 'real' issues underlying the lack of coherence between policy areas must be brought to light and addressed first, and these include silo thinking, power differences in the policy arenas and lack of democratic inclusion through bottom-up governance processes. It is imperative to establish better (more transparent and inclusive) decision-making processes to balance conflicts between different stakeholders.

Finally, the concept of RD has not yet been fully integrated into Slovenian policy (and likely has not been in most other CEECs). Rurality is still understood mainly as an extension of farming, while countries seem more strongly inclined to support a regional approach (albeit also weakly implemented and substantiated) due to the amount of funding available through Cohesion policy. Meanwhile, emancipating rural areas from agriculture under the CAP and applying an adequately differentiated territorial approach in public policies addressing rural areas remains a challenge. And without such an approach, the LTVRA will remain but a vision.

References

Agriculture act [Zakon o kmetijstvu]. (2008). http://www.pisrs.si/Pis.web/preglедPredpisa?id=ZAKO4716

Asai, M., Dwyer, J., Antón, J., & Garcilazo, E. (2023). Fostering agricultural and rural policy dialogue, 197. https://doi.org/10.1787/d36fcbad-en

Barbič, A., Udovč, A., & Medved, A. (2004). Protection of the environment and biodiversity for sustainable future of rural areas : The case of planned Regional park Trnovski gozd. *Slovenia. Sociologija Sela, 165–166*(3–4), 277–307.

Bedrač, M., Kožar, M., Moljk, B., Pintar, M., Volk, T., Zagorc, B., Belaj, S., Polak Benkič, T., Cerjak, M., Cvelbar, J., Čadonič Špelič, V., Erjavec, J., Filipi, P., Hočevar, V., Hrastar, T, Jurcan S., Korbar, U., Požar, M., Ravnikar, L., & Stanonik Rotar, K. (2014). Poročilo o stanju kmetijstva, živilstva, gozdarstva in ribištva v letu 2013. Ministrstvo za kmetijstvo in okolje. Kmetijski inštitut Slovenije. https://www.kis.si/f/docs/Porocila_o_stanju_v_kmetijstvu_OEK/ZP-2013-splosnopriloge.pdf

Bedrač, M., Bele, S., Brečko, J., Hiti, A., Kožar, M., Moljk, B., Travnikar, T., & Zagorc, B. (2020). Poročilo o stanju kmetijstva, živilstva, gozdarstva in ribištva v letu 2019. Ministrstvo za kmetijstvo, gozdarstvo in prehrano. Kmetijski inštitut Slovenije. https://www.kis.si/f/docs/Porocila_o_stanju_v_kmetijstvu_OEK/ZP_2019_splosno__priloge_net.pdf

Bedrač, M., Bele, S., Brečko, J, Hiti Dvoršak, A., Kožar, M., Ložar, L., Moljk, B., Telič, V., Travnikar, T., & Zagorc, B. (2023). Poročilo o stanju kmetijstva, živilstva, gozdarstva in ribištva v letu 2022. Ministrstvo za kmetijstvo, gozdarstvo in prehrano. Kmetijski inštitut Slovenije. https://www.kis.si/f/docs/Porocila_o_stanju_v_kmetijstvu/ZP_2022_splosno__priloge_2.pdf

Bizjak, I., Gantar, D., Cotič, B., Gulič, A., Koblar, S., Kozamernik, J., Mušič, B., Mujkić, S., Nikšič, M., & Sendi, R. (2021). Poročilo o prostorskem razvoju 2021 (V. Slabe, Ed.). Ministrstvo za okolje in prostor, Direktorat za prostor, graditev in stanovanja.

CoA. (2012). Sistem izvajanja evropske kohezijske politike v Republiki Sloveniji. https://www.rs-rs.si/fileadmin/user_upload/revizija/519/EUSkladi_SP06-11.pdf

CoA. (2020). Regionalni razvoj. https://www.rs-rs.si/fileadmin/user_upload/Datoteke/Revizije/2020/RRA/RRA_SP14-17.pdf

Cigale, D., & Lampič, B. (2023). Aspects of tourism sustainability on organic farms in Slovenia. *Journal of the Geographical Institute Cvijic, 73*(2), 251–267. https://doi.org/10.2298/IJGI2302251C

Dax, T. (2002). Rural development—A challenge for European inter-disciplinary research. *Ländlicher Raum,* 1.

DG REGIO. (2016). Degree of Urbanisation. https://ec.europa.eu/regional_policy/information-sources/maps/degree-urbanisation_en

DG REGIO. (2019). Tracking cohesion policy investment by type of territory. https://cohesiondata.ec.europa.eu/stories/s/Tracking-cohesion-investments-by-type-of-territory/kff5-7ask

DG REGIO. (2022). 2021–2027: Initial cohesion policy EU budget allocations. https://cohesiondata.ec.europa.eu/stories/s/2021-2027-EU-allocations-available-for-programming/2w8s-ci3y/

Dwyer, J., Baldock, D., Beaufoy, G., Bennet, H., Lowe, P., & Ward, N. (2003). Rural development in an Enlarging European Union.
ESPON. (2003). The Territorial Impact of CAP and Rural Development Policy—Third Interim Report. https://www.espon.eu/sites/default/files/attachments/3.ir_2.1.3-full.pdf
EU Monitor. (2018). Regional Development and Cohesion Policy beyond 2020: Questions and Answers. https://www.eumonitor.eu/9353000/1/j9vvik7m1c3gyxp/vkorldekh7qy?ctx=vgb8kauhgays
European Commission. (2010). The CAP towards 2020: Meeting the food, natural resources and territorial challenges of the future. https://eur-lex.europa.eu/LexUriServ/LexUriServ.do?uri=COM:2010:0672:FIN:en:PDF
European Commission. (2017). The future of food and farming. https://eur-lex.europa.eu/legal-content/EN/TXT/PDF/?uri=CELEX:52017DC0713
European Commission. (n.d.). European Commission. (n.d.). New Cohesion Policy. https://ec.europa.eu/regional_policy/2021-2027_en
European Union. (2013). Regulation (EU) No 1303/2013 of the European Parliament and of the Council of 17 December 2013 laying down common provisions on the European Regional Development Fund, the European Social Fund, the Cohesion Fund, the European Agricultural Fund for Rural Development and the European Maritime and Fisheries Fund and laying down general provisions on the European Regional Development Fund, the European Social Fund, the Cohesion Fund and the European Maritime and Fisheries Fund and repealing Council Regulation (EC) No 1083/2006. https://eur-lex.europa.eu/legal-content/EN/TXT/?uri=CELEX%3A02013R1303-20230301
European Union. (2021). Regulation (EU) 2021/1060 of the European Parliament and of the Council of 24 June 2021 laying down common provisions on the European Regional Development Fund, the European Social Fund Plus, the Cohesion Fund, the Just Transition Fund and the European Maritime, Fisheries and Aquaculture Fund and financial rules for those and for the Asylum, Migration and Integration Fund, the Internal Security Fund and the Instrument for Financial Support for Border Management and Visa Policy. https://eur-lex.europa.eu/legal-content/EN/TXT/PDF/?uri=CELEX:32021R1060
European Union. (2021b). Regulation (EU) 2021/1058 of the European Parliament and of the Council of 24 June 2021 on the European Regional Development Fund and on the Cohesion Fund. https://eur-lex.europa.eu/legal-content/EN/TXT/?uri=CELEX:32021R1058
Faludi, A. (2000). The European spatial development perspective—What next? *European Planning Studies, 8*(2), 237–250. https://doi.org/10.1080/096543100110866

Féret, S., Berchoux, T., Requier, M., Abdelhakim, T., Slätmo, E., Chartier, O., Nieto, E., & Miller, D. (2020). Framework providing definitions, review and operational typology of rural areas in Europe (SHERPA Project Deliverable 3.2).

Glumac, R., Franić, R., & Udovč, A. (2017). Stakeholders' expectations from the agri-environmental programme in Slovenia and Croatia. *Journal of Environmental Planning and Management, 60*(1), 67–91. https://doi.org/10.1080/09640568.2016.1140633

Guštin, Š., & Potočnik Slavič, I. (2015). Identification and spatial distribution of conflicts in rural areas. *Geografski vestnik, 87*(1), 81—101. https://doi.org/10.3986/GV87105

Hubbard, C., Gorton, M., & Hubbard, L. (2007). The Introduction of EU Rural Development Policy in Central and Eastern Europe. EAAE 100th Seminar, June 21–23, 2007, Novi Sad, Serbia and Montenegro.

Jelen, N. (2010). Vodenje sodobne podružnične šole – izziv za raznolikost. In Peček, Polona (Ed.), Zbornik 14. strokovnega posveta Vodenje v vzgoji in izobraževanju, 55—61. https://solazaravnatelje.si/ISBN/978-961-6637-26-8/055-061.pdf

Kotnik, E. (2022). Vloga mladih pri soustvarjanju podeželja: Primer občine Kidričevo. *Geografski Obzornik, 69*(1–2), 27–37.

Kovač, N., & Petrič, M. (2023). Spremljanje storitve pomoči za družino: Storitev pomoč na domu – Analiza stanja v letu 2022, končno poročilo. Inštitut RS za socialno varstvo. https://irssv.si/wp-content/uploads/2023/10/Analiza-izvajanja-PND-v-2022.pdf

Klemenčič, M. M., Lampič, B., Potočnik Slavič, I. (2008). Življenjska (ne)moč obrobnih podeželskih območij v Sloveniji. Znanstvena založba Filozofske fakultete Univerze v Ljubljani.

Kull, M., Voutilainen, O., Christopoulos, S., & Reimets, R. (2014). The Rural under the Common Agricultural Policy of the European Union: Sustainable Rural Development aspects of Pillar II in Finland and Estonia.

Logar, E. (2019). Primerjalna analiza učinkov druženja in sodelovanja v prostovoljnih gasilskih društvih na primerih podeželskih skupnosti z Gorenjske in Sauerlanda. *Geografski Vestnik: Časopis Za Geografijo in Sorodne Vede, 91*(2), 39–51. https://doi.org/10.3986/GV91202

LTVRA. (2021). Communication from the Commission to the European parliament, the Council, the European Economic and Social committee and the Committee of the Regions. A Long-Term Vision for the EU's Rural Areas—Towards Stronger, Connected, Resilient and Prosperous Rural Areas by 2040. https://eur-lex.europa.eu/legal-content/EN/TXT/?uri=celex:52021DC0345

MAFF. (2015). Program razvoja podeželja Republike Slovenije za obdobje 2007–2013. https://skp.si/wp-content/uploads/2013/06/PRP_07-13_9._spr.pdf

MAFF. (2023). Program razvoja podeželja RS za obdobje 2014–2020. https://skp.si/wp-content/uploads/2023/07/Programme_2014SI06RDNP001_16_1_sl.pdf

MAFF. (2023b). Poročilo o strateškem načrtu SKP za leto 2021. https://skp.si/wp-content/uploads/2023/10/Strateski-nacrt-SKP-2023-2027-2.-sprememba-1.pdf

MAFF. (2023c). Objava Uredbe o izvajanju lokalnega razvoja, ki ga vodi skupnost, v obdobju do leta 2027. https://skp.si/novice/objava-uredbe-o-izvajanju-lokalnega-razvoja-ki-ga-vodi-skupnost-v-obdobju-do-leta-2027?utm_source=mailpoet&utm_medium=email&utm_campaign=nove2-e-novice-mreze-za-podezelje-23-6-2022_110

Matthews, A. (2006). The CAP and the Regions: The Territorial Impact of the Common Agricultural Policy. *EuroChoices, 5*(1), 42–44. https://doi.org/10.1111/j.1746-692X.2006.00026.x

MKRR. (2023). Evropska kohezijska politika. https://www.gov.si/teme/sredstva-evropske-kohezijske-politike/

MKRR. (n.d.). Opis sistema izvajanja. Retrieved 3 April 2024, from https://evropskasredstva.si/izvajanje/opis-sistema-izvajanja/

Nared, J., Horvat, K. P., & Visković, N. R. (2019). Demografske spremembe in regionalni razvoj. https://omp.zrc-sazu.si/zalozba/catalog/view/1553/6503/824-1

Nared, J., Hudoklin, J., Kavaš, D., & Zavodnik Lamovšek, A. (2019b). Povezovanje prostorskega in razvojnega načrtovanja na regionalni ravni v Sloveniji (Vol. 29). ZRC SAZU, Založba ZRC. https://doi.org/10.3986/9789610501558

Nared, J. (2020). Regional Development in Slovenia. In D. Perko, R. Ciglič, & M. Zorn (Eds.), *The Geography of Slovenia: Small but diverse* (pp. 291–302). Springer International Publishing. https://doi.org/10.1007/978-3-030-14066-3_19

Nared, J. (Ed.) (2021). *Atlas on Quality of Life in Slovenia*. ESPON.

Nared, J., Repolusk, P., Zavodnik Lamovšek, A., Foški, M., Mrak, G. (2023). *Demografska analiza in projekcije za podeželska in urbana območja v Sloveniji*. Založba ZRC.

National Assembly. (2010). Resolucija o strateških usmeritvah razvoja slovenskega kmetijstva in živilstva do leta 2020 – »Zagotovimo.si hrano za jutri«. http://www.pisrs.si/Pis.web/pregledPredpisa?id=RESO80

National assembly. (2020). Resolucija o nacionalnem programu o strateških usmeritvah razvoja slovenskega kmetijstva in živilstva »Naša hrana, podeželje in naravni viri«. http://www.pisrs.si/Pis.web/pregledPredpisa?id=RESO125

OECD. (2016). RURAL 3.0. OECD. https://doi.org/10.1787/9789264260245-en

Operativni program za izvajanje Evropske kohezijske politike v obdobju 2014–2020. (2023). https://www.eu-skladi.si/sl/dokumenti/kljucni-dokumenti/op_slo_web.pdf

Organisation and Financing of Education Act. (2023). http://pisrs.si/Pis.web/pregledPredpisa?id=ZAKO445

Ostrožnik, P. (2020). Vpliv podružnični šol na razvoj podeželja: Primer Zasavske statistične regije. *Georafski Obzornik, 67*(3–4), 41–50.

Papadopoulos, A. G. (2015). The Impact of the CAP on Agriculture and Rural Areas of EU Member States. *Agrarian South: Journal of Political Economy: A Triannual Journal of Agrarian South Network and CARES, 4*(1), 22–53. https://doi.org/10.1177/2277976015574054

Partnership Agreement between Slovenia and the European Commission for the period 2014–2020. (2014). https://www.eu-skladi.si/sl/dokumenti/kljucni-dokumenti/partnership-agreement-english-version.pdf

Pečar, J. (2020). Cilji regionalne politike Slovenije v obdobju 2021–2027. UMAR. https://www.umar.gov.si/fileadmin/user_upload/publikacije/dz/2020/DZ3_2020.pdf

Penko Seidl, N., Pintar, M., & Bončina, A. (2017). Strokovna podpora fokusnim skupinam v sklopu priprave strategije prostorskega razvoja slovenije 2050: podeželje in zelena infrastruktura. https://www.gov.si/assets/ministrstva/MNVP/Dokumenti/Prostorskirazvoj/SPRS/podezelje_zelena_infrastru ktura_zakljucki.pdf

Potočnik Slavič, I. (2009). Slovenian rural areas and social capital. *Dela, 31*, 21—36. https://doi.org/10.4312/dela.31.21-36

Potočnik Slavič, I. (2010). Neoendogenous in- and output of selected rural areas: The case of economic cycles in Slovenia. Revija za geografijo, 5(1), 75—90. https://www.dlib.si/details/URN:NBN:SI:doc-4NJXYEGB

Potočnik Slavič, I. (2019). Staranje na podeželju: Dejstva, pričakovanja in prostorske razsežnosti. In J. Nared, K. Polajnar Horvat, & N. Razpotnik Visković (Eds.), Demografske spremembe in regionalni razvoj. ZRC SAZU.

Potočnik Slavič, I., Cunder, T., Šabec Korbar, E., Bedrač, M., & Šoster, G. (2022). Izvajanje pristopa LEADER/CLLD v Sloveniji. Znanstvena založba Filozofske fakultete Univerze v Ljubljani.

Program za izvajanje Evropske kohezijske politike v obdobju 2127–2027. (2022). https://evropskasredstva.si/app/uploads/2022/12/Program-evropske-kohezijske-politike-sprejeta-verzija-12.-12.-2022.pdf

Rac, I., Černič Istenič, M., Erjavec, E., Ule, I., Šoster, G., Letina, D., & Tomažič, P. (2022). *Social dimension of rural areas: MAP position paper*. University of Ljubljana. https://doi.org/10.5281/zenodo.7249630

Rac, I., & Erjavec, E. (2020). Slovenian rural development vision: long-term vision for rural area: contribution from 20 science-society-policy platform: map position paper - multi-actor platform SVARUN.

ilustr. https://rural-interfaces.eu/wp-content/uploads/2022/03/MAP_Position-Paper_SL_LTVRA_update.pdf

Resolution on the national social assistance programme 2022—2030. (2022). http://www.pisrs.si/Pis.web/pregledPredpisa?id=RESO137

Richardson, T. (2000). Discourses of rurality in EU spatial policy: The European spatial development perspective. *Sociologia Ruralis, 40*(1), 53–71. https://doi.org/10.1111/1467-9523.00131

RRA GIZ. (2023). Slovenija pred uvedbo regionalnega prostorskega planiranja. https://www.rra-giz.si/aktualno/novice/slovenija-pred-uvedbo-regionalnega-prostorskega-planiranja

RRA GIZ. (2023b). *Nujna krepitev regionalnih razvojnih agencij*. https://www.rra-giz.si/aktualno/novice/nujna-krepitev-regionalnih-razvojnih-agencij

Rules on standards and norms for social assistance services. (2022). http://www.pisrs.si/Pis.web/pregledPredpisa?id=PRAV10060

Social Assistance Act. (2023). http://pisrs.si/Pis.web/pregledPredpisa?id=ZAKO869

SRRS. (2023). Letno poročilo 2022 Slovenskega Regionalno razvojnega sklada. https://www.srrs.si/wp-content/uploads/2023/11/16_3_LP22_20230602_revidirano_poNS_poMF_SVZ_cistopis.pdf

SURS. (2023). https://pxweb.stat.si/SiStatData/pxweb/sl/Data/-/0972107S.px

SVRK. (2017). Strategija razvoja Slovenije 2030. Služba Vlade Republike Slovenije za razvoj in evropsko kohezijsko politiko.

SVRK. (2021). Poročilo o izvajanju evropske kohezijske politike 2014–2020 za obdobje od januarja 2014 do konca decembra 2020 Cilj: Naložbe za rast in delovna mesta.

SVRK. (2022). Partnership Agreement between Slovenia and the European Commission 2021–2027. Available at: https://commission.europa.eu/publications/partnership-agreement-slovenia-2021-2027_en

Tiran, J. (2015). Urbano proti ruralnemu: (nov) razcep v slovenskem političnem prostoru?. Teorija in Praksa, *52*(1–2).

ZSRR-2. (2011). Promotion of Balanced Regional Development Act [Zakon o spodbujanju skladnega regionalnega razvoja]. http://www.pisrs.si/Pis.web/pregledPredpisa?id=ZAKO5801. Slovenian Spatial Management act (ZUreP-3)

CHAPTER 4

Long-term Vision of EU Rural Areas via Policy Cycle Innovation: Lithuania-Specific Future Trajectories

Rita Lankauskienė and Živilė Gedminaitė-Raudonė

1 The Evolving Importance of Science and Society in the Invention of Policy Cycles

The profound changes occurring worldwide at the onset of the twenty-first century have presented democracy with unforeseen problems, necessitating the development of novel models of governance. The process of digitalization, along with the rapid dissemination of knowledge, has significantly transformed political, economic, and social interactions. This transformation is occurring simultaneously with the changing roles of

R. Lankauskienė (✉) · Ž. Gedminaitė-Raudonė
Lithuanian Centre for Social Sciences, Institute of Economics and Rural Development, Vilnius, Lithuania
e-mail: rita.lankauskiene@ekvi.lt

Ž. Gedminaitė-Raudonė
e-mail: zivile.gedminaite@ekvi.lt

D. Barjolle et al. (eds.), *Innovation and the Future of Rural Development in Europe*,
https://doi.org/10.1007/978-3-032-22570-2_4

governments, society, and science. The ongoing transformations have shown the inconsistency of hierarchical state-based systems, leading to new demands from modern society (Howlett et al., 2021; Mourik et al., 2021; Shiffer, 2021; Vohland et al., 2021; Chartier & Wu, 2023). The growing recognition of the importance of science and the changing role of society in ongoing processes are speeding up the development of discussions across many scientific fields. Open science, society, and policy have been identified as areas where innovation has led to a recent increase in citizen science, as noted by Hecker et al. (2018), Moedas (2018), Bush (2020), and Vohland et al. (2021). The field of political science has expanded its traditional participatory method to include a thorough analysis of the complex interactions between research, society, and policy, aiming to understand the comprehensive advantages that arise from these interactions. Recent studies by Cheng (2020), Šūmane et al. (2021), and Vohland et al. (2021) have contributed to this enrichment of the participatory approach.

The rural development policy underwent significant transformations during the second half of the twentieth century. These changes were primarily driven by industrialization, mechanization of agricultural work processes, implementation of irrigation and amelioration systems, electrification of farms, adoption of chemical production technologies, increased productivity, and various other advancements (Tovey, 2016). The current period of the European Union regional policy, as outlined by the European Commission in 2016, is closely linked to the concept of a 'knowledge society'. This period emphasizes the importance of sustainable development in rural regions, which relies on their capacity to implement innovative solutions and approaches as key factors for success. Various studies, including those by Šira et al. (2020), Klessova et al. (2020), and Turk (2021), have highlighted this connection. Additionally, research by Beer (2014), Vilkė (2017), Vilkė and Šarkutė (2018), Gerlitz et al. (2020), Szymańska et al. (2021), Vilkė et al. (2021), Lankauskienė and Gedminaitė-Raudonė (2024) has further emphasized the significance of these factors. The utilization of knowledge through science-society-policy interfaces and various collaborative decision-making methods in multi-level governance represents policy cycle innovation by consistently involving stakeholders. This serves as a pivotal catalyst for the shaping of European rural policy and the advancement of European regions in the near future (Wellbrock et al., 2013; European Commission, 2016; Sallter et al., 2018; Buonanno & Nugent, 2020; Davies et al., 2021).

The European Commission has been observing the flaws in the European Union's policy formation and implementation process. As a result, they have recently been promoting the use of innovative approaches to improve the transnational multi-level policy formation cycle. This is being done through the Horizon Research and Innovation programme. Various large-scale projects have been initiated in European member states to explore new approaches to participative multi-level governance. These projects aim to develop innovative methods for policy cycle innovation. For instance, the Science Cafés were employed as an interactive technique for establishing the agenda in the context of the InSPIRES H2020 project (Balázs et al., 2020). The project aimed to gather the perspectives of influential individuals in the green care sector in Hungary, to create joint research initiatives on green care services, and to launch public discussions on green care in Hungary. The primary research inquiry was: how can we collaboratively develop a research agenda on green care through the active participation of engaged individuals and experts in an inclusive and democratic environment? The application of Science Cafés as a methodology for policy cycle innovation has been further examined by scholars. Another example is the application of science-society-policy interfaces, which are examined in the Horizon 2020 Research and Innovation programme's project MOVING—"Mountain Valorisation Through Interconnectedness and Green Growth" (Coro, 2022). The project aimed to enhance capabilities and collaboratively construct policy frameworks throughout Europe. The objective was to create or enhance value chains in order to enhance the resilience and sustainability of alpine areas in the face of climate change (MOVING, 2020–2024). One more case for policy cycle innovation is the Horizon 2020 project "Sustainable Hub to" Engage into Rural Policies with Actors (referred to as the SHERPA project). This project utilized science-society-policy interfaces to develop a Position Paper on the Long-Term Vision for EU Rural Areas (see Chapter 2 in this volume, and Chartier et al., 2021a, 2021b). The primary concept of the SHERPA project was rooted in the belief that the European Union's forthcoming rural policy requires a fresh direction that will significantly alter the current structure and procedure of EU rural policy formulation (European Commission, 2016; DG Agri, 2017). The proposed EU rural policy-making model relies on the expertise and perspectives of multi-actor platforms (MAPs) in different regions of the EU. These

MAPs facilitate collaboration between science, society, and policy through science-society-policy interfaces.

In this chapter we explore the policy cycle innovation through science-society-policy interfaces, based on the Horizon 2020 project SHERPA practice. The goal of our research is to demonstrate, based on the Lithuanian case, how it is possible to engage stakeholders at various levels of the EU multi-level governance mechanism for the collaborative participatory creation of a long-term vision (in this particular case—for the Long-term vision of EU rural areas until 2040), which considers the perspectives and opinions of all EU member states, including Lithuanian stakeholders. The purpose was achieved by the application of systemic study of scientific literature, document analysis, the six-step Delphi technique, descriptive statistical analysis, and generalization approaches.

2 Theoretical Framework for Policy Cycle Innovation

To further consolidate the conceptual discussion on the evolving role of science and society in governance, it is essential to establish a coherent theoretical framework that explains how policy cycle innovation is operationalized within the SHERPA approach. The framework builds upon the concepts of reflexive governance, open and participatory innovation, and multi-level policy learning, positioning science-society-policy interfaces as the central mechanism through which knowledge is co-created and transformed into practical policy outcomes.

Based on the synthesis of earlier research (Carayannis & Campbell, 2014; Carayannis & Rakhmatullin, 2014; Chartier et al., 2021a, 2021b; Howlett et al., 2021; Vohland et al., 2021), five key pillars can be identified as constituting the foundational conceptual model for policy cycle innovation in the European Union's multi-level governance system (Table 1). These pillars provide both the analytical and operational logic for participatory policy formation applied in this chapter.

This theoretical framework provides the structural bridge between the conceptual rationale for participatory governance and the methodological application of the Delphi-based MAP approach. It highlights the multidimensional nature of policy cycle innovation, where learning, experimentation, and co-creation converge through science-society-policy interfaces. Within this framework, MAPs operate not only as coordination mechanisms but also as dynamic environments for knowledge

Table 1 Conceptual model: theoretical pillars of policy cycle innovation in multi-level governance

Pillar	*Conceptual focus*	*Theoretical basis*	*Function in policy innovation*
Science–Society–Policy Interfaces	Interactional arenas that link scientific knowledge, societal needs, and policymaking practices (e.g., SHERPA Multi-Actor Platforms)	Open Innovation; Reflexive Governance	Translate scientific evidence and stakeholder knowledge into actionable policy recommendations
Multi-Actor Platforms (MAPs)	Institutional mechanisms enabling co-learning and dialogue among diverse stakeholders across EU regions	Multi-level Governance Theory; Co-creation and Foresight	Facilitate participatory knowledge exchange and feedback loops between local and EU levels
Policy Cycle Innovation	Redefinition of policy-making as an iterative, adaptive, and collaborative process rather than a linear one	Policy Learning and Governance by Experimentation	Enable continuous improvement and responsiveness in governance structures

(continued)

Table 1 (continued)

Pillar	*Conceptual focus*	*Theoretical basis*	*Function in policy innovation*
Quadruple Helix Engagement	Involvement of academia, government, business, and civil society in joint knowledge production	Quadruple Helix Innovation Model	Ensure legitimacy, inclusiveness, and diversity of perspectives in policy design
Place-Based Knowledge	Recognition of regional and local contexts as the core source of innovation and strategic planning	Territorial Innovation Systems; Place-Based Development	Tailor European-level strategies to specific regional needs and assets

Source Authors' elaboration

transformation, enabling stakeholders to co-produce long-term visions, validate regional evidence, and shape future policy agendas within the EU's evolving governance landscape.

3 Establishing the Boundaries of Methodology for Innovation in the Policy Cycle

As previously mentioned, in the second decade of the twenty-first century, the science-society-policy interfaces gained recognition as effective means of engaging in collaborative participation at many levels of government. From a methodological perspective, there are numerous pivotal stages that significantly influence the outcomes of activities involving the interfaces of science, society, and policy. At first, it is assumed that the agreement is expected on how to define the long-term vision for rural areas. Therefore, it is suitable to use the Delphi technique during this cycle of policy innovation. In literature, the Delphi technique is recommended for situations when a certain arrangement of components is required and collective agreement needs to be obtained from a panel of experts (e.g., Fish & Busby, 1996; Chrisp et al. 1997; Okoli & Pawlowski,

2004; Galanis, 2018; Rahmani et al., 2020; Barrios et al., 2021). The Delphi technique can be implemented in various modes, involving a specific number of steps. These steps, derived from multiple sources, include: conducting desk research to define the problem, identifying the required expertise and selecting experts, conducting initial interviews with experts, analyzing the interview data, conducting a second round survey and consultation with experts, analyzing the survey results, holding a consensus meeting to validate the results, and making final corrections if necessary (e.g., Barrios et al., 2021; Chartier et al., 2021a, 2021b; Rahmani et al., 2020).

In this research a 6-step Delphi technique was utilized to acquire its findings, employing a blend of quantitative and qualitative research approaches. The SHERPA project approach has implemented the 6-step Delphi technique uniformly throughout all EU member states to develop the Long-term vision for European rural areas until 2040 (Chartier et al., 2021a, 2021b). This research provides a detailed explanation of how the 6-step Delphi technique was implemented in the Lithuanian case, intending to achieve a consensus on the Long-term vision for Lithuanian rural areas until 2040 (Gedminaite-Raudone & Vilke, 2020b). The study was devoted to contributing to the Long-term vision of rural areas in the European Union (Chartier et al., 2021a, 2021b).

The following Delphi method represents the policy cycle innovation, step-by-step implemented in Lithuania while building the Long term vision of Lithuanian rural areas until 2040. These steps were implemented from March to October 2020.

1. Conducting a thorough examination of documents and analyzing the surrounding circumstances (duration: 3 months);
2. Conducting interviews with specialists during 2 expert group sessions (duration: 1 month);
3. Summarizing the outcomes of the expert group meetings, debates on the Lithuanian rural vision till 2040, report preparation, and creation of a semi-structured questionnaire for the expert survey (duration: 2 months);
4. Conducting a survey of experts by distributing a questionnaire (duration: 2 months);
5. Analyzing the results of the survey (duration: 1 month);
6. Validating the results through a Consensus meeting (duration: 1 month).

During the first step of the Delphi technique, the analysis of scientific literature, data sets and different documents was done. The outcomes of the 1st Delphi stage concerning the primary patterns of growth and progress in Lithuanian rural regions are summarized in the next section of this chapter.

The more challenging from a methodological point of view was the second Delphi step. It was crucially important to accurately identify stakeholders who are important to the subject at hand. This entailed selecting the specific specialists who would be part of the multi-actor platform in the science-society-policy interface, where they would collectively examine the specific topic—Long-term vision for Lithuanian rural areas until 2040. Previously implemented studies (e.g., Virkkala and Mariussen, 2021; Hegyi & Mariussen, 2021) outline the advantage of a combination of two approaches in the expert selection phase:

1. Quadruple Helix innovation approach (Carayannis & Campbell, 2014; Carayannis & Rakhmatullin, 2014);
2. Stakeholder salience model (Mitchell et al., 1997).

Lithuanian expert selection was conducted based on both above-outlined criteria. The initial criterion for expert selection was the specific field of work, namely *the helix*, which pertains to the formulation and execution of policies related to rural development. The Quadruple Helix approach (Carayannis & Campbell, 2014; Carayannis & Rakhmatullin, 2014; González-Martinez et al., 2023) was applied in this stage. The Quadruple Helix approach aims to form a group consisting of individuals with expertise from four different sectors: government, society, business, and academia. The purpose of this diverse group is to ensure the representation of various perspectives and to reach a consensus on the long-term vision, specifically tailored to the context of Lithuanian rural areas (Roman et al., 2020; Virkkala et al., 2020). In this research, following the SHERPA methodological advice, business is considered to represent society's interests and goes together into the same helix.

The second criterion for selecting appropriate experts in Lithuania's rural development policy design and implementation is their ability to exert influence, address pressing issues, and possess legitimacy. The Stakeholder Salience Model (Mitchell et al., 1997) approach was used to measure these features. The development of stakeholder salience theory (Mitchell et al., 1997) was derived from an analysis of corporate strategy. The stakeholder was classified based on their role as a strategic leader inside the organization. The approach is to accumulate assistance. According to Mitchell (1997), to uphold a dynamic theory of stakeholder identification and salience, it is necessary to take into account many additional consequences related to *power, legitimacy,* and *urgency*. Each attribute is a variable, not a constant, and can change for each specific entity or stakeholder-manager connection. Furthermore, the presence or extent of each feature is subject to different interpretations and is a product of human perception rather than being inherently "objective". Furthermore, it is possible for an individual or entity to lack awareness of carrying the trait, or if aware, to choose not to engage in any associated activities. The stakeholder attributes discussed in this theory are crucial for understanding how stakeholders can become more or less important to an organization's managers. Firstly, these attributes are not fixed but can change over time. Secondly, they are not based on objective facts but are influenced by social factors. Lastly, the presence or absence of consciousness and intentional action can vary. Mitchell (1997) classifies stakeholders into three distinct categories: latent, moderate, and definitive. This categorization is of significant importance. The importance of these categories rests in their capacity to enable the activation of stakeholders, shifting them from a passive position to a more positive and moderate stance, and ultimately into a key advocate. The level of stakeholder salience determines the measurement of this dynamic. Stakeholder salience will be low (dormant, discretionary, or demanding) when managers perceive that only one of the stakeholder attributes—power, legitimacy, or urgency—is evident. Low salience refers to a situation where an individual's actions are significant to the organization's leader, but they do not have any connection to the organization itself or its strategy. Inactive stakeholders are commonly known as dormant entities. They have the potential to inadvertently harm or weaken the organization, or they may unknowingly engage in actions that benefit the company. They hold significant importance, although remain unattainable at present. Stakeholder salience will be moderate when managers sense the presence of two stakeholder attributes: power, legitimacy, and urgency, which might be characterized as dangerous, dominant, or dependent. The organization relies on dominant stakeholders who possess both power and legitimacy. An astute leader will maintain close proximity to them. Dependent stakeholders are individuals or groups who rely on the organization and operate within its sphere of influence. They could perhaps be discerning customers or users of the organization's services. Both of them belong to a strong alliance. A stakeholder who possesses both power and legitimacy is inherently a part of a firm's dominant coalition, according to the definition. Managers are obligated to promptly address and prioritize the claim of a stakeholder when it is urgent. The most frequent event is likely to be the transition of a dominating stakeholder into the "definitive" classification. The stakeholder salience theory provides a useful starting point for comprehending the competition between established systems and emergent clusters.

In this research, Lithuanian experts were selected from the fields of science (universities and research institutes), society (private sector and civil society organizations such as NGOs), and policy (public sector). The selection process was primarily aimed at determining whether stakeholders were involved in the implementation of rural development measures either directly or indirectly. A scale ranging from 0 to 2 was employed, with 0 representing a weak role, 1 indicating a moderate role, and 2 denoting an important (crucial) role in the creation and implementation of rural development policy in Lithuania. The selection of experts for the relevant specialists' list for the MAP of Lithuania was done by measuring their power, urgency, and legitimacy according to the above-described scale. An optimal approach typically involves a combination of elements tailored to the specific needs of each stakeholder group (Virkkala et al., 2020). Ministries tend to have a higher level of legitimacy, while private enterprises often exhibit a greater sense of urgency. Additionally, the distribution of power can vary among different stakeholders. The Lithuanian MAP consisted of 12 experts who were specialists selected based on the aforementioned several criteria. The Vision for Lithuanian rural areas till 2040 was developed by reaching a consensus within the following group of specialists: science—4 experts; civil society and business—4 experts, and political representatives—4 experts.

During the initial SHERPA policy innovation cycle, the SHERPA project coordination and implementation team maintained regular communication with the MAPs, including Lithuanian MAP. They first invited the MAPs to engage in discussions and address relevant issues within smaller groups, utilizing interactive collaboration platforms such as Microsoft Teams and Cisco Webex. The purpose was to share experiences, challenges, and solutions within individual MAPs, as well as to reflect on the activities and problems faced by other MAPs in their search for solutions based on best practices. Another step in the process involved using a simple monitoring and evaluation tool in Microsoft Excel. This tool included a semi-structured questionnaire that experts used to provide feedback on the completed SHERPA process. The questionnaire was regularly completed by all MAPs facilitators and monitors, including Lithuania, to ensure the process's quality and ongoing improvement. The initial assessment of the inaugural SHERPA cycle was completed in March 2021 and deliberated upon by SHERPA collaborators during an April 2021 workshop.

During step 3, the semi-structured questionnaire (with a 5-level Likert scale) was prepared, which was used to rate the core findings from step 2. During step 4, experts were surveyed individually. Every question contained an open option to mention any additional issue-relevant remarks, which were not listed in the questionnaire. Step 5 entailed the analysis of survey results, and the final step 6 was organized in the form of face-to-face meeting, aiming to validate the reached consensus on the main findings regarding the Long-term vision for Lithuanian rural areas until 2040, gathered from experts via step 2 and step 4. The final version of the Long-term vision of Lithuanian rural areas until 2040 was ready by mid-October 2020.

4 Policy Cycle Innovation Performed in Lithuania: Formulating the Long-Term Vision for Lithuanian Rural Areas Until 2040

Subsequent parts present the results of employing the SHERPA innovative policy cycle, based on the Delphi technique, devoted to formulating the long-term vision for rural areas in Lithuania 2040 (Gedminaite-Raudone & Vilke, 2020b). The initial Delphi research phase yielded a concise systematization of crucial findings from scientific literature, statistics, and document analysis (for more thorough information please see the Discussion Paper on the Long-term Vision for Lithuanian Rural Areas (Gedminaite-Raudone & Vilke, 2020a)). This will serve as a foundation for subsequent research endeavors. In addition, the interviews revealed numerous obstacles, opportunities, and the envisioned future of Lithuanian rural areas. Furthermore, specialists delineated the potential strategies to combat the encountered difficulties in achieving the Lithuanian rural vision for the year 2040.

Evidence Regarding the Primary Patterns of Growth and Progress in Lithuanian Rural Regions

The rural development perspectives in Lithuania primarily address the significant changes occurring in Lithuanian rural areas, including:

- demographic transition,
- climate change and environmental services,
- transformation of rural economy and diversification of production,
- infrastructure and essential services,
- digitalization and the development of smart rural areas,
- inequalities and the well-being of rural communities.

Demographic transition. The most notable aspect when evaluating the situation in rural parts of Lithuania is the decline in the Lithuanian rural population. The decrease in the rural population has a direct influence on the overall population. The primary causes of population decline are the adverse rate of natural population growth and persistent net emigration. Due to these demographic changes, the composition of the country's population is undergoing little alteration: the population is seeing an increase in age, while the number of young and working-age individuals is declining.

Climate change and environmental services. Lithuania has undertaken certain international obligations to support the achievement of climate change mitigation objectives. The influence of livestock farming on climate change has diminished; but, greenhouse gas (GHG) emissions from the crop subsector continue to rise, contributing to the overall increase in GHG emissions from agricultural activities. The occurrence of severe climatic events has led to a rise in agricultural losses, a decrease in output reliability, and a heightened interest in farming as well as a greater willingness to support the sector's development and modernization efforts in order to combat climate change. Lithuania falls well behind the EU average in terms of renewable energy production per hectare of usable land. The energy efficiency of agriculture and forestry in Lithuania continues to rise.

Transformation of rural economy and diversification of production. In Lithuania, the agricultural production sector is primarily controlled by small-scale producers. This sector is characterized by fragmentation, while the food processing industry and retail trade exhibit a high level of concentration. The amount of collaboration among farmers is insufficient. The participation of farmers in market-driven production paradigms is transforming. In Lithuania, there has been a notable surge in efforts to enhance the local food system and establish shorter food supply chains through the use of several direct sales techniques for agricultural and food goods. Community-led local development is playing an increasingly significant role in the rural economy. Volunteering, community projects, and partnerships, actively cultivated in rural parts of the country, provide untapped potential to enhance the rural economy and simultaneously address the issues of unemployment and social inclusion among the rural people in Lithuania.

Infrastructure and essential services. The overall condition of Lithuanian infrastructure has been enhanced since joining the European Union. The primary challenge in coordinating the delivery of services in rural parts of Lithuania is the decline in population density, which has resulted in a fall in the number of service recipients. This has increased the expenses associated with public services, as the provision of these services is concentrated in a few regional institutions. The restricted availability of public transit, education, health, and social services in rural areas of Lithuania results in social isolation and the exacerbation of other socioeconomic problems.

Digitalization and the development of smart rural areas. The key trends associated with the growth of digitalization and smart ruralities in Lithuania can be observed from two main perspectives. Firstly, there is a general digitalization of rural areas, which involves daily internet access and the utilization of e-services. Secondly, there is a digitalization of agriculture. Internet connectivity and e-public services are currently in favourable conditions, with broadband availability in Lithuanian rural areas reaching 98%. The use of new technology and digitalization in Lithuanian agriculture is currently limited. It is imperative to incentivize farmers in the country to embrace the potential benefits offered by these advances.

Inequalities and the well-being of rural communities. The persistence of Lithuanian farming traditions, the development of public values in the future, and the sustainability of rural areas are all at risk due to negative demographic trends. The issue of unemployment in rural parts of

Lithuania persists due to inadequate vocational training, insufficient qualifications, and a lack of entrepreneurial skills. The low income of the rural population and social exclusion stems from persistent reliance on social benefits, limited social integration, and a lack of proactive efforts to combat unemployment. Additionally, there is a lack of motivation and desire to pursue affluence.

The initial phase of the Delphi process involved organizing and categorizing the distinctive rural development patterns specific to Lithuania, which have had an impact on rural areas in the country. These findings were then incorporated into the subsequent stage of the Delphi process.

Examining the Challenges and Opportunities That Lithuanian Rural Communities Will Face in the Upcoming Two Decades

Rural areas in Lithuania encompass a substantial portion of the country's land, characterized by diverse physical, economic, sociological, environmental, and cultural attributes. The rural areas of Lithuania, like the rest of Europe, have experienced significant changes in recent decades. These changes can be attributed to various factors such as economic and demographic shifts, technological advancements, socio-economic changes, and policy developments at both the national and EU levels. An analysis of the difficulties and opportunities in rural areas in Lithuania is essential for formulating future development strategies for these regions. In addition, the expert group discussion identified important difficulties specific to rural communities in Lithuania.

Demographic change was envisaged through a decrease in population size and an increase in the proportion of older individuals. Rural areas in Lithuania are experiencing depopulation due to the internal migration of young residents to urban areas and external migration for employment opportunities abroad. The rural population is experiencing an aging trend, leading to a decline in population as older individuals make up the majority of residents in rural areas.

The main issues concerning infrastructure and basic services are as follows: (1) sparsely populated rural areas, resulting in low population density; (2) high costs associated with infrastructure maintenance; (3) limited availability of services in rural areas, such as the location of kindergartens, primary and secondary schools, post offices, hospitals, and supermarkets; (4) subpar quality of education services provided by primary and secondary schools; (5) challenges faced by the elderly in accessing necessary services located outside their place of residence; (6) insufficient digital literacy skills among the elderly, hindering their ability to utilize digital resources; (7) the problem of abandoned and unused buildings and houses in rural areas, which disrupt the rural landscape and diminish the appeal of living in a village.

Regarding the diversification of the rural economy, Lithuanian rural areas are primarily seen as locations where farming operations take place, either on farms or in firms associated with agriculture. An important task is to promote economic diversification in rural areas by encouraging the development of various economic activities in the services, industry, and construction sectors. This is particularly relevant in Lithuania, where the expanding opportunities for remote labour due to digitization have opened up new possibilities. Small farms and other projects might diversify their activity by offering additional services. In many instances, the lack of connectivity and communication between rural people and farmers hinders the successful development of rural areas.

There are numerous issues concerning the competencies of rural residents and the public agencies responsible for implementing rural policy in Lithuania. First, the elderly population encounters difficulties in utilizing the opportunities provided by digitalized services. Second, farmers and individuals residing in rural communities have a deficiency in information, which hinders their ability to generate innovative ideas and solutions. Third, public institution employees cannot effectively respond to the diverse requirements of stakeholders in rural areas. A huge lack of motivation to stay updated with new information was observed.

The poor intents of rural dwellers for integration, cooperation, and co-creation are problematic. The presence of both low motivation and low self-confidence was noted, particularly regarding the lack of confidence between different generations. While there is support for projects aimed at young people, there is a lack of trust from the old towards the younger generation, which extends to areas such as farming activities and decision-making processes.

The decision-making process for rural regions in Lithuania was also found problematic, firstly considering the inadequate strategic planning for rural areas. There are gaps in communication and coordination between many institutions, including national decision-makers, municipalities, local representatives, local communities, and other actors in rural areas.

The survey results regarding the issues faced by rural areas in Lithuania are presented in Fig. 1. The respondents rated the importance of these challenges on a 5-point Likert scale, ranging from 1 (not important at all) to 5 (extremely important).

The survey results indicate that the primary challenges faced by rural areas in Lithuania are the demographic shift (11 experts rated as 'Very important' or 'Fairly important'), the competencies of rural inhabitants (all experts rated as 'Very important' or 'Fairly important'), infrastructure and basic services, and the diversification of the rural economy (10 experts rated as 'Very important' or 'Fairly important' in both options).

To summarize, the following primary obstacles were identified in achieving the vision for the future of rural areas in Lithuania by 2040:

1. The absence of a comprehensive and strategic planning procedure for rural areas in Lithuania that takes into account the outcomes of elections. Not only when prioritizing visual development in rural areas, but also in other fields as well. The regional innovation strategy is excessively expansive.

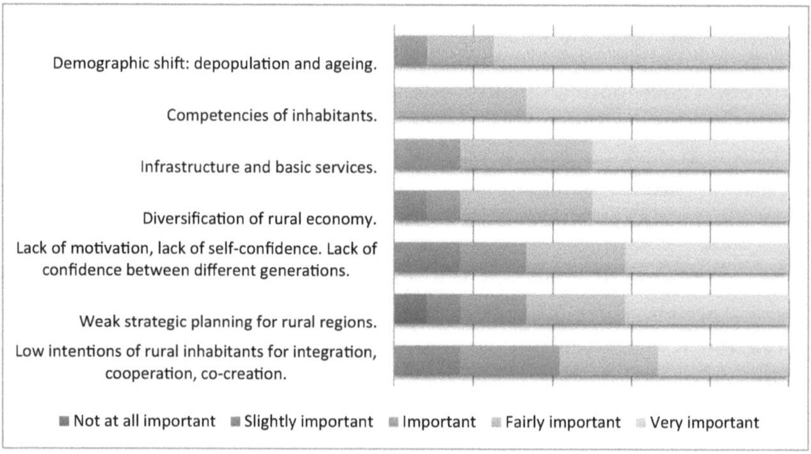

Fig. 1 Key challenges and opportunities faced by Lithuanian Rural Communities in the forthcoming two decades. *Source* Authors' elaboration based on research findings

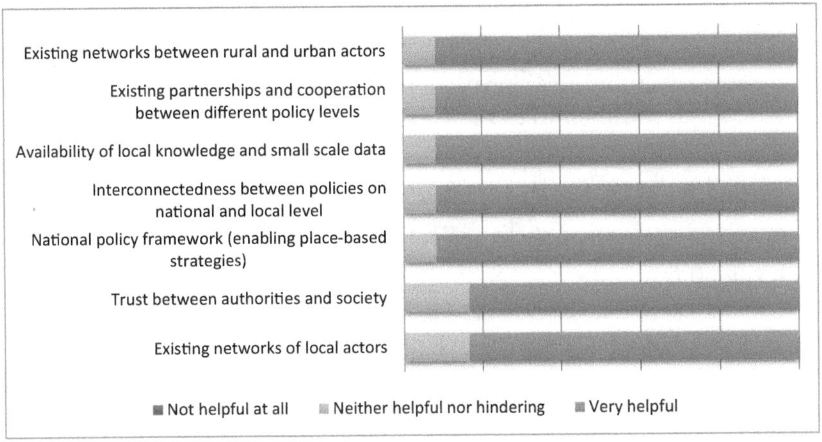

Fig. 2 Presents the factors that contribute to the realization of the vision for rural areas in Lithuania by 2040. *Source* Authors' elaboration based on research findings

2. Disparity in the ability of rural actors to exert influence on the decision-making process in Lithuania. Urban citizens in Lithuania are not actively engaged in the decision-making process for strategic planning on the future of rural areas. Only by creating a vision in which all actors clearly identify their roles in rural areas can we ensure that it is both viable and effectively implemented.
3. Insufficient education, skills, and expertise across all participants in the helix. The strategy lacks emphasis on implementing innovative initiatives and practices that can effectively promote the prosperity of rural communities, drawing inspiration from successful projects both locally and internationally. Within society, there is a significant need for the analysis of exemplary models, as well as the provision of coaching and mentorship. The scientific community should make an effort to be informed about new programs and methods for including students and the elderly in lifelong learning, in order to keep up with current trends.

Almost all identified facilitators have been acknowledged as highly beneficial in achieving the long-term vision of Lithuanian rural areas. These include the establishment of networks connecting rural and urban areas, partnerships and collaboration among various levels of policy-making, the enhancement of existing networks of local actors, and the cultivation of trust between authorities and society. Additional facilitators have been translated into possibilities to achieve the Lithuanian rural vision for 2040.

Potential Prospects for Rural Areas in Lithuania During the Course of the Next Two Decades

Following the deliberation of the expert groups, specific opportunities for rural areas in Lithuania were identified. The potential of digitalization was found promising for the extensive infrastructure of fast broadband services. The process of digitizing activities and providing access to internet services aims to bridge the connection gap between remote rural areas and cities. Personnel management identified individuals who are focus-driven and diligent. Contemporary university programs are designed to address the specific requirements of rural areas, such as agriculture. Concerning the robust urban–rural interconnections, urban dwellers have robust connections with rural regions, either because they or their parents were former residents of rural areas. The goal of visiting rural places is mostly associated with engaging in nature-based leisure activities, such as slow tourism, transformative tourism, ecological tourism, and other similar pursuits. Additionally, visiting rural areas may also involve reconnecting with family or friends residing in these areas, as well as engaging in numerous other activities.

Indeed, it should be highlighted, that the COVID-19 pandemic has created a need for finding locations outside urban areas that offer more living space and opportunities to spend time in natural surroundings. Rural areas provide an ideal setting for employees from various professions to engage in remote work, facilitated by high-speed broadband internet connectivity. The local food industry can enhance the local food market by establishing a short supply chain for local food, which can also contribute to the development of tourism. Promote the consumption of products made in Lithuania.

Experts highly valued the opportunities presented by the Green Deal, a program started by the European Union by directing attention towards the fields of bio-economy and circular economy. Strategies aimed at developing rural areas in Lithuania should prioritize ecological farming and other environmentally friendly efforts, with a focus on reducing pollution and meeting environmental requirements.

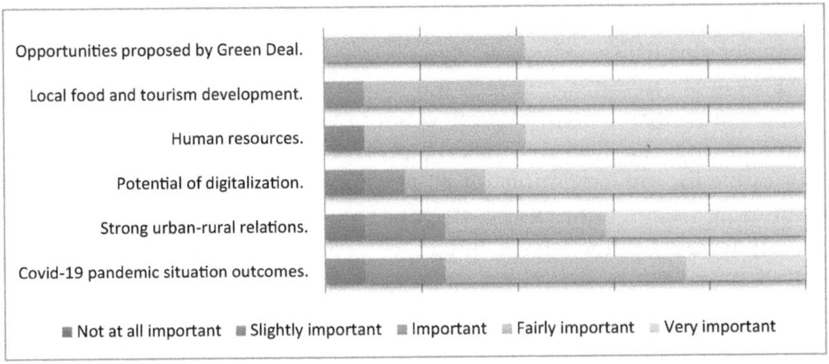

Fig. 3 Potential prospects for rural areas in Lithuania during the course of the next two decades. *Source:* Authors' elaboration based on research findings

The survey findings from experts regarding the potential for rural areas in Lithuania during the next 20 years, up to 2040, are presented in Fig. 3. The experts rated the importance of these chances on a 5-point Likert scale, ranging from 1 (not at all important) to 5 (extremely significant).

The survey results have shown that the most significant prospects for rural areas in Lithuania over the next 20 years are the opportunities presented by the Green Deal (all experts rated it as 'Fairly important' or 'Very important'), followed by local food and tourism development (11 experts rated it as 'Fairly important' or 'Very important'), and human resources (91.7% of respondents rated it as 'Fairly important' or 'Very important').

Envisioned Future of Lithuanian Rural Areas in 2040

The ongoing discourse over the ideal future for rural areas in Lithuania is expected to persist in the years to come. This is due to the fact that a significant portion of Lithuania's land is comprised of rural areas, with cities occupying just a small fraction of the territory. Approximately one-third of the population resides in rural regions of Lithuania. Another segment of the urban population maintains a strong connection with rural areas due to the fact that their parents or grandparents either used to reside in rural areas or currently reside there. A significant number of urban and rural individuals have proficient abilities in cultivating vegetables and fruits, as well as engaging in countryside activities.

Rural areas in Lithuania strongly support large farms, as they have a significant impact on the rural economy and possess effective means of influencing the decision-making process with the public authorities responsible for implementing agricultural policy in the country. Small and medium farms and entities also attempt to determine their role, but their capacity to exert influence is comparatively limited or less significant than that of other actors. In recent decades, rural villages in Lithuania have experienced increased activity and witnessed successful growth. These communities have been known for their intriguing projects, greater local involvement, and even the attraction of new residents to live in these areas. In rural areas of Lithuania, there is a growing popularity of new initiatives such as slow, educational, or transformative tourism. These initiatives involve the establishment of new business models by city residents who have chosen to move to villages. These models include various culture-uncommon thematic villages, local food restaurants, therapy centers, and more. Additionally, there are networking initiatives that aim to connect urban and rural areas, such as the "rent a piece of garden" project and the delivery of food baskets to homes. Exemplary instances of good practice might serve as a source of inspiration for aspiring individuals who are seeking opportunities to engage in meaningful activities in the rural regions of Lithuania.

Another trend observed in rural parts of Lithuania is the migration towards suburban areas near major cities, driven by the desire to live in proximity to nature, have larger living spaces, and maintain convenient access to essential infrastructure.

The Covid-19 pandemic has sparked further debate, particularly regarding its impact on rural communities. Rural places in Lithuania are considered appealing and secure for individuals who have the ability to work remotely, as they are equipped with high-speed broadband internet coverage across all regions. Furthermore, this circumstance has created further prospects for prioritizing the domestic food market and enhancing the efficiency of local food supply chains. This can be achieved by utilizing various strategies to establish connections between rural areas and urban centers, facilitating the consumption of locally produced food.

Considering the issues outlined above, experts emphasized the desired future of rural communities with the following characteristics:

- Rural locations include individuals from diverse professions, as rurality does not solely revolve around farming. Instead, these areas offer a range of economic activities that can be pursued on-site or remotely. Residents or immigrants have the option to concentrate on novel inventive projects that utilize the distinct natural or cultural resources of this location, such as slow, transformative tourism. Alternatively, they can establish a new non-agricultural enterprise, such as small or medium food processing organizations or wood construction.
- Development of necessary infrastructure in the region and at the local level. Public authorities should evaluate regulations on the establishment or upkeep of essential infrastructure in the region. This includes determining the required travel time to reach facilities such as hospitals, post offices, supermarkets, schools, and kindergartens. The infrastructure in villages should be improved to address the issue of non-utilized ancient residential dwellings and abandoned farm buildings. These neglected structures discourage newcomers from considering the village as a potential new home. Finding effective solutions to repurpose these buildings is essential to make the community more appealing.
- Regional specialization. Rural inhabitants in Lithuania should select a specific area of focus for their territory in order to optimize resource utilization. This could involve regions specializing in agriculture, regions with distinctive natural resources suitable for various forms of tourism, or regions emphasizing non-agricultural activities such as social business, agricultural product processing cooperatives, or wood processing companies.
- Execution of the smart specialization approach. The main focus is on providing support for the bio-economy and circular economy. Nutrient-rich food for consumers. Food is cultivated using environmentally-friendly and sustainable technologies. Biologically significant for humans, the ecosystem, and biodiversity.
- Local food has the ability to enhance the local food industry by utilizing a short supply chain and promoting tourism development. Promote the consumption of products made in Lithuania. Enhance educational proficiency regarding the advantages of locally sourced food for customers. Reduce the transportation of imported products and prioritize the consumption of locally sourced meals.

- Higher education in tertiary institutions. Requirement for innovation intermediaries and guides. The necessity of distant learning arises from the desire to acquire new skills and enhance knowledge in areas of personal interest. The importance of ongoing professional development.

The survey results have shown that all six topics for the desirable future of rural areas in Lithuania, as presented by the experts in the Focus group sessions, were highly placed in the poll. In fact, 83 percent or more of the experts claimed that these areas were either 'Fairly significant' or 'Very important'.

The Long-term vision for Lithuanian rural areas has been established based on the specified desirable future statements, and formulated as following: *"A vision for rural areas of Lithuania up to 2040—rural regions with modern villages in a partnership as an attractive place to live and work."* (Gedminaitė-Raudonė & Lankauskienė, 2021).

Experts have emphasized the forthcoming progress of rural regions in Lithuania by endorsing three categories of villages (refer to Fig. 4).

Recently developed or refurbished settlements located near cities, commonly referred to as urban villages. Two examples of these villages include (1) newly developed smart villages and (2) newly established villages that prioritize the utilization of attractive natural resources in rural locations. Excellent opportunity for remote employment. The inhabitants

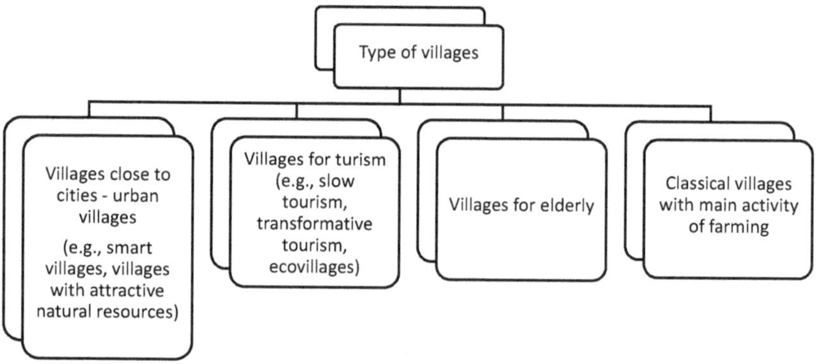

Fig. 4 The types of villages for future development of Lithuanian rural areas. *Source* Authors' elaboration based on research findings

of these villages are city people who choose to reside near urban areas and utilize urban infrastructure while still enjoying a natural environment. The COVID-19 pandemic has prompted city inhabitants to increasingly consider relocating to rural areas, where they can live in private residences surrounded by nature and with larger plots of land, as opposed to residing in apartment buildings.

Villages that prioritize tourism include those that specialize in so called slow tourism, transformative tourism, and ecovillages. Many of the innovative initiatives in Lithuania are carried out by urban dwellers. Newly established or preexisting villages have a great opportunity to participate in new services by offering essential services for new businesses. Additional services such as 'Walk with a ranger' and 'Walk on food in Labanoras forest' are now available. The establishment of a robust community can be the outcome.

Senior villages: These specialized living communities offer senior individuals the opportunity to relocate to a new residence where they can access a range of social services tailored to their needs. Older individuals who are capable of self-care have the option to reside in specialized villages. The presence of these villages can greatly diminish the expenses associated with social services that they require. Additionally, these villages offer highly appealing living conditions for this demographic, as well as opportunities for social interaction through the provision of open spaces designed to cater to their specific needs, such as gardens, cafes, and various activities like handicrafts.

Rural communities are characterized by traditional agricultural practices and a range of economic activity such as services, industry, and construction. The arrival of new residents in small villages often brings with it novel ideas, innovations, and other forms of inspiration, which might motivate the existing community to collaborate on implementing new initiatives. The emphasis should be on providing consumers with biologically valuable food that is grown using ecological and clean technologies. Additionally, promoting products that have recognized quality schemes at the European or national level, such as protected designations of origin or geographical indications, and guaranteed agricultural products of exceptional quality, would not only improve the eating habits of the population but also support the long-term growth of producers specializing in high-quality products. By adopting a multifunctional agricultural approach, farmers or firm owners can adapt their skills to engage in new activities, for instance pharmacist can integrate their job with the cultivation of herbs. The agricultural expertise possessed by farmers can also be utilized for consultancy, design work, journalism, and other related fields.

Lithuanian specialists emphasized the significance of adopting a concept of smart villages, particularly in the context of rural Lithuania. Smart villages concept gives rural communities a framework to prepare a specific strategy for development. In these villages, individuals not only live and work, but also invest their time and money in the community life. For instance, the residents of these villages, including farmers, craftspeople, and other enterprises, can collaborate and work together using renewable resources to create local products. These products are then sold to customers and such approach can guarantee the safeguarding of biodiversity and the establishment/conservation of diverse environments.

Conclusions and Future Insights

Rural residents, their activities, and rural areas as a whole have undergone substantial changes in recent decades in Lithuania and across Europe. These changes can be attributed to various significant factors, such as economic and demographic shifts, technological advancements, socioeconomic changes, and alterations in national and EU policies. The prospects for rural areas in Europe and Lithuania remain uncertain.

The outcomes of the conversations conducted in the Lithuanian multi-actor platform (MAP) indicate that experts from the three helixes' groups—science, society, and policy—emphasized similar opportunities and challenges for rural areas in Lithuania in the next two decades, extending until 2040. The experts have identified several significant recent challenges in rural areas of Lithuania. These challenges include depopulation and aging, infrastructure and basic services, diversification of the rural economy, characteristics of human resources (such as inadequate competencies, low intention for cooperation, lack of motivation and self-confidence), and the decision-making process. The suggested opportunities revolve around the potential for digitalization, human resources, strong urban–rural relations, the local food market, tourism growth, ideas from the Green Deal, and new opportunities arising from the COVID-19 pandemic.

The Lithuanian experience demonstrates that stakeholders were highly satisfied with the outcome and their contribution to the published Position Paper on Lithuanian Rural Vision 2040 (Gedminaite-Raidone & Vilke 2020b) and the Long-Term Vision for EU Rural Areas until 2040 (Chartier et al., 2021a, 2021b). All Lithuanian MAP specialists have submitted input on the MAP process, specifically regarding the teamwork inside the MAP. The aggregated survey findings reveal positive collaboration trends inside the Lithuanian MAP. During the subsequent survey steps, Lithuanian MAP specialists were asked to give their feedback on the different outputs produced in the policy cycle innovation, including the Discussion Paper (Gedminaite-Raudone & Vilke, 2020a), Position Paper (Gedminaite-Raudone & Vilke, 2020b), and SHERPA Position Paper (Chartier et al., 2021a, 2021b). The results reveal that half of Lithuanian MAP experts expressed extreme satisfaction, while the other half of them expressed normal satisfaction, with the MAP position paper on the Long Term Vision for Lithuanian Rural Areas (Gedminaite-Raudone & Vilke, 2020b). In reference to the Sherpa Position Paper on the Long Term Vision for Rural Areas (Chartier et al., 2021a, 2021b), Lithuanian MAP specialists confirmed its high relevance to the findings of their work in MAP in Lithuania. It is worth noting that all Lithuanian professionals have went through the SHERPA position paper on the Long Term Vision for Rural Areas (Chartier et al., 2021a, 2021b) carefully and they acknowledge the contribution of Lithuanian Long term vision of rural areas until 2040 to the Long Term Vision for European rural areas (Chartier et al., 2021a, 2021b). Survey showed that together 90.0% of Lithuanian MAP specialists agreed that this EU document accurately and effectively reflects the input of Lithuanian MAP, and 10.0% found it satisfactory.

Engaging in the science–society–policy interface through the MAP offered Lithuanian experts several personal benefits that strengthened their own work. The key sources of added value, confirmed by the survey study, were:

- Informing policy design. Almost all experts regarded contributing to policy-making as their most significant personal contribution.
- New knowledge and understanding. Acquiring fresh insights was valued as highly as networking, with most experts considering these personal benefits essential.

- Networking. Building professional connections ranked among the most appreciated forms of added value.
- Relevance to daily practice. Most experts found the topics addressed relevant, and a substantial share regarded them as highly significant in their professional lives.
- Opportunity to share views. Experts expressed strong satisfaction with the chance to voice their ideas, which they attributed to high ethical standards in the debates, mutual respect among participants and effective moderation. By contrast, advocating for one's own interests was seen as the least significant personal contribution among the recognised sources of added value.

The SHERPA policy-cycle innovation prompted diverse reflections on how these experiences related to the experts' routine work. During the monitoring and evaluation survey, Lithuanian experts actively engaged with additional issues raised in the first monitoring cycle, offering constructive feedback and encouraging thoughtful analysis of the areas under study.

The anticipated results of the work carried out in the Lithuanian MAP at the European policy level are considered to be high and ambitious, according to experts. Primarily, Lithuanian experts expect that European policymakers and decision-makers will receive accurate and comprehensive information regarding the perspectives that have been carefully examined and determined at the local level. Furthermore, it was expected that the ideas will be incorporated into the forthcoming programming period, ensuring implementation and contemplation aligned with the long-term, grassroots perspective for rural areas in Europe. Lithuanian experts anticipated that their insights and observations, as expressed in the Lithuanian MAP, can contribute to the advancement and execution of shared European policies. Anticipated are the identification of policies aimed at enhancing the desirability and advantages of rural communities in all aspects—economic, social, and environmental. This could contribute to the achievement of sustainability goals and the objectives of the European Green Deal. The project's insights, in their opinion, could be applied across many levels of public administration, ensuring the project's wider impact. Finaly, Lithuanian MAP experts expressed their appreciation for the opportunity to participate in the MAP events, exchange their knowledge and perspectives, and be given a platform to express their opinions, using the "anything else" option as a contingency plan. This way, a participatory framework introduced by SHERPA enabled the contribution to the formulation of EU policy on the long-term strategic direction for rural areas. Both the follow-up and the execution of concepts introduced to the MAP reflected a strong determination to achieve project goals with a great success.

The SHERPA policy cycle innovation approach, which involves ongoing stakeholder engagement through science-society-policy interfaces, is regarded as a promising and comprehensive model for formulating new policies in multi-level governance systems in various domains, both at the national and EU levels.

At the regional level, the findings highlight the importance of developing territorial governance models that translate participatory policy design into actionable regional programmes. Strengthening regional innovation ecosystems through the creation of Multi-Actor Platforms (MAPs) at county or municipal levels would allow bottom-up knowledge and stakeholder perspectives to feed directly into regional development plans. Moreover, regional authorities could act as intermediaries for policy learning, facilitating the exchange of best practices between local communities and national policymakers. Finally, promoting locally tailored capacity-building measures, particularly in digital skills, entrepreneurship, and circular economy practices, would enhance the resilience and competitiveness of rural regions, ensuring the continuity of participatory governance.

Acknowledgements This research was funded by European Commission, Horizon 2020 grant number 862448, Project "SHERPA—Sustainable Hub to Engage into Rural Policies with Actors".

References

Balázs, B., Horváth, J., & Pataki, G. (2020). Science-society dialogue from the start: Participatory research agenda-setting by Science Cafés. *European Journal of Futures Research, 8*(1), 5. https://doi.org/10.1186/s40309-020-00164-75

Barrios, M., Guilera, G., Nuño, L., & Gómez-Benito, J. (2021). Consensus in the Delphi method: What makes a decision change? *Technological Forecasting and Social Change, 163*, Article 120484. https://doi.org/10.1016/j.techfore.2020.120484

Beer, A. (2014). Leadership and the governance of rural communities. *Journal of Rural Studies, 34*, 254–262. https://doi.org/10.1016/j.jrurstud.2014.01.007

Buonanno, L., & Nugent, N. (2020). Policies and policy processes of the European Union. *Bloomsbury Publishing*. https://doi.org/10.1007/978-1-137-30527-5

Bush, V. (2020). Science, the endless frontier. *Princeton University Press*. https://doi.org/10.1515/9780691201658-002

Cai, Y., & Lattu, A. (2022). Triple helix or quadruple helix: Which model of innovation to choose for empirical studies? *Minerva, 60*(2), 257–280. https://doi.org/10.1007/s11024-021-09451-y

Carayannis, E. G., & Campbell, D. F. J. (2014). Developed democracies versus emerging autocracies: Arts, democracy, and innovation in Quadruple Helix innovation systems. *Journal of Innovation and Entrepreneurship, 3*(1), 1–23. https://doi.org/10.1186/2192-5372-3-12

Carayannis, E. G., & Rakhmatullin, R. (2014). The Quadruple/Quintuple Innovation Helix and Smart Specialisation Strategies for sustainable and inclusive growth in Europe. *Journal of the Knowledge Economy, 5*(2), 212–239. https://doi.org/10.1007/s13132-014-0185-8

Cartier, C., & Wu, P. (2023). From the administrative hierarchy to the system of administrative divisions. In *Handbook on local governance in China* (pp. 30–47). Edward Elgar Publishing. https://doi.org/10.4337/9781800883246.00010 .

Chartier, O., Salle, E., Irvine, K., Kull, M., Miller, D., Nieto, E., & Vestergård, L. O. (2021a). Long-Term Vision for Rural Areas: Contribution from SHERPA science-society-policy platforms. *SHERPA Position Paper. Available Online:* https://doi.org/10.5281/zenodo.4557440

Chartier, O., Salle, E., Irvine, K., Kull, M., Miller, D., Nieto, E., Vestergård, L. O., Potters, J., Slätmo, E., Zomer, B., & Iadecola, F. (2021). Long-Term Vision for Rural Areas: Contribution from SHERPA science-society-policy platforms. SHERPA Position Paper. https://doi.org/10.5281/zenodo.4557440. Available online: https://rural-interfaces.eu/wp-content/uploads/2021/02/SHERPA_PositionPaper-LTVRA.pdf.

Cheng, H. (2020). Bridging the science-society-policy interface: A comparative case study on citizen science for policies. Master Thesis, Delft University of Technology, The Netherlands. Available online: https://repository.tudelft.nl/islandora/object/uuid%3A61d261d7-4850-4e7b-972a-2582362dd568.

Coro, G. (2022). Tools for science–society–policy interfaces (D3.3). Horizon 2020 MOVING Project. Available online: https://www.moving-h2020.eu.

Crisp, J., Pelletier, D., Duffield, C., Adams, A., & Nagy, S. (1997). The Delphi method? *Nursing Research, 46*(2), 116–118. https://doi.org/10.1097/00006199-199703000-00010

Davies, C., Chen, W. Y., Sanesi, G., & Lafortezza, R. (2021). The European Union roadmap for implementing nature-based solutions: A review. *Environmental Science & Policy, 121*, 49–67. https://doi.org/10.1016/j.envsci.2021.03.004

DG Agri (2017). EIP-AGRI. Horizon 2020 Multi-Actor Projects. European Commission, DG Agri, EIP-Agri, 2017; pp.8. Available online: https://ec.europa.eu/eip/agriculture/sites/default/files/eip-agri_brochure_multi-actor_projects_2017_en_web.pdf

European Commission (2016). A Strategic approach to EU Agricultural Research & Innovation: Final Paper. pp.40. Available online: https://ec.europa.eu/newsroom/horizon2020/items/33294.

EU MAP (2023). SHERPA Rural Science-Society-Policy Interfaces. Available online: https://rural-interfaces.eu/eu-map/.

Fish, L. S., & Busby, D. M. (1996). The delphi method. *Research Methods in Family Therapy, 469*, 482.

Galanis, P. (2018). The Delphi method. *Archives of Hellenic Medicine, 35*(4), 564–570.

Gedminaitė-Raudonė, Z., Lankauskienė, R. (2021). MAP Position Paper (Lithuania)–Change in production and diversification of the rural economy. https://doi.org/10.5281/zenodo.5920891

Gedminaite-Raudone, Z., & Vilke, R. (2020a). Discussion Paper on Long-Term Vision for Lithuanian Rural Areas. 2020. Available online: "Circular Bio-economy—Lithuania". https://rural-interfaces.eu/wp-content/uploads/2020/10/MAP_Discussion-Paper_LT.pdf.

Gedminaite-Raudone, Z., & Vilke, R. (2020b). Long-Term Vision for Rural Areas: Contribution from 20 science-society-policy platforms. Lithuanian MAP Position Paper. Available online: https://rural-interfaces.eu/wp-content/uploads/2021/02/MAP_Position-Paper_LT_LTVRA.pdf.

Gerlitz, L., Meyer, C., & Prause, G. (2020). Methodology approach on benchmarking Regional Innovation on Smart Specialisation (RIS3): A joint macro-regional tool to regional performance evaluation and monitoring in Central Europe. *Entrepreneurship and Sustainability Issues, 8*(2), 1359–1385. https://doi.org/10.9770/jesi.2020.8.2(80)

González-Martinez, P., García-Pérez-De-Lema, D., Castillo-Vergara, M., & Hansen, P. B. (2023). Determinants and performance of the quadruple helix model and the mediating role of civil society. *Technology in Society, 75*, Article 102358. https://doi.org/10.1016/j.techsoc.2023.102358

Hecker, S., Haklay, M., Bowser, A., Makuch, Z., Vogel, J., & Bonn, A. (2018). Innovation in open science, society and policy–setting the agenda for citizen science. *Citizen Science: Innovation in Open Science, Society and Policy*, 1-23. https://doi.org/10.2307/j.ctv550cf2.8

Hegyi, F. B., & Mariussen, Å. (2021). Connecting urban and regional innovation ecosystems to enhance competitiveness. *The Palgrave Encyclopedia of Urban and Regional Futures*. https://doi.org/10.1007/978-3-030-51812-7_130-1

Howlett, M., Capano, G., & Ramesh, M. (2021). Governance styles: Re-thinking governance and public policy. In *The Routledge handbook of policy styles* (pp. 204–213). Routledge. https://doi.org/10.1057/9781137477972.0007

Rural Interfaces. (2023). SHERPA Rural Science-Society-Policy Interfaces. Available online: https://rural-interfaces.eu/rural-interfaces/

Janowski, T., Estevez, E., & Baguma, R. (2018). Platform governance for sustainable development: Reshaping citizen-administration relationships in the digital age. *Government Information Quarterly, 35*(4), S1–S16. https://doi.org/10.1016/j.giq.2018.09.002

Klessova, S., Botterman, M., Cave, J., & Engell, S. (2020). *Collaboration in a globally networked knowledge society.* ICT policy, research, and innovation: Perspectives and prospects for EU-US collaboration (pp. 3-19). https://doi.org/10.1002/9781119632481.ch1

Lankauskienė, R., & Gedminaitė-Raudonė, Ž. (2024). Challenges and Prospects for the Determinants of Socioeconomic Development in Rural Areas: Evidence from Lithuania. *European Countryside, 16*(1), 10–25. https://doi.org/10.2478/euco-2024-0002

MAPs Monitoring and Evaluation. (2023). SHERPA Rural Science-Society-Policy Interfaces. Available online: https://rural-interfaces.eu/news-or-events/maps-monitoring-evaluation-workshop/.

MAPs—Multi-Actor Platforms. (2023). SHERPA Rural Science-Society-Policy Interfaces. Available online: https://rural-interfaces.eu/multi-actor-platforms/.

Mariussen, Å., Mäenpää, A., & Virkkala, S. (2019). Revealing the innovation potential in the Baltic sea region: A comparative analysis. Available online: https://osuva.uwasa.fi/bitstream/handle/10024/9766/mariussen-m%C3%A4enp%C3%A4%C3%A4-virkkala_2019a_comparative%20analysis.reportfinal.pdf?sequence=5

Mitchell, R. K., Agle, B. R., & Wood, D. J. (1997). Toward a theory of stakeholder identification and salience: Defining the principle of who and what really counts. *Academy of Management Review, 22*(4), 853–886. https://doi.org/10.2307/259247

Moedas, C. (2018). Citizen science: Innovation in open science, society and policy. *UCL Press*. https://doi.org/10.2307/j.ctv550cf2.2

Mourik, R. M., Sonetti, G., & Robison, R. A. V. (2021). The same old story–or not? How storytelling can support inclusive local energy policy. *Energy*

Research & Social Science, *73*, 101940. https://doi.org/10.1016/j.erss.2021.101940

MOVING—MOuntain Valorisation through INterconnectedness and Green growth (2020–2024). Horizon 2020 Project internet site. Available online: https://www.moving-h2020.eu

Okoli, C., & Pawlowski, S. D. (2004). The Delphi method as a research tool: An example, design considerations and applications. *Information & Management*, *42*(1), 15–29. https://doi.org/10.1016/j.im.2003.11.002

Rahmani, A., Vaziri Nezhad, R., Ahmadi Nia, H., & Rezaeian, M. (2020). Methodological principles and applications of the Delphi method: a narrative review. *Journal of Rafsanjan University of medical sciences*, *19*(5), 515–538. https://doi.org/10.29252/jrums.19.5.515

Roman, M., Varga, H., Cvijanovic, V., & Reid, A. (2020). Quadruple Helix models for sustainable regional innovation: Engaging and facilitating civil society participation. *Economies, 8*(2), 48. https://doi.org/10.3390/economies8020048

Sattler, C., Loft, L., Mann, C., & Meyer, C. (2018). Methods in ecosystem services governance analysis: An introduction. *Ecosystem Services, 34*, 155–168. https://doi.org/10.1016/j.ecoser.2018.11.007

SHERPA annual conference. SHERPA Rural Science-Society-Policy Interfaces. 2023. Available online: https://rural-interfaces.eu/news-or-events/sherpa-conference-2022/

SHERPA—Sustainable Hub to Engage into Rural Policies with Actors (2019–2023). Horizon 2020 Project internet site. Available online: https://rural-interfaces.eu/what-is-sherpa/.

Shiffer, V. (2021). Local Collaborative Governance: Could It Bypass Outdated Legal Structures? *Collaborative governance: Theory and lessons from Israel* (pp. 103-125). https://doi.org/10.1007/978-3-030-45807-2_5

Šírá, E., Vavrek, R., Kravčáková Vozárová, I., & Kotulič, R. (2020). Knowledge economy indicators and their impact on the sustainable competitiveness of the EU countries. *Sustainability*, *12*(10), 4172. https://doi.org/10.3390/su12104172

Smart-Up BSR (2023). An overview of smart specialization strategy in Lithuania. Available online: https://smartup-bsr.eu/wp-content/uploads/2021/06/O2.6-Lithuania-RIS3.pdf

Szymańska, E., Kołoszko-Chomentowska, Z., & Stepaniuk, K. (2021). Innovative mobility solutions in Baltic Sea region rural areas. *EPPM 2021*, 104. https://doi.org/10.3390/su14116603

Šūmane, S., Ortiz Miranda, D., Pinto-Correia, T., Czekaj, M., Duckett, D., Galli, F., Grivins, M., Noble, C., Tisenkopfs, T., Toma, I., & Tsiligiridis, T. (2021). Supporting the role of small farms in the European regional food systems:

What role for the science-policy interface? *Global Food Security, 28*, 100433. https://doi.org/10.1016/j.gfs.2020.100433

Tovey, H. (2016). Rural sustainable development in the knowledge society. *Routledge*. https://doi.org/10.4324/9781315607214

Turk, Ž. (2021). On Knowledge Society in Europe 2021. Available online: https://doi.org/10.2139/ssrn.3899876

Vilkė, R., Vidickienė, D., Gedminaitė-Raudonė, Ž, Simonaitytė, V., & Ribašauskienė, E. (2021). *Rural Economic Developments and Social Movements: A New Paradigm*. Palgrave Macmillan. https://doi.org/10.1007/978-3-030-71983-8

Vilkė, R., & Šarkutė, L. (2018). Lithuanian local action groups: spatial initiatives or mobilized potential for rural development? *Viešoji politika ir administravimas = Public Policy and Administration*. T. 17, Nr. 4, p. 510–525; online ISSN 2029–2872; print ISSN 1648–2603; https://doi.org/10.13165/VPA-18-17-4-02

Vilkė, R. (2017). Participatory development of local communities in the context of farmers' social responsibility. *Public Policy and Administration, 16*(2), 245–263. https://doi.org/10.13165/VPA-17-16-2-06

Virkkala, S., & Mariussen, Å. (2021). Networks of Innovation: Measuring Structure and Dynamics between and within Helices, Regions and Spatial Levels. Empirical Evidence from the Baltic Sea Region. *Triple Helix, 8*(2), 282–328. https://doi.org/10.1163/21971927-bja10019

Virkkala, S., Mariussen, Å., & Mäenpää, A. (2020). Quadruple helix relations in innovation networks in EU macro-region. Comparative analysis of regional innovation potential in Baltic Sea Region. In *The 18th triple helix conference conference proceedings* (Vol. 15, p. 78).

Vohland, K., Land-Zandstra, A., Ceccaroni, L., Lemmens, R., Perelló, J., Ponti, M., & Wagenknecht, K. (2021). The science of citizen science evolves. In K. Vohland, A. Land-Zandstra, L. Ceccaroni, R. Lemmens, J. Perelló, M. Ponti, & K. Wagenknecht (Eds.), *The science of citizen science* (pp. 1–12). Springer. https://doi.org/10.1007/978-3-030-58278-4_1

Wellbrock, W., Roep, D., Mahon, M., Kairyte, E., Nienaber, B., García, M. D. D., & Farrell, M. (2013). Arranging public support to unfold collaborative modes of governance in rural areas. *Journal of Rural Studies, 32*, 420–429. https://doi.org/10.1016/j.jrurstud.2013.09.011

CHAPTER 5

Promoting the Transition to Carbon Neutrality in Specialized Agricultural Systems: Insights from the Emilia-Romagna Multi-Actor Platform

Emilia Pellegrini, Meri Raggi, Stefano Targetti, and Davide Viaggi

1 Introduction

In this chapter, we present the results of a multi-actor approach carried out in the Emilia-Romagna region (North-East of Italy) from 2021 to 2022 to investigate what types of transformational change is appropriate

E. Pellegrini (✉) · S. Targetti · D. Viaggi
Department of Agriculture and Food Sciences, University of Bologna, Bologna, Italy
e-mail: emilia.pellegrini2@unibo.it

S. Targetti
e-mail: stefano.targetti@unibo.it

D. Viaggi
e-mail: davide.viaggi@unibo.it

D. Barjolle et al. (eds.), *Innovation and the Future of Rural Development in Europe*,
https://doi.org/10.1007/978-3-032-22570-2_5

and feasible to contribute to transitions to climate neutrality by 2050. Transformational changes in agri-food systems are needed across Europe to achieve the ambitious objectives established by the European Green Deal,[1] the Farm to Fork[2] and the Biodiversity Strategy.[3] The IPCC defines transformation as "The alteration of fundamental attributes of a system" (IPCC, 2012); however, it is more realistic to think of transformation as a continuous process that allows small, in-depth changes, where new modes of governance play a key role (Termeer Dewulf & Biesbroek, 2017). Moreover, interpretations and narratives of required transformational changes differ across the EU depending on national and regional specificities and on specific interests and priorities of different (types of) rural actors. In this chapter, the focus is placed on a region characterized by a strong agri-food sector, which generates significant benefits for the regional economy, but has also caused a high territorial fragmentation, land use change, and intensification. Moreover, the unstable weather pattern, with series of late frosts, droughts, and flood events, is severely damaging farmers' profitability and the livelihood of rural areas. Hence, through the multi-actor approach designed by the Horizon project SHERPA, we investigated the priorities, challenges, and opportunities perceived as most relevant by regional stakeholders in the process of transition to climate neutrality and formulated a list of recommendations to EU rural policy and research agenda. The chapter is organized as follows: Section 2 describes the main aspects of the Italian strategy for a climate-neutral agriculture, Section 3 sets out the description of the studied area with a focus on the main trends in land use and climate patterns, and the method adopted to carry out the stakeholders' consultation. Section 4 summarizes and discusses the main results, while Section 5 provides some conclusive remarks.

M. Raggi
Department of Statistical Sciences, University of Bologna, Bologna, Italy
e-mail: meri.raggi@unibo.it

[1] COM(2019) 640 final.

[2] COM(2020) 381 final.

[3] COM(2020) 380 final.

2 The Italian Strategy towards a Climate-Neutral Agriculture

The Italian strategy towards a climate-neutral agricultural sector is built upon the EU legislation of which we recall some key elements. The European Green Deal aims to make Europe climate-neutral by 2050, and to make this goal legally binding, the Commission has proposed the European Climate Act (EU Reg. No. 2021/1119) which also sets an additional and more ambitious goal of reducing net greenhouse gas emissions by at least 55% by 2030 compared to 1990 levels. To fulfil this objective the Commission issued Regulation No. 2023/839 (amending Regulation 2018/841) which set a net greenhouse gas absorption target for 2030 in the Land Use, Land Use Change, Forestry sector (LULUCF) of 310 million tons of CO2 equivalent through specific national commitments. Moreover, in 2021 the Commission approved the Communication on Sustainable Carbon Cycles (European Commission, 2021) where it outlines the principles, short- and medium-term actions and rules needed to store carbon dioxide in nature with the use of appropriate soil management practices and innovative technological solutions.

Moreover, the new green architecture of the 2023–2027 CAP deploys three main instruments that can contribute towards a more carbon-neutral agriculture, these are (i) the conditionality (including the greening), (ii) the eco-schemes (both under the I Pillar), and (iii) the agri-environmental-climate measures (AECMs) under the II Pillar. Another import novelty of the 2023–2027 CAP is the New Delivery Model (NDM) which is a new governance structure that should allow a shift from the compliance-based approach to a results-based approach, where performance plays a central role. The Strategic Plan (SP) drafted by each Member State represents a crucial element, as it transfers significant responsibilities from the European Union to the Member States, allowing them to design and implement strategies more freely.

Looking at the Italian strategy to fulfil the above-mentioned targets, the national SP was approved in December 2022 by the EC and came into force in January 2023. The fourth specific objective of the SP is dedicated to climate action including strategies for GHG emissions reduction, improving carbon sequestration, and promote sustainable energy (MIPAAF, 2022). Specifically, the Italian SP provides several interventions including eco-schemes, AECMs, and investment measures, which directly or indirectly aim to:

- **GHG reduction** through (i) the maintenance or adoption of more extensive land uses, (ii) the adoption of practices and technologies useful for energy and fertilizer use efficiency/reduction, (iii) the production of renewable energy from products and by-products of agricultural, livestock and forestry origin.
- **Promote carbon sequestration in soils** through interventions that support (i) the adoption of practices that reduce the intensity of tillage; (ii) the transition/maintenance to more extensive and/or less impactful cropping systems; (iii) the use of organic soil conditioners, with a view to recycling of waste materials and by-products; (iv) the conservation and/or integration of crop residues; (v) the introduction of cover crops and/or grassing of permanent crops; (vi) the adoption of techniques and practices to protect existing carbon stocks.
- **Increasing the resilience and adaptation of the primary sector to climate change** through interventions that support (i) agricultural diversification; (ii) water efficiency and savings; (iii) agro-ecosystems conservation including recovery actions resulting from disaster events.
- **Curb land degradation and erosion** through (i) agro-forestry interventions; (ii) non-productive investments; (iii) infrastructural interventions for rural areas and environmental purposes.

With the Regulation No. 2023/839, for Italy the absorption target has changed from - 21 to - 35.8 MtCO2eq. As reported by the Institute for Environmental Protection and Research (ISPRA) in the National Greenhouse Gas Inventory (ISPRA, 2023), in 2021 in Italy, the LULUCF sector absorbed −27.5 MtCO2eq. achieving the previous target. Based on the scenario reported in the National Integrated Energy and Climate Plan (updated in 2023), the LULUCF sector will be able to absorb −34.9 MtCO2eq by 2030, therefore almost reaching the Italian target for the sector of −35.8 MtCO2eq., as set by the EU Regulation No. 2023/839 (Falconi & Amato, 2023).

Finally, it is worth mentioning that the Bioeconomy is recognised as crucial for achieving carbon neutrality as underlined in the Communication on Sustainable Carbon Cycles (European Commission, 2021). The second Italian Bioeconomy Strategy (BIT II) was published in 2019 with the general objective of increasing by 15% the current performance of the Italian Bioeconomy by 2030 (currently about EUR 330 billion/

y and about 2 M of people working in bioeconomy sectors) (BIT II Bioeconomy in Italy, 2019). The strategy envisages to interconnect the main bioeconomy sectors "to build longer, more sustainable and locally routed value chains". If implemented, the BIT II should contribute to the achievement of carbon neutrality especially through the development of technologies and practices that intervene on various aspects of soil quality improvement, carbon accumulation in soil, and decarbonization.

3 Materials and Methods

Study Area

Emilia-Romagna is a region (NUTS2) of the North-East of Italy and it is one of the most developed in the country, with a regional GDP higher than the national average' (Regione Emilia-Romagna e Agriconsulting, 2013). The North-East is the first macro-region in Italy in terms of gross added value by agricultural sector, and it is among the first ten in Europe (EUROSTAT, 2021). The rural areas of Emilia-Romagna are very heterogeneous (Fig. 1). The areas located in the Po plain (medium-light grey in Fig. 1) are mainly specialized in the production of cereals; notably, about one third of the national production of soft wheat is concentrated in the region (Regione Emilia-Romagna e Agriconsulting 2013). Moreover, an important share of the regional UAA is devoted to fodder crops (e.g., alfa-alfa, maize) linked to the Grana Padano and Parmigiano Reggiano supply chain, which are among the main Protected Designation of Origins at the regional and national level (Mantovi Dal Prà Pacchioli & Ligabue, 2015). The hilly mountainous areas along the Apennines ridge (dark grey in Fig. 1) are, instead, characterised by the presence of smaller farms specialized in valuable crops (eg, vines, fruit) and for which an important source of income derives from other activities such as agritourism, forestry, and food processing. The agricultural sector has suffered from contraction over the past decades that, although sharper in predominantly rural areas, has concerned the whole region (Regione Emilia-Romagna e Agriconsulting, 2013). These trends had consequences for the reconfiguration of the rural territories of the region. In particular, an increase in farm concentration (increasing UAA per holding and decreasing number of holdings) and intensification in plain areas have exacerbated land-use competition, homogenisation of agricultural landscape structure and fragmentation. This trend of specialization of cropping systems, with the subsequent disappearance of traditional farm livestock activities, has led to a significant increase in soil erosion in hilly areas, while a constant decrease in soil organic carbon (SOC) has been observed in flat areas (Regione Emilia-Romagna, 2020).

The region also experiences a progressive change in climatic conditions, particularly with an increase in regional temperatures (plus 1.1 C° on average) and a significant variation in seasonal precipitation (drier summers and wetter autumns) (Arpae Emilia-Romagna, 2017). Moreover, over the last 20 years, several droughts have hit the Po River Basin making water crises a structural problem for agriculture and other water-related activities. Extremely severe drought has been observed in 2022 which has caused dramatic yields drop for almost all crops, with losses reaching–40% for soft wheat and - 50% for maize (Regione Emilia-Romagna, 2013). In addition, rising temperatures are causing significant consequences for the feed industry and dairy supply chain due to mycotoxin contamination of corn caused by thermophilic pests. Therefore, water scarcity and the increase in average temperature, on the one hand,

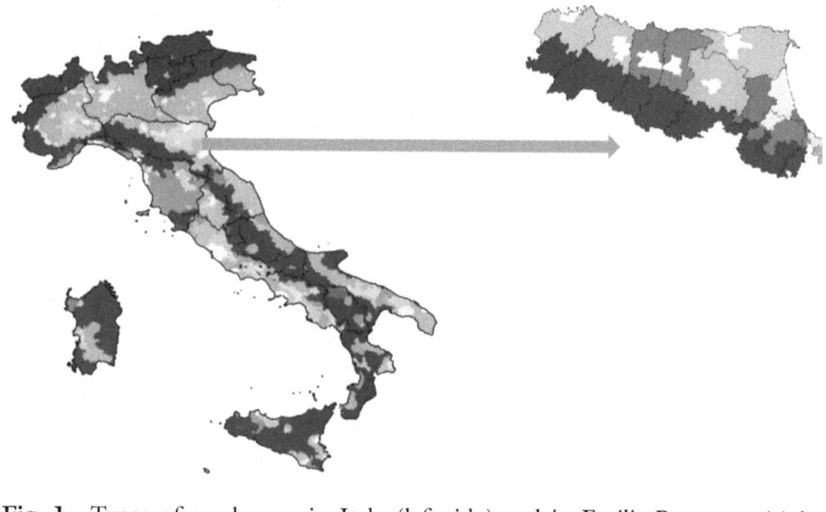

Fig. 1 Types of rural areas in Italy (left-side) and in Emilia-Romagna (right-side). Dark grey: Predominantly rural areas; Medium gray: intermediate areas; Light grey: Urban-rural transitional areas; White: urban areas. Source: adapted from Reterurale.it

jeopardize the degree of forage self-sufficiency of farms, while on the other, promote the shift to other crop systems.

Eventually, it is worth saying that in 2023 a flood of exceptional intensity hit the region causing deaths and enormous damage to residents while also compromising many productive activities. At the time of the flood, the MAP activities were already over, and issues related to soil erosion and risk management were not highlighted during the discussion. However, it is likely that these issues would have attracted more attention nowadays.

The Multi-Actor Approach

The Horizon 2020 project SHERPA originates from two needs: to improve the use of knowledge gained from investment in research, and to empower key actors and stakeholders in the development of public policy. Therefore, the project has acted as an intermediary of knowledge between two groups generally identified in knowledge transfer processes as knowledge producers and knowledge users (Contandriopoulos, Lemire, Denis, & Tremblay, 2010). In SHERPA, in fact, knowledge producers are represented by the EU-funded projects whose main outputs were synthetised in research summaries called SHERPA Discussion paper, while the group of knowledge users is represented by the 41 local Multi-actor Platforms (MAPs) (plus one at the EU level), created by the project across 19 EU countries plus Scotland, and composed of rural stakeholders belonging to science, society, and policy domains. The process of knowledge exchange established by SHERPA is well described in Fig. 2. The summery of research results, indeed, fed the discussion in the MAPs, and the inputs collected during the interactions within the MAP were reformulated in terms of recommendations for EU rural policy and research agendas to develop the MAP Position papers.

The Emilia-Romagna MAP (ERMAP) was invited to follow this process to discuss the topic of what types of transformational change is appropriate and feasible in the regional context to contribute to transitions to climate neutrality by 2050. More in detail, the discussion was articulated in two main phases:

Scoping phase. At the first stage, a summary of the SHERPA Discussion paper "Climate change and environmental sustainability" (Miller et al., 2021) was provided to the ERMAP. The paper offers a comprehensive overview of policy strategies as well as findings derived from EU research projects on interventions supporting mitigation and adaptation

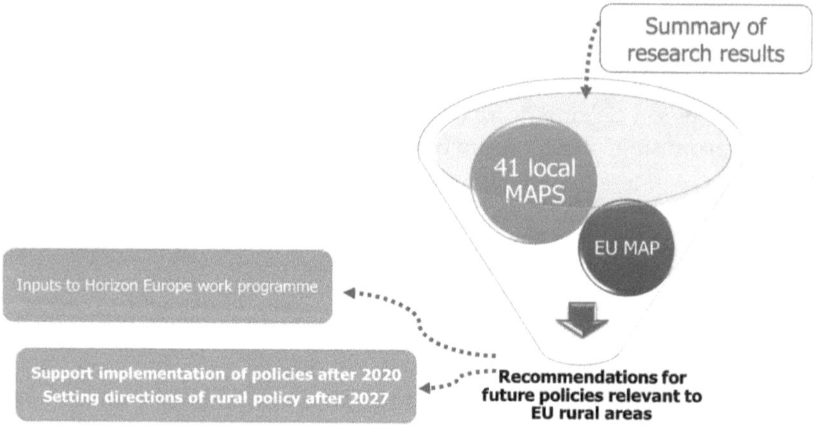

Fig. 2 SHERPA knowledge exchange process. Source SHERPA

in rural areas. In particular, the paper identifies five areas of intervention that are: Land use and water, Social innovation and partnerships, Food and diet, Business and finance, Open science and citizen science. After providing this background information, a first online workshop was organized with the ERMAP on July 2021. Ten stakeholders participated in the online workshop, coming from research and consultancy (five), public bodies (four), and one representative of a Local Action Group. Through an online survey, the ten stakeholders were asked to rate which areas of intervention perceived as most relevant in the regional context to boost the transition to carbon neutrality. After the vote, the ERMAP was invited to discuss the identified priorities with a focus on what policy interventions would enable or facilitate the transition and what are the main research needs and gaps. The information collected during the first workshop was processed to develop a preliminary version of the ERMAP Position paper that was discussed and improved during the second on-line focus workshop held in October 2021 whose inputs were used to finalize the ERMAP Position paper. In this first stage (both workshops), 17 stakeholders participated in the process with the following composition: five actors from science and consultancy, five from civil society (four from business and one from a Local Action Group), and seven from policy.

Deepening phase. In 2022 the MAPs were given the possibility to delve further into one of the identified priorities discussed during the scoping phase. Hence, the ERMAP decided to focus on the topic of "Climate change and land use" and, again, the starting input for the discussion was provided by the SHERPA Discussion paper specifically addressing this topic (Miller et al., 2022). Six online interviews were conducted with the ERMAP members followed by an online workshop to discuss the results of the interviews and collect additional input. The six experts interviewed represent a smaller group of "core actors", while invitations to the workshop were sent to a larger group that included all participants in the scoping phase. The interviews and workshop focused on: (i) regional priorities in relation to land use and climate change, (ii) policy interventions already in place and recommended by MAP members, (iii) knowledge gaps and research needs. The final composition of the ERMAP was made up of a regional officer, three representatives from research and consultancy, and four representatives from civil society. This group was the most heterogeneous with two actors from irrigation boards, one from a cooperative farm, and one private citizen.

The outcomes of both phases are summarized in two ERMAP Position papers (Pellegrini et al., 2021, 2022) whose main results are described in the following sections.

4 Results and Discussion

Identified Priorities

Intervening on "Land use and Water management", and "Social innovation and partnerships" were the key priorities identified by the ERMAP through the online survey (Fig. 3). While land use and water management were discussed in relation to their contribution to mitigation and adaptation and the main points raised by the ERMAP are described below, the topic of social innovation and partnerships was discussed as a crosscutting approach that should underlie the transition process and, for this reason, is described in Section 4.3 on recommendations to policy and research.

Priorities for Land Use

Within the overarching umbrella of land use, two priorities were identified as particularly urgent in the regional context. The first focuses on soil with the aim of improving the mitigation potential generated by agriculture. In particular, there is a need to promote agricultural practices

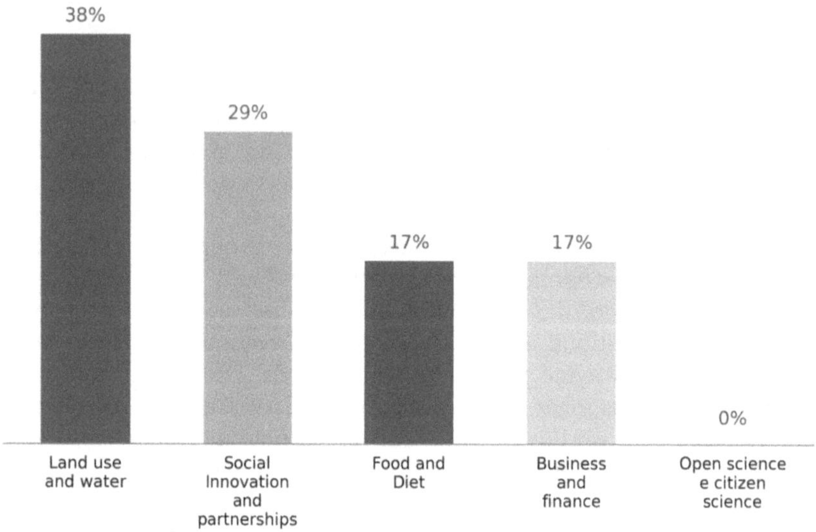

Fig. 3 Results of the on-line survey: priority issues for the transition to climate neutrality in Emilia-Romagna

and techniques to increase SOC, given also the fact that higher temperatures tend to accelerate its loss. Some of the practices mentioned by the ERMAP include change in land use, vegetation management, crop rotation, nutrient management (e.g. organic soil conditioners), and reduced tillage intensity.

The second priority is to improve the adaptation capacity of agricultural sector by promoting the adoption of more resilient crop choices. As some stakeholders have observed, farmers are already changing their crop choices but there is the need to support them in building new supply chains. Building sustainable and profitable supply chains requires time but, at this moment—it was argued - not much attention is dedicated to this with the risk of being unprepared when these changes inevitably will happen.

However, the MAP also highlighted the importance of acknowledging the possible trade-offs that mitigation and adaptation strategies may entail. It is widely recognized, for instance, that deep tillage does not favour the storage of SOC and that it should be reduced where possible. Nevertheless, the rise in temperature makes deep tillage necessary in specific cases to counteract the spread of pests. This is the case for maize, where specific guidelines suggest the removal of crop residues through deep tillage to reduce the spread of thermophilic pests. Therefore, it is important to be aware of these potential trade-offs and to design policy measures accordingly.

Priorities for Water Management
In the face of an increasing frequency of extreme events (e.g., drought and floods), the ERMAP highlighted the need to rethink water management towards a more efficient use of water resources. Within this priority, the many aspects discussed by the MAP can be summarized in two key points. On the one hand, there are still some areas of the region characterized by highly inefficient use of water resources. For instance, the experts provided examples of rice and maize productions grown on permeable soils (e.g., gravel) which are significantly inefficient for these water-intensive crops. On the other, the economic damages borne by farmers are significant as reported by the director of a cooperative farm. In 2020, due to a late frost, the farm lost about 13,000 quintals of its orchard production; moreover, with the drought of 2022, wheat yields drop by approximately 15–20%. Therefore, there is the need to increase the preparedness towards extreme climate events and to adopt a long-term, future-oriented approach, moving from crisis management to a risk management, focusing on preventive strategies, taking into account the characteristics of the affected water bodies and basins and the expected changes in the environmental, socio-economic, and cultural spheres.

Opportunities and Challenges

Given these priorities, the discussion with the ERMAP moved to the identification of opportunities and challenges that the transition to carbon neutrality may entail for the agri-food sector and, more in general, for the regional rural areas. The MAP recognized that the increasing awareness of consumers about the footprint generated by agri-food systems is pushing companies to showcase how they contribute to emission reduction targets. Moreover, the attention placed by the new CAP on result-based approaches to the delivery of agro-environmental goods is also driving the demand for environmental reporting of agri-food products. Hence, according to the ERMAP, markets for carbon credits, carbon footprint labelling and, more generally, environmental reporting could become more widespread in the future. These opportunities also concern water management, as it will be increasingly important to reduce the incidence of energy consumption at the various stages of the water cycle (capture, transport, distribution) and assessment tools, such as Life Cycle Assessment, and certification schemes, such as the Environmental Product Declaration, could help to measure and demonstrate the reduction of water-related emissions. If, on the one hand, this can generate the opportunity to monitor the commitment of companies towards climate mitigation targets and, ideally, ensuring a greater accountability, on the other hand, there are several challenges associated with the spread of environmental reporting. The first relates to providing reliable measurements of the impacts (or impacts' reduction) of agricultural practices on SOC dynamics or other environmental parameters. However, currently, at the regional level, the predictive models used to simulate the dynamics of SOC in relation to different farming practices are quite simplistic and only a few long-term field measurements are available. Moreover, environmental reporting entails the collection, management, and transmission of a large amount of data that would require an improvement in the data management structure, in order to make data as uniform as possible across the supply chain so that each segment can collect and transmit data in a way that is usable in the markets.

Recommendations

Recommendations for Policy and Research Agendas

The topics arising from the activities conducted with stakeholders in Emilia-Romagna are also discussed in the literature, although in some cases knowledge on these topics is still in its early stages. Hence, this section wants to put the raised issues into a broader discussion to emphasize key research and policy recommendations. The problems raised by the ERMAP in relation to environmental reporting are very similar to those highlighted by Deconinck Jansen & Barisone (2023) who identify three main concerns linked to the adoption of environmental labels. These encompass conceptual issues (i.e. which impacts to include), technical issues (i.e. how to measure or estimate these impacts), and administrative issues (i.e. how to avoid a fragmentation of approaches leading to high transaction costs). As highlighted by the authors these issues generate numerous research questions to which applied research, and in particular agricultural economists, could contribute. For instance, what institutional setups allow to measure and communicate environmental impacts while avoiding excessive transaction costs. Moreover, it is unclear what socio-economic effects these certifications will have on consumers and producers and, likewise, what will be the effects on the supply chains. Finally, as already mentioned, questions around potential trade-offs (or synergies) among policy objectives should be further explored. Related to this last point, results from a pan-European survey on the willingness to participate in four innovative contractual solutions for the efficient and effective provision of agri-environment-climate public goods (i.e., result-based, collective, value chain, and land tenure contracts) highlight that the poor adoption of innovative contract solutions is not explained by a general farmers' reluctance towards these instruments, but rather is related to the potential trade-offs that these contracts may entail (D'Alberto et al., 2024). For result-based contracts, in fact, the study suggests that a greater involvement of farmers in the measurement of the results could enable the design of locally tailored contract solutions, more flexible and acceptable for farmers.

The systemic review of Raina et al. (2024), who screened about 40 global case studies on various types of incentive mechanisms for carbon farming contracts, arrives at similar results. The authors found that the primary challenges in designing effective carbon-based payments include the cost and reliability of monitoring, reporting, and verification tools, ensuring "additionality" of the schemes (i.e., that mitigation would not have occurred in the absence of the carbon farming project), and overcoming the barriers to scaling up such projects. Acknowledging that, the authors conclude that the success of carbon farming relies on understanding the complexities of contract design attributes and fostering collaboration among farmers and other stakeholders, while also learning from ex-post analysis of successful cases.

Regarding the priorities for water management, there is already a portfolio of policy instruments to steer farming choices towards a more efficient use of water resources, ranging from incentivizing water pricing to regulations, and some of them are explicitly required by the EU legislation with the Water Framework Directive (WFD, 2000/60/EC). However, as highlighted by several studies, pricing needs to be included in a broader set of tools to be used according to local specificities from environmental, hydrological, land-use, and socio-economic perspectives (Pellegrini et al., 2023). Moreover, in a future likely characterized by a rise in extreme events, the effectiveness of water pricing policies may diminish if not integrated within a broader management framework that engages users through participatory systems (Berbel & Expósito, 2020). Hence, with the increasing climate variability, policies should address a wide range of solutions like, for instance, infrastructures (e.g., retention basins), water reuse, and efficient irrigation techniques. Hard measures, however, are not sufficient in contexts of increasing water scarcity but attention should also be placed on governance arrangements (e.g. norms, contract solutions, policy) that can ease collaboration among water users. Thus, socio-economic research is the key to studying potential conflicts that can arise during water crises and support the identification of effective governance solutions.

To wrap-up, based on the above-mentioned issues, a general recommendation can be drawn to enhance evidence-based policymaking. Policy instruments that can contribute to climate neutrality and more efficient water management (e.g. carbon farming, environmental labelling, result-based payments, water pricing, etc.) entail numerous decisions on indicators, measurement, costs of implementation/monitoring, and data management where each choice is likely to be subject to trade-offs. For this reason, policymaking may benefit from multi-actor and participatory approaches to get a clearer understanding of local specificities and potential barriers, opportunities and challenges to implement these instruments.

Cross-Cutting Approaches to Enable the Transition at the Regional Level

As highlighted, the transition to a carbon neutral agricultural sector does not only require the implementation of practices targeting soil and water management, but it should be framed also within a new governance model. As emerged from the survey (Fig. 3), in fact, the ERMAP identified "Social innovation and partnerships" as priorities in the process of transition. This new governance model should consist of at least three approaches. The first relates to the need for policies that support a "Territorial approach" which, according to the OECD definition, is the capacity to tap the underutilised regional potentials and, building on existing territorial strengths, to rethink strategies and priorities (OECD, 2020). For instance, one MAP member argued that the great heterogeneity of rural areas of the Emilia-Romagna could favour the development of compensation mechanisms between more polluting productive districts and areas of the territory that can accumulate it (e.g. through pilot projects of agroforestry management, forest management, pasture management). However, this type of strategy requires policy frameworks that acknowledge the inner resources of a territory and enhance what scholars define as "territorial capital" which includes both physical assets and human, social, relational capital and cooperative networks of a region (Camagni & Capello, 2013). The second aspect, that is also linked to the first, concerns policies that support the creation of networks, partnerships, and collaboration (i.e. collaborative approach). Policies should encourage the creation and longevity of networks and collaboration that can be motivated by proximity (e.g. coordinated action within the same river basin) or by purpose (e.g. coordination in data collection and management along agri-food supply chains for environmental reporting). It is interesting to note that several notable examples of collaborative networks have emerged as the region faces increasing exposure to extreme climatic events. The recent drought, in particular, has fostered stronger collaboration among water-use sectors, leading to the co-development of a Drought Management Plan and to a growing number of meetings and platforms aimed at coordinating responses to drought conditions. Another noteworthy example in water resource management is the establishment of collective reservoirs among farms, funded through the latest Rural Development Programme. These shared reservoirs enhance farms' resilience to the rising risks associated with drought. The third, as mentioned in the previous section, relates to policymaking processes based on place-based and participatory approaches for the design of appropriate instruments that can target specific environmental problems while also taking into account local management inefficiencies. As represented in Table 1, these cross-cutting approaches frame the priorities, opportunities, challenges, and recommendations characterizing the process of transition to carbon as emerged from the consultation with the ERMAP.

5 Conclusions

The multi-actor approach adopted in this study allowed the identification of three main priorities - and of related opportunities, challenges, and recommendations - to steer the transition to carbon neutrality in a territory that can be representative of other intensive agriculture systems of Europe. Certainly, the consultation conducted with the MAP presented some intrinsic limitations. One concerns the representativeness of the ERMAP: for instance, agricultural stakes were over-represented compared

Table 1 Synthesis of the key messages emerged from the ERMAP

Territorial approach					Bottom-up and
Collaborative approach	Priorities	Improving the maintenance of SOC	More efficient management of water resources	Steering the transition to alternative crop choices	Place-based approaches
	Opportunities	Markets for carbon credits; carbon footprint labelling.	Environmental reporting	New income opportunities	
	Challenges	Providing reliable measurements; Coordinated data management.	Providing reliable measurements; Coordinated data management; Addressing inefficient water uses.	Building new supply chains.	
	Recommendations	Evidence-based policymaking benefiting from multi-actor and participatory approaches to get a clearer understanding of local specificities and potential trade-offs among policy objectives.			

to environmental issues. Likewise, most of the actors involved operate in intensive agricultural areas, while predominantly rural areas were less represented in the ERMAP. While acknowledging these limitations, we believe that this study can contribute to understanding future trajectories of rural areas and agri-food systems towards the objective of climate neutrality.

The identified priorities for land use and water management underscore the intricate interplay between mitigation and adaptation strategies in the face of climate change impacts. Soil improvement initiatives, aimed at enhancing carbon sequestration through agricultural practices, and resilient crop choices to bolster adaptation capacity emerge as urgent imperatives. Similarly, addressing water management challenges necessitates a paradigm shift toward efficient resource utilization, coupled with long-term, proactive strategies to mitigate economic losses incurred by extreme weather events.

Among these priorities lie both opportunities and challenges for the agri-food sector and rural areas. The growing awareness of consumers about their environmental footprints presents opportunities for market-driven initiatives such as markets for carbon credit and environmental reporting. However, a number of challenges emerge around these instruments pertaining to reliability, standardization of measurement tools, monitoring and implementation costs that might hinder their effectiveness in contributing to carbon neutrality targets. For this reason, the recommendations proposed for policy and research agendas underscore the imperative for evidence-based policymaking that benefit from multi-actor and participatory approaches to get a clearer understanding of local specificities and potential barriers, opportunities and challenges to implement these instruments. A new governance model that supports territorial approaches, collaborative networks, and participatory decision-making processes is crucial to navigate the complexities of the transition to a carbon-neutral agricultural sector.

References

Arpae Emilia-Romagna. (2017). Atlante climatico dell'Emilia-Romagna 1961–2015.

Berbel, J., & Expósito, A. (2020). The theory and practice of water pricing and cost recovery in the water framework directive. Water. *Alternatives*, *13*(3), 659–673. Retrieved from www.water-alternatives.org

BIT II Bioeconomy in Italy. (2019). BIT II Bioeconomy in Italy. Retrieved April 15, 2024, from https://cnbbsv.palazzochigi.it/media/1951/bit-italiano-14feb2020.pdf

Camagni, R., & Capello, R. (2013). Regional competitiveness and territorial capital: A conceptual approach and empirical evidence from the European Union. *Regional Studies, 47*(9), 1383–1402. https://doi.org/10.1080/00343404.2012.681640

Contandriopoulos, D., Lemire, M., Denis, J., & Tremblay, É. (2010). Knowledge exchange processes in organizations and policy arenas: A narrative systematic review of the literature. *Milbank Quarterly, 88*(4), 444–483.

D'Alberto, R., Targetti, S., Schaller, L., Bartolini, F., Eichhorn, T., Haltia, E., et al. (2024). A European perspective on acceptability of innovative Agri-environment-climate contract solutions. *Land Use Policy, 141*(May 2023), 107120. https://doi.org/10.1016/j.landusepol.2024.107120

Deconinck, K., Jansen, M., & Barisone, C. (2023). Fast and furious: The rise of environmental impact reporting in food systems. *European Review of Agricultural Economics, 50*(4), 1310–1337. https://doi.org/10.1093/erae/jbad018

Emilia-Romagna, R. (2020). *2020.* La qualità dell'ambiente in Emilia-Romagna.

European Commission. COMMUNICATION FROM THE COMMISSION TO THE EUROPEAN PARLIAMENT AND THE COUNCIL. Sustainable Carbon Cycles, Pub. L. No. COM. (2021) 800 final COMMUNICATION (2021). Brussels. doi: https://doi.org/10.1142/9789812791924_0004

Eurostat. (2021). Economic accounts for agriculture. Retrieved April 2, 2024, from https://ec.europa.eu/eurostat/data/database

Falconi, I., & Amato, A. (2023, December). La sfida del Carbon farming. Pianeta PSR (Web Magazine). Retrieved from https://www.pianetapsr.it/flex/cm/pages/ServeBLOB.php/L/IT/IDPagina/2998#Note .

IPCC. (2012). Summary for policymakers. IPCC special report on managing the risks of extreme events and disasters to advance climate change adaptation. In *Managing the risks of extreme events and disasters to advance climate change adaptation (Cambridge).*

ISPRA. (2023). Italian Greenhouse Gas Inventory 1990–2021 National Inventory Report 2023 (ISPRA, Rap). Retrieved from www.isprambiente.gov.it

Mantovi, P., Dal Prà, A., Pacchioli, M. T., & Ligabue, M. (2015). Forage production and use in the dairy farming systems of northern Italy. *Grassland Science in Europe, 20*(April), 508.

Miller, D., Irvine, K., Nijnik, M., Garcia, B., Panoutsopoulos, H., Martino, G., & Schwarz, G. (2022). *SHERPA Discussion Paper CLIMATE CHANGE AND LAND USE.* https://doi.org/10.5281/zenodo.6671041

Miller, D., Nijnik, M., Irvine, K., Chartier, O., Martino, G., Bourneix, J., et al. (2021). Climate change and environmental sustainability. *SHERPA Discussion Paper, 862448*. https://doi.org/10.5281/zenodo.4905655

MIPAAF. (2022). PIANO STRATEGICO DELLA PAC 2023–2027. Documento di Disntesi. Agroecología. https://inea.org/la-pac-2023-2027-2/. Último acceso: 16/07/2023.

OECD. (2020). A territorial approach to the sustainable development goals. Retrieved from https://www.oecd-ilibrary.org/sites/e86fa715-en/1/1/1/index.html?itemId=/content/publication/e86fa715-en&_csp_=6d42c3e04d6f0b50b2439e764fde242b&itemIGO=oecd&itemContentType=book.

Pellegrini, E., Raggi, M., Viaggi, D., & Targetti, S. (2021). *MAP position paper (Emilia- Romagna, Italy)-climate change and environmental sustainability*. https://doi.org/10.5281/zenodo.5920887

Pellegrini, E., Dalmazzone, S., Fasolino, N. G., Frontuto, V., Gizzi, P., Luppi, F., et al. (2023). Economic analysis under the water framework directive: The state of the art and way forward. *Water (Switzerland), 1–24*. https://doi.org/10.3390/w15234128

Pellegrini, Emilia, Raggi, M., Davide, V., & Targetti, S. (2022). MAP position paper CLIMATE CHANGE, (862448). doi: https://doi.org/10.5281/zenodo.7249343.

Raina, N., Zavalloni, M., & Viaggi, D. (2024). Incentive mechanisms of carbon farming contracts: A systematic mapping study. *Journal of Environmental Management, 352*(September 2023), 120126. https://doi.org/10.1016/j.jenvman.2024.120126

Regione Emilia-Romagna e Agriconsulting. (2013). analisi del contesto socioeconomico dell'agricoltura e dei territori rurali della regione analisi swot e fabbisogni di intervento per la programmazion e 2014–2020.

Termeer, C. J. A. M., Dewulf, A., & Biesbroek, G. R. (2017). Transformational change: Governance interventions for climate change adaptation from a continuous change perspective. *Journal of Environmental Planning and Management, 60*(4), 558–576. https://doi.org/10.1080/09640568.2016.1168288

PART II

Territorial Dynamics and Regional Pathways

CHAPTER 6

Future Pathways for Mediterranean Mountains: A Comparative and Participatory Foresight Approach

Andreas Vavvos, Manola Colabianchi, Catarina Esgalhado, Sofia Triliva, Michele Moretti, Teresa Pinto-Correia, Eugenia Petropolou, and Gianluca Brunori

1 Introduction

Mountains cover approximately 27% of the Earth's land surface and have been recognized globally as a distinctive category in the sphere of public action, at least since the 1992 United Nations Conference on Environment and Development in Rio de Janeiro (Debarbieux & Rudaz, 2010). Over the past decade, there has been a renewed interest in these areas because of their valuable contribution to the provision of both public and

A. Vavvos (✉) · S. Triliva
Department of Psychology, University of Crete, Crete, Greece
e-mail: vavvosandreas@gmail.com

D. Barjolle et al. (eds.), *Innovation and the Future of Rural Development in Europe*,
https://doi.org/10.1007/978-3-032-22570-2_6

private goods (Price, 2015). Mountain regions are particularly vulnerable to climate change due to their fragile ecosystems, low adaptive capacity, and high sensitivity (Mehzabin & Mondal, 2021), but this vulnerability also makes them ideal settings for innovation and regeneration (De Rossi, 2016). Mediterranean regions face critical challenges, including land and vegetation degradation from past and present grazing pressures, biomass accumulation, and land-use conflicts, all aggravated by projected drier and warmer climates (Cramer et al., 2018).

In response to these mounting socio-environmental pressures, growing debate has emerged around whether rewilding, ecological restoration, or

S. Triliva
e-mail: triliva@uoc.gr

A. Vavvos
Department of Social Anthropology, University of Saint Andrews, St Andrews, United Kingdom

M. Colabianchi · M. Moretti · G. Brunori
Department of Agriculture, Food and Environment, University of Pisa, Pisa, Italy
e-mail: manola.colabianchi@phd.unipi.it

M. Moretti
e-mail: michele.moretti@unipi.it

G. Brunori
e-mail: gianluca.brunori@unipi.it

C. Esgalhado
Mediterranean Institute for Agriculture, Évora, Portugal
e-mail: cesg@uevora.pt

T. Pinto-Correia
MED–Mediterranean Institute for Agriculture, Environment and Development CHANGE–Global Change and Sustainability Institute Departamento de Paisagem Ambiente e Ordenamento, Escola de Ciências e Tecnologia, Universidade de Évora, Évora, Portugal
e-mail: mtpc@uevora.pt

E. Petropolou
Department of Sociology, University of Crete, Crete, Greece
e-mail: petrope@uoc.gr

human intervention are the most effective means of safeguarding biodiversity, soil quality, and the regional cultural legacy (García-Ruiz et al., 2020). In some Mediterranean areas, the continuous decline in human presence and agricultural activities has led to the expansion of wooded and forested areas, a trend considered favourable and compatible with EU environmental regulations. However, the degradation of local agricultural systems in Mediterranean countries is often linked to negative impacts on conservation measures. For example, in Italy, as local conservation and harvesting activities recede, the escalating demand for imported forest goods contributes to the erosion of national forest heritage (Lanfredi et al., 2023). Furthermore, land-use conflicts in Mediterranean areas stem from a combination of scattered and fragmented land ownership, climate-driven extreme events and wildfires, and land dispossession due to renewable energy projects (Delattre et al., 2020; Korfiati, 2020; Lanfredi et al., 2023). Research in the Asteroussia Mountains in Crete has highlighted the gradual disintegration of social capital and solidarity ties, subsidy distribution through clientelist networks, and a longstanding disregard for the inherent value of the biophysical environment since the 1980s (Kizos et al., 2014). These trends suggest that, in Mediterranean mountainous regions, unsustainable social practices are as critical as environmental and land-related pressures.

Ongoing policy challenges include the ambiguous relationship between Common Agricultural Policy (CAP) subsidies and landscape preservation, inadequate capacity and staffing in agencies, unreliable environmental data, and inefficient administration (Canessa et al., 2022; Delattre et al., 2020; Lanfredi et al., 2023). Mediterranean regions also remain marginalized in European policy debates (Delattre et al., 2023; Goussios & Lerin, 2021). These complex political dynamics call for the formation of social and scientific forums that tackle the distinctive and shared challenges local communities in these areas face. A notable example of a comprehensive mountain policy in the Mediterranean is Cyprus's National Development Strategy of Mountainous Communities (ESAOK), which advocates for more active involvement of local stakeholders in policy making (Goussios, 2019). In a similar vein, Italy's *Strategia nazionale per le Aree interne* (hereafter, SNAI: National Strategy for Inner Areas), launched in 2012, seeks to promote development in rural areas distant from service centers but rich in cultural and environmental resources (Barca et al., 2014).

Adequate and equitable policies for the Mediterranean require foresight into social, environmental, and economic trends. Climate models predict an increase in forest fires in Southern Europe, as well as less precipitation and higher temperatures in Mediterranean mountains (Bravo et al., 2008; Lanfredi et al., 2023). The future of the Mediterranean mountains is likely to be shaped by the decline of the agricultural sector, including land abandonment and fewer job opportunities, along with rural imaginaries deeply entrenched in recreational and tourism-related activities (Tzanopoulos et al., 2011). In Greece's Zagori region, the scenario of agricultural liberalization, where mass tourism prevails and agricultural activity declines under free market pressures, is considered the most likely, even as certain stakeholder groups pursue alternatives (Tzanopoulos et al., 2011). Additionally, a scenario with scattered governance and a diminishing rural population appeared to be the most likely scenario for several foresight groups from across Europe (Salle et al., 2022). Despite the EU's vision for stronger, connected, resilient, and prosperous rural areas (European Commission, 2021), the aforementioned trends point to disruptive and tension-ridden dynamics in rural Mediterranean regions. It is therefore imperative to comprehend what needs to be done across various scales in order to align local initiatives with international aspirations of rural justice.

Under EIP-AGRI's Agricultural Knowledge and Innovation System (AKIS), consistent efforts have been undertaken to critically integrate various forms of knowledge through partnerships among multiple actors (EU SCAR AKIS, 2019). Based on this multi-scalar logic, the chapter outlines how a multi-actor participatory foresight analysis can contribute to integrating the Long-term Vision for the EU's Rural Areas with the goals of human and planetary flourishing. A primary aim of this chapter is "ensuring alignment and complementarity between international, national and local policies" (European Commission, 2021 p.14), as set forth in the Rural Pact, a formal platform designed to enhance cooperation among national, regional and local authorities, civil society organizations, economic stakeholders, the scientific community, and local populations (European Commission, 2022).

Within this frame of reference, we explore how multi-stakeholder partnerships can unveil complex future trajectories and promote collective action. The backbone of our research relies on three multi-actor platforms (hereafter, MAPs) from the Mediterranean mountain regions, each focusing on a distinct value chain: carob flour in Central Rethymno, Crete (CR); chestnut flour in Alta Versilia (Tuscany), Italy (AV); and Serra da Estrela PDO cheese in Portugal (SE). With the aim of comparing the foresight groups related to these value chains, the chapter is organized as follows. It opens with an overview of the MOVING project's participatory design, followed by a discussion of the formation of the MAPs and their associated value chains. The fourth section outlines the foresight methodology and provides a detailed, step-by-step comparison of the policy implications derived from the three foresight groups. The final sections summarize the main findings and explore the transformative role of the participatory foresight approach in the preparation of European policies for rural justice.

2 The MOVING Project's Participatory Structure

Participatory methods enhance decision-making, improve effectiveness, and facilitate the integration of diverse forms of knowledge (Reed et al., 2017). Normative arguments in support of participatory methods frame research as a human right (Appadurai, 2013) and decision-making as a democratic right (Reed, 2008). However, participatory approaches face several limitations, including time constraints, stakeholder fatigue, declining engagement, limited implementation within centralized systems, and a tendency to neglect emancipatory ideals (Reed, 2008). The political implications of participatory frameworks can also be contentious. Henderson (2015, p. 130) argues that participatory frameworks like communities of practice (hereafter, CoPs) often rely on a romanticized view of community that is "colonized by an arguably delusional ideology of home, harmony, homogeneity, regeneration, innovation, and unified purpose." This lack of critical reflection is further complicated by the limited availability of empirical evidence and theoretical frameworks to systematically assess participatory approaches' drawbacks and benefits (Reed et al., 2017).

The H2020 MOVING project adopted a participatory approach to more effectively fulfill its aims of contributing to the resilience and sustainability of mountain areas. Research activities were conducted at three distinct levels—regional, interregional, and pan-European—to gain comprehensive insight into processes and dynamics across various scales. The simultaneous operation of multiple MAPs over an extended timeframe, supported by extensive data on participation and outcomes, offers a foundation for evaluating the contributions of MAPs in social research and for responding to the current lack of evidence-based participatory practices.

As defined by Wenger et al. (2011), CoPs are collaborative learning partnerships among individuals who recognize the value of engaging in a specific domain and benefit from each other's practical experiences. In the MOVING project, CoPs served as a Science-Society-Policy interface across Europe, bringing together stakeholders to enhance resilience to climate change and other socio-economic trends (e.g., depopulation) affecting mountain value chains (Fig. 1). MOVING consisted of 23 regional Multi-Actor Platforms (MAPs) across 23 Reference Regions and one European-level Multi-Actor Platform (EU MAP). The main objective of the EU MAP was to assist project partners in integrating insights and outcomes from the regional MAPs, which involved stakeholders such as policymakers, producers, researchers, and agricultural businesses. The overarching aim was to promote the exchange of knowledge and expertise, facilitate mutual learning, and foster co-created knowledge through bottom-up collaboration. However, as noted by Krantz and Gustafsson (2023), MAPs may face challenges from disputes between conflicting worldviews, highlighting the importance of careful navigation and conflict resolution.

3 Three Mountain Value Chains and the Formation of MAPs

This chapter focuses on the MAPs of three Mediterranean mountain areas: Crete in Greece, Alta Versilia in Italy, and Serra da Estrela in Portugal (see Fig. 2). In Crete, the main area of focus was Central Rethymno, specifically, the semi-mountainous region situated between the island's two major massifs: the White Mountains and Mount Psiloritis (Ida). For the foresight analysis, the target area was expanded to the mountainous regions of Crete, where agro-silvo-pastoral land use systems predominate. The value chain examined was carob flour. Carob, a drought-resistant and hardy species, has been integral to agroforestry since ancient times. Some farmers still practice "symisiaka," a cooperative sharecropping harvest method that originated in the Byzantine era. Production declined sharply after the 1960s, but the recent extension of the carob value chain renewed interest among producers and consumers, as carob flour is now used in a range of food products.

The Alta Versilia case study focused on two municipalities in the northern Tuscan Apennines. The landscape features steep mountain slopes, a dense network of watercourses, and forests that have been

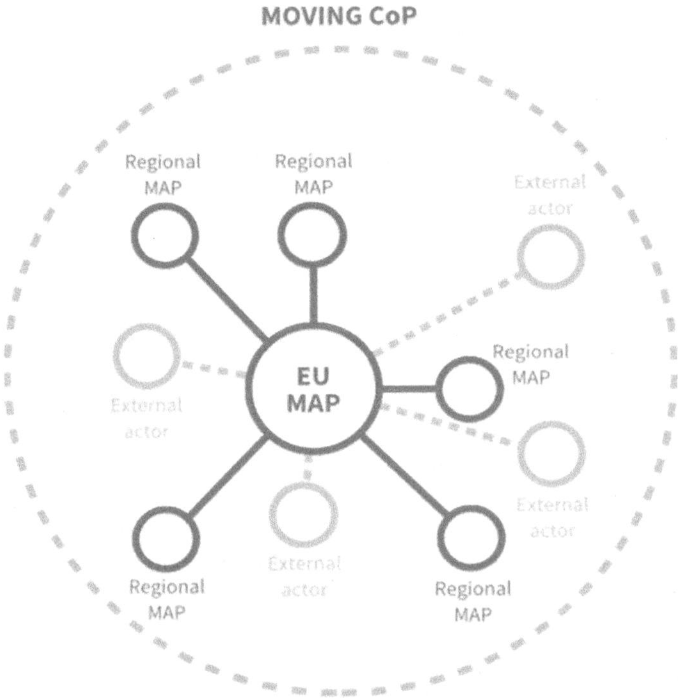

Fig. 1 Scheme of the MOVING Participatory Structure

Fig. 2 Location of the three Case Studies and Associated Value Chains

partially privatized since the 19th century. Chestnut trees form the traditional forest system of the area and have enabled centuries-old land use and cultivation techniques. The MOVING MAP was primarily concerned with the chestnut flour value chain. To take a more comprehensive approach, foresight analysis extended its geographical scope to the mountainous areas of northern Tuscany. Across the region, chestnut flour production has traditionally played a pivotal role in sustaining local livelihoods, supporting economic stability, and preserving cultural heritage. Despite recurring cycles of agricultural land abandonment in the region, contemporary chestnut cultivation remains integral to multifunctional agricultural activities in northern Tuscany, providing ecological services that extend beyond purely economic benefits.

Serra da Estrela is located in central-eastern Portugal, marking the transition between temperate and Mediterranean climates. Its cultural traditions, land use systems and socio-economic dynamics are well aligned with those of regions in the Mediterranean basin. The study area includes the Municipality of Manteigas, and parts of the municipalities of Seia and Covilhã, covering the central plateau. For the foresight analysis, the target area was expanded to the whole area of Serra da Estrela, as delimited by the borders of the National Park with the same name. The landscape features a mosaic of forest patches mixed with meadows and low-density shrubs on the rockier slopes. The value chain examined was Serra da Estrela cheese. This cheese is produced from the raw milk of two native sheep breeds. Historically, these sheep grazed in the mountains, maintaining the open landscape. However, with greater availability of lowland pastures within the PDO area, the traditional high-altitude grazing by shepherds and their flocks has gradually declined.

Although common guidelines were implemented, contextual characteristics account for differences in the composition of MAPs and foresight groups. In Serra da Estrela, despite efforts to maintain a balanced MAP, involving producers and cheesemakers proved more difficult than engaging office workers. Similarly, the Cretan MAP comprised mainly policymakers and representatives from agricultural businesses. In Serra da Estrela, key expectations focused on improving communication among shepherding, forestry (conservation), and tourism stakeholders, as well as fostering networking and developing local and regional initiatives. Conversely, stakeholders in Alta Versilia aimed to support small farmers and deliver tangible benefits to the chestnut flour value chain. Their work included preserving the community mill, assisting in reopening metati—traditional stone-roofed buildings for drying and smoking chestnuts—and addressing the lack of funding for chestnut grove maintenance. In the project's final phase, the participation of farmers and stakeholders from small farm businesses across Tuscany rekindled a sense of regional identity. Similarly, the MAP in Central Rethymno initially focused on urgent, short-term challenges but shifted toward community empowerment and broader engagement of local communities as the initiative progressed.

Across all three case studies, both administrative and accessibility barriers posed challenges to sustained engagement at a broader geographical scale. While associations and cooperatives engage stakeholders across the mountain areas, collective action tends to occur predominantly on the local scale. Although collective action beyond local boundaries remains limited, the three MAPs consolidated effective community-level support and collaboration networks. For instance, in Serra da Estrela, key findings from the MOVING project have been fully integrated into project proposals developed by MAP members. In a similar vein, in Alta Versilia, MAP members actively engaged in a Local Action Group (LAG) project. The main impact of the three MAPs appears to lie in their potential to strengthen networking opportunities and provide transformative spaces for meaningful participation by producers, policymakers, and farmers.

4 Foresight Exercise in the three EU MAPs

Each MAP undertook the task of identifying vulnerabilities, strategic resources, constraints, and key value chains across the mountain region. A series of interactive workshops covering critical topics such as youth engagement and vulnerability analysis laid a strong foundation for the foresight exercise (hereafter, FE). These workshops encouraged exploration, anticipation, and critical analysis regarding the future of mountainous areas. The Joint Research Centre (JRC) of the European Commission (EC) characterizes FEs as structured, systematic, participatory, and inclusive. This approach informs present decision-making and promotes collaborative actions through various methods, including trend analysis, expert consultation, Delphi methods, and scenario planning (Joint Research Centre, n.d). Van Notten (2005, p. 7) defines scenarios as "coherent descriptions of alternative hypothetical futures that reflect different perspectives on past, present, and future developments, which can serve as a basis for action." This methodology empowers citizens and organizations, encouraging and facilitating participatory processes (Mietzner & Reger, 2005; Salewski, 2012). In the context of climate change, scenarios provide collaborative settings for rehearsal, experimentation, and improvisation, allowing stakeholders to navigate the profound uncertainties of the Anthropocene (Tyszczuk, 2021). By fostering such engagement, scenarios help explore innovative alternatives, strengthen the adaptive capacity of mountain regions, and draw on local wisdom.

In MOVING, scenario development provided an effective method for exploring future alternatives, adaptation strategies, and the impacts of climate change. Since future outcomes depend on intersecting and uncertain social and environmental factors, FEs were primarily exploratory. According to Tanner et al. (2009), climate change is only one dimension within a broader set of interconnected natural, social, and economic crises. Therefore, strategies focusing solely on climate risks may overlook the full range of community needs and priorities. Additionally, in their participatory foresight study on Mediterranean agricultural systems, Faysse et al. (2012) identified several complex challenges, including stakeholder reluctance to consider the long-term effects of climate change, as well as power dynamics that hindered equitable participation—particularly among farmers and other less-educated groups. Overall, participants in this study voiced doubts about the applicability of the workshop-generated insights into urgent social challenges.

The MOVING project employed a participatory FE designed to help participants rehearse and prepare for a range of desirable and plausible futures in mountainous areas. Consistent with the project's interactive methodology, researchers and stakeholders created civic spaces to foster critical consciousness-raising at the community level (see Fig. 3). Before launching the FEs, each research team defined the geographic scope and selected participants for the foresight groups. Three workshops were conducted between January and April 2023. In the Italian and Portuguese case studies, the second and third workshops were held on the same day. The workshops eventually adopted the following format:

- The first workshop began with validating a baseline scenario—a projection for 2050, assuming no new policies. Each group then identified two long-term, important, and uncertain forces expected to affect the region's future. These forces were instrumental in generating the matrix and developing the four scenarios, forming the following phase of the foresight methodology.

- In the second workshop, the foresight group refined the four scenarios by providing constructive feedback and selecting the preferred scenario. Identifying the most desirable scenario for mountain region resilience required in-depth deliberation on strategic policy options linked to each scenario.
- The third workshop focused on translating the preferred scenario into policy options, strategies, and roadmaps for transformative change. Both near-term and long-term actions were outlined to ensure the realization of the long-term vision. During this phase, comprehensive policies were developed to create a supportive environment, enabling the transition from selected measures and scenarios to concrete actions.

The research teams actively sought to recruit a balanced group, including the most engaged MAP members, as well as experts from social, environmental, economic, and cultural fields, along with policymakers at regional and national levels. As demonstrated in Fig. 4, each team successfully maintained a core group of at least six active members across the three sessions, although a few withdrew during the process, and new stakeholders were invited at later stages when their input was deemed crucial.

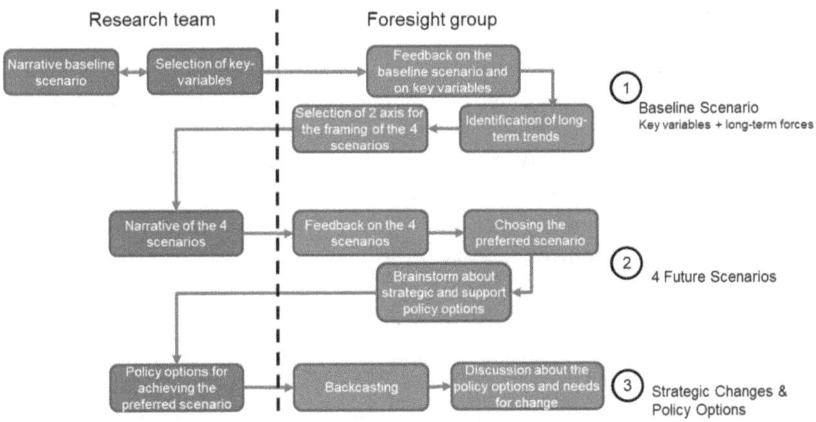

Fig. 3 A Common Methodological Approach to the Foresight Exercise

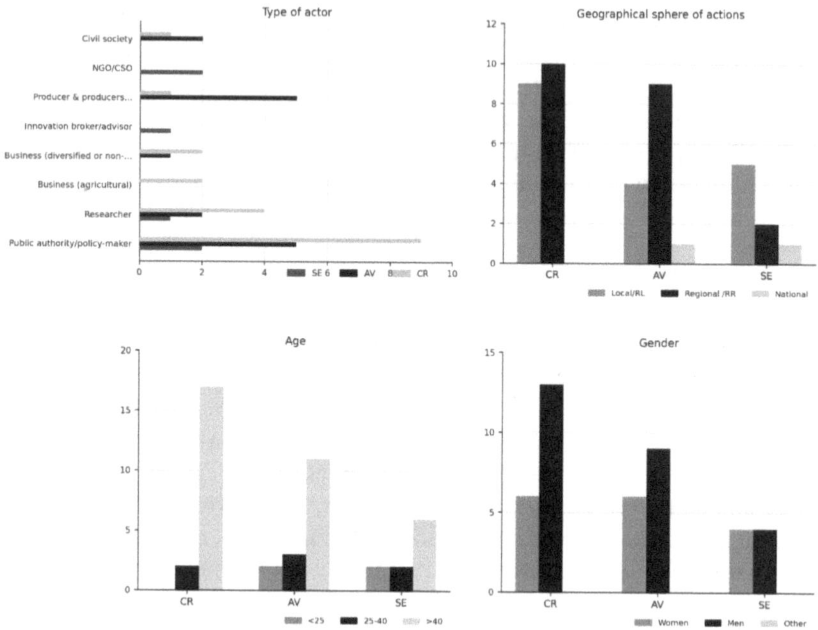

Fig. 4 Graphs of MAPs' Composition in the three Case Studies

Public officials, policymakers, and researchers made up the majority of participants in the foresight groups, except during the second and third workshops in Alta Versilia, which included seven producers. Most participants were local or regional actors. Despite concerted efforts to ensure gender and age diversity, women remained underrepresented in most workshops, and there were no participants under 25 years of age. The following analysis is organized by the sequence of foresight workshops and aims to identify both commonalities and differences across the three case studies.

Establishing a Baseline Scenario

The baseline scenario, which served as the foundation for the first workshop, was characterized by similar socio-political dynamics across the three case studies (for a detailed description of the baseline scenario in each region, see Appendix A). Without targeted policy support, the rural family farming model is expected to become obsolete by 2050, leading to a crisis in small-scale agriculture and favoring the growth of large-scale urban farming enterprises. These projections also predict growing distrust towards political institutions, ongoing social stigmatization and exclusion, and limited educational opportunities for mountain residents. Common challenges include poorly designed mountain policies, an increase in climate change events such as heat waves and wildfires, and an irreversible rural exodus. Despite these shared challenges, clear differences emerged in the case studies. In Crete, the foresight group identified heightened conflicts over land use among farmers, livestock producers, tourism companies, and renewable energy firms. In contrast, land abandonment was considered the main threat in Portugal and Italy.

The following workshop activity involved identifying two long-term forces expected to have a significant impact on each region's future. As illustrated in Table 1, participants chose the forces highlighted in grey from several options and ranked them according to importance and uncertainty. Central and regional governance and climate change were identified as the main driving forces in Crete. To better capture participants' perspectives, the research team redefined these long-term forces as "value systems," encompassing individual and community norms tied to cultural heritage and environmental stewardship, and "economic growth," reflecting the direction of future economic policies. In Alta Versilia, the key long-term forces selected were demographic changes—particularly migration trends toward foreign countries and larger cities—and the decline of traditional forest management practices, such as chestnut tree pruning and the planting or grafting of new trees. In Serra da Estrela, the most significant and unpredictable forces were people's willingness to pay for ecosystem services, reflecting public support for landscape management, and the relationship between cheese production and the mountain region as opposed to the neighboring lowlands.

Exploratory Scenario Development

The second workshop began with a discussion centered on the four scenarios each group developed (see also Appendix B). As shown in Figure 5, these scenarios are positioned within quadrants defined by two long-term forces, which were identified as the main axes in the previous workshop. Each quadrant label corresponds to the title of a specific scenario.

Table 1 Long-term forces ranked by importance and uncertainty

Category (STEEPV)	*Long-term element*	*Importance*	*Uncertainty*	*Region*
Economic	Inflation	0	4	SE
	Attractiveness of the agricultural and cheese sectors	1	1	SE
	Coastal over-tourism	0	2	CR
Economic & political	Public expenditure	1	2	AV
Political	Capacity of the local governance	1	3	AV
	Central and regional governance	11	1	CR
	Land use change	8	0	SE
	Landholding system	0	0	SE
Social	Demographic trends (presence of young inhabitants)	4	1	AV
	Urbanization	1	4	CR
Technological	Use of technology/ automation	1	0	AV
	Use of technology/ automation	0	4	SE
Values	Willingness to pay for ecosystem services / Society's environmental awareness	4	3	SE
	Link between cheese and mountainous territory	3	1	SE
	Dietary Changes	0	2	SE
Environmental	Chestnut grove maintenance (lack of)	4	1	AV
	Climate change	4	4	CR

In all three cases, one axis was associated with environmental and ecosystem-related factors, highlighting stakeholder concerns about social awareness, environmental stewardship, and efforts to address climate change. Issues such as ecological degradation, loss of ecosystem services, and the decline of the biophysical environment were repeatedly raised in the foresight groups. The second axis, which varied more across the three regions, encompassed trends including the ongoing presence of rural dwellers in mountainous areas, the need for targeted economic initiatives, and the insufficient integration of cultural heritage with local value chains.

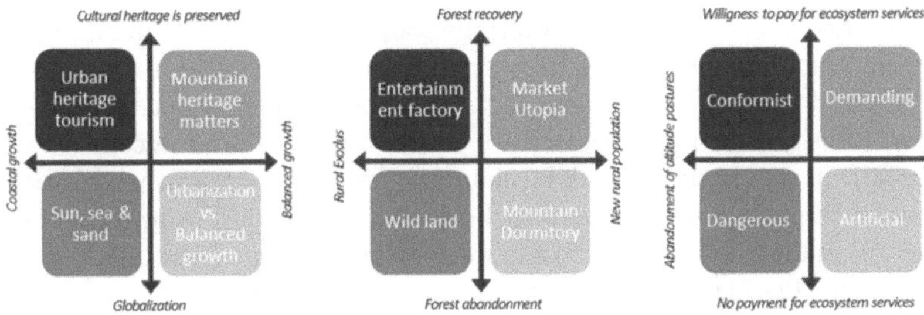

Fig. 5 Matrix of the three Case Studies in Order: Crete, Alta Versilia, and Serra da Estrela

Strategies and Policy Options for the Preferred Scenario

Each foresight group subsequently selected its preferred scenario, which in nearly all cases was the most optimistic projection for the future. In Crete, the chosen scenario was "Mountain heritage matters," which envisioned balanced economic growth between coastal and mountainous areas with a focus on sustainably conserving natural and cultural heritage. However, since coastal development has dominated the Cretan economy in recent decades, balanced growth now seems unattainable. In Alta Versilia, the preferred scenario was a synthesis of two workshop scenarios, anticipating harmonious coexistence between newcomers and the natural environment. Residents are expected to collaborate with newcomers to create services and activities that enhance local cultural identity, prioritize forest preservation, and protect shared resources for future generations. In Serra da Estrela, the preferred scenario envisions continued use of high-altitude pastures and an open landscape. Shepherds are respected stakeholders, PDO cheese remains a vital resource for the region, and tourism is a complementary sector. The strong link between PDO cheese and the mountainous territory ensures that the area is managed in ways that preserve cultural traditions, such as utilizing native breeds and local expertise, thus contributing significantly to the maintenance and openness of the landscape.

In the last workshop, each foresight group developed customized strategies and regulatory approaches to guide progress toward their preferred scenarios. Despite regional differences, several common priorities emerged. Notably, all three strategies focused on sustainable practices in mountainous regions and emphasized community engagement and collaboration. This involved fostering cooperation among smallholder farmers, engaging both new and established residents in forest stewardship, and creating collective spaces and community associations. The Cretan foresight group advocated for more horizontal and decentralized processes at the regional and local levels. In Alta Versilia, participants discussed the active involvement of both newcomers and long-term residents in managing forest ecosystems and restoring abandoned land. In Serra da Estrela, the foresight group explored the establishment of collective spaces and associations to act as intermediaries between local communities and bureaucratic institutions.

5 Discussion

This study revealed significant differences between baseline and preferred scenarios, suggesting that current strategies are inadequate for promoting resilience in mountainous regions (Jiménez-Olivencia et al., 2021; MacDonald et al., 2000). Land abandonment (Lasanta et al., 2017; MacDonald et al., 2000; Salle et al., 2022) and land-use conflicts (Delattre et al., 2020; Korfiati, 2020; Lanfredi et al., 2023), both well-documented in existing research, represented contrasting but interlinked threats identified by stakeholders in the foresight groups. While the preferred scenarios in all three cases align to some extent with the EU's long-term vision for Strong, Connected, Resilient, and Prosperous rural areas (EC, 2022), persistent shared challenges need to be addressed in the next Rural Policy cycle. For example, strengthening Agricultural Knowledge and Innovation Systems (AKIS) remains a shared priority for all three regions. Kierem and Prager (2015) described the three national AKIS as fragmented, with disconnected and uncoordinated knowledge networks. Overcoming this compartmentalization requires enhancing extension services, improving education and training for farmers, and raising public awareness of the value of mountain ecosystems. Developing interpersonal skills and stronger community ties is also crucial for empowering social cooperatives and other collaborative efforts.

The three foresight groups anticipated a shift in value chains away from rural smallholders toward large-scale agricultural enterprises in urban centers by 2050. Reversing this economic trend depends on ensuring small farmers have equitable participation in the networks shaping future agricultural policies. Low-income farmers, often lacking access to educational resources and systematically marginalized in decision-making, viewed participation in our foresight groups as essential for transformative praxis. From this perspective, applying the foresight method in the next Rural Policy period may empower marginalized low-income farmers to navigate current challenges and contribute to the long-term flourishing of both communities and ecosystems. Small-scale agricultural producers, positioned as primary beneficiaries under CAP 2023–2027, could use these networks to strengthen their collective agency. Kochskämper et al. (2016) also suggested that, although the creation of MAPs under the European Water Framework Directive (WFD) had a limited impact, the networking and information sharing among diverse stakeholders fostered political spaces for collaborative practices. Similarly, a significant achievement of our foresight groups was their ability to popularize critical climate change discourses and instill a long-term ecological vision in both institutional politics and grassroots practices.

The participatory foresight method holds significant political potential to transform social relations and rural policies. However, integrating it into upcoming Rural Policy planning requires overcoming entrenched structural barriers. A persistent challenge across all three cases was sustaining genuine engagement from foresight stakeholders throughout every phase of the FEs. Critically examining our social positionality as researchers reveals that the FEs remained somewhat researcher-driven. This limited opportunities for stakeholder-led initiatives and preserved hierarchical distinctions between academic researchers and foresight stakeholders. These power imbalances threaten to curtail the foresight groups' potential for radical grassroots mobilization once academic support and external funding are withdrawn. Achieving this transformative goal depends on the ongoing involvement of state officials and relevant stakeholders in participatory foresight initiatives. Similarly, Nesheim et al. (2021) noted that while nine MAPs within the WFD cultivated collaborative practices, their long-term sustainability is contingent upon institutional, top-down support.

Our FEs centered on social transformation understood as progress toward justice, equality, and the well-being of communities inhabiting mountainous regions. These challenges emerge from entrenched social, economic, and political power dynamics that uphold the existing social order (Gass, 2012). The ultimate task of transformative social change is to restructure these power systems by addressing the shared anxieties raised by participants in horizontal foresight groups, but this endeavor is not attainable through disconnected local groups and reclusive initiatives. To exert real influence on rural policies, bottom-up foresight groups must establish strategic alliances with top-down institutional actors that hold decision-making power.

6 Conclusions

This chapter employed a comparative approach to critically assess the long-term visions collectively mobilized by foresight groups in three Mediterranean mountain regions. The process of stimulating critical foresight began with an analysis of a local value chain, recognized for its ecological regeneration potential but constrained by ongoing challenges in an unequal and unstable global economy. The three foresight groups identified overlapping threats to local communities, natural resource management, and ecosystem services, highlighting the complex interplay between social and biophysical systems. By moving beyond disciplinary silos and present-focused perspectives, the groups drew from diverse knowledge systems to implement significant transformations within social-ecological systems, challenging established norms and relational dynamics.

The analysis highlighted key underlying dynamics among MAPs in the three territories. While a one-size-fits-all solution for all Mediterranean regions seems unlikely, shared characteristics among territorial clusters suggest potential avenues for collaboration. In each case, the value chains are associated with products that are both highly valued and characterized by low carbon footprints, embedded within traditional, multifunctional farming systems—models that are prominently featured in regional development strategies. However, the baseline scenarios developed by the foresight groups predict that these native crops will face considerable challenges by 2050, including profit-driven monoculture practices, intensified mass tourism, and the privatization of common resources. These trends directly contradict locally and politically expressed aspirations for sustainable territorial development, as external pressures increasingly undermine the long-term viability of these value chains.

Instead of assuming local challenges can be easily scaled globally, the foresight groups emphasized the need for MAPs that capture and interpret place-based dynamics. Despite the complexities of these collaborations, the three foresight groups successfully developed local strategies aimed at strengthening social capital, cultural heritage, and psychosocial resilience, while promoting policy agendas and value systems that prioritize environmental justice and ecosystem services. In the context of rising global authoritarianism, consolidating transregional democratic forums that can analyze shared conditions and advance critical EU-relevant policies is also essential. Our long-term engagement with Mediterranean foresight groups indicates that, while stakeholders in mountain areas face deep-rooted inequalities, integrative and multi-scalar approaches that support the self-determination of local communities and foster territorially connected alliances offer a promising path to rural justice.

Acknowledgments Special thanks to all the MOVING experts and partners who participated in the interviews and expressed interest and support for our study. We are also deeply indebted to the Origin for Sustainability team for providing high-quality training for the foresight analysis and to all stakeholders for their active participation in the MAPs.

Funding The research was supported by the H2020 European Project MOVING. This project has received funding from the European Union's Horizon 2020 research and innovation programme under grant agreement No. 862739. This publication reflects only the authors' views. The European Commission is not responsible for any use that may be made of the information it contains.

Data Availability Statement Data collected for this paper are available in the public reports of the H2020 European MOVING project, complemented by available data collected for this paper by the authors.

Appendix A: Summary of the Baseline Scenarios

Baseline scenario for Crete

By 2050, mountainous communities in Crete are expected to experience rapid and dramatic demographic decline, extreme weather events, urbanization-driven land use changes, increasing social marginalization, population aging, and widespread abandonment of agriculture. Only a handful of processing businesses in urban centers will remain profitable, while most farmers and small agribusinesses in rural areas will face precarious socioeconomic conditions. The agricultural crisis will worsen traditional farming practices, erode local knowledge, and dwindle institutional support for farmers. Subsidy policies have fostered dependence, hampered innovation, and severely harmed smallholder farmers, making it impossible for them to compete against cheaper imported crops. Meanwhile, the expansion of mass tourism in Crete will increasingly dominate the local economy, further undermining the primary sector.

Baseline scenario for Alta Versilia

By 2050, the effects of climate change—rising temperatures and droughts—will have increased the instability of agricultural production even in mountainous areas. Historic chestnut groves will experience decreased yields; some ancient trees in the sunny valleys will dry out, while others will collapse. The Italian national policy for the development of inland areas (SNAI) will have only a marginal impact on the socio-economic trends of marginal areas. The inability of regional and local politicians to invest the resources promoted by the National Recovery and Resilience Plan (PNRR) will foster general distrust in public institutions and uncertainty regarding economic investments. Furthermore, small-scale agriculture will remain heavily penalized by difficulties in accessing land, despite widespread landscape abandonment, which will increase risks of soil erosion, fires, and biodiversity loss. The initiative promoted by the Banca della Terra will produce only marginal results in Tuscany. Young people will continue their "rural exodus" toward big cities in search of a stable future or will migrate to Northern Europe. The national average age, 46.2 in 2022, will rise to about 53 by 2050.

Baseline scenario for Serra da Estrela

By 2050, the aging population and lack of support for small and medium enterprises will lead to greater concentration of production, processing, and distribution structures in the cheese sector. There are fewer certified PDO cheese dairies, and the family business model of transformation is virtually extinct, with those that persist choosing not to be certified. Sales are primarily made through two channels: supermarket chains and the international market. People living in the Serra do not have a strong connection to the territory, and few are linked to the primary sector. There are fewer shepherds, and remaining herds have become larger. Changes in precipitation and temperature have decreased the available pastureland at low altitudes. Conflicts have increased both among herders and between herders and landowners over access to pastures and the use of access roads. Tourism is growing in importance as an economic activity. However, there is no concerted strategy of active land management to ensure the interconnection between agriculture, grazing, forestry, and tourism.

Appendix B: Four Scenarios

Four scenarios in Crete

1. ***Urban heritage tourism***

Cultural and natural heritage are transformed into resources aimed at addressing sustainability challenges. However, this is mainly true for coastal areas, where heritage becomes a vital asset for the sustainable growth of urban destinations.

2. ***The discontents of "sun, sea, and sand"***

In this scenario, a value system that prioritizes urbanized, globalized lifestyles dominates, along with an economic growth model that relies primarily on coastal mass tourism.

3. ***Mountain heritage matters***

This scenario promotes balanced economic growth alongside a lifestyle that responsibly preserves the region's natural and cultural heritage.

4. ***Rapid urbanization vs. balanced growth***

An urban and globalized lifestyle is promoted by the prevailing value system, while central government and regional authorities encourage balanced growth, resulting in two antagonistic and countervailing forces.

Four scenarios in Alta Versilia

1. ***Mountain dormitory***

The decline in urban quality of life has driven a population shift to rural Northern Tuscan Apennines. Local authorities struggle to meet growing demands. The region's failure to adapt to environmental and socio-economic risks, particularly in the agricultural sector, limits its capacity to leverage climate change opportunities.

2. ***Wild land***

Depopulation and land abandonment lead to reoccupation of territories by native vegetation and wildlife. As villages become increasingly deserted and young people migrate to urban centers, depopulation emerges as a significant challenge.

3. ***Entertainment factory***

Several mountain communities in northern Tuscany suffer demographic decline, and villages empty. Deteriorating infrastructures give way to modern, efficient buildings, while an urban mentality is established with intrusive lighting, paved roads and expanding car parks. The mountain areas of the region increasingly function as recreational spaces for tourists.

4. ***Market Utopia***

The decline in urban quality of life drives a return to mountainous areas in northern Tuscany. This trend results in the sale and privatization of formerly communal resources such as forests, leading to the need for boundary fences and access restrictions.

Four scenarios in Serra da Estrela

1. ***Demanding***

Altitude pastures are actively used, and the landscape is maintained open. Shepherds are valued stakeholders, the PDO cheese is an important asset to the mountain territory, and tourism a complementary activity.

2. *Conformist*

Landscape is kept open and there is a higher number of non-native grazers. Fewer people act as landscape stewards, while pressure for rewilding and carbon offsetting increases.

3. *Dangerous*

An increase in forest area and biomass has led to greater fire intensity. The PDO cheese loses market value, and the associated local wisdom is eroded.

4. *Artificial*

Shepherding is valued primarily as a tourist attraction, but it is optimized to benefit the mountainous ecosystems, which increases pressure to adopt alternative territorial management strategies such as rewilding and reforestation for carbon offsetting.

References

Appadurai, A. (2013). *The future as cultural fact: Essays on the global conditions*. Verso.

Barca, F., Casavola, P., & Lucatelli, S. (2014). A strategy for inner areas in Italy: Definition, objectives, tools and governance (Materiali UVAL, Issue 31). UVAL.

Bravo, D. N., Araújo, M. B., Lasanta, T., & Moreno, J. I. (2008). Climate change in Mediterranean mountains during the 21st century. *Ambio: A Journal of the Human Environment, 37*(4), 280–285. https://doi.org/10.1579/0044-7447(2008)37[280:ccimmd]2.0.co;2

Canessa, C., Vavvos, A., Triliva, S., Kafkalas, I., Vrachioli, M., & Sauer, J. (2022). Implementing a combined Delphi and focus group qualitative methodology in Nexus research designs—the case of the WEFE Nexus in Apokoronas, Crete. *PLOS ONE, 17*(7). https://doi.org/10.1371/journal.pone.0271443

Cramer, W., Guiot, J., Fader, M., Garrabou, J., Gattuso, J.-P., Iglesias, A., Lange, M. A., Lionello, P., Llasat, M. C., Paz, S., Peñuelas, J., Snoussi, M., Toreti, A., Tsimplis, M. N., & Xoplaki, E. (2018). Climate change and interconnected risks to sustainable development in the Mediterranean. *Nature Climate Change, 8*(11), 972–980. https://doi.org/10.1038/s41558-018-0299-2

De Rossi, A. (2016). Una nuova stagione per le Alpi? 10 tesi e 6+1 ontologie per il progetto del territorio alpino contemporaneo. In D. Del Curto, R. Dini, & G. Menini (Eds.), *Alpi e architettura. Patrimonio, progetto, sviluppo locale* (pp. 319–332). Mimesis.

Debarbieux, B., & Rudaz, G. (2010). *Les faiseurs de montagne: Imaginaires politiques et territorialités*. CNRS.

Delattre, L., Debolini, M., Paoli, J. C., Napoleone, C., Moulery, M., Leonelli, L., & Santucci, P. (2020). Understanding the relationships between extensive livestock systems, land-cover changes, and CAP support in less-favored Mediterranean areas. *Land, 9*(12), 518. https://doi.org/10.3390/land9120518

EU SCAR AKIS. (2019). *Preparing for Future AKIS in Europe*. European Commission.

European Commission (EC). (2022). *A long-term vision for the EU's rural areas: Building the Future of Rural Areas Together.* European Commission. https://ec.europa.eu/info/strategy/priorities-2019-2024/new-push-european-democracy/long-term-vision-rural-areas_en

European Commission (EC). (2021). *A long-term Vision for the EU's Rural Areas-Towards stronger, connected, resilient and prosperous rural areas by 2040*, COM(2021) 345 final, 30.06.2021.

Faysse, N., Rinaudo, J.-D., Bento, S., Richard-Ferroudji, A., Errahj, M., Varanda, M., Imache, A., Dionnet, M., Rollin, D., Garin, P., Kuper, M., Maton, L., & Montginoul, M. (2012). Participatory analysis for adaptation to climate change in Mediterranean agricultural systems: Possible choices in process design. *Regional Environmental Change, 14*(S1), 57–70. https://doi.org/10.1007/s10113-012-0362-x

García-Ruiz, J. M., Lasanta, T., Nadal-Romero, E., Lana-Renault, N., & Álvarez-Farizo, B. (2020). Rewilding and restoring cultural landscapes in Mediterranean mountains: Opportunities and challenges. *Land Use Policy, 99*, 104850. https://doi.org/10.1016/j.landusepol.2020.104850

Gass, R. H. (2015). Social influence, sociology of. *International Encyclopedia of the Social & Behavioral Sciences, 348–354*. https://doi.org/10.1016/b978-0-08-097086-8.32074-8

Goussios, D. (2019). *National strategy for the development of mountain communities of Cyprus*. Papadouri Foundation for the Republic of Cyprus.

Goussios, D., & Lerin, F. A. (2021). A European conference on insular mountain territories in the Mediterranean. In D. Goussios, D. Gaki, A. Garnier, & F.

Lerin (Eds.), *Mountain areas of large Mediterranean islands. European issues, national and regional policies and local mechanisms* (pp. 13–16). University of Thessaly Press. https://utpress.uth.gr/images/ebooks/TroodosEN_web.pdf
Henderson, M. (2015). The (mis)use of community of practice: Delusion, confusion, and instrumentalism in educational technology research. In S. Bulfin, N. F. Johnson, & C. Bigum (Eds.), *Critical perspectives on technology and education* (pp. 127–140). Palgrave Macmillan.
Jiménez-Olivencia, Y., Ibáñez-Jiménez, Á., Porcel-Rodríguez, L., & Zimmerer, K. (2021). Land use change dynamics in Euro-Mediterranean Mountain regions: Driving forces and consequences for the landscape. *Land Use Policy, 109*, 105721. https://doi.org/10.1016/j.landusepol.2021.105721
Joint Research Centre. (n.d.). *Foresight: What, why and how*. Knowledge4policy. https://knowledge4policy.ec.europa.eu/sites/default/files/foresight_briefme.pdf
Kizos, T., Detsis, V., Iosifides, T., & Metaxakis, M. (2014). Social capital and social-ecological resilience in the Asteroussia Mountains, southern Crete, Greece. *Ecology and Society, 19*(1). https://doi.org/10.5751/es-06208-190140
Kochskämper, E., Challies, E., Newig, J., & Jager, N. W. (2016). Participation for effective environmental governance? Evidence from Water Framework Directive implementation in Germany, Spain and the United Kingdom. *Journal of Environmental Management, 181*, 737–748. https://doi.org/10.1016/j.jenvman.2016.08.007
Korfiati, I. P. (2020). Classifying like a state: Land dispossession on Eastern Crete's contested mountains. *Antipode, 52*(5), 1331–1350. https://doi.org/10.1111/anti.12640
Krantz, V., & Gustafsson, S. (2023). Regional collaboration for the Sustainable Development Goals: Experiences from developing a multi-actor platform in Sweden. *Sustainable Development, 1–12*. https://doi.org/10.1002/sd.2580
Lanfredi, M., Coluzzi, R., Imbrenda, V., Nosova, B., Giacalone, M., Turco, R., Prokopovà, M., & Salvati, L. (2023). In-between environmental sustainability and economic viability: An analysis of the state, regulations, and future of Italian forestry sector. *Land, 12*(5), 1001. https://doi.org/10.3390/land12051001
MacDonald, D., Crabtree, J. R., Wiesinger, G., Dax, T., Stamou, N., Fleury, P., Gutierrez Lazpita, J., & Gibon, A. (2000). Agricultural abandonment in mountain areas of Europe: Environmental consequences and policy response. *Journal of Environmental Management, 59*(1), 47–69. https://doi.org/10.1006/jema.1999.0335
Mehzabin, S., & Mondal, M. S. (2021). Assessing impact of climate variability in southwest coastal Bangladesh using livelihood vulnerability index. *Climate, 9*(7), 107. https://doi.org/10.3390/cli9070107

Mietzner, D., & Reger, G. (2005). Advantages and disadvantages of scenario approaches for strategic foresight. *International Journal of Technology Intelligence and Planning, 1*(2), 220. https://doi.org/10.1504/ijtip.2005.006516

Nesheim, I., Sundnes, F., Enge, C., Graversgaard, M., van den Brink, C., Farrow, L., Glavan, M., Hansen, B., Leitão, I. A., Rowbottom, J., & Tendler, L. (2021). Multi-actor platforms in the water–agriculture nexus: Synergies and long-term meaningful engagement. *Water, 13*(22), 3204. https://doi.org/10.3390/w13223204

Price, M. F. (2015). *Mountains: A very short introduction.* Oxford University Press.

Reed, M. S. (2008). Stakeholder participation for environmental management: A literature review. *Biological Conservation, 141*(10), 2417–2431. https://doi.org/10.1016/j.biocon.2008.07.014

Reed, M. S., Vella, S., Challies, E., de Vente, J., Frewer, L., Hohenwallner-Ries, D., Huber, T., Neumann, R. K., Oughton, E. A., Oughton, E. A., & del Seno, J. S. (2017). A theory of participation: What makes stakeholder and public engagement in environmental management work? *Restoration Ecology, 26*(S1), S7–S17. https://doi.org/10.1111/rec.12541

Salewski, C. (2012). *Dutch new worlds scenarios in physical planning and design in the Netherlands, 1970-2000.* 010 Publishers.

Salle, E., Zomer, B., Iadecola, F., & Arcuri, S. (2022). Foresight exercise. In *Alternative rural futures: how to get there?* Paper. https://doi.org/10.5281/zenodo.6474919

Skulska, I., Montiel-Molina, C., & Rego, F. C. (2020). The role of forest policy in Mediterranean mountain community lands: A review of the decentralization processes in European countries. *Journal of Rural Studies, 80*, 490–502. https://www.sciencedirect.com/science/article/pii/S0743016719316067?via%3Dihub

Tanner, T., Lazcano, J., Molina, F., Molina, G., Rodriguez, G., Tribunalo, B., & Seballos, F. (2009). Children's participation in community-based disaster risk reduction and adaptation to climate change. In M. Garcia (Ed.), *Community-based adaptation to climate change* (pp. 54–64). International Institute for Environment And Development.

Tyszczuk, R. (2021). Collective scenarios: Speculative improvisations for the Anthropocene. *Futures, 134*, 102854. https://doi.org/10.1016/j.futures.2021.102854

Tzanopoulos, J., Kallimanis, A. S., Bella, I., Labrianidis, L., Sgardelis, S., & Pantis, J. D. (2011). Agricultural decline and sustainable development on mountain areas in Greece: Sustainability assessment of future scenarios. *Land Use Policy, 28*(3), 585–593. https://doi.org/10.1016/j.landusepol.2010.11.007

Van Notten, P. (2005). *Writing on the wall: Scenario development in times of discontinuity*. Universal-Publishers.

Wenger, E., Trayner, B., & Laat, M. D. (2011). *Promoting and assessing value creation in communities and networks: A conceptual framework (Ruud de Moor Centrum Rapporten)*. Open Universiteit. https://www.betterevaluation.org/sites/default/files/Wenger_Trayner_DeLaat_Value_creation.pdf

CHAPTER 7

Different Problems, Various Coping Solutions and the Same Hopes. Diversity of Rural Areas and Their Future Trajectories in Poland

Barbara Wieliczko, Katarzyna Gizińska, Agnieszka Kurdyś-Kujawska, and Paweł Chmieliński

1 Introduction

Contemporary rural areas in Europe are undergoing dynamic and complex changes resulting from the impact of social, economic, environmental and technological megatrends. These transformations are particularly significant in Central and Eastern European countries, where historical development conditions, regional diversity and the pace of institutional change influence today's social and economic structures. Poland

B. Wieliczko (✉) · P. Chmieliński
Institute of Rural and Agricultural Development, Polish Academy of Sciences, and European Rural Development Network, Warsaw, Poland
e-mail: bwieliczko@irwirpan.waw.pl

D. Barjolle et al. (eds.), *Innovation and the Future of Rural Development in Europe*,
https://doi.org/10.1007/978-3-032-22570-2_7

is a particularly interesting case study for these processes, as it is characterised by a marked heterogeneity of rural areas—from the metropolitan areas of Mazowiecki, through mountainous areas with a scattered settlement structure, to post-collectivised and post-industrial areas in the north-west.

Over the last two decades, rural development has become one of the most important priorities of European Union policies. Reforms of the Common Agricultural Policy, the European Green Deal, Smart Villages concepts, as well as place-based approaches to territorial planning emphasise the importance of innovation (technological, organisational, social and institutional) as a key mechanism for building the long-term resilience of local communities. The literature on the subject increasingly points out that it is precisely the capacity for adaptation, the ability to cooperate across sectors and the involvement of residents in the process of co-creating public policies that will determine the future paths of development of European rural areas (Bock, 2012; Dax & Fischer, 2018; Neumeier, 2012).

From a European perspective, social innovations play a particularly important role, enabling the creation of new forms of cooperation, the mobilisation of resources, the strengthening of social capital and the development of local institutions, especially in regions with low population density, limited access to public services and little economic diversity (Bock, 2012; Jungsberg et al., 2020). Research indicates that investing in

P. Chmieliński
e-mail: pchmielinski@irwirpan.waw.pl

K. Gizińska
Institute of Economics and Rural Development, Lithuanian Centre for Social Sciences, Vilnius, Lithuania

European Rural Development Network, Warsaw, Poland

K. Gizińska
e-mail: katarzyna.gizinska@erdn.eu

A. Kurdyś-Kujawska
Faculty of Economics, Koszalin University of Technology, Koszalin, Poland
e-mail: agnieszka.kurdys-kujawska@tu.koszalin.pl

European Rural Development Network, Warsaw, Poland

the competences of local communities, strengthening intermediary institutions, developing multi-level dialogue and creating structures conducive to co-decision-making are the foundation of policies supporting territorial cohesion and socio-economic resilience (Steiner & Atterton, 2015). At the same time, not all rural areas have equal development resources—there is a growing gap between dynamic areas linked to large agglomerations and peripheral areas affected by depopulation and spatial exclusion (Copus & de Lima, 2015).

These differences are particularly evident in Poland. Regions such as Mazowieckie combine processes of metropolisation with intensive suburbanisation, while the Bieszczady are an example of peripheral mountain areas with low infrastructure accessibility, and part of the Zachodniopomorskie is still struggling with the consequences of structural transformation following the collapse of state-owned farms. The SHERPA project selected three Polish regions representing these different development trajectories: Mazowieckie (MAP Zielone Sąsiedztwo), Podkarpackie (MAP Bieszczady) and Zachodniopomorskie (MAP Zachodniopomorskie). Multi-actor research platforms (MAPs) have become a place for analysing social perceptions of challenges, local resources and visions of the future formulated by residents, social organisations, local governments and experts.

This chapter presents an interpretation of the results of this work in a broader European theoretical and political context. It includes a discussion of the importance of innovation in rural development, an analysis of the diversity of challenges and development strategies in three Polish regions, an assessment of their resilience, and a reflection on the future of rural policies in the EU.

2 Theoretical Foundations of Innovation in Rural Development

Innovation as a Driver of Change in the European Countryside

In European research on rural areas, innovation is understood broadly—not only as new technologies or technical solutions, but also as new forms of organisation, cooperation and management. Dargan and Shucksmith (2008) point out that innovations in rural areas are now seen as the result of a joint, co-evolutionary learning process that is generated through interaction and cooperation within networks of various rural actors. In rural areas, social and organisational innovations play a particularly important role, enabling the development of public services where the market does not provide them, as do ecological innovations that support the sustainable use of natural resources (Dargan & Shucksmith, 2008; Neumeier, 2017). Social innovation, resulting from cooperation between civil society actors, is recognized as a response to social problems, thereby gaining recognition as a key driver of sustainable development. Their role is to strengthen civic attitudes, which is particularly important in marginalized rural areas. These areas often struggle with both a lack of public funding and constraints resulting from the natural environment and the weakness of market mechanisms (Kluvankova et al., 2021). In many regions of Europe, digital innovations are also crucial—mechanisms that facilitate access to education, public administration, the labour market and health services, which are slowly changing the role of technology in the lives of local communities (OECD, 2025).

The Concept of Rural Resilience

Territorial resilience, derived from ecology, has been adapted to social research as a concept describing the ability of local systems to cope with disruptions, adapt to new conditions and transition to new development models when existing paths become insufficient. The literature emphasises that resilient rural areas are able to maintain stability in the face of shocks, adapt to new conditions and transform institutional and economic structures if the long-term interests of the community so require (Berkes & Ross, 2013; Meuwissen et al., 2019).

When assessing the resilience of rural areas, factors such as human and social capital, the level of self-organisation, economic diversification, institutional flexibility, the quality of technical and digital infrastructure, and the quality of cooperation at local, regional and national levels are important. A combination of these factors makes it possible to identify development potential and barriers that determine the possibilities for change and adaptation of local structures (Soriano et al., 2023; Steiner & Atterton, 2015).

European Framework Supporting Innovation in Rural Areas

The European Union has a comprehensive institutional system in place to support innovation in rural development, covering both sectoral policies and horizontal programmes. The European Green Deal emphasises the need for ecological transformation, which requires innovative technological and organisational solutions, especially in agriculture and spatial economy (EC, 2019). The Common Agricultural Policy, following reforms for 2023–2027, places greater emphasis on the role of innovation, digitalisation, biodiversity and climate resilience. The Smart Villages concept promotes the use of digital technologies and social innovation to improve the quality of life of residents in sparsely populated areas, while the LEADER approach and community-led local development (CLLD) increase the participation of residents in decision-making processes. In turn, the European Innovation Partnership EIP-AGRI supports co-creation of innovation through operational groups bringing together farmers, scientists, local authorities and entrepreneurs (ENRD, 2021).

Poland Among European Types of Rural Areas

Polish rural areas stand out on a European scale due to their complex socio-economic structure, which is influenced by both historical processes and the latest demographic and infrastructural trends. Firstly, regional polarisation is more pronounced than in many Western European countries, which is due to the large gap between metropolitan areas and the periphery (Stanny et al., 2018). Secondly, the family farming model plays an important role, dominating most regions outside the north-western part of the country, where a significant part of rural areas are former state-owned farms affected by a combination of social and economic problems (Śleszyński et al., 2019). Thirdly, suburbanisation processes around the largest cities are blurring the boundaries between urban and rural areas, generating new types of challenges, especially in the sphere of public services. Finally, the development of local institutions, in particular non-governmental organisations, rural women's clubs and local action groups, creates a favourable ecosystem for the development of social innovation and the building of local resilience.

3 Diversity of Challenges, Strategies and Visions for Rural Development in Poland in the European Context

The development of rural areas in Poland is characterised by marked spatial and institutional diversity, reflecting both the diversity of geographical conditions and the different historical trajectories of individual regions. When compared to European typologies of rural areas—which differentiate them according to their level of accessibility, economic structure, demographic dynamics or social capital—Poland's regional mosaic fits in with trends observed across Europe, but at the same time reveals unique combinations of factors that make the country a particularly interesting analytical case. The three regions analysed within the MAP platforms of the SHERPA project represent a cross-section of these differences: Mazowieckie as a strongly polarised metropolitan-peripheral space, Bieszczady as an example of a mountainous area with a dispersed settlement network and multicultural heritage, and Zachodniopomorskie as an area of post-1989 transformed post-state farm structures, where processes of marginalisation and depopulation are intertwined with intensive modernisation of the agricultural sector.

Mazowieckie and the "Green Neighbourhood" MAP: Metropolitan Areas and Peripheral Distance

Socio-economic Conditions of the Region

Mazowieckie is the region with the greatest internal socio-economic polarisation in Poland and one of the most diverse in Central and Eastern Europe. The presence of Warsaw—a metropolis with international economic links and significant human capital—contrasts with areas further away from the centre, which are characterised by limited access to public services, depopulation and difficulties in maintaining local economic functions. The phenomenon of metropolisation intensifies these differences: the development of suburban areas and related service functions runs parallel to the marginalisation of areas on the outskirts of the region, which is described in the literature as a growing development gradient between the core and the periphery (ESPON, 2017).

The region also plays an important role in national agricultural production, especially in fruit growing and milk production. However, the structure of farms, often smaller than the national average, combined with growing regulatory and climate requirements, means that many of them do not have sufficient investment capacity to implement new technologies and sustainable agricultural practices. In the European context, this is a typical problem for regions with a large number of small farms, where the intensification of modernisation processes face capital and institutional barriers (Ciaian & Swinnen, 2009).

Vision of Development in Terms of MAP

The members of MAP Zielone Sąsiedztwo (Green Neighbourhood) formulate a vision of Mazowieckie's development as an area offering a high quality of life, combining natural values with full access to public services and employment opportunities. In their view, attractive rural areas are those that effectively integrate environmental, social and economic elements within a single sustainable development model. In particular, they emphasise the need to invest in public transport, digitalisation and the development of social services, which serve as infrastructure enabling innovation and entrepreneurship. In European literature, this approach is considered a key condition for the development of "smart villages"(Komorowski, 2025), where public and digital infrastructure becomes the basis for implementing bottom-up social and economic innovation (ENRD, 2021).

An important element of the MAP vision is also the development of short food supply chains and local food production, which is in line with EU strategies on food security, biodiversity and the resilience of food systems. These concepts are particularly relevant for metropolitan regions, where there is a growing demand for locally produced food and environmentally sustainable supply chains (EC, 2021). At the same time, this orientation requires the development of innovative business models, cooperation between farmers and local processors, and an adequate financial support system, which, according to MAP members, is often lacking.

Key Challenges

The most important challenges identified by MAP members include an ageing population, climate change, growing social and spatial inequalities, and insufficient access to public transport. These factors reinforce the processes of peripherisation, which are described in the literature as the weakening of rural areas' ability to participate in the economic flows generated by metropolitan centres (Copus, 2001). Limited mobility, lack of social infrastructure and insufficient support for entrepreneurship create conditions in which innovation can only develop in selected locations.

MAP Bieszczady: peripherality, Local Communities and the Role of Social Capital

Regional Context

The Bieszczady region, located in south-eastern Poland, is characterised by a unique combination of environmental, historical and social factors. Scattered settlements, extensive protected areas, low population density and limited transport accessibility create conditions of peripherality in both geographical and functional terms. At the same time, it is an area of high natural value, developing tourism and a dynamically growing number of grassroots social initiatives, including non-governmental organisations and rural housewives' circles.

The region's historical heritage—including post-war resettlements and the destruction of the traditional ethnic structure—has shaped local communities as heterogeneous, complex and lacking a uniform identity rooted in the long term. The literature indicates that regions with this profile often have lower levels of bridging capital but higher potential for creating new forms of social cooperation that can turn into social innovation (Bock, 2012; Putnam, 2000).

Vision of Development from the Perspective of Local Communities

The members of MAP Bieszczady formulate a vision of development centred around values related to locality, natural heritage and quality of life. In their view, the future of the region should be based on the sustainable use of natural resources and the strengthening of the local community as the basis for institutional development. The idea of a "small homeland" plays a special role here, understood as a space for social bonds, joint action and a sense of rootedness, which is an important element in shaping local resilience (Berkes & Ross, 2013).

This vision is also strongly oriented towards the development of social capital, both in institutional (NGOs, local organisations) and informal forms. In practice, this translates into numerous grassroots initiatives, from the construction of local recreational infrastructure to the creation of new cultural events and shared meeting spaces. Although these activities are micro-innovations, their cumulative potential is significant and fits in with European concepts of social innovation as a tool for building resilience (Neumeier, 2017).

Key Challenges for the Region

The Bieszczady are primarily struggling with depopulation, the outflow of young people and a lack of transport infrastructure, which limits access to education and public services. These problems are typical of European mountainous and peripheral regions, where spatial isolation weakens the adaptive capacity of communities and at the same time reinforces dependence on seasonal sectors of the economy, such as tourism (Sarkki et al., 2025). MAP members also highlight difficulties in accessing finance, the small scale of local labour markets and occasional conflicts between nature conservation and economic needs.

MAP Zachodniopomorskie: The Legacy of Transformation and Socio-economic Diversity

Characteristics of the Region

The Zachodniopomorskie region is one of the most interesting examples of transformation after 1989, when the collapse of state-owned farms led to rapid socio-economic restructuring. This legacy is still visible today: many localities are characterised by an accumulation of social problems, low employment, weak social capital and limited mobility of residents. The infrastructure gap is particularly acute, manifesting itself in poor public transport and insufficient access to broadband internet, which deepens the digital and communication divide. At the same time, the region has great agricultural potential, a high level of mechanisation and a growing number of organic farms.

Zachodniopomorskie combines elements of peripherality and modernisation, making it an example of a complex territorial system in which processes of marginalisation coexist with dynamic development in selected locations, especially in coastal areas and around larger cities. In rural areas, marginalization is particularly visible in the form of weak local institutions, an aging population, and a lack of mechanisms making the youth stay, which prevents building the strong social capital necessary to generate grassroots innovation.

Vision for Development Presented by the MAP Zachodniopomorskie
MAP Zachodniopomorskie members emphasise the need to build strong, well-connected and resilient rural communities in the region through investment in infrastructure, the development of digital skills and the strengthening of cooperation between residents and public institutions. In their view, a key element of future development is the creation of 'vibrant' rural areas—places that not only retain residents but also attract new initiatives and businesses. To achieve this goal, investment is needed in transport, electronic communications, local markets for organic products and support systems for entrepreneurs.

This vision reflects the European approach to territorial planning, according to which interventions should strengthen local economic networks, build partnerships and develop social capital as a foundation for innovation (Steiner & Atterton, 2015). Importance is also attached to the role of agricultural advisory services and business support institutions, which act as a bridge between science and practice, enabling the transfer of innovation and knowledge.

Main Challenges
The most important problems in the region include limited spatial mobility, weak functional links between rural areas and urban centres, technical infrastructure deficits, low levels of public services and insufficient social cohesion. Many localities suffer from social fragmentation and low levels of civic participation. This is particularly evident in the former state-owned farm areas, which currently a significant part of the region's peripheral areas. Unemployment and poverty are concentrated in these areas, leading to the creation of "poverty enclaves". This constitutes a serious barrier that prevents the effective development of local ownership and thus significantly hinders the implementation of social innovation. Such problems are often observed in post-collectivised regions throughout Central Europe, where sudden economic changes have led to persistent forms of marginalisation (Lelkes, 2006).

4 Comparative Analysis: Resilience and Adaptive Capacities of Three Regions

A comparison of the three MAPs reveals both clear similarities and significant differences between the regions. The similarities include insufficient access to public services, demographic problems and limited transport mobility, which are typical challenges for rural areas in Europe. The differences, on the other hand, concern social capital, institutional capacity and innovation potential.

Mazowieckie has the highest level of infrastructure and economic capital, but at the same time is experiencing strong polarisation processes. Bieszczady are characterised by dynamic social capital and great potential for grassroots initiatives, although they are limited by their peripheral location and depopulation. Zachodniopomorskie, on the other hand, is undergoing a process of structural transformation in which the role of institutions supporting innovation is growing, but the weakness of social structures in many localities is still evident.

Identified problems and long-term vision for rural areas in the three Polish MAPs are strikingly similar despite significant geographical and historical divisions. This seems to be related with the perceived strengths, weaknesses, opportunities and threats of these localities (SWOT analysis) which can also be seen as an assessment of resilience capacity and its attributes.

Resilience capacity can only be qualitatively assessed at this stage. Further studies building reference points and benchmarks can help in estimating the resilience capacity in quantitative terms. We apply the qualitative capacity assessment as the study framework - the list of resilience attributes presented in relation to farming systems, proposed in the study by Soriano et al. (2023). Table 1 presents the resilience attributes and the assessment of their presents in the study MAPs.

Resilience attributes of the Polish MAPs can be grouped into three main categories, reflecting the adaptive capacity and transformative potential of rural areas. These are social and human capital, institutional and political support, and economic structure and its sustainability (Fig. 1).

Social and human capital refers to a community's ability to organize, learn, and build internal and external relationships. It is the foundation for implementing social innovation. This group of resilience attributes includes social self-organization, human capital building, reflective and collaborative learning, and supporting rural life. Only one attribute

Table 1 Rural resilience attributes' assessment in Polish MAPs

Resilience attributes	*Definition*	*MAP Zielone Sąsiedztwo*	*MAP Bieszczady*	*MAP Zachodniopomorskie*
Builds human capital	The system takes advantages of, and builds on, resources that can be mobilized through social relationships and membership social networks	5	4	5
Socially self-organized	The social components of the system can form their own configuration based on their needs and desires	5	5	5
Appropriately connected	Connectedness describes the quantity and quality of relationships with actors outside the system	4	4	4
Response diversity	Range of responses of social components to environmental change	5	2	3
Optimally redundant	Critical components and relationships with the systems are duplicated in preparation of failure	4	2	3
Carefully exposed to disturbance	The system is exposed to discrete, low-level events that cause disruptions without pushing the system beyond critical thresholds	4	4	3

(continued)

Table 1 (continued)

Resilience attributes	*Definition*	*MAP Zielone Sąsiedztwo*	*MAP Bieszczady*	*MAP Zachodniopomorskie*
Reflective and shared learning	Individuals and institutions learn from past experiences and present experimentation to anticipate change and create desirable futures	5	3	3
Honors legacy	The current configuration and future trajectories and investments of systems are influenced and informed by past conditions and experiences	4	3	3
Reasonably profitable agriculture	People involved in agriculture can make a livelihood from the work they do without relying too heavily on subsidies	2	2	3
Reasonably profitable non-agricultural sectors	Entrepreneurs can make a livelihood from their work and can sustain their business activities	4	3	3
Diverse policies	Policies stimulate all three capacities of resilience, i.e. robustness, adaptability, transformability	4	3	5

(continued)

Table 1 (continued)

Resilience attributes	*Definition*	*MAP Zielone Sąsiedztwo*	*MAP Bieszczady*	*MAP Zachodniopomorskie*
Infrastructure for innovation	Existing infrastructure facilitates knowledge and adoption of cutting-edge technologies (e.g. digital)	4	3	4
Supports rural life	The activities in the FS attract and maintain a healthy and adequate workforce, including young, intermediate and older people	4	4	3

Scale 1–5: 1—institutional system has a destructive effect on hitherto existing resilience; 2—system does not help maintain existing resilience 3—system is neutral to resilience; 4—system supports the maintenance of resilience; 5—system supports increasing resilience.
Source Study findings, Adopted from Soriano et al. (2023)

achieved the maximum score in all three MAPs: social self-organization. This means that in all the regions studied, the social component of the system (i.e., residents, local groups, organizations, enterprises) is able to independently determine its structures and relationships and can decide how to organize itself to meet challenges or take advantage of opportunities and thus contribute to increasing the resilience of these regions. The system uses and relies on resources mobilized through social relations, which contributes to increasing the resilience of rural areas in Mazowieckie and Zachodniopomorskie. The systems in both regions actively support the increase of this capital. In Mazowieckie, this is due to the strong metropolitan environment, while in Zachodniopomorskie it is the result of support for transformation in rural areas. In the Bieszczady Mountains, this system only contributes to maintaining existing resilience.

When it comes to reflective and collaborative learning (the ability to anticipate change), this attribute was rated the highest in Mazowieckie, which is typical for a metropolitan region with a strong academic base. The system supports the enhancement of this ability. The other regions are neutral in this respect, suggesting that their institutions do not

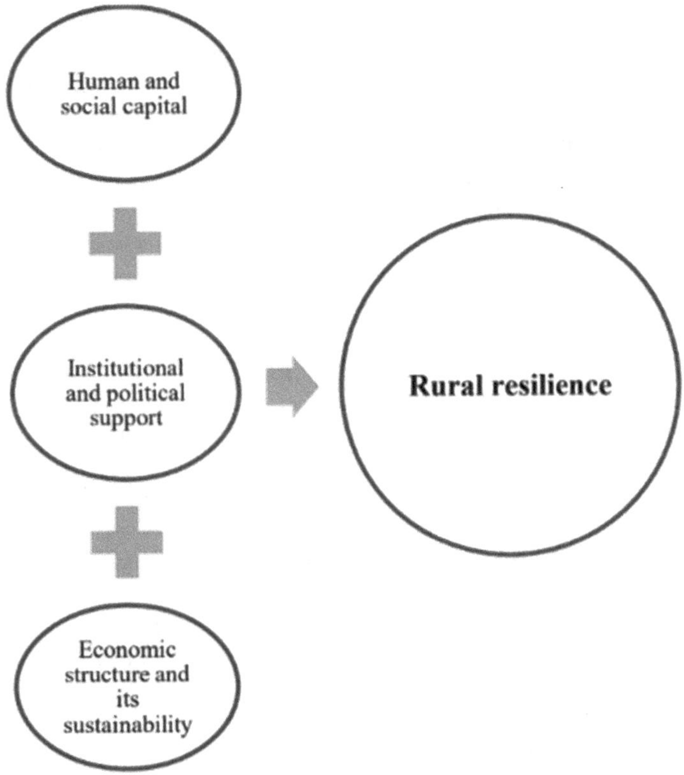

Fig. 1 Attributes of rural resilience. (*Source* Own elaboration)

fully exploit the potential of learning to generate innovation, which may significantly hamper the development of resilient rural areas. The capacity to support rural life (attracting and retaining labor, including young people) was rated highest in Mazowieckie and Bieszczady, meaning that the system supports the maintenance of resilience. In Zachodniopomorskie, the system is neutral, reflecting the region's problems in attracting and retaining an adequate workforce, especially in peripheral and post-collectivization areas.

Institutional and political support refers to the extent to which the political framework and technical infrastructure are conducive to maintaining and increasing the adaptive capacity of regions. Within this group, the following attributes of resilience were identified: policy diversity, infrastructure for innovation, appropriately connected, cautiously exposed to disruption, and honoring heritage. The role of institutions and political support or lack thereof is crucial also in building social capital (Mazur et al., 2018). Policies that stimulate all three resilience capacities (robustness, adaptability, transformability) were rated the highest in Zachodniopomorskie. This means that this region has the best-suited and most comprehensive systemic support for increasing the resilience of rural areas. In Mazowieckie, the diversity of policies only supports the maintenance of resilience, while in the Bieszczady Mountains they are neutral towards resilience. The existing infrastructure facilitating knowledge and the adoption of modern technologies (e.g., digital) in Mazowieckie and Zachodniopomorskie supports the maintenance of the resilience of these areas. However, an infrastructure gap is still visible in Zachodniopomorskie. The Bieszczady Mountains are neutral in the case of resilience, which is consistent with their limited transport accessibility. In all MAPs, the quantity and quality of relations with actors outside the system contribute to supporting resilience in rural areas. In Mazowieckie and the Bieszczady Mountains, the system is exposed to discrete, low-level events that cause disruptions without exceeding critical thresholds, which supports the maintenance of resilience, while in Zachodniopomorskie it is neutral. The region's heritage also has an impact on increasing the resilience of rural areas. In Mazowieckie, the use of the region's heritage supports the maintenance of resilience. In the Bieszczady Mountains (heritage of resettlement) and Zachodniopomorskie (heritage of state-owned farms), it is neutral to resilience. This indicates that institutional systems do not fully transform this difficult historical heritage into a factor of development.

Economic structure and its sustainability refer to the economic stability of agriculture and non-agricultural sectors and the ability of regions to adapt in the event of a crisis. It includes attributes such as reasonably profitable agriculture, optimal redundancy, diversity of response, and profitable non-agricultural sectors. A key common weakness is the low profitability of agriculture, which is rated low in all three MAPs. The institutional system in Mazovia and Bieszczady does not help to maintain existing resilience. Low profitability, linked in Mazowieckie to the structure of small farms, forces farmers to rely excessively on subsidies. This low profitability necessitates the diversification of agricultural family income. Reasonably profitable non-agricultural sectors, providing entrepreneurs (including farmers and their family members) with decent incomes, can contribute to increasing the resilience of rural areas. In Mazowieckie, the system supports the maintenance of profitability, which is understandable given its metropolitan market. In the Bieszczady Mountains and Zachodniopomorskie, the system is neutral in terms of resilience, which indicates barriers to activities supporting entrepreneurship outside agriculture. The ability to adapt to disruptions, measured by optimal redundancy (duplication of critical components) and diversity of response (range of responses to change), is most weak in the Bieszczady Mountains. The system there does not help to maintain the reproduction of critical components, which increases their vulnerability as a peripheral region. In Mazowieckie, the system supports maintenance, while in Zachodniopomorskie it is neutral. The Bieszczady Mountains are characterized by the lowest level of response of social components to change, and the system does not help maintain this capacity. In Mazowieckie, on the other hand, the system supports increasing the capacity for diverse adaptation. The diversity of policies that stimulate all three resilience capacities (robustness, adaptability, and transformability) is key to building resilience. In Zachodniopomorskie, policy diversity supports increased resilience, in Mazowieckie it contributes to its maintenance, and in Bieszczady, policy diversity is neutral towards resilience.

An analysis of resilience attributes reveals three distinct models for building adaptive capacity in rural areas, reflecting the different historical, geographical, and economic contexts of each of these regions. In Mazowieckie, resilience is based on strong human capital and learning capacity. Thanks to its strong metropolitan environment, the institutional system actively supports the increase of this knowledge and resources mobilized through social networks. This is the region with the greatest potential for transformation. The biggest challenge for building resilient rural areas is the lack of adequate support for the economic viability of agriculture. The low rating of this attribute indicates that the system does not help to maintain the profitability of farms (often small), forcing farmers to rely excessively on subsidies. In the Bieszczady Mountains, resilience is based almost exclusively on grassroots social self-organization. The institutional system in this area supports the growth of local initiatives. The region struggles with structural peripheral problems, where the system does not help to maintain resilience in key areas: low profitability of agriculture, poor adaptability (diversity of responses), and low optimal redundancy. This makes the Bieszczady Mountains most vulnerable to external shocks due to their spatial isolation and limited range of alternative economic solutions. In Zachodniopomorskie, resilience is strongly supported by a variety of policies that actively promote the enhancement of all three resilience capacities, as well as by the development of human capital. This confirms the region's efforts in managing the transition after the state-owned farms. Support for rural life, in terms of attracting and retaining a healthy workforce and its impact on building the resilience of rural areas, is the region's greatest weakness.

5 Summary

The analysis of three Polish regions—Mazowieckie, Bieszczady and Zachodniopomorskie—shows that contemporary rural development in Europe, and especially in Central and Eastern Europe, increasingly depends on the capacity of local communities to adapt, cooperate and create new forms of innovative activity. In the Polish context, this capacity reflects both historical conditions and diverse local resources, as well as the influence of European policies supporting territorial resilience and the sustainable transformation of rural areas. The literature clearly indicates that the attractiveness of rural areas and the well-being of their inhabitants, stem not only from the availability of public services and infrastructure, but also from the quality of social relations and opportunities to participate in local and supra-local decision-making processes (Chmieliński & Wieliczko, 2023).

Each of the analysed regions represents a different developmental trajectory, which makes this study particularly valuable for understanding the complexity of the Polish countryside. Mazowieckie illustrates the dual nature of metropolisation processes: on the one hand, the rapidly developing surroundings of the capital city generate opportunities for modernisation, while on the other hand they deepen existing spatial inequalities. In this region, investments in social and digital infrastructure and the strengthening of public services are crucial prerequisites for maintaining attractiveness and fostering innovation.

Bieszczady, in contrast, exemplify a specific model of development based on endogenous resources, a strong sense of locality, and the importance of social ties in shaping adaptive capacity. Although the region, like many mountainous areas in Europe, struggles with depopulation and limited availability of services, it stands out due to its growing potential for social innovation resulting from residents' engagement and dynamic bottom-up initiatives.

Zachodniopomorskie represents a post-industrial region whose contemporary challenges largely stem from the legacy of systemic transformation. Weak social capital, insufficient mobility and poorly developed public service infrastructure coexist there with a modernising agricultural sector and the rise of ecological initiatives. This diversity makes coherent regional development difficult and points to the need for substantial institutional support and stronger cooperation structures.

All three regions, despite their differences, confirm the broader research thesis that multifunctional rural development requires a complex combination of infrastructural, social, economic and institutional interventions. As noted by Chmieliński (2019), rural entrepreneurship and its institutional environment are key elements of multifunctional rural development, determining the ability to generate innovation and build stable foundations for long-term progress.

First, the future of rural development in Poland depends on the ability to combine technological innovations with social and organisational innovations. The latter, as demonstrated by Bieszczady, may serve as a durable foundation for development even in regions affected by long-standing marginalisation. Social innovations based on local cooperation and residents' engagement strengthen territorial resilience by building relationships, institutions and competencies crucial for responding to change.

Second, interventions aimed at reducing spatial inequalities are indispensable. Mazowieckie shows that even a region containing the country's largest metropolis may face serious developmental challenges if areas distant from the centre lack access to transport, education and social infrastructure. Public policies must utilise metropolitan potential to strengthen the peripheries, rather than the reverse.

Third, post-industrial and post-transformational areas such as parts of Zachodniopomorskie require particularly robust institutional support. The legacy of the collapse of former economic structures has created persistent challenges that cannot be resolved through infrastructural investment alone. Rebuilding social capital and strengthening cooperation among public, private and civic sectors are necessary to overcome developmental barriers.

Fourth, ecological and digital transformation may serve as a driving force for modernisation, but only if implemented with attention to local resources and regional specificity. In each of the analysed regions, this transformation takes a different form and requires a distinct set of tools: Mazowieckie needs digital integration of public services, Bieszczady require support for innovative bottom-up initiatives, while Zachodniopomorskie needs ecological education and the development of technological competencies.

Fifth, the Polish countryside—despite its diversity—possesses significant developmental potential that can strengthen the European model of territorial resilience. Enhancing this potential requires modern place-based policies, co-governance and investment in people. European literature emphasises that the attractiveness of rural areas and the quality of life of their inhabitants depend on the synergy between infrastructure, the social environment and opportunities for co-decision-making (Chmieliński & Wieliczko, 2023). In this sense, Polish rural areas may not only benefit from European policies but also contribute to shaping them by providing innovative solutions and practices.

References

Berkes, F., & Ross, H. (2013). Community resilience: Toward an integrated approach. *Society & Natural Resources, 26*(1), 5–20.

Bock, B. B. (2012). Social innovation and sustainability: How to disentangle the buzzword and its application in the field of agriculture and rural development. *Studies in Agricultural Economics, 114*(2), 57–63.

Bock, B. B. (2016). Rural marginalisation and the role of social innovation; A turn towards nexogenous development and rural reconnection. *Sociologia Ruralis, 56*(4), 552–573.

Chmieliński, P. (2019). *Przedsiębiorczość i polityka gospodarcza w wielofunkcyjnym rozwoju obszarów wiejskich w Polsce* (Vol. 175). IERiGŻ PIB.

Chmieliński, P., & Wieliczko, B. (2023). Diversification of rural economy in times of green transition in the eyes of rural stakeholders. Case study of the Polish Mazowieckie region. *Rural Areas and Development, 18*(2023), 99–106. https://doi.org/10.61517/RAD/2023/18.0700

Ciaian, P., & Swinnen, J. (2009). Credit market imperfections and the distribution of policy rents. *American Journal of Agricultural Economics, 91*(4), 1124–1139.

Copus, A. K. (2001). From core–periphery to polycentric development: Concepts of spatial and aspatial peripherality. *European Planning Studies, 9*(4), 539–552.

Copus, A. K., & de Lima, P. (2015). *Territorial cohesion in rural Europe. The relational turn in rural development*. Routledge.

Dargan, L., & Shucksmith, M. (2008). LEADER and innovation. *Sociologia Ruralis, 48*(3), 274–291.

Dax, T., & Fischer, M. (2018). An alternative policy approach to rural development in regions facing population decline. *European Planning Studies, 26*(2), 297–315.

EC (European Commission). (2019). *The European Green Deal*. EC.

EC (European Commission). (2021). *Food supply chains are of key importance for a sustainable future*. EC.

ENRD. (2021). *Smart villages and rural development*. European Network for Rural Development.

ESPON. (2017). Shrinking rural regions in Europe. ESPON EGTC.

Jungsberg, L., Byskov Herslund, L., Nilsson, K., Perjo, L., Copus, A., Randall, L., & Berlina, A. (2020). Key actors in community-driven social innovation in rural areas in the Nordic countries. *Journal of Rural Studies, 79*, 276-285.

Kluvankova, T., Nijnik, M., Spacek, M., Sarkki, S., Perlik, M., Lukesch, R., Melnykovych, M., Valero, D., & Brnkalakova, S. (2021). Social innovation for sustainability transformation and its diverging development paths in marginalised rural areas. *Sociologia Ruralis, 61*(2), 344–371. https://doi.org/10.1111/soru.12337

Komorowski, Ł. (2025). Smart villages jako koncepcja rozwoju obszarów wiejskich (Smart villages as a concept for rural development). Instytut Rozwoju Wsi i Rolnictwa PAN.

Lelkes, O. (2006). Social exclusion in Central and Eastern Europe: Concepts, measures and policy interventions. *European Centre for Social Welfare Policy and Research*.

Mazur, M., Czapiewski, K., Janc, K., & Konopski, M. (2018). Władza lokalna na obszarach wiejskich—zróżnicowanie w przestrzeni i zmiana w czasie profilu samorządowca (Local authorities in rural areas—diversification in space and change in the profile of self-government officials over time). *Studia Obszarów Wiejskich, 51*, 7–26. https://doi.org/10.7163/SOW.51.1

Meuwissen, M., Feindt, P., Midmore, P., et al. (2019). A framework to assess the resilience of farming systems. *Agricultural Systems, 176*, Article 102656.

Neumeier, S. (2012). Why do social innovations in rural development matter and should they be considered more seriously in rural development research? Proposal for a stronger focus on social innovations in rural development research? *Sociologia Ruralis, 52*(1), 48–69.

Neumeier, S. (2017). Social innovation in rural development: Identifying the key factors. *The Geographical Journal, 183*(1), 34–46. https://doi.org/10.1111/geoj.12180

OECD. (2025). *Rural innovation pathways*. OECD Publishing.

Putnam, R. D. (2000). *Bowling alone: The collapse and revival of American community*. Simon & Schuster.

Sarkki, S., Lynn, T., Hiedanpää, J., Vizzarri, M., Christoforidi, I., Brnkalakova, S., Crisan, V., Egli, A., Gültekin, P., Selman Gültekin, Y., Jokinen, M., Monteiro, A. T., Nastran, M., Özdemir, H., Pelyukh, O., Sulc, I., Živojinović, I., & Ficko, A. (2025). Polytraps in European rural mountainous regions: An expert view. *European Planning Studies, 33*(5), 757–777.

Śleszyński, P., Komornicki, T., & Solon, J. (2019). Post-state farm localities in Poland: Legacy and transformation. *Geographia Polonica, 92*(4), 427–447.

Soriano, B., Garrido, A., Bertolozzi-Caredio, D., Accatino, F., Antonioli, F., Krupin, V., Meuwissen, M. M. P., Ollendorf, F., Rommel, J., Spiegel, A., Tudor, M., Urquhart, J., Vigani, M., & Bardají, I. (2023). Actors and their roles for improving resilience of farming systems in Europe. *Journal of Rural Studies, 98*, 134–146. https://doi.org/10.1016/j.jrurstud.2023.02.003

Stanny, M., Rosner, A., & Komorowski, Ł. (2018). *Monitoring rozwóju obszarów wiejskich, etap III: struktury społeczno-gospodarcze, ich przestrzenne zróżnicowanie i dynamika:(wersja pełna)* (Monitoring rural development, stage III: socio-economic structures, their spatial diversity and dynamics: (full version)). Fundacja Europejski Fundusz Rozwoju Wsi Polskiej.

Steiner, A., & Atterton, J. (2015). Exploring the contribution of rural enterprises to local resilience. *Journal of Rural Studies, 40*, 30–45.

CHAPTER 8

Contribution of a Science-Society-Policy Platform to the Long-Term Vision for Rural Areas. The Perspective from a Peripheral Region of Southern Europe (Galicia, Spain)

María Amparo Ferreira-Golpe, Mar Pérez-Fra, Ana Isabel García-Arias, Beatriz Guimarey-Fernández, and Edelmiro López-Iglesias

1 Introduction

Rural areas in Spain are very diverse in their climatic and biophysical conditions, and also in their economic and social structure and dynamics. But most of them are characterized by the continuity of the depopulation process in recent decades, increasing ageing, and emigration of young people (Banco de España, 2021; Molinero & Alario, 2022).

M. A. Ferreira-Golpe (✉) · B. Guimarey-Fernández
University of Santiago de Compostela, Escola Politécnica Superior, Lugo, Spain
e-mail: mariaamparo.ferreira@usc.gal

B. Guimarey-Fernández
e-mail: beatriz.guimarey@usc.gal

D. Barjolle et al. (eds.), *Innovation and the Future of Rural Development in Europe*,
https://doi.org/10.1007/978-3-032-22570-2_8

Galicia, a region located in the Northwest of Spain, has historically been an eminently rural region with a relatively high demographic density in the Spanish context (Dubert, 2008), but in the last decades it has experienced a strong demographic and economic decline of rural areas. It faces typical challenges of peripheral regions in Europe, like rural depopulation and ageing, reinforced by the emigration of young people. The region (NUT2) covers 29,574 km^2 in which 2,690,464 people reside in 2022, with an average density of 90.8 inhabitants per km^2. Rural areas present a growing deagrarianisation and a high population dispersion, which makes it difficult to provide basic services. Its bioclimatic conditions characterise Galicia as prone to forest fire risk, with catastrophic events happening during last years (namely 2006, 2017 and 2025). Climate change scenarios seem to worsen that situation.

Considered in the Spanish context, Galician rural areas present notable specificities, among which we can highlight: the existence until the mid-20th century of high demographic densities, among the highest in Spain, supported by an intensive traditional agrarian system; the sharp decline of the rural population in the last 60 years and the continuity of this process in recent decades, in parallel to the late but accelerated decline in agricultural employment; a very strong dispersion of rural habitat, which is reflected in the fact that Galicia, which occupies 6% of the Spanish territory, has half of the population entities (settlements) in Spain (Atance et al., 2010; López Iglesias, 2019a; Molinero & Alario, 2022).

M. Pérez-Fra
Institute for Research in Global Health and Sustainable Development, iTERRA, University of Santiago de Compostela, Campus Terra, Lugo, Spain
e-mail: mariadomar.perez@usc.gal

A. I. García-Arias
University of Santiago de Compostela, CISPAC, Escola Politécnica Superior, Lugo, Spain
e-mail: anaisabel.garcia@usc.gal

E. López-Iglesias
University of Santiago de Compostela, Facultade de Ciencias Económicas e Empresariais, Santiago de Compostela, Spain
e-mail: edelmiro.lopez@usc.gal

Focused on this region, Galician rural areas currently present a strong heterogeneity, which makes it advisable to have a classification of the territory as a background. For this purpose, the typology created in the *Galician Green Infrastructure Strategy* (Díaz-Varela et al., 2019) is considered. This typology is based on the territories of the 24 Local Action Groups (LAGs) existing in the region in the period 2014-2022 and characterizes them according to four groups of variables: trends in land use, urban-rural gradient, agricultural activity and economic and business dynamism. The resulting classification differentiates four types of rural areas (Fig. 1), although for our study we can simplify it into the three main ones: urbanized and forested, active (agrarian), and abandoned rural areas.

This chapter summarizes the results of a study whose aim was to contribute to the process promoted by the European Commission of designing the long-term vision for rural areas (LTVRA) [1]. The specific objectives were to identify the main challenges and opportunities, to design the desirable future for 2040 and to set out the actions needed to achieve this desirable future for Galician rural areas.

After this introduction, the chapter is organized into five sections: research methodology and sources (Sect. 2); key trends of Galician rural areas (Sect. 3); main challenges and opportunities for these areas in the next 20 years (Sect. 4); vision of the desirable future for the Galician rural areas in 2040 (Sect. 5); priority actions to achieve the desirable rural in 2040 (Sect. 6). Finally, in Sect. 7 we summarize the main conclusions.

2 Methods

The results were obtained by applying a Delphi method through five steps. The method involved the members of a Multi-Actor Platform (MAP) and external actors. A Galician MAP was set up under the SHERPA[2] (Sustainable Hub to Engage into Rural Policies with Actors) project. It covers the entire territory of Galicia. The institution responsible is the University of Santiago de Compostela (USC) with the support

[1] https://rural-vision.europa.eu/index_en.

[2] The EU-funded SHERPA project (https://rural-interfaces.eu/) https://doi.org/10.3030/862448

of the Galician Association of Local Action Groups (GALAGs). This association brings together a broad representation of rural actors (more than 1,500 entities are involved in the 24 LAGs), belonging to a variety of economics sectors, civil society, and local public institutions. Starting with this association, and incorporating other actors, a MAP was established composed of 17 members representing society (10 members), public institutions (4 members) and research organizations (3 members).

The five steps of the Delphi method are explained below.

- 1st step: Online questionnaire

To gather some preliminary insights for the first MAP meeting, its members replied to an online questionnaire in February 2020, in which they evaluated the priority of a list of challenges for rural areas of Galicia. These challenges were aligned with the 10 objectives of the 2021-2027 CAP (Common Agricultural Policy). They were also asked to point out the most important ones and propose potential actions to address them.

- 2nd step: Desk research

The USC team developed desk research and context analysis to identify the current and probable trends of the Galician rural areas, focusing on 8 specific topics: 7 proposed by the SHERPA project, and another suggested by MAP members in the online questionnaire (the dynamics of the agri-food and forestry sector). For this purpose, a collection and analysis of statistical data was carried out, complemented with the results of research projects and reports supporting the characterisation of trends of the Galician rural areas.

- 3rd step: First MAP meeting

The first MAP meeting was conducted online on 11th June 2020, attended by 12 of the 17 members: society (7 members), policy (2) and science (3). The agenda of the meeting was organised in two parts:

- Trends, challenges, and opportunities of rural areas in Galicia. We began by summarising the data collected in the 2nd step and the results obtained through the online questionnaire. Then, by applying

the Delphi method, the MAP members re-evaluated the challenges included in the questionnaire.
- Vision for the future of rural areas in 2040. In this part the MAP members set out their vision of the desirable future of rural Galicia in 2040.

The results were collected into a document (MAP Discussion Paper) that was sent to MAP members for review in late June 2020. Following this review, a new topic was added: Governance and participation.

- 4th step: Survey of external actors of the MAP

Afterwards, we conducted a survey of external actors in order to broaden the views provided by MAP members. We surveyed 61 people, receiving 33 responses. The list included representatives of society, policy, and science. In the survey, people assessed the main challenges and opportunities resulting from the MAP work and the desk research.

Combining the results obtained at the first meeting and the responses to the survey of external actors, a first draft MAP Position Paper was prepared and sent to the MAP members.

- 5th step: Second (consensus) MAP meeting

The second MAP meeting was held in person on 25th September 2020, attended by 9 of the 17 members: society (6), policy (2) and science (1). The agenda was organised in three parts:

- Opportunities in Galician rural areas: based on the previous results, MAP members proceeded to order the opportunities according to their importance.
- Desirable rural (horizon 2040): the desirable rural defined in the first meeting was characterised by a set of 29 ideas and MAP members proceeded now to choose the 10 ideas they found most desirable and rank them.
- Priority actions to achieve the desirable rural: the members were divided into two discussion groups to refine and complete the list of 52 priority actions drawn up from the previous MAP work.

Afterwards, they proceeded to choose the 10 actions considered as priorities and to vote on them.

As a result, the whole process ended with three ranked lists: opportunities for Galician rural areas, most desirable features of Galician rural areas in 2040 and actions to achieve the desirable rural. This resulted in the final MAP Position Paper (Guimarey-Fernández et al., 2021).

3 Key Trends of Galician Rural Areas; Review of Data and Previous Studies

Demographic shift: decrease and ageing of the rural population

Following the DEGURBA classification developed by Eurostat, we identify thinly populated areas (TPAs) as rural areas, in which 240 of Galicia's 313 municipalities are located. With this demarcation, Galician Institute of Statistics (IGE) data for 2022 show the rural areas occupy 4/5 of the territory (81.8%) but only 1/4 of the population (26.3%) reside there, with a mean density of 30 inhabitants per km^2. Depopulation is particularly acute in low-density thinly populated areas (TPA low): 65.2% of the surface area but only 14.2% of the population, with the density limited to 21 inhab/km^2 (IGE, 2023). These low densities are added to by increasingly accentuated ageing.

Sex differences in life expectancy mean that the rural population presents a feminisation in old age brackets, in contrast with the masculinisation among young people and adults, as a consequence of recent migrations. The confluence of ageing and low fertility causes negative natural growth, tendency accentuated over the last 15 years. With data from 2021, the natural growth rate of the rural population presents a negative value of 11.9‰, double the Galician average. This means that, in the absence of migration, this population will suffer an annual decline of 1.19% due to natural causes. In addition to ageing, this is influenced by an especially low fertility rate. The mean number of children per women is 0.94 in rural areas, which is lower than the Galician average (1.01), and in the least populated rural areas (TPA low) it falls to 0.89 (IGE, 2023). This lower rural fertility rate suggests the existence of specific factors in these areas which disincentivise the decision to have children, factors linked to the limited employment opportunities and deficiencies in access to basic services (López Iglesias, 2019a).

With respect to migratory flows, the emigration to urban areas continues, compensated for the arrival of returning emigrants and of immigrants. The result for rural areas as a whole is a migratory balance approximately in equilibrium, but one which masks large differences by municipality, age and gender. Specifically, the data indicate an important rural emigration of the young population, compensated by the return of people of middle and old age. As such, the greatest rates of emigration are recorded in the age bracket of 25–34 years, the initial stage of working life, and this affects women to a greater degree (Toxo & García Arias, 2018).

Deagrarianisation and Limitations on the Economic Diversification of Rural Areas

The loss of demographic and economic weight of rural areas in recent decades has been accompanied by a growing deagrarianisation, a reduction in the importance of agricultural activity (López Iglesias, 2019a). Social Security data provide evidence of this reality: in 2022, of the employed residents in rural municipalities (TPAs), only 11.9% had their principal activity in the agricultural sector (including forestry and fishing); 9.8% worked in construction, 15.2% in industry and 62.4% in the services sector (IGE, 2023). The same applies to low-density TPAs, where people who work mainly in agriculture constitute a minority (15.5%), with a clear predomination of the services sector (59.9%).

The dynamics of Galician rural areas are marked by the accelerated fall in agricultural employment: the population employed in the agricultural sector reduced by 95% in the period from 1950 to 2020, and in the last 35 years alone, since the integration into the European Union, the fall has been almost 90%. This led to a parallel decline in its weight in total employment: this percentage decreased in Galicia from 70% in 1950 to 4.5% in the present day (López Iglesias, 2019b). The other factor which defines the dynamic of rural employment is the limited development of the agri-food industry, other industrial branches, and services. This has meant that the contraction in agricultural employment has only been compensated by the generation of jobs in other activities to a limited extent (López Iglesias & Pérez Fra, 2004). Therefore, the specificity of

Galicia compared to other Spanish and European regions originate from these two factors: agricultural employment continues to decrease at very high rates, markedly above the Spanish and EU averages, and this is accompanied by a weak development of industrial and services activities in rural areas (López Iglesias, 2019a).

The data on the number of companies also reflect the low economic dynamism of Galician rural areas: 100.8 companies/1,000 inhabitants in urban areas compared to 79.9 in peri-urban municipalities and 69.0 in rural areas. The low labour productivity in the agricultural sector, together with the limited development of industrial and services activities, result in a low GDP per inhabitant in rural areas. The situation is not so unfavourable in terms of disposable income, but with the cost of a strong dependence on public transfers, mainly Social Security pensions (IGE, 2023).

Dynamics of the Agri-Food and Forestry Sectors

Despite the transformations of recent decades, the agricultural sector continues to present strong deficiencies, especially in the territorial base of holdings (small size and fragmentation of the area of holdings) and in land uses, and this is reflected by low labour productivity. This productivity is currently limited to 80% of the average for Spanish agriculture and a similar percentage of the average for the Galician economy (López Iglesias, 2019b).

According to the 2020 Agricultural Census, the region currently has around 75,500 farms, with an average agricultural area of 7.9 ha (less than 1/3 of the Spanish average). But families who work and live mainly from agriculture are limited to around 25,000, while land ownership is divided among 1.7 million owners (López Iglesias, 2019b). The reduced average size of holdings is accompanied by high ageing of the holders: in 2020 just 3.5% were aged under 35 years, while 48.3% were aged over 64 years.

To the structural deficiencies of the agricultural sector, we must add the weakness of agri-food industry, which limits employment and the value added generated by the agri-food chain (Sineiro, 2009). This chain remains centred on the production of raw materials, with limited development of the transformation industry. As such, while the agri-food industry in Galicia adds €0.57 to each euro of GVA of agricultural production, in Spain and in the EU the figure exceeds €1 and in more developed

European countries approaches €2. The result of the deficiencies of the agricultural sector and the agri-food industry is expressed in Galicia recording a deficit in its agri-food trade balance. Counting interregional and international trade, net exports are recorded for livestock raw materials and simple by-products (packaged milk and meat), but this is more than counteracted by the net imports of other products (López Iglesias, 2019b; Valdês & López Iglesias, 2008).

The forestry sector has expanded as deagrarianisation progressed, and its productive chain accounts for 1.7% of GDP and 2.3% of employment in Galicia in 2020. Forestry production specialises in pulpwood, especially *Eucalyptus globulus* and *Pinus pinaster*, which is mainly used for the manufacture of paper pulp and boards. The timber chain is focused on first transformation industries, while the development of second transformation industries is limited. The 2008-2013 financial crisis severely affected this production chain, due to its connection with the construction sector, whilst in recent years we have observed a gradual recovery.

Infrastructure and Basic Services

Just as relevant as the weakness of the productive fabric is that rural areas in Galicia continue to record large deficiencies in access to basic services for the population and companies. This problem is exacerbated by the dispersed structure of the habitat, which makes it difficult for people who do not reside in centres of a certain size to access services (Fernández & Peón, 2017). This strong dispersity is reflected in the fact that, while occupying 6% of the territory, Galicia has half of Spain's population settlements (more than 30,000 in absolute terms), the large majority of them very small in size (91.0% have less than 100 inhabitants).

A phenomenon which conditions both the economic structure and the provision of services in rural areas is the growing volume of daily mobility flows (commuting). According to the 2001 Population Census, 37.8% of employed people in Galicia worked in a different municipality to the one where they reside, a percentage which increased to 59.4% in 2021. Mobility throughout the Atlantic Corridor, the most dynamic and urbanized axis of the region, and the nearby rural areas is notable, but the attraction of the two inland provincial capitals (Lugo and Ourense) and certain county centres is also observed (López-Iglesias et al., 2018).

Digitalisation and Smart Ruralities

4G coverage reached almost 100% of Galicia's population settlements in 2019, but with varying quality. Coverage of satellite access is 100%. Furthermore, 84% of settlements had fibre-optic trunk networks in their surroundings in 2018, a fundamental element for deploying the 5G network, which has started from 2020 (Government of Spain, 2020). According to the official statistics, 89% of Galician households had internet access in 2018 (91% in Spain), almost all of them (88%) with broadband access. The percentage of rural households with broadband access was slightly lower (76%), although the strong increase in recent years (OSIMGA, 2019).

In terms of the real level of digitalisation, 70% of rural Galician households used the internet in the past three months in 2018, with the overall percentage at 80% in Galicia and 87% in Spain. This percentage masks a significant rift based on age and educational level, such that in rural households with people under the age of 45 and with a higher educational level (secondary education or above) the use of the internet in the past three months exceeds 90% (OSIMGA, 2019). The main reasons cited for not using the internet in rural areas are the lack of need (57% of households that do not use internet), followed by a lack of knowledge (1/3). The cost of the equipment and the service represents an obstacle for 10% and the lack of availability of the service is only cited as a reason by 1.7% (OSIMGA, 2019). As such, the lower use detected in rural areas appears to be due less and less to technological barriers and more to other problems: suitability of the services to needs, lack of knowledge about the possibilities of digitalisation and abilities to take advantage of them – particularly among the older and/or less educated population.

In the business sphere, the level of digitalisation of key sectors of rural Galicia is still low. The implementation of Industry 4.0 has barely occurred in the forestry sector and the familiarity of companies from this sector with emerging technologies is low. The diagnosis is similar in the agriculture and livestock sector and in the agri-food industry, although with nuances based on company size (IGAPE, 2017).

Inequalities and Social Well-being

As occurs in general in EU countries, the gender gap in employment rates is greater in rural areas of Galicia than in urban areas, but the differences are moderate. In addition, in the last decade the gap between the male and female employment rate has tended to reduce: while it amounted to 12 percentage points in Galicia in 2010 (14 in rural areas), in 2019 it had fallen to 7 points in both cases (IGE, 2023). Despite this recent improvement, overall, the data corroborate the limited employment opportunities for women in rural areas. The reduction of the gender gap in the recent period is partly related to greater female rural emigration.

The percentage of people at risk of poverty or social exclusion has reduced slightly in Galicia in the last decade, standing at 19.2% in 2021. This rate has traditionally been somewhat higher in rural areas, but in recent years it records values similar and even lower than the regional average (18.2% in 2021) (IGE, 2023). Life expectancy at birth in rural areas is 82.6 years and the high ageing of the population means that the weight of pensions and other social transfers in Gross Disposable Income (39.8%) is clearly above the Galician average (35.6%), with a notable increase over the last two decades (IGE, 2023).

Land-use Change

Land-use data show that farmers currently only manage 29% of the surface of Galicia, and only 21% is devoted to crops and pastures. Of the remaining 71%, 41% is forested or abandoned land in the hands of non-agricultural owners, 23% corresponds to communal lands and 7% is devoted to urban use, infrastructure, and other non-agricultural land. This is a very different situation to the one 60 years ago, when the area devoted to crops, grassland and livestock pasture comprised half of the territory. This is combined with a strong division of ownership: there are currently more than 1.7 million landowners, the vast majority of the regional population (2.7 million) (López-Iglesias et al., 2013).

These overall data on land use mask growing internal disparities which can be summarised as the existence of three different rural Galicias: rural urbanised and forested, characteristic of the Atlantic Corridor, the coastal strip and other peri-urban municipalities; active rural, composed of inland counties with recent expansion and a high weight of agricultural land (crops and pastures); and abandoned rural, defined by the strong weight of shrubland, characteristic of mountainous areas (Corbelle & Crecente, 2014a). These three groups generally correspond to the three rural Galicias which are also portrayed by the demographic and socioeconomic indicators (Fig. 1).

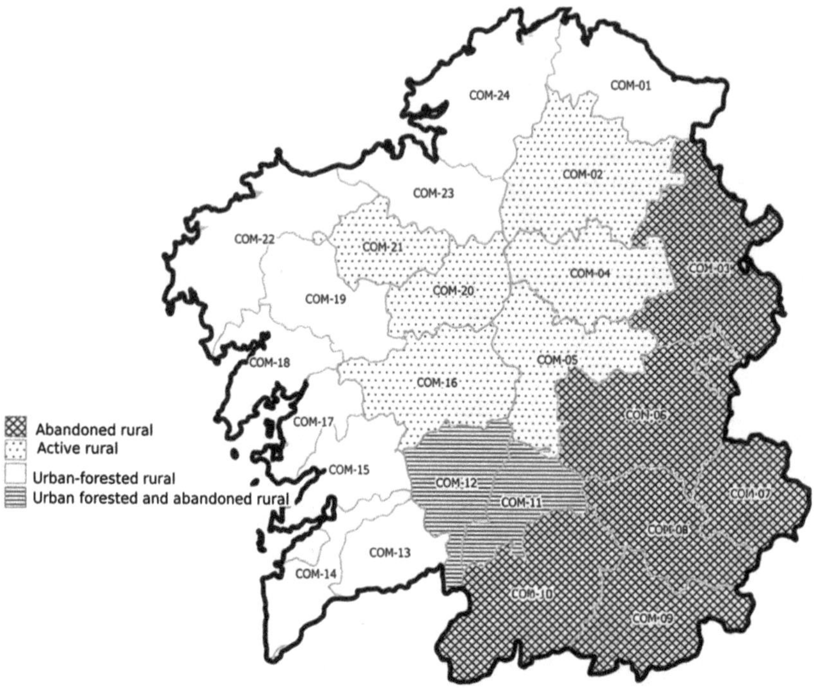

Fig. 1 Typology of the rural areas of Galicia. *Source* Díaz-Varela et al. (2019)

The current panorama is the result of important land-use changes over the past half century and specifically in recent decades, which can be summarised in three phenomena: forestation, urbanisation and abandonment. Wooded forest areas recorded a notable expansion and currently occupy 35% of the surface area. Other relevant changes were the conversion of areas of seminatural vegetation to pastures, the inverse phenomenon resulting from the abandonment of agricultural land, and the occupation of land for urban and industrial uses (Corbelle & Crecente, 2014a, 2014b; Fernández & Corbelle, 2018).

In the geography of Galicia, current land use follows a gradient from coastal areas in the northwest to the mountainous areas in the east, where the abandonment of land is concentrated. Forestation also follows a northwest-southeast gradient, which affects the type of forest species. In the northwest, the lower-altitude areas are dominated by fast-growing species (particularly *Eucalyptus spp.*), while the highest-altitude areas of the southeast are mainly occupied by autochthonous trees, generally without commercial exploitation (Corbelle & Tubío, 2018). In low-intensity agricultural systems, abandonment is associated with the loss of traditional, environmentally valuable landscapes. In addition, the expansion of vegetation linked to abandonment increases the risk of forest fires (Sil et al., 2019; Montiel et al., 2019).

Environment and Ecosystem Services

The main environmental problem faced by rural areas in Galicia are forest fires. The area burned annually stands at 18,000 ha on average in the last 15 years and the number of fires at 3,200 annually. This chronic problem over the past five decades is closely linked to land-use changes and the absence of land-use planning. More recently, to this we must add the influence of climate change, which aggravates extreme events (Montiel et al., 2019).

Other important environmental problems are related to the intensification of livestock farming in certain areas and the management of liquid manure, the spread of plastics of agricultural origin and the loss of animal and plant biodiversity (Soto et al., 2016). The proliferation of invasive species is also related to climate change. At the same time, climate change forecasts envisage important changes in the productivity of a range of crops.

Water pollution does not appear to be a significant problem, with bodies of water generally in good health: 87% of surface water and almost 86% of groundwater is of good quality (< 25 NO_3 mg/L), although this percentage has decreased slightly in the past ten years. On the other hand, Galician agriculture is not highly demanding of groundwater: extraction for agricultural use amounts to less than 1% of the Spanish total. GHG emissions originating from the agricultural sector represent around 10% of the total.

4 Challenges and Opportunities in the Next 20 Years

Based on recent trends, the future of rural areas in Galicia will depend on the capacity of private actors and public policies to make progress on two main challenges (López Iglesias & Pérez Fra, 2017): i) improving employment opportunities, income levels and the provision of services for the population and companies, and ii) respond to the current demands of society, as a basis for employment and income generation. That includes four types of demands:

a. Traditional functions: supply of food, timber, and other raw materials.
b. Production of other goods and services paid by the market: handcrafts and local industry, renewable energy, tourism and leisure, etc.
c. Environmental functions: preservation of landscape, water, air and soil quality, biodiversity, climate change mitigation.
d. Social-territorial functions: conservation of heritage and contribution to territorial balance.

Of these four types of demands, the dynamics of the first two will depend on the capacity of the rural population and companies to offer products with adequate quality and price conditions. However, the other two types of functions (environmental and socio-territorial) are not remunerated by the market, as they are public goods. This means that their provision, and the effects on the local population, will depend on public policies (Andrade & Vázquez, 2016).

This determines the main economic and environmental challenges for rural areas in Galicia over the next two decades. Adequate fulfilment of the first type of functions involves resolving the structural deficiencies of the agricultural sector, in particular addressing the problem of land use and land management, and further development of the agri-food industry. In this same area, pending challenges also include the improvement of forest management, species diversification and the consolidation of industries involving the second transformation of timber. Opportunities offered by demand trends include the potential for the development of organic farming, currently limited to 3.6% of the utilised agricultural area but with important growth in the last 10 years (López Iglesias, 2019b).

In relation to the second group of functions, the challenge is to advance in the diversification of the local business fabric and/or the activities of the resident population. In this regard it is important to stress the growing importance of commuting for work reasons, a phenomenon that will continue to grow over the next 20 years. On the other hand, Galicia's rural areas have great potential for renewable energy, especially wind and hydropower, but also biomass energy (Andrade & Vázquez, 2016).

About environmental functions, in Galicia just 11.9% of the surface area lies in Natura 2000 areas and 1.9% has been declared a Natural Park. This protected area, with calls for it to be increased, offers an opportunity for the provision of ecosystem services, and must also serve to generate new employment and income opportunities for the local population.

Following these challenges and opportunities, we can underscore four issues which will condition the future of rural areas in Galicia in the 2040 horizon (Fernández & Peón, 2017; López Iglesias, 2019a):

a. The role of the agri-food and forestry sectors and of other activities in the economic future of the "three rural Galicias".
b. The management of complementarities and trade-offs between activities and land uses, making land-use planning a core issue.
c. The habitat structure and the model for territorial organisation, provision of services and governance of rural areas. Regarding this, the high dispersity of the population constitutes a challenge, as does the adaptation of the administrative and government structure to a different reality to the one of the mid nineteenth century (when the current municipal map was established).
d. The need to organise new relations between the rural population and rural space and between landowners and land users. The basic fact that needs to be considered is the increasingly complex relationship between three groups which up until the mid-twentieth century could almost be considered one and the same: residents in each municipality, landowners and actors interested in exploiting the land.

Based on the online questionnaires completed by MAP members and other actors, and the subsequent re-evaluation of the results at MAP meetings, we can highlight the importance of the challenges related to the 10 objectives of the 2021-2027 CAP from the Galician perspective. *Fostering vibrant rural areas* and *Ensuring a fair income for farmers* are considered the most important challenges. There is also consensus on the less relevant challenges: *Increasing the competitiveness of companies* and *Climate change action* are the lowest rated by both groups (Table 1).

Table 1 Score obtained for the 2021-2027 CAP objectives (Maximum 5/ Minimum 1)

Challenges	*Average MAP*	*Average external actors*
Fostering vibrant rural areas	4.4	4.6
Ensuring a fair income to farmers	4.2	4.5
Supporting generational renewal of farms	4.2	4.4
Fostering knowledge and innovation	4.1	4.2
Protecting food and health quality	4.1	4.3
Environmental care	3.9	4.3
Preserving landscapes and biodiversity	3.8	4.2
Rebalancing the power in the food chain	3.8	4.5
Increasing the competitiveness of companies	3.5	3.9
Climate change actions	3.5	4.1

Based on the work carried out by the MAP, a list of opportunities comprising 16 items was constructed. These opportunities were prioritised by MAP members and external actors. They are a combination of productive, social, and environmental aspects and a large part of them require public policy decisions or actions (Table 2).

Social actors stress public policies which improve the quality of life in rural areas, as well as the generation of conditions for creating and consolidating economic activities. The strengthening of public services which contribute to making the territory more attractive, making internet access widespread and promoting digitalisation, improving training, and land-use management are among the most rated aspects both by the MAP and the external panel.

Economic diversification is highlighted among the opportunities. However social actors believe that the agriculture and forestry sectors, and the processing industry linked to them, must also play an important role in the future of Galician rural areas, as long as they are capable of progressing towards production models which involve greater environmental sustainability, and which focus on differentiation and quality.

The incorporation of environmental values into productive activities is identified as an opportunity. There is also an explicit reference to the need to remunerate the ecosystem services provided by the agricultural and forestry sectors. The actors believe that this remuneration should be supported by public policies.

Table 2 Opportunities for Galician rural areas in the next 20 years (Maximum 5/Minimum 1)

Opportunities	*Average MAP*	*Average external actors*
Increasing the attractiveness of rural areas by strengthening basic public services (health, education, welfare services for the elderly, welfare services for children, etc.)	4.8	4.5
Improving internet access and promoting digitalisation	4.5	4.5
Develop the agri-food and forestry industry oriented towards higher value-added products	4.4	4.5
Improving productive use of land	4.3	4.7
Improving the environmental sustainability of agricultural and forestry systems	4.2	4.3
Economic diversification of rural areas	4.2	4.0
Limiting individual landowners' actions through land use management mechanisms	4.1	4.5
Improve the training of people working in the agricultural and forestry sector and of the rural population as a whole	4.1	4.2
Remuneration of ecosystem services provided by agricultural and forestry producers through public policies	4.0	4.2
Curbing the disappearance of farms	4.0	3.9
Product differentiation and quality as a basis for improving the competitiveness of agri-food and forestry production	3.9	4.4
Exploiting the potential of the Galician rural areas to produce renewable energy	3.9	3.3
New residents of urban origin and/or immigrants and returnees	3.5	3.8
Increasing the role of rural women by helping them overcome traditional gender roles	3.3	3.7
Improving roads and other transport networks	3.1	2.7
Concentration of the rural population in county and municipal centres of a certain size	2.3	3.0

This list of challenges and opportunities for the future does not include demographic problems. The reason is that, while acknowledging the gravity of demographic trends, the participants consider that these are the consequence rather than the cause of the weaknesses of rural areas. Therefore, limiting or reverting these trends will not depend on demographics, but rather on socioeconomic factors, mainly improving employment opportunities and access to services.

5 Desirable Future for 2040

The MAP members' vision of the desirable future for the Galician rural areas in 2040, for each of the nine key topics identified,[3] is summarised in the 29 elements listed in order of priority (Table 3).

The results confirm the relevance of two topics (Dynamics of the agri-food and forestry sectors, Governance and participation). The desirable rural for 2040 designed by the MAP includes a significant number of elements related to these topics, and in prominent positions. Specifically, among the first 10 prioritized elements there are 3 related to the dynamics of the agri-food and forestry sectors, and one (in second place) related to improving the governance of rural areas.

In the top 10 positions we also find elements of desirable rural for 2040 linked to six other of the nine topics. Among those elements are a dynamic rural from a demographic perspective which manages to maintain the small villages; a rural with a land-use planning that rationalises land use and addresses environmental criteria; rural areas which manage to take economic advantage from the ecosystem services they provide; well-connected rural areas with widespread broadband access; a rural with services that differ from urban areas, but which allow for an adequate quality of life.

6 Actions to Achieve the Desirable Rural in 2040

As a result of the online questionnaire to MAP members and the survey of external actors, we drew up a list of 52 actions considered important to move towards the desirable future. This list was expanded to 65 proposals at the second MAP meeting. Table 4 shows the results of the prioritisation by MAP members, with the list of the 22 actions that obtained the highest score.

The proposed actions have a very uneven level of specificity, and many of them would need more precise elaboration. But their interest derives from the fact that they reflect the vision of the MAP members.

[3] This includes the eight topics analyzed in section 3, plus an additional one (Governance and participation) that was added for future foresight as a proposal from MAP members.

Table 3 Elements of the desirable future for the Galician rural areas in 2040 (maximum 45 points)

Topic	*Vision*	*Total score*
Dynamics of the agri-food and forestry sectors	Rural areas which produce raw materials sustainably, with differentiated, healthy, high-quality products linked to the territory	29
Governance and participation	Population that can participate socially and is involved in the governance of its territories	26
Dynamics of the agri-food and forestry sectors	Forest management that diversifies species, to achieve higher environmental performance and increased production of high-quality timber	22
Demographic shift: decrease and ageing of the rural population	Dynamic rural areas from a demographic perspective	20
Land-use change	Land-use planning that rationalises land use and addresses environmental criteria	20
Deagrarianisation and limitations on the economic diversification of rural areas	More developed agri-food industry	18
Demographic shift: decrease and ageing of the rural population	Rural areas able to maintain their small villages to ensure adequate management and conservation of the environment	18
Deagrarianisation and limitations on the economic diversification of rural areas	Rural areas that maintain/increase the current level of agricultural activity	17
Dynamics of the agri-food and forestry sectors	Better use of the territory by farms	14
Digitalisation and smart ruralities	Well-connected rural areas with widespread broadband access	13
Environment and ecosystem services	Rural areas which manage to take economic advantage (employment and income generation) from the ecosystem services they provide	13
Infrastructure and basic services	Services that differ from urban areas, but which allow for an adequate quality of life	13
Deagrarianisation and limitations on the economic diversification of rural areas	Increased production of renewable energy	10
Infrastructure and basic services	Higher level of publicly provided population services	10
Infrastructure and basic services	Local governments sharing services and infrastructures to take advantage of synergies and offer improved quality of life	8
Dynamics of the agri-food and forestry sectors	Food sovereignty	8

(continued)

Table 3 (continued)

Topic	*Vision*	*Total score*
Inequalities and social well-being	Public services which permit work-life balance and gender equality	8
Land-use change	Lower percentage of abandoned land than at present	8
Environment and ecosystem services	Rural areas harnessing climate change concerns to give value to and promote extensive livestock production systems	8
Deagrarianisation and limitations on the economic diversification of rural areas	Greater presence of private companies providing services to the rural population	7
Governance and participation	There is cooperation between SMEs for putting development strategies into practice	7
Dynamics of the agri-food and forestry sectors	Short distribution channels for agricultural products have greater weight	7
Land-use change	Value environmental land use and take it into account in the design of public policies	5
Demographic shift: decrease and ageing of the rural population	Differentiated demographic dynamics (peripheral/intermediate/remote municipalities) are reduced	3
Demographic shift: decrease and ageing of the rural population	Less population dispersion	3
Deagrarianisation and limitations on the economic diversification of rural areas	More companies from the tourism sector	3
Infrastructure and basic services	Rural areas that have overcome the rural/urban confrontation	2
Environment and ecosystem services	Areas subject to environmental protection are managed with the participation of the local population	1
Dynamics of the agri-food and forestry sectors	Rural areas that are part of a society with urban consumers who understand the agricultural reality	1

Improving basic services–education, health, social services, culture, sport and mobility – is a course of action which most actors prioritise. They included in this group internet access, although this element constitutes also an important condition for consolidating business activity in rural areas. In relation to the issue of quality of life, the measures which permit work-life balance are also among the prioritised actions, and social actors consider this to be an especially important item for the viability of

Table 4 Actions required to achieve the desirable rural in 2040 (maximum 45 points)

Action	*Total score*
Actions to improve basic services, with special attention to internet access, education, health, social services, culture, sport, and mobility	27
Actions aimed at facilitating the installation of young people of non-rural origin and measures to incentivise the permanence of the current population	19
Land-use planning and management	16
Changes in forest management	12
Actions to support agri-food industry and service sector based on the social economy	12
Measures which permit work-life balance with a special emphasis on farmers	12
Actions aiming at the sustainable use of abandoned land	12
Actions to improve the competitiveness and/or diversification of the agri-food and forestry sectors	12
Actions to improve governance and social participation in the management of rural development. Further promotion of the bottom-up approach in public policies through the LEADER method	12
Creation of a strategic plan to foster innovation and product differentiation based on quality, including actions aimed at improving training and technical consultancy, as well as the establishment of economic and tax incentives	11
Creation of a housing bank and a land bank aimed at both residents and non-residents	11
Measures to promote renewable energies and to use by-products, waste, and other non-food raw materials to foster the development of the bioeconomy	10
Conservation and enhancement of the value of the territory in terms of heritage, art, and culture	8
Improving the quality of life through the creation and renewal of services, facilities, and infrastructure	8
Implementation of a tax policy to encourage the establishment of businesses in rural areas	7
Promotion of remote work in rural areas	7
Actions to promote the multifunctional use of forests	7
Actions to utilise and rationalise farm by-products. Specific measures for liquid manure	6
Support measures for owners of sites of environmental value to ensure their conservation	6
Improvement of the quality of life	6
Reduction of bureaucracy	6
Adaptation of land use to the different realities of rural Galicia	6

farms. The inclusion of this type of action on the list of priorities contrasts with the lack of importance given to the topic of *Inequalities and social well-being* when defining the vision of the desirable rural.

To progress towards achieving a dynamic rural from a demographic perspective, actions aimed at facilitating the installation of young people of non-rural origin are suggested, as well as measures to increase the permanence of the current population. Furthermore, it is presented more as a desire than as a set of detailed specific actions to achieve this. In fact, the only concrete proposal prioritised is the creation of a housing bank and a land bank aimed at both the resident and non-resident population.

The need to improve land-use planning and management is also highlighted. As such, the MAP once again points to land-use planning, the sustainable use of abandoned land and to changes in current forest management as important areas of action.

Consistent with the vision of the desirable rural, the agricultural and forestry sectors occupy a prominent position in the prioritisation of the actions. In addition to agriculture and forestry productions being the main sectors benefited by land-use planning and management, the importance given to these sectors is once again made clear. Thus, within the top 10 it is proposed as well to improve the competitiveness and/or diversification of the agri-food and forestry sectors. Also, worth stressing is the disagreement of part of the MAP with the current forestry management model (focused on fast growing species), which appears as an obstacle to progress towards the desirable future.

Economic diversification also appears as a clear course of action. The MAP points to the need to implement measures to support agri-food industry and service sector based on the social economy or the creation of a strategic plan to foster innovation and differentiation of products based on quality, which includes actions aimed at improving training and technical consultancy, as well as establishing economic and tax incentives.

Finally, the improvement of governance and social participation in managing rural development is an element considered to be important, pointing to the need to give greater impetus to the bottom-up approach in public policy through the LEADER[4] method.

[4] For a better understanding of the LEADER methodology and its impact on European rural areas,the Special Report of European Court of Auditors LEADER and community-led local developmentfacilitate local engagement, but additional benefits still

7 Conclusions

MAP members agree with the vision of the "three rural Galicias" proposed by the USC team (see Fig. 1), and therefore consider policies adapted to these different realities to be necessary. Starting from that, the Galician MAP shows a high level of agreement with the ten 2021-2027 CAP objectives. Among them, two are highlighted as the main challenges: *Fostering vibrant rural areas* and *Ensuring a fair income for farmers*. In the review of the key trends in Galician rural areas and to design the desirable future, MAP members consider it necessary to add two new topics to the seven established in the SHERPA project: *Dynamics of the agri-food and forestry sectors* and *Governance and participation*.

Based on these results, we can summarise the main challenges of the Galician rural areas over the next 20 years. In the productive sphere, there is the resolution of the structural deficiencies of the agricultural sector, the consolidation and diversification of forestry production, the development of the agri-food industry and the timber chain and taking advantage of opportunities in other activities such as renewable energy. Regarding social conditions and quality of life, we have the improvement of services and also of the working conditions for the young population and women, as requirements for curbing the depopulation of rural areas. Finally, in the environmental realm, we can stress the need to tackle problems such as forest fires, the effects of climate change and the loss of biodiversity, with the MAP members viewing the European Green Deal as an opportunity for the Galician rural areas in this regard.

The opportunities identified cover productive, social and environmental aspects, highlighting the following: economically strengthening and diversifying rural areas, by taking advantage of the potential of the agricultural and forestry sectors and developing the agri-food industry; new sources of income linked to the sustainable use of natural resources; and the improvement of infrastructure and services as a means to increasing the attractiveness of rural areas.

The Galician MAP desires a future for rural areas of the region in 2040 in which: (i) these areas produce healthy and high-quality food and raw materials in a sustainable way, with further development of the local agri-food processing industry; (ii) rural society is empowered and involved in

not sufficiently demonstrated can be consulted (https://op.europa.eu/webpub/eca/special-reports/leader-10-2022/en/).

the governance of its territories; (iii) small villages are maintained as a guarantee of sustainable landscape management; (iv) land-use planning leads to rational and sustainable use of land, taking advantage of the valuation of ecosystem services; (v) and finally where there is truly universal and high-quality access to broadband internet for rural communities.

Regarding to the actions required to advance towards this desirable future, the initial proposals of the MAP stress policies in three areas: adequate provision of basic services and improving the quality of life of the population in a highly dispersed rural habitat; consolidating the agricultural and forestry sectors and supporting new entrepreneurial initiatives in other activities; and improving governance and social participation.

Acknowledgements We are grateful for the work developed by the MAP Members. In addition, we would also like to thank the collaboration of the people who responded to the online survey launched in July 2020.

Funding This work was supported by the SHERPA project (https://rural-interfaces.eu). SHERPA receives funding from the European Union's Horizon 2020 research and innovation programme under grant agreement number 862448.

References

Andrade Calvo, J.M., Vázquez Rodríguez, M.X. (2016). *Novas demandas para o rural galego*. Document 18/2016. Foro Económico de Galicia. https://api.foroeconomicodegalicia.es/uploads/FEG/originals/0a324f64-94cc-4362-a624-336c76fc6083.pdf

Atance, I., Garcia Corral, A., Martínez Jávega, M. T., Pujol, R., & Urruela, J. (2010). La población rural en España: un enfoque a escala municipal. *Economía Agraria y Recursos Naturales, 10*(1), 35–57. https://doi.org/10.7201/earn.2010.01.03

Corbelle Rico, E., & Crecente Maseda, R. (2014a). Urbanización, forestación e abandono. Cambios recentes na paisaxe de Galicia, 1985-2005. *Revista Galega de. Economía, 23*(1), 35–52. https://doi.org/10.15304/rge.23.1.2445

Corbelle Rico, E., & Crecente Maseda, R. (2014b). Evaluating IRENA indicator "Risk of Farmland Abandonment" on a low spatial scale level: The case of Galicia (Spain). *Land Use Policy, 38*, 9–15. https://doi.org/10.1016/j.landusepol.2013.10.013

Corbelle Rico, E., & Tubío Sánchez, J. M. (2018). Productivismo y abandono: dos caras de la transición forestal en Galicia (España), 1966-2009. *Bosque, 39*, 457–467. https://doi.org/10.4067/S0717-92002018000300457

Banco de España. (2021). La distribución espacial de la población en España y sus implicaciones económicas. In *Informe anual 2020* (pp. 269-318). Banco de España. https://www.bde.es/f/webbde/SES/Secciones/Publicaciones/PublicacionesAnuales/InformesAnuales/20/Fich/InfAnual_2020-Cap4.pdf

Díaz-Varela, E., Ferreira-Golpe, M. A., García-Arias, A. I., Pérez-Fra, M. M., López-Iglesias, E., & Rodríguez-Morales, B. (2019). *Estratexia Galega de Infraestrutura Verde. 7.1. Estratexias para o aproveitamento das potencialidades da infraestrutura verde para o desenvolvemento socioeconómico.* Unpublished.

Dubert, I. (2008). Vejez, familia y reproducción social en España, siglos XVIII-XX. *Revista de Demografía Histórica*, 26(2), 87122. https://www.adeh.org/revista/2008,%202/DUBERT.pdf

European Commission. (2024). *The long-term vision for the EU's rural areas: key achievements and ways forward.* COM(2024) 450 final. https://eur-lex.europa.eu/legal-content/EN/TXT/PDF/?uri=CELEX:52024DC0450

Fernández, M., & Peón, D. (2017). *Desafíos dunha sociedade avellentada e en declive: desequilibrios territoriais e prestación de servizos*. In *Document 20/2017*. Galicia. https://api.foroeconomicodegalicia.es/uploads/FEG/originals/b7abd754-ae3b-42f3-9417-eb5dff9a7085.pdf

Fernández Nogueira, D., & Corbelle Rico, E. (2018). Land Use Changes in Iberian Peninsula, 1990-2012. *Land*, *7*(3), 99. https://doi.org/10.3390/land7030099

Government of Spain. (2020). *Datos particularizados de cobertura de banda ancha en Galicia a 30 de junio de 2019. Ministerio de Asuntos Económicos y Transformación Digital.*. https://avancedigital.gob.es/banda-ancha/cobertura/datos2019/Galicia.pdf

Guimarey-Fernández, B., Ferreira-Golpe, M., Pérez-Fra, M., García-Arias, A. I., & López-Iglesias, E. (2021). *Long-term vision for rural areas: contribution from 20 science-society-policy platforms. Map Position Paper Galician Rural Interfaces.*. https://rural-interfaces.eu/wp-content/uploads/2021/02/MAP_Position-Paper_ES_Galicia_LTVRA.pdf

IGAPE. (2017). *Oportunidades Industria 4.0 Galicia. Diagnóstico sectorial: Alimentación e bio.* IGAPE-Xunta de Galicia. http://www.xornadas.igape.es/gl/component/k2/item/1529-oportunidades-industria-4-0-en-galicia

IGE. (2023). *Panorama rural urbano.* https://www.ige.gal/web/mostrar_seccion.jsp?idioma=gl&codigo=0701

Lasanta, T., Nadal-Romero, E., & Arnáez, J. (2015). Managing abandoned farmland to control the impact of re-vegetation on the environment. The state of the art in Europe. *Environmental Science & Policy, 52*, 99–109. https://doi.org/10.1016/j.envsci.2015.05.012

López Iglesias, E. (2019a). Realidade actual e retos futuros do medio rural en Galicia. In *Pasado, presente e futuro do mundo rural. Feiraco, un modelo cooperativo de 50 anos* (pp. 75-106). Editorial Galaxia. https://www.researchgate.net/publication/334168442_Realidade_actual_e_retos_futuros_do_medio_rural_en_Galicia

López Iglesias, E. (2019b). O sector agrario e agroalimentario en Galicia; balance das transformacións desde a integración europea, 1986-2016. *Revista Galega de Economía, 28*(3), 1–20. https://doi.org/10.15304/rge.28.3.6168

López Iglesias, E., & Pérez Fra, M. (2004). Axuste agrario e despoboación rural: as tendencias recentes en Galicia. *Grial. Revista Galega de Cultura, 162*, 36–43.

López Iglesias, E., & Pérez Fra, M. (2017). *Unha estratexia para a Galicia rural do século XXI. Diagnóstico e propostas para o debate*. Document 22/2017. Foro Económico de Galicia. https://doi.org/10.13140/RG.2.2.28021.27365

López-Iglesias, E., Peón, D., & Rodríguez-Álvarez, J. (2018). Mobility innovations for sustainability and cohesion of rural areas: A transport model and public investment analysis for Valdeorras (Galicia, Spain). *Journal of Cleaner Production, 172*, 3520–3534. https://doi.org/10.1016/j.jclepro.2017.05.149

López-Iglesias, E., Sineiro-García, F., & Lorenzana-Fernández, R. (2013). Processes of farmland abandonment: land use change and structural adjustment in Galicia (Spain). In D. Ortiz-Miranda, A. M. Moragues-Faus, & E. Arnalte-Alegre (Eds.), *Agriculture in Mediterranean Europe. Between Old and New Paradigms* (pp. 91–120). https://doi.org/10.1108/S1057-1922(2013)0000019007

Molinero, F., & Alario, M. (2022). *Una mirada geográfica a la España rural. Revives.*. https://revives.es/wp-content/uploads/2022/05/UNA-MIRADA-GEOGRAFICA-A-LA-ESPANA-RURAL-Revives_Alta-resolucion.pdf

Montiel Molina, C., Karlsson Martín, O., & Galiana Martín, L. (2019). Regional fire scenarios in Spain: Linking landscape dynamics and fire regime for wildfire risk management. *Journal of Environmental Management, 233*, 427–439. https://doi.org/10.1016/j.jenvman.2018.12.066

OSIMGA. (2019). *A Sociedade da Información no rural galego.* Xunta de Galicia. http://www.osimga.gal/sites/w_osimga/files/documentos/201911_rural_2019.pdf

Sil, A., Fernandes, P. M., Rodrigues, A. P., Alonso, J. M., Honrado, J. P., Perera, A., & Azevedo, J. C. (2019). Farmland abandonment decreases the fire regulation capacity and the fire protection ecosystem service in mountain landscapes. *Ecosystem Services, 36*, 100908. https://doi.org/10.1016/j.ecoser.2019.100908

Sineiro García, F. (2009). Los complejos de actividades agroalimentarias y de la madera. In *Proyecto Galicia. Economía. Tomo LXI. Los sectores y actividades productivas* (pp. 19–55). Hércules.

Soto Fernández, D., Infante-Amate, J., Guzmán, G. I., Cid, A., Aguilera, E., García, R., & González de Molina, M. (2016). The social metabolism of biomass in Spain, 1900-2008: From food to feed-oriented changes in the agro-systems. *Ecological Economics, 128*, 130–138. https://doi.org/10.1016/j.ecolecon.2016.04.017

Toxo, R., & García Arias, A. I. (2018). Caracterización das migracións no rural galego do século XXI. *Semata, 30*, 123–143. https://doi.org/10.15304/s.30.5365

Valdês Paços, B., López Iglesias, E. (2008). *Análise do complexo de produción agroalimentario galego a través das táboas input-output*. Fundación Caixa Galicia-Centro de Investigación Económica y Financiera. https://doi.org/10.13140/2.1.1428.9283

CHAPTER 9

What Is the Future of Mountain Areas? Participatory Scenario Building for the 2050 Horizon in the Northern Apennines and Corsica

Tarek Allali, Sabrina Tomasi, Manola Colabianchi, Francesco Felici, Michele Moretti, Chiara Mignani, Marie Noëlle Ottavi, Jean-Michel Sorba, Olivier Mora, and Gianluca Brunori

1 Introduction

Mountain and rural areas constitute essential pillars of Europe's socio-economic fabric. Indeed, the rich material and immaterial cultural heritage, the traditional know-how and the local productions, the biodiversity, the human relationships shaping the human and social capital, and the related rural-urban interconnections characterise the diverse landscape

T. Allali (✉) · S. Tomasi · M. Colabianchi · F. Felici · M. Moretti · C. Mignani · G. Brunori
Department of Agriculture, Food and Environment, University of Pisa, Pisa, Italy
e-mail: tarek.allali@agr.unipi.it

D. Barjolle et al. (eds.), *Innovation and the Future of Rural Development in Europe*,
https://doi.org/10.1007/978-3-032-22570-2_9

of Europe's rural and mountainous areas. Nevertheless, these regions face multifaceted challenges, such as depopulation and abandonment, economic stagnation, environmental degradation, and inadequate access to essential services. In this regard, more recently, there has been progressive attention, at the European level and—to a certain extent—also at the national levels, to support these areas—which several times correspond to inner areas—in facing their specific challenges in terms of policy, strategies and dedicated funding.[1]

S. Tomasi
e-mail: sabrina.tomasi@agr.unipi.it

M. Colabianchi
e-mail: manola.colabianchi@phd.unipi.it

F. Felici
e-mail: francesco.felici75@gmail.com

M. Moretti
e-mail: michele.moretti@unipi.it

C. Mignani
e-mail: chiara.mignani@agr.unipi.it

G. Brunori
e-mail: gianluca.brunori@unipi.it

M. Moretti
Department of Engineering Management, University of Antwerp, Antwerp, Belgium

M. N. Ottavi · O. Mora
INRAe, Paris, France
e-mail: marie.ottavi@inrae.fr

O. Mora
e-mail: olivier.mora@inrae.fr

J.-M. Sorba
INRAe, Corsica, France
e-mail: jean-michel.sorba@inrae.fr

[1] In the case of Italy, it is worth mentioning the National Strategy for Inner Areas by Barca, F., Casavola, P., and Lucatelli, S. (2014). Strategia nazionale per le aree interne: definizione, obiettivi, strumenti e governance (SNAI) edited by

Such policy initiatives put efforts to boost agricultural sustainability and innovation, enhance rural infrastructure and connectivity, support, maintain and increase economic liveliness, improve access to education, healthcare and mobility services, safeguard cultural heritage, and promote sustainable tourism. These are often supported by EU funding mechanisms, such as the Common Agricultural Policy (CAP),[2] the European Structural and Investment Funds (ESIF) and the Cohesion Policy,[3] and Horizon Europe,[4] which aim to catalyse transformative change in mountain and rural landscapes. Moreover, some of them aim to emphasise the importance of participatory governance and partnership-based approaches, calling for the engagement of diverse stakeholders, including local authorities, civil society organisations, and private sector actors. By fostering collaboration and co-creation, the objective is to leverage collective intelligence and effectively mobilise resources.

Fabrizio Barca, Paola Casavola e Sabrina Lucatelli. The SNAI is a territorial policy aimed at improving the quality of citizen services and economic opportunities in inner territories at risk of marginalisation, first contemplated in the 2014 National Reform Programme (NRP) and defined in the 2014–2020 Partnership Agreement. The strategy was also confirmed in the 2021–2027 cycle. More info is available at this link: https://politichecoesione.governo.it/it/politica-di-coesione/strategie-tematiche-e-territoriali/strategie-territoriali/strategia-nazionale-aree-interne-snai/ (last retrieved: 30/03/2024). As for France, a relevant policy intervention is represented by the Mountain Law: LOI n° 2016-1888 du 28 décembre 2016 de modernisation, de développement et de protection des territoires de montagne, available at: https://www.legifrance.gouv.fr/jorf/id/JORFTEXT000033717812 (last retrieved: 30/03/2024).

[2] Common Agricultural Policy (CAP) and its contribution to the Long Term Vision for Rural Areas (LTVRA) available at: https://agriculture.ec.europa.eu/news/contribution-cap-strategic-plans-long-term-vision-eus-rural-areas-2023-09-21_en (last retrieved: 30/03/2024).

[3] 3 EU Cohesion Policy: European Structural and Investment Funds supported SMEs, employment of millions of people and clean energy production, available at: https://ec.europa.eu/commission/presscorner/detail/en/ip_23_389 and https://ec.europa.eu/regional_policy/policy/what/investment-policy_en (last retrieved: 30/03/2024).

[4] Horizon Europe, research and innovation funding programme, available at: https://research-and-innovation.ec.europa.eu/funding/funding-opportunities/funding-programmes-and-open-calls/horizon-europe_en (last retrieved: 30/03/2024).

The Long-Term Vision for Rural Areas

One of the most relevant policy initiatives is the so-called European Long-Term Vision for Rural Areas (LTVRA), launched in 2021.[5] The initiative outlines a strategic framework for the creation of future perspectives for rural areas towards 2040 based on holistic and place-based approaches able to empower rural communities to thrive socially, economically, and environmentally. The strategy is based on foresight and wide consultations with citizens and other actors in rural areas and focuses on four action areas to make rural areas (1) stronger, (2) connected, (3) resilient, and (4) prosperous, all related to 10 shared action goals. It originated a series of related initiatives, such as the Rural Pact and a Rural Action Plan.[6] In the LTVRA, rural areas are considered vibrant living spaces: there is a need to build strategies that allow for maintaining and fostering social cohesion, enhance access to quality services and create opportunities for meaningful inclusive employment, particularly for youth and women, people with disabilities and at-risk of social exclusion. The rural heritage and the cultural diversity form part of the vision as they are seen as essential components of Europe's identity. Therefore, preserving and valorising them through initiatives that foster local communities' cultural awareness, preservation of natural and cultural heritage—including traditional practices—and the promotion of culture-based sustainable and responsible tourism is necessary. This also relates to economic diversification and innovation: rural areas can become hubs for entrepreneurship, creativity, and technological advancement while pursuing rural development through sustainable land use and environmental stewardship. This entails promoting agroecological practices, mitigating climate change impacts, and conserving biodiversity.

In this perspective, the European Rural Pact and the European Rural Action Plan represent a collaborative effort to revitalise and empower rural areas across Europe. Both policy initiatives consider inclusive governance and participatory decision-making processes as key pillars to involve rural stakeholders in shaping policies and strategies affecting

[5] Long Term Vision for rural areas: for stronger, connected, resilient, prosperous EU rural areas, available at: https://ec.europa.eu/commission/presscorner/detail/en/IP_21_3162 and https://rural-vision.europa.eu/index_en (last retrieved: 30/03/2024).

[6] Rural Pact and Rural Action Plan: European Commission. (2021). A Long-Term Vision for Rural Areas: Rural Pact. Retrieved from: https://ec.europa.eu/info/sites/default/files/rural-pact-communication_en.pdf.

their communities. This calls for an approach based on accountability, transparency, and responsiveness to the needs and aspirations of rural residents.

Moreover, the Rural Pact prioritises efforts to strengthen rural resilience and vitality through targeted investments and support mechanisms. This includes initiatives to stimulate economic diversification, foster entrepreneurship, and improve access to essential services such as healthcare, education, and digital infrastructure.

As mentioned, at the basis of the LVTRA, the EU Rural Pact and Rural Action Plan are the outcomes of an open public consultation, and several conversations were held through a robust foresight exercise involving European local communities (Bock & Krzysztofowicz, 2021), that aimed to define common actionable goals, which already produced several results after 30 months of activity (European Commission, 2024). Among these results, rural populations were engaged in the rural revitalisation platform launched in 2023 to work in a policy lab to tackle depopulation in rural areas, with over 100 participants and 20 good practices; more than 60 research and innovation (R&I) projects were funded through Horizon EU, addressing rural development drivers. As an example, Horizon EU funded R&I projects for agricultural and rural digitalisation for more than EUR 100 million. Support to 27 rural energy communities has been provided by the dedicated REC Advisory Hub. Initiatives targeting rural youth and childhood, gender balance, migrant inclusion and services for people with disabilities in rural areas have been addressed through dedicated action plans, research projects and networking platforms funded through several instruments. Projects to develop the social economy in rural areas have been supported. Data availability was also improved, also through the launch of an EU rural observatory in 2022. The Rural Pact Community to address the related goals fostered networking, interactions, mutual learning and good practice exchanges at the EU level for rural communities by carrying out several events and establishing thematic groups to tackle specific challenges. The involved members in 2023 were 2350. A Rural toolkit has also been launched to ease access to EU funding for rural areas and optimal combination to EU funding for rural areas (European Commission, 2024).

Foresight Exercises: A Tool to Shape Participatory Rural Policies

The adoption of foresight exercises to shape rural policies at the EU level demonstrates the relevance of such methods to gather useful context-based insights by directly involving rural actors. This might contribute to setting up punctual interventions responding to local needs for the present and the future of these areas.

In general, for many years, foresight and scenario-building techniques have been applied to a wide range of fields (e.g., health, agriculture, security, etc.), at different levels (i.e., local, regional, national, and global), and by many different actors (e.g., universities, research centres, NGOs, etc.) around the world (Andreescu et al., 2013; Bingley, 2014). These are also perceived as a strong tool to communicate uncertainties in decision-making (Kwakkel et al., 2013). Indeed, foresight exercises have been widely applied to policy-making, as they are systematic participatory processes that create collective intelligence about the medium- to long-term future (Störmer et al., 2020).

In this context, scenario techniques support decision-making as they enable the identification of "drivers of change"—namely, the developments that might take place in a certain group/society and that could induce a system's change. Therefore, in this perspective, they play a pivotal role as they allow a systemic understanding of the changing conditions and their potential impacts (Bock & Krzysztofowicz, 2021). By involving and mobilising actors to think about possible futures they also inform present-day decisions and foster joint actions (Störmer et al., 2020).

Scenarios are usually divided into three main categories (Reilly & Willenbockel, 2010; Wiebe et al., 2018):

1. *Predictive scenarios*: these are based on existing knowledge to estimate future conditions. They build their forecast (e.g.: projection as a baseline scenario) by extrapolating the future conditions based on current specific trends (e.g.: long-term forces) and project their forecast accordingly;
2. *Exploratory scenarios*: designed to explore possible futures. They start from the present and investigate the interdependencies of long-term forces in a complex system (e.g. changes in the system);
3. *Normative scenarios based on* a particular desired vision of the future and working backwards in time to identify pathways to that

future. They build the vision by developing narratives for the system to achieve specific goals. Desirable future situations or goals are defined through an agreement that emerges from discussions among relevant actors and stakeholders encompassing participatory components, such as inclusiveness and consensus (Andreescu et al., 2013). This kind of scenario is constructed to intervene in changing and influencing the course of events in an attempt to shape the future and to understand relevant impacts, potential interventions, and their applicability through time (Bingley, 2014; Wuijts et al., 2022).

In general, scenarios lead to a series of assumptions about key relationships and driving forces that describe how the future may develop (Nakicenovic & Swart, 2000). Schoemaker et al. (2013) claim each scenario should offer more than a mere description of a final state but also underlining its dynamic and storyline.

In this sense, the practice of labelling scenarios (e.g., best, acceptable, worst scenario, etc.) as utilised by Önkal et al. (2013), enhances the acceptance of the forecast exercise outcomes and strengthens practitioners' confidence in their predictions and choices.

Following this thread, several EU-funded projects involving a policy-level contribution started including foresight and scenario exercises as ways to involve rural stakeholders in thinking about possible futures (Brunori et al., 2020), as they are found useful to treat complex as well as wicked problems (Navarro et al., 2008).

More recently, the Horizon 2020 project MOVING (Mountain Valorisation through Interconnectedness and Green Growth) undertook a foresight exercise.

This chapter presents and discusses the results of a foresight exercise that took place in 2023 to identify pathways to enhance mountain areas' resilience through an analysis of climate change and socio-economic scenarios in the 2050 horizon. It compares the results from two areas, considering the chestnut flour value chains (VC) from Italy (Tuscany, Northern Apennines) and central Corsica (France).

In line with EU-related policies, this study aims to highlight what challenges and potential actions could be implemented for the future of rural mountain areas by drawing upon the contents emerging from the participatory discussion that took place during the foresight exercises run in the context of the MOVING project. After describing the Methods adopted and the Background contexts from the two investigated chestnut VCs, the Results and the Discussion paragraph focus on the contents emerging from the exercise, discussed according to the ten LTVRA goals. Besides reflections upon the future of the specific VCs, local stakeholders were able to identify potential opportunities and advancements for the future of the mountain area, in addition to the related commitments. Therefore, results provide useful insights to policymakers at the local and EU level, in terms of bottom-up and shared policy recommendations.

2 Background Context

The MOVING Project

The Horizon 2020 MOVING[7] project aims to co-develop relevant policy frameworks for mountainous areas across Europe through bottom-up participatory processes. By taking specific contexts and value chains into consideration and involving the related public-private actors in the conversation, the project establishes the so-called "multi-actor platforms" (MAPs) involving diverse mountain regions from 16 countries. The MAPs are centred around specific value chains that insist at the local level. Two out of these 23 produce chestnut flour: the Northern Apennines[8] and the Corsica VCs.[9]

The project involves researchers from institutions located close to the interested VC to run extended VC analysis and to investigate mountainous areas and VCs' vulnerability, resilience and sustainability. Among other activities, the project also included a participatory multi-level foresight, which results are the focus of this study. The exercise aimed at identifying the key variables and long-term forces (social, environmental, technological, policy-related, etc.) shaping the future of VCs and producing scenario narratives by 2050 that could support strategic action plans for the evolution of mountain VCs at European and regional levels.

[7] HORIZON 2020, MOVING Project: www.moving-h2020.eu (last retrieved: 30/03/2024).

[8] MOVING Northern Apennines MAP: https://www.moving-h2020.eu/reference_regions/northern-apennines-italy/ (last retrieved: 30/03/2024).

[9] MOVING Corsica MAP: https://www.moving-h2020.eu/reference_regions/corsica-france/ (last retrieved: 30/03/2024).

Description of the Involved Mountain Regions and Related Chestnut Flour VCs

Northern Apennines—Alta Versilia

The Mountain Reference Landscape (MRL) for our case study is called Alta Versilia, situated in the Apuan Alps, a part of the Northern Apennines.

The Apuan Alps are a mountain range in northwestern Tuscany known for its extraordinary natural and cultural heritage. The MRL includes two municipalities (Seravezza and Stazzema) with a population barely exceeding 15,000 inhabitants (Fig. 1). The population mostly lives near the coast, while a third of the population still lives in 26 small villages in the mountainous area, counting on average of less than 200 inhabitants each. The mountainous area is crisscrossed by a dense network of streams and canals, with the steep mountain slopes covered mainly by forests, which have been privatised since the nineteenth century. One of the traditional forest systems, both in historical and cultural value, is the chestnut tree. The first traces of chestnut trees (Castanea Sativa Mill) in the Apennines date back to the Palaeolithic era. Marco Apicio, an ancient Roman gastronomy-related author (I century B.C.–I century A.C.) was probably the first one who mentioned chestnut production in the area. Cultivation was probably initiated during the Roman Empire (Apicio, 2018), but only in the early mediaeval age (8th–9th centuries), under the Lombards, chestnut trees started to be selected and planted systematically in Lucca and the MRL (Giambastiani et al., 2004). Moreover, traditional chestnut production has allowed the same land uses and cultivation techniques to be maintained over the past centuries.

In the MRL, the chestnut flour value chain (VC) involves mainly local actors generating limited economic impact. In 2023, about 100 chestnut flour producers produced 9000 kg of chestnut flour using 11 dryers located in 8 villages. The VC is characterised by an overall gender balance, especially in the production and distribution phases and it is managed by mainly mid-aged actors above 40 years old. Some of the activities are carried out collectively and by hand (e.g.: chestnut collection and selection, drying and transformation) and are also recognised by the local actors as meaningful moments for social gathering. Despite numerous efforts to improve value chain performance, mainly led by members of local associations, (e.g., restoring abandoned chestnut

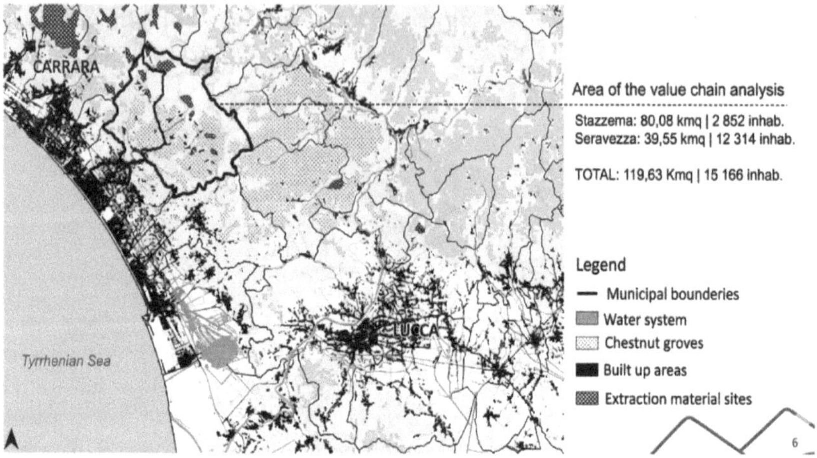

Fig. 1 Northern Apennines—Alta Versilia MRL (*Source* Authors' elaboration on Tuscany Region GIS Layers)

groves, revitalising disused mills and dryers, implementing pest monitoring initiatives, and promoting the creation of a territorial brand) persistent fragilities and unresolved issues are still in place, also burdened by climate change effects (droughts, increased hydrogeologic risks, higher temperatures, etc.) which affect the VC development. Moreover, demographic changes and generational gaps are leading to knowledge losses and abandonment of chestnut groves. The related lack of maintenance (pruning, regular cleaning, grafting, etc.) is causing the substitution of chestnut trees for other species. Furthermore, some other issues threatening the sustainable development of this VC are legal framing (for land possession, management, and access), financial support, and infrastructure development.

Corsica

Corsica is an island in the Mediterranean Sea with a great diversity of landscapes, including wide plains, rolling hills and dramatic steep valleys. Historically, it has been a centre of transhumant herding of small ruminants. Since the sixteenth century, chestnut groves and their production have been a vital part of Corsica's mountain villages: their products are key in the traditional Corsican diet.

The whole island in 2022 counted 349,465 inhabitants. The MRL is the result of a partnership between the three municipalities of Bucugnà (367 inhabitants in 2021), Ghisoni (226 inhabitants in 2021) and Nuceta (66 inhabitants in 2009) and is part of a larger project led by a group of municipalities (GAL-Leader, and communities of municipalities) in central Corsica (Fig. 2). The assembly of these mountain communes created links between the departments of Haute-Corse and Corse-du-Sud to investigate the diversity of professional and non-professional activities. The MOVING MAP includes researchers from INRAE (LRDE-UMR Selmet).

"The breadfruit tree" has shaped the architecture and fed a system of exchange of foodstuffs between the micro-regions. The golden age

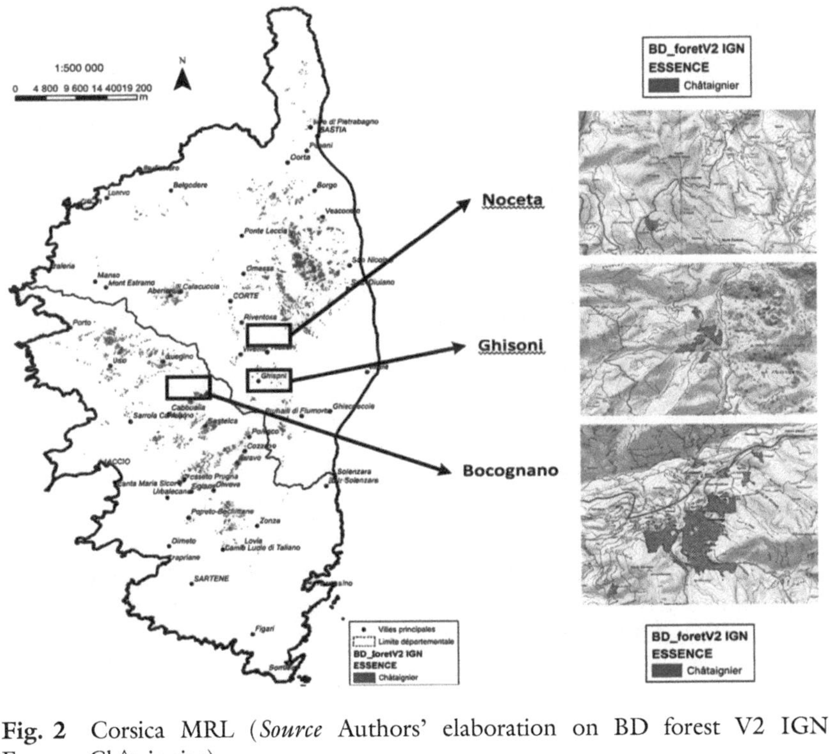

Fig. 2 Corsica MRL (*Source* Authors' elaboration on BD forest V2 IGN Essence Châtaignier)

of chestnut was between 1729 and 1830, with a peak during the nineteenth century in terms of ha occupied by chestnut groves (more than 30,000 ha), number of varieties (more than 45) and population density in the area (Pomponi & Arrighi, 1978). Then, a long period of decline hit Corsican chestnut groves, due to economic changes and tree diseases, resulting in demographic loss, rural exodus and change in consumption habits (Perry, 1984).

Nevertheless, in the 1970s, the attractiveness of the countryside and Corsican identity products revived, and chestnut production restarted through the commitment of younger generations. Since 1983 the chestnut fair has taken place in Bucugnà, organised by the Foyer Rural, entailing a chestnut flour competition. The fair showcased local and forgotten practices. In 2003, 30,000 people visited the fair, with 15 tons of chestnut flour sold. The fair encouraged producers to come together and create the Groupement Régional de Producteurs et de Transformateurs de Châtaignes et Marrons (GRPTCMC) in 1991.

In 2001, a syndicate was formed to begin the process of obtaining the certification of quality and major regulations. In 2010, the flour was awarded the AOP/PDO label, the first in France. This boosted the realisation of new products (pastries, confectionery, beers) and chestnut groves represented a food resource for pigs breeding with related 3 PDO products (*Prisuttu*, *Coppa* and *Lonzu*) and beekeeping (PDO *Mele di Corsica*) as well as for heating wood. All the PDO products adhere to the Organic Agriculture (AB) scheme. Chestnut flour is produced from a very small part of the existing orchards which have been regenerated after severe fungal diseases (Phytophthora and Cryphonectria). This also led to a requalification of the chestnut orchards. Nevertheless, some challenges emerged: food gentrification, namely the high prices removed the chestnut flour popular character; the PDO for the charcuterie from pigs finished in chestnut groves poses coexistence problems between breeding and chestnut production. In addition, contemporary food issues (renewal of food crops, search for better food, and attractiveness of local productions) open a new way of valuing the fruit from new plantations. Besides all this, climate change issues emerge.

3 Methodology

This section presents the methodology adopted during the foresight exercise in both Corsican (CVC) and Northern Apennines VCs (NAVC) (Barjolle et al., 2022).

An integrated method was adopted, where every step of the exercise included the three main categories of scenarios previously mentioned (predictive, exploratory and normative).

Three in-presence subsequent workshops were carried out, with different but related objectives.

The predictive approach was mainly applied during the first workshop, the exploratory one characterised the second workshop while the normative approach was identified to conduct the third step of foresight exercises in the two chestnut flour VCs analysed (Andreescu et al., 2013; Reilly & Willenbockel, 2010; Wiebe et al., 2018). The aim was to identify pathways to enhance mountain areas' resilience through an analysis of climate change and socio-economic trend scenarios in the 2050 horizon.

This methodological framework considered the interactions between the specific VCs and the Socio-Ecological System (SES) in which the different stages of the VC and their practices take place. The SES is a complex system further organised into interconnected (at different levels) subsystems: the social system (people) is included in and interacts with an ecological system according to given norms and rules. This also entails the ecosystem's provision of services for the benefit of human beings (McGinnis & Ostrom, 2014; Ostrom, 1990, 2009). Such a framework inspired the development of the MOVING conceptual framework by Moretti et al. (2023) (Fig. 3) that took as a reference point the four first-level core subsystems of an SES and represented the basis upon which VCs were analysed, before the foresight exercises, also in terms of vulnerability and resilience.

Participatory approaches were applied to the foresight exercises as it was crucial to include different local stakeholders, particularly the VC's actors, responding to the need to investigate and build a bottom-up shared vision of a desirable future for more sustainable and resilient mountain areas.

The foresight exercise was carried out by two research teams involved in the MOVING project, one from the University of Pisa, Department of Food, Agriculture and Environment (Tuscany case, Italy) and one from

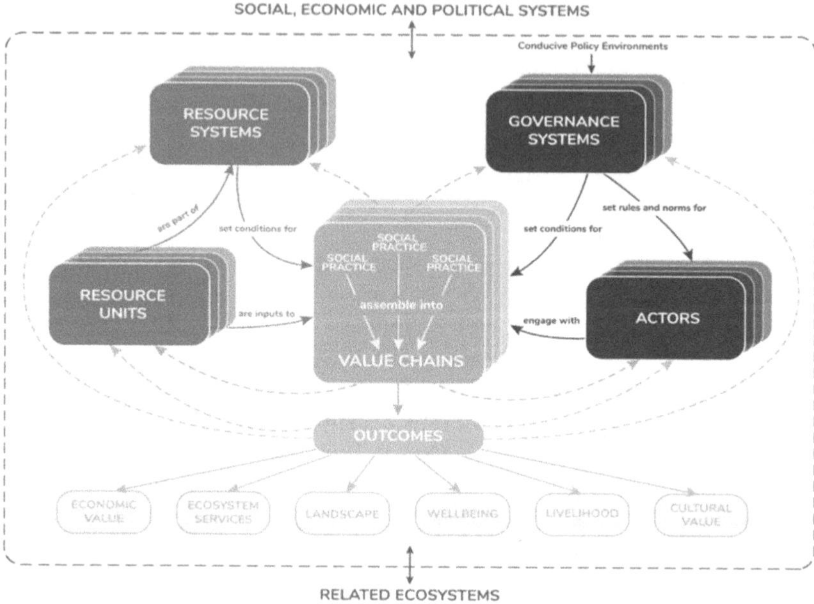

Fig. 3 The MOVING conceptual framework by Moretti et al. (2023)

INRAE, the National Research Institute for Agriculture, Food and Environment—INRAE (Corsica case, France). They had the role of inviting local key actors, organising, moderating, and reporting the activities of the foresight exercise.

Participants, defined as the "foresight group", were categorised according to several typologies, namely:

- Chestnut VCs actors: i.e., producers, and processors;
- Experts: i.e., researchers, Local Action Group (GAL) representatives, producers' associations members, etc.;
- Policy network members: i.e., municipality representatives, regional advisors, representatives of other public entities working at the local level, etc.

The two long-term forces enabled the establishment of the parameters (axes) for constructing the narrative of the four possible scenarios towards 2050, foreseen in the second workshop.

Based on the results of this first workshop, the second workshop applied an exploratory approach. Four scenarios were built through the application of a 2 × 2 matrix (Rhydderch, 2017), where the two axes represented the two long-term forces selected during the first workshop (high importance; high uncertainty), and the four spaces defined by their intersection represented four different and well-contrasted narratives of exploratory scenarios. The objective of this workshop was to discuss the four scenarios and engage participants in commenting on the key variables and their role in each scenario, adding missing elements and reflecting upon the reasons behind the opinions generated. Finally, they had to choose and consolidate the description of the most preferred scenario (more probable and desired future).

The third workshop, with a normative approach, had the objective of engaging participants in a discussion to refine the preferred scenario and its related strategic changes and policy options, by prioritising the changes needed for its occurrence. A backward approach was employed. Starting from the vision of the ideal scenario back to the current situation, they had to define the most urgent interventions to implement along a timeline till the year 2050.

The workshops have been recorded, transcribed and then analysed. The analysis compared the information collected and reported by the research team on the foresight exercises of Tuscany and Corsica, and building on the discussions emerging from the three related workshops. The authors conducted the analysis based on a qualitative coding approach (Gibbs, 2018; Saldaña, 2021), and commented on the results by taking the LVTRA goals as a reference point (Table 1).

4 Results and Discussion

This section describes the results stemming from discussions and debates during the three workshops conducted in both regions of our study.

Table 2 presents an overview of the 3 workshops in each investigated area. Following, the outcomes of each workshop will be reported.

Table 1 LTVRA shared goals for 2040

Goal N.	*Action area*	*LTVRA shared goals (Rural areas as…)*	*Description*
1	**Stronger**		
	Empowered communities Access to services Social innovation	Attractive spaces, developed in harmonious territorial development	Unlocking the potential of specific places to provide opportunities and solutions at the local level to tackle the effects of global challenges
2	**Stronger**		
	Empowered communities Access to services Social innovation	Engaged in multi-level and place-based governance	Developing integrated strategies using collaborative and participatory approaches, benefitting from tailor-made policy mixes and interdependencies between urban and rural areas
3	**Prosperous**		
	Diversification of economic activities Sustainable food production	Providers of food security, economic opportunities, goods and services for wider societies	Development and use of bio-based materials and energy but also local, community-based high-quality products, and renewable energy, retaining a fair share of the value generated
4	**Stronger**		
	Empowered communities Access to services Social innovation	Dynamic communities focusing on well-being	Considering aspects related to livelihoods, fairness, prosperity and quality of life, where all people live and work well together, with adequate capacity for mutual support
5	**Resilient**		
	Social resilience	Inclusive communities	Inter-generational solidarity, fairness and renewal, open to newcomers and fostering equal opportunities for all
6	**Resilient**		
	Resilience to climate change Environmental resilience	Flourishing sources of nature	Enhanced by and contributing to the objectives of the Green Deal, including climate neutrality, as well as sustainable management of natural resources
7	**Connected**		

(continued)

Table 1 (continued)

Goal N.	*Action area*	*LTVRA shared goals (Rural areas as...)*	*Description*
	Digital connectivity Transport links and new connectivity	Fully benefiting from digital innovation	With equal access to emerging technologies, widespread digital literacy and opportunities to acquire more advanced skills
8	**Prosperous**		
	Diversification of economic activities Sustainable food production	Entrepreneurial, innovative and skilled people	Working together to co-create technological, ecological and social progress
9	**Stronger**		
	Empowered communities Access to services Social innovation	Lively places equipped with efficient, accessible and affordable public and private services	Including cross-border services, and providing tailored solutions (such as transport, education, training, health and care, including long-term care, social life and retail business)
10	**Stronger**		
	Empowered communities Access to services Social innovation	Places of diversity	Making the most out of their unique assets, talents and potential

Source Authors elaboration from EU Rural Vision: https://rural-vision.europa.eu/rural-vision/shared-goals_en, last retrieved: 30/03/2024

Discussing the Key Variables

The first workshop employed a serious game format, which, in the case of the NAVC, was based on key variables that represented the essential needs of value chain-specific actors and their well-being. Whereas, in the case of CVC the serious game considered a VC-related timeline from the late 1970s to 2020s (Figs. 4 and 5).

Discussions and exchange between the research team and the foresight group in Tuscany resulted in a short list of five long-term elements that were ranked according to (i) their importance, (ii) the uncertainty of their occurrence, and (iii) the level of their impact on the key variables. The workshop resulted in a set of community-centred key variables with some

Table 2 Overview of the three workshops in Northern Apennines and Corsica

	Northern Apennines	*Corsica*
1st workshop		
Date and venue	February 2nd 2023—University of Pisa Conference Hall	January 26th 2023—INRAE SELMET LRDE, Corté (salle de réunion)
Number of participants according to category	13, 3 VC actors, 4 experts, 3 from policy network, 3 stakeholders (civil society, NGO)	14, 4 VC actors, 5 experts, 3 from policy network, 2 stakeholders (researcher, NGO)
Description of the activity	1st part: serious game. Discussion on key variables and long-term forces based on local actors' social/well-being needs. 2 groups, each chose a character from a set of 12 cards with a short bio, representing an ideal actor from the region connected to the VC. The discussion made emerge 5 long-term forces (Fig. 2) *** 2nd part: discussion upon 2 pre-designed baseline scenarios (1 optimistic, 1 pessimistic). Participants modified the presented scenarios according to their perspectives. This led to identifying the two long-term forces, prioritised according to uncertainty, importance, and influence on the key variables.	1st part: presentation of 1 baseline scenario. Participants discussed its potential verification and commented on related modifications. 2nd part: serious game. Participants discussed a series of driving variables presented about a VC timeline from the late 1970s to the 2020s and the influences between the key variables and the potential bodies that can act on them (Fig. 3). They identified the most influential key variables on the baseline scenario and finally, discussed and chose two long-term forces, prioritised according to uncertainty and significance.
2nd workshop		
Date and venue	March 23rd 2023 (morning)—Visitors' centre of the Park of the Alpuan Alps, in Bosa di Careggine	March 9th 2023—INRAE SELMET LRDE, Corté (salle de réunion)

(continued)

Table 2 (continued)

	Northern Apennines	*Corsica*
Number of participants according to category	13, 5 VC actors, 2 experts, 3 from policy network, 4 stakeholders (farmers and producers/processors from the Garfagnana area, devoted to chestnut flour production, with a different type of VC organisation)	14, 6 VC actors, 4 experts, 2 from policy network, 2 stakeholders (researcher, NGO)
Description of the activity	Presentation of the 4 scenarios, disposal of the 2 × 2 matrix on the flour. One group per scenario, before rotating to discuss each scenario (pros and cons; probability of their occurrence)	
3rd workshop		
Date and venue	March 23rd 2023 (afternoon)—Visitors' centre of the Park of the Alpuan Alps, in Bosa di Careggine	April 7th 2023—INRAE SELMET LRDE, Corté (salle de réunion)
Number of participants according to category	13, 5 VC actors, 2 experts, 3 from policy network, 4 stakeholders (farmers and producers/processors from the Garfagnana area)	16, 5 VC actors, 4 experts, 4 from policy network, 3 stakeholders (researcher; NGO, farmer in a chestnut-flour complementary VC)
Description of the activity	Discussion on the list of actions and paths to adopt for the implementation of the scenario they agreed upon by the end of the second workshop: selection of milestones, obstacles and opportunities to co-construct a transition trajectory and then a regional strategy.	

Source Authors' elaboration

references to the chestnut VC. The CVC participants took a more VC-oriented approach, instead (Fig. 6).

In both cases, aspects related to climate change and environmental issues were discussed: the Corsicans mentioned Climate change and Biological economy that somehow corresponded to some aspects considered by Tuscans in Supply stability and Environmental quality (within the Health key variable). While the Tuscan mentioned economic-related variables in terms of VC stability and the employment opportunity offered by the VC, the Corsicans pointed out aspects related to the socio-technical system, the governance of the VC (VC organisation, management and land rules), and local policy. Moreover, the Tuscan research

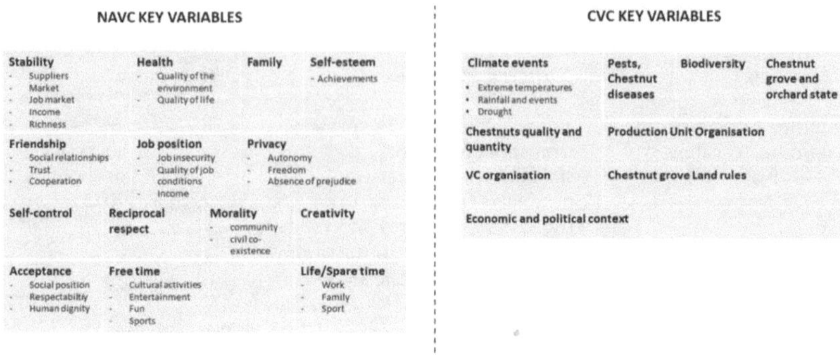

Fig. 4 Key variables identified by NAVC and CVC foresight group during the first workshop (*Source* Authors' elaboration)

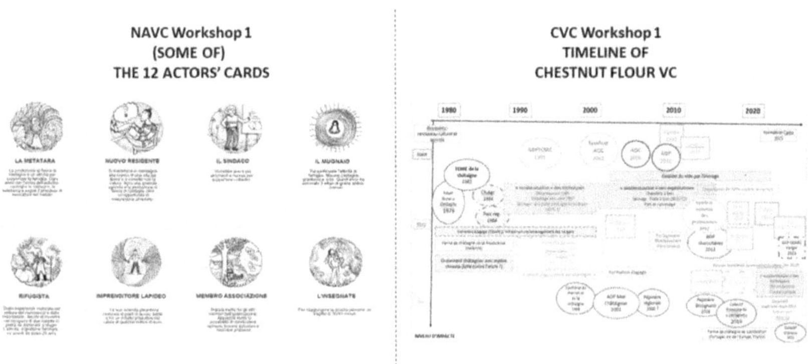

Fig. 5 Materials from NAVC and CVC's first workshop (*Source* Authors' elaboration)

team supported a discussion that specifically considered human well-being-related variables as pivotal: social relations, self-esteem, autonomy and leisure.

Ranking the Long-Term Forces

For the selection of the most influential long-term forces on the key variables, NAVC participants examined the correlation between the variables

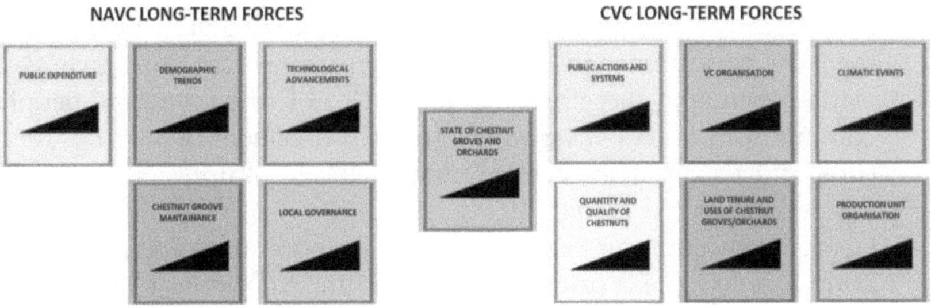

Fig. 6 Long-term forces identified by NAVC and CVC foresight group during the first workshop (*Source* Authors' elaboration)

(well-being needs) and their fluctuations about five primary long-term forces: public expenditure, demographic trend, (low) capacity of the local governance, use of technology/automation, (lack of) chestnut groves maintenance. The latter originated from the discussion and was added during the workshop.

The two long-term forces that ranked higher were related to social and environmental elements:

1. Demographic trends (presence of young inhabitants): historical outmigration. Demographic trends have shown strong patterns of migration towards foreign countries and the plains. However, in the past, the broad family structure ensured a continuous transfer of knowledge and effective management of chestnut groves. Unfortunately, nowadays, the generational transition has become increasingly challenging. Many people in this profession today come from urban areas. Since there is no generational change in the local population, the only way to maintain production is to work alongside people from other backgrounds. Consequently, there is an urgent need for renewal, rather than relying solely on family ties. This long-term force influences the key variables in terms of shortage of labour during cultivation, harvesting, processing, and marketing; impoverishment of knowledge and innovation with negative effects on the territory's ability to adapt to changes; decline in the number of future chestnut farmers, processors, and distributors. Some adaptive capacities to face the influence of the long-term force have been

proposed: the promotion of agriculture and rural activities, investment in education and skills development, which also serve as a way to train and, therefore, include in the VC the interested people coming from other backgrounds; the reinforcement of links between rural and urban areas, preservation of local culture, and access to finance and micro-credit;

2. (Lack of) chestnut grove maintenance: abandonment and neglecting crucial tasks (e.g., pruning, clearing undergrowth, planting/re-planting (also other species), targeted irrigation, etc.) in forest management. Abandonment of chestnut groves was one of the primary causes of negative impacts on the chestnut ecosystem. The only positive aspect of the lack of maintenance could be correlated to a slow re-naturalisation of less accessible areas, that are also less suitable for chestnut cultivation. The abandonment also counteracted the spread of chestnut as a monoculture, thus supporting a certain return of the mixed forest, with the coexistence of several species. Participants in the NAVC workshops highlighted the need for new technologies to optimise such activities and to consider undertaking relevant agroforestry co-productions (e.g.: edible mushrooms, honey, forage, organic litter, healthy plants, etc.). This long-term force might negatively influence the key variables in terms of loss of biodiversity, increased wildfire risk, soil erosion and degradation, forest management and fire protection plan, biodiversity conservation, soil conservation and erosion control. Also in this case, some adaptive capacities related to the influential power of this long-term force emerged: the forest management and fire protection plan, considering that the chestnut tree is more resistant to fire than other species, biodiversity conservation, soil conservation and erosion control.

In the case of Corsica, the key variables corresponded to the long-term forces. CVC participants chose two among them, with economic relevance:

1. "Biological Economy": dreadful state of chestnut groves. In this perspective, chestnut trees are no longer recoverable and productive, pests persist in pockets of abandoned chestnut trees, and it is impossible to renew the chestnut trees. This might lead to the loss

of natural resources, biodiversity and chestnut groves, in resilience, productivity and competitiveness as well as to increases in market prices.

2. Sociotechnical and governance systems: it entails production unit organisation; VC organisation; land tenure and uses of chestnut groves/orchards. Its influence in the long-term might result in an increase in processing costs and time, shortage of labour, loss of attractiveness of the profession, increase in multi-activity, professionalisation and production issues, loss of financial resources, of VC resilience, conflicts in land use, chestnut land blocked, continuing deterioration, predatory practices and customs (breeding). This could have impacts in terms of loss of producer number, especially of small producers, of leadership and development, of chestnut surfaces, with an increase in water issues and agropastoral conflicts.

Discussing and Adopting the Baseline Scenario

In the case of NAVC, two baseline scenarios (Fig. 7), one more optimistic and one more pessimistic were presented and discussed by participants, following the discussion about key variables and long-term forces. On the contrary, the CVC participants discussed their baseline scenario (Fig. 8) before the key variables and long-term forces part of the workshop.

NORTHERN APENNINES VC – BASELINE SCENARIOS BY 2050

Hypothesis 1 – Optimistic

- Biodiversity and forest restoration supported "coppice governance" (a sustainable form of forestry management) to ensure the continuous regeneration of broad-leaved trees following a traumatic impact;
- Limited impact of the Italian national policy for developing inner areas (Barca et al 2014), on socio-economic trends (e.g.: generational renewal and population ageing) of marginal areas.
- Ad hoc incentives and resources allocated by Tuscany's regional policies to these areas. Anyway, distrust towards policymakers for their inability to ground resources and uncertainty in economic investments;
- Increased virtuous social innovations (e.g., "Chestnut VC Community" linking production and distribution along the VC) as a reaction and resulting in less dependence on public institutions;
- "Youngsters rural exodus" reversed: new training/job paths developed in the area based on local resources; tenders and public funding supporting new businesses and startup innovation; renewed access to land and rural assets (e.g.: real estate, cottages, land) for agricultural production purposes.

Hypothesis 2 – Pessimistic

- Climate change effects - rising temperatures and droughts - increased the instability of agricultural production in mountainous areas. Historic chestnut grove production decreased, ancient trees dried out and some collapsed. New chestnut plantations = artificial irrigation systems = significant impacts and costs;
- No real impact of the Italian national policy for developing inner areas (Barca et al 2014) on socio-economic trends of marginal areas but it produced a solid system of maintaining the political machine;
- Distrust towards local/regional policymakers due to their inability to invest the available resources from the Next Generation Europe funds and uncertainty in economic investments.
- Difficulties in land accessibility despite a widespread abandonment with risks of soil erosion, increased fires and biodiversity weaknesses. Banca della Terra initiative produced marginal results, almost null in Tuscany.
- "Youngsters rural exodus" continues, towards the big cities or to Northern Europe, in search of a stable future. Increase in the national average age, reaching 53 in 2050.

Fig. 7 NAVC—baseline scenarios by 2050 (*Source* Authors' elaboration)

CORSICAN VC – BASELINE SCENARIO BY 2050

Baseline scenario

As the summer of 2049 draws to a close, chestnut groves are suffering the combined effects of rising temperatures and drought. Irrigation is needed to maintain fruit size, but it is becoming difficult to achieve a balance between size and sweetness, which is jeopardising the typicality of the flour.

The ageing of the trees is reducing regional production and trees outside the station (adret < 600/700 m) are disappearing.

The frequency of extreme weather events and uncontrolled livestock farming practices have led to almost irreversible soil degradation, prohibiting any new plantations. The new soil and climate conditions are leading to a proliferation of pathogens and pests.

Production has fallen below a level that can no longer generate an income. Several socio-technical innovations opened the way to a few corrective measures (choice of varieties, mycorrhizae, orchard management, mills).

Low scrubland is replacing the chestnut-growing landscape, reducing the use value of the chestnut groves and increasing land tenure disorder.

The remaining chestnut groves, the highest ones, are the subject of conservation measures to protect the heritage landscape and biodiversity.

Chestnut growing and the status of producers is back to where they were in the 1980s, with brand names replacing the PDO. The result has been a gentrification of chestnut flour consumption, with very narrow niche markets.

Maize *pulenta* has become widespread and is a substitute for chestnut flour in Corsican culinary culture.

Fig. 8 CVC—baseline scenario by 2050 (*Source* Authors' elaboration)

The discussion on the baseline scenarios helped the NAVC to identify place-specific political decisions and initiatives that impact the present and future perspective of the mountainous area. For example, the dissolution, at the National level, since 2008, of territorial bodies—the "*Comunità Montane*"—established in the Seventies whose goal was to manage dedicated resources to shape and implement initiatives for mountainous areas. This led to forestry management being managed at the regional level, with a substantial decrease in the capacity and availability of resources dedicated to forests and a loss of place-based perspective in managing such resources. Participants also agreed on the fact that, when it comes to local development, different governance levels should contribute to an integrated policy implementation. Finally, the "Banca della Terra" (Land Bank) project, a regional initiative to promote the use and resilience of abandoned lands and facilitate social and economic benefits for local communities, was mentioned as a success story. It consisted of a complete inventory of public and private land available for rental or other contractual arrangements, available through a web portal. Anyway, participants stated the project requires improved procedural coordination and simplification. These measures are essential to streamline the project's implementation and ensure its effectiveness.

According to the baseline scenario proposed, CVC participants reflected on the difficult situation of small producers. While large farmers are still capable of holding out. A potential perspective to enter new markets could be meeting the demand for gluten-free and organic products, which represent a strong trend in food consumption. They also discussed issues related to the loss of heritage trees, biodiversity, and productive chestnut groves due to an increase in competitive agro-pastoral practices and risky situations such as predation phenomena (e.g.: impact of pig and cow farm divagation). Finally, in terms of knowledge and know-how, the discussion brought out a potential loss of traditional farming practices about chestnut and chestnut flour production in the long term.

Discussing the Four Exploratory Scenarios

The second workshop allowed participants to choose two long-term forces that would represent the two axes of the 2 × 2 matrix enabling the proposal of four exploratory scenarios that the research team designed.

In the case of NAVC, the X axis represented "Demographic trends", with the following extremes "new population/rural exodus"; while the Y axis represented the "chestnut grove maintenance", with "recovery/abandonment" as extremes. The resulting quadrants presented four different scenarios for the foresight group to be discussed: (1) market utopia; (2) entertainment factory; (3) wild land, and (4) mountain dormitory (Fig. 9).

In the case of NAVC, the foresight group expressed its thoughts highlighting its views about aspirations and difficulties faced by each scenario, while in a second session of the workshop, the group delved into the four proposed scenarios through the lens of the two selected long-term elements and potential related consequences. The discussion allowed participants to point out several considerations transversally emerging from the different scenarios:

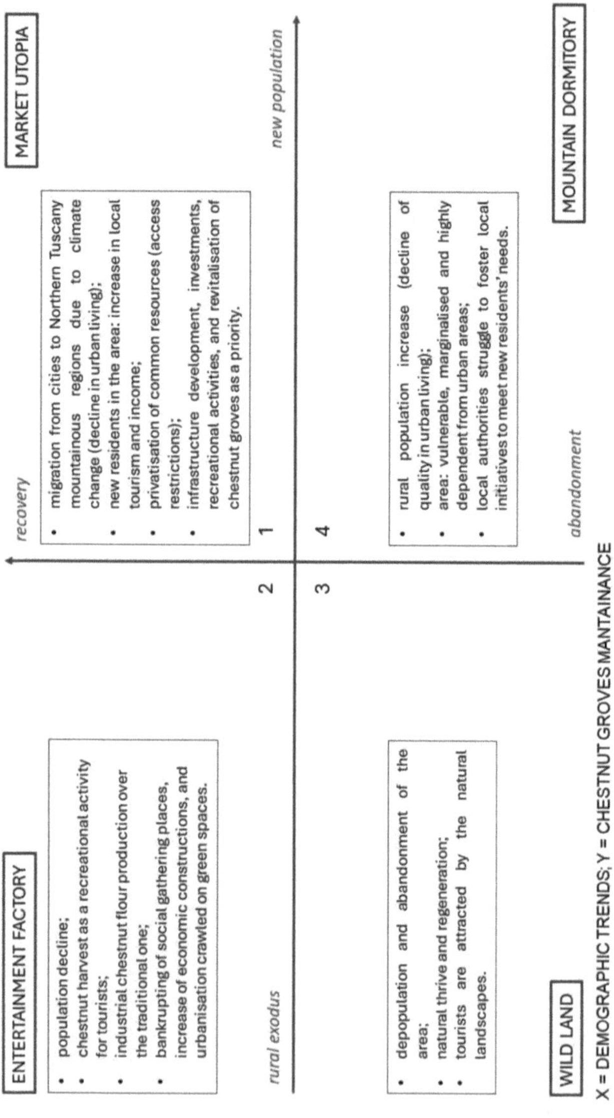

Fig. 9 The NAVC 2 × 2 matrix adopted in the second workshop (*Source* Authors' elaboration from Rhyderch (2017))

- A general decline in institutional support and services in the mountain regions;
- Essential services in villages (e.g.: small grocery shops; schools; pharmacies; bakeries, etc.) play an important role in terms of economic circuit and social perspective (community aggregation/cohesion/identity);
- Direct connections between consumers and producers, even on a global scale are becoming increasingly relevant and are motivated by the desire for transparency, accountability in the supply chain, and a preference for locally sourced and sustainable products;
- Digital marketing and online sales channels opportunities: they facilitated connectivity with the wider world making rural areas visible (also local productions) and allowing people in rural regions to access goods and services that may not have been readily available otherwise;
- Living in rural areas is increasingly becoming a deliberate lifestyle choice for both new and long-time residents. They are drawn to the advantages of community, sustainability, and a stronger connection to the land that rural living offers.

In the case of CVC, the two long-term forces that emerged from the first workshop were "Biological economy", translated as "VC organisation" and included as X axis in the 2 × 2 matrix with the following extremes: "multi-activity system/PDO-centred system" and "Sociotechnical and political organisation", translated as "State of chestnut grove" (Y axis in the 2 × 2 matrix) with these extremes: "interventionist management/conservationist management". The resulting quadrants presented four different scenarios for the foresight group to be discussed: (1) Agroecology; (2) Social and biotechnical innovations; (3) Village producers, and (4) Conservation (Fig. 10).

In the case of CVC, the discussion on the four scenarios made some transversal elements emerge:

- Pressing and crucial climate change situation;
- Interventionist approaches are preferred, with the development of strong PDO-centred actions;
- Two types of strategies for productive and non-productive areas can support facing ecological and agroecological issues;

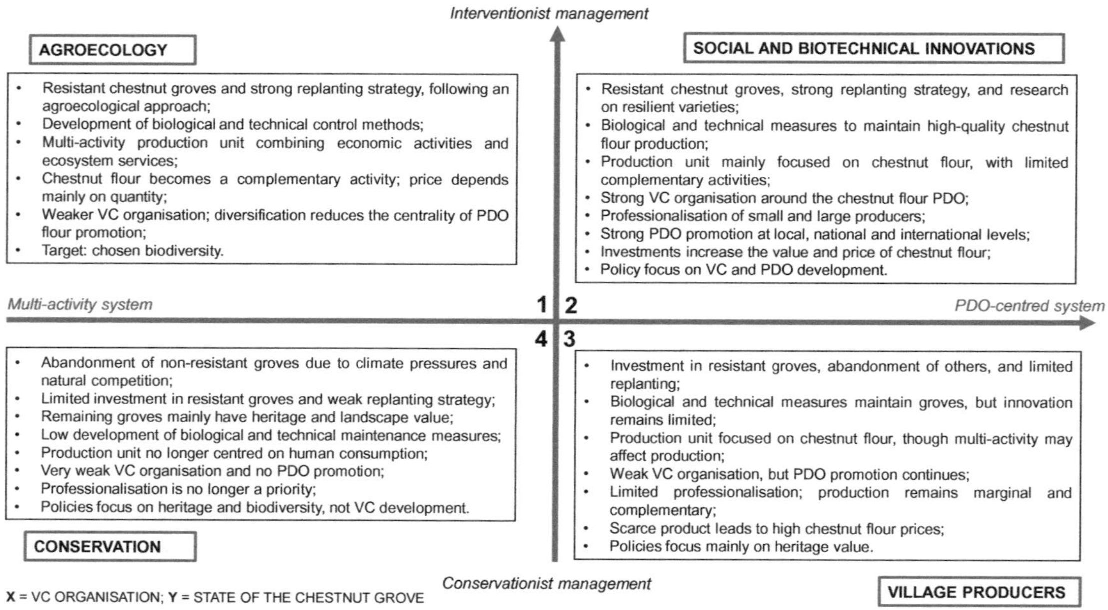

Fig. 10 The CVC 2 × 2 matrix adopted in the second workshop (*Source* Authors' elaboration from Rhydderch (2017))

- The need to maintain income-generating activities in mountain areas and to make them attractive emerged;
- Focus on multi-activity in the chestnut groves (already a major trend).

Discussing the Preferred Scenario and the Related Strategies and Action Paths: NAVC Results

The following discussion enabled the reflection upon the most preferred scenario.

The NAVC foresight group reflected upon a combination of two extreme scenarios: Market Utopia + Wild Land (Table 3).

The emerging new combined scenario for NAVC has the following characteristics:

- Well-balanced coexistence of new inhabitants and wild nature in the mountainous areas of northern Tuscany;
- New residents seeking to live in harmony with the land, escaping from a deteriorating quality of life due to elevated temperatures and air pollution in urban areas;
- Increase in sustainable tourism practices with low impact on the natural environment. Locals + new residents build sustainable infrastructure to favour the fruition of the natural heritage;
- Forest and other resources: preservation and protection. Management and recovery of chestnut groves and forests for both productive and recreational purposes (new residents);
- The local traditional practices of chestnut flour production are accepted and passed on;
- The area becomes a model for sustainable living, with a focus on self-sufficiency and a low environmental impact;
- Responsible and nature-based tourists interested in supporting the local community and natural resources' preservation. Wild land regeneration: higher attractive destination.

This brought to a final discussion related to Strategy building and the definition of actions and milestones by 2050.

In general, the NAVC strategy is characterised by sustainable living and tourism practices in the mountainous regions of northern Tuscany,

Table 3 Characteristics of the Market Utopia and Wild Land scenarios as discussed by the foresight group

Scenarios	*Aspirations*	*Difficulties*	*Long-term elements*		*Consequences*
			Demographic trend	*Grove maintenance*	
MARKET UTOPIA (+,+)	• Use of plant species to define groves • Rigorous regulations to recover land • More extension and training services • Less bureaucracy	• Uncontrolled population flows and mountain areas distortion • Absence of local institutions to accompany and help actors	• People move back to mountain areas • Arrival of new residents	• Priority to maintain and recover chestnut groves • Development of infrastructure	• Growth of the tourism sector • Regional economic growth • Cultural conflicts between residents • Privatisation of public goods
WILD LAND (−,−)	• Slow tourism • Emphasis of mountain identity • More support for small activities • More adequate taxes • More controlled wilderness	• Abandonment of groves • Population exodus	• Youth migration to urban areas	• Shift from groves active management to landscape natural regeneration	• Abandonment of communities • The wild landscape becomes a key attraction

Source Authors' elaboration

with a focus on preserving and protecting the natural environment. Self-sufficiency, low environmental impact, and the active participation of both new residents and locals in the management and recovery of chestnut groves and forests and tourism activities is at the basis of this strategy. The target tourist appreciates and supports the preservation of the natural environment:

- By 2025, at a policy level, new funding will be dedicated to "Mountain Custodians" a regional initiative dedicated to existing or newly established farms (above 500 mlsm, in mountain areas affected by depopulation) that receive incentives to provide forest management services for the benefit of the community, besides their core activities. Moreover, the "Land Bank" regional initiative will be improved, by also considering training and technical assistance to farmers or cooperatives, enabling them to sustainably recover and manage the land acquire through lease or purchase. Finally, promoting sustainable tourism will entail guided nature tours, educational programs about local flora and fauna, and promotion of sustainable practices among tourists during their stay.
- By 2030, the promotion of small-scale farms that use traditional and environmentally-friendly farming practices, such as organic farming and crop rotation, to produce a variety of crops and livestock. Focus on chestnut flour quality. At a policy level, the "Technical committee on rural areas" will be established: context-based and targeted rural development initiatives entailing sustainability and life quality aspects. Additionally, improvement of cultural awareness, knowledge and know-how transfer (schools + public institution). Chestnut groves are valued as cultural heritage, through education, cultural events and initiatives.
- By 2040, policy interventions focus on resources: low taxes in high-altitude lands and sparsely populated areas to enhance sustainable entrepreneurial initiatives. New legal framework for civic uses: water, forests, and pastures to be managed by communities.
- By 2050, the Regional Apuan Alps Park becomes a technical support office for the local communities.

Discussing the Preferred Scenario and the Related Strategies and Action Paths: CVC Results

In terms of preferred scenario, the CVC foresight group supported an integration of different from the all the 4 scenarios. Besides their different perspectives and roles within the CV, strong consensus emerged around a scenario allowing all ambitions to coexist for the resilience of CV and the natural resource by 2050.

The emerging new combined scenario has the following characteristics:

- Chestnut groves contributed to the income of 487 rural people, of which 270 chestnut VC-related jobs + additional related activities (agriculture, craftmanship and hospitality);
- Chestnut groves as a means of fire prevention and biodiversity preservation;
- Regional Strategy Action Plan (2025) to revive the Corsican chestnut grove is bearing fruit: ecosystem resilience to face drought and other extreme events, with 20% of the area productive again (planting, regeneration and renovation) against 40% of the chestnut area lost since 2020;
- Expert mappings identify strategic chestnut-growing areas (ESC) (relevant areas for recovery—600 to 1200 m) and regional nursery supplies trees to young growers and houses a rich collection of varieties used to run tests and multifactorial experimental protocols in pilot farms. Related to the experiments, an interdisciplinary platform brings training, development and research organisations and VC and PDO actors together;
- Multi-active farmers and new forms of organisation (inspired by the Italian examples of joint farms) are bearing fruit;
- Regional Ministry of Agriculture: a guide specifies good and bad practices and defines eligibility depending on the proper use of chestnut groves;
- Recognition of the chestnut tree as of public interest: increase in the visibility of chestnut groves and flours starting being produced based on varietal associations interesting to the market.
- Associated marketing based on chestnut grove products' diversification and innovation along the VC (e.g.: flour, honey, charcuterie, crafts, etc.).

Related to this, some proposals emerged:

- Need for training in the chestnut flour production steps: collectively define modalities (traditional vs. modern);
- Support system for farmers: catalogue/platform for regional aids, capacity building activities; technical information and resources (e.g.: techniques, varieties, mapping, replanting strategies, usages of chestnut groves, management, etc.);
- PDO specifications: changes needed (e.g.: irrigation and access to water, maintenance practices, varietal reinforcement, chestnut quality maintenance, multi-active farmers status recognition, including non-professionals in the PDO management;
- Chestnut groves "heritage landscape" value to be integrated. Recovery of the landscape to increase rural demography (return to villages in the long run): landscape desolation relates to depopulation and marginalisation;
- Need to define activities and strategies for chestnut groves multi-functionality of chestnut groves: livestock; areas used for food, tourism and heritage purposes, etc.

The CVC Strategy and action path towards 2050 is characterised by a chestnut-growing socio-ecosystem in rural mountain areas, described as sustainable in terms of production and PDO systems, for the cultivation and replanting practices, for biodiversity, and for the preservation and valuing of heritage areas. Collective practices (e.g.: associations of users, inter-professional committees, rural village associations, etc.) are sustained through policy initiatives. Moreover, chestnut production will be boosted by identifying preferential areas and localised experiments. Chestnut conservation will be promoted through a regional inventory that will collect, test and select several resilient and resistant varieties, and will multiplicate seedlings and certificate them. Finally, the multi-activity chestnut-growing profession will be fostered through training initiatives, through tutoring.

- By 2030, several new chestnut VC-related policy interventions will be created. Some of them will have a more institutional rationale. This is the case with the establishment of the scientific, and technical committee; the innovation platform for data collection and management and health monitoring and the observatory for the Corsican chestnut grove (e.g.: know-how, collection, etc.). Some interventions to provide policy and operational directions will be designed: a management strategy for productive and non-productive chestnut-growing areas (including identification of heritage landscape, regional interest trees, etc.); the establishment of the right of experimentation (through Mountain Law); debate on a policy integration to regulate agropastoral practices in chestnut groves. Some interventions directly support entrepreneurs' activities in the field, such as the establishment of a multi-partner incubator, the provision of training and tutoring services for chestnut and forestry workers and the development of related equipment.

- By 2040, a series of interventions will be designed to boost the chestnut flour VC and to boost the related management and organisational processes. On the one hand, priority housing in chestnut-growing areas will be renovated and the local chestnut variety will be certificated. Moreover, a process for diversification of the PDO production will be undertaken. A chestnut land policy will be implemented aiming at de-compartmentalising the land associations. In this context, a new association will be also created to foster sustainable management, multifunctionality and public utility initiatives. Multi-activity will be also fostered with some dedicated initiatives. On the other hand, the needs of the rural population will be addressed, through the launch of a dedicated support plan.
- By 2050, a series of development plans will be launched. One will be the multifunctional management plan for chestnut areas, considering agroforestry, beekeeping, livestock farming, tourism, education, and conservation as complementary activities to chestnut/chestnut flour production. Some other plans concern conservation: (1) Chestnut conservation and development plan and (2) Heritage Trees Plan. These are also linked to the Development plan for productive and non-productive chestnut areas. Based on good practice in the chestnut flour VC, the aid system will be revised.

The Long-Term Vision for Mountain Areas: Perspectives and Recommendations from Northern Apennines and Corsica

The foresight exercise enabled both NAVC and CVC groups to discuss the future perspectives of the rural mountain areas in which the respective VCs are located. By taking into account the most influential key variables and long-term forces, the exercise allowed participants to select a preferred and newly integrated future scenario upon which to build an action plan that identifies specific milestones by 2050. This was done after discussing four pre-designed potential scenarios resulting from the intersection of the two main long-term forces.

Overall, during the first workshops both VCs' participants referred to climate change and environmental issues as key variables with several related risks such as an increase in natural disasters, proliferation of plant pathogens, loss in biodiversity, air and water pollution, etc. that could negatively influence the quantity and quality of chestnut productions. Additional risks are related to VC organisation and stability variables' risks, e.g.: difficulties in production processes management (higher costs, time, availability of human resources); attractiveness of the sector (low employment opportunities; insufficient income; lack of skills and training); land management risks (land use block; conflicts related to predatory practices/costumes); supply stability (uncertainty in flour supplies, volatility and fluctuations in prices and demand). Social needs also emerged as key variables, especially in the NAVC foresight group, related to a risk of loss in social cohesion and connected to negative demographic trends (outmigration and ageing).

The following steps of the foresight exercise pointed out potential concrete answers presented both in the preferred scenarios and in the action plans and commented according to the specific long-term forces identified. In this regard, it is interesting to notice that, among the latter, both VC foresight groups highlighted those related to chestnut VC production management and aspects connected with plants and groves' biological status-related aspects, e.g.: lack of chestnut grove maintenance (NAVC); "biological economy" (state of chestnut groves and orchards, quantity and quality of chestnuts) and sociotechnical and political organisation (production unit organisation; VC organisation; land tenure and uses of chestnut groves/orchards) (CVC). Moreover, the NAVC group highlighted aspects related to demographic trends that might influence the VC activities and the liveliness of local communities.

In both cases, the preferred scenarios and action plans touched on the following general points:

- Promoting initiatives to improve VC management through a more sustainable and systematic approach to the cultivation and resource management practices,
- Overcoming organisational issues by:
- Approaching diverse markets and income sources, by also considering multifunctionality;
- Improvements in the processing techniques and technological advancements;
- Increased collaboration among stakeholders, to strengthen existing and build new partnerships also with experts and technical and scientific bodies;
- Education and knowledge exchange to spot new employment opportunities in the field, by also fostering entrepreneurship and increasing technical knowledge and professionals' availability needed to face the identified organisational risks;
- Improving the governance system, political change and improved/new dedicated policy initiatives (subsidies and technical support, connection to international markets, certification processes) also in response to risks of conflicts and erosion of social trust and cohesion at the local level;
- Active participation in the decision-making processes of non-public bodies (e.g.: local organisations related to the VC, local associations and members from the local community), due to their direct and high interest in the discussed matters and the need to increase a shared sense of responsibility and activate the political agency potential of local communities;
- Scientists and experts are to be involved in the governance system, especially for the support they can provide on technical matters.

These premises enable a discussion based on the ten goals of the LTVRA and account for the considerations made by the two mountain regions' foresight groups.

Goal 1 (STRONGER action area) relates to the creation of attractive spaces, developed in harmonious territorial development. This goal is here addressed by considering the chestnut flour VC not only as an economic activity but also as an economic activity able to enhance social relationships and to open up new opportunities for inhabitants to keep staying in the area or for new inhabitants to arrive. The VC entails a series of processes carried out collectively and can enhance social gathering and cohesion. Indeed, the "metato" and—in some cases—the "mill" represent a meeting point for locals engaged in the VC. Moreover, both VC foresight groups highlighted that the future of the area depends on the services available at the local level and farms' multifunctionality and complementary forest management-related activities. This increases the perspective of locals and new residents to undertake new entrepreneurial activities and the potential establishment of missing basic services. As an example, small new grocery stores, bakeries, bars, and other types of shops open to the public represent a way to create a lively economic and social circuit and to reinforce the relationships at the local level. Moreover, in both cases, the chestnut grove itself, which in some cases has the characteristics of commonly recognised cultural heritage, if well managed, creates a new perspective of cultural and sustainable valorisation for the area, both for fostering community cultural awareness and for pushing forward the interest and commitment of new residents and responsible tourists.

Goal 2 refers to rural areas engaged in multi-level and place-based governance (STRONGER action area). It is clear, from the foresight exercise, that public bodies must work closely with local stakeholders involved in the VC, to set up dedicated policy interventions. Associations of producers and users, inter-professional committees, and rural village associations can be the key intermediaries able to bring about the specific needs to be addressed by the different policies. Existing interventions might be improved by accounting for the practical experiences of former beneficiaries' practical experiences (e.g.: "Bank Land" and "Mountain Custodians", NAVC). New initiatives at a regional, inter-municipal and municipal level can be created to address specific issues and challenges through the establishment of new dedicated entities (e.g.: observatories, committees; support systems; incubators) for the design of development and management plans and data monitoring. These are needed to consider resource management, dedicated tax schemes and public incentives and the integration of different funding sources. Certifications processes management; productive/non-productive lands mapping and management and redistribution; business/technical support and training to farmers, also in a multifunctionality and ecosystem services-oriented perspective; technological advancements to optimise processes in the VC; initiative for intergenerational exchange, knowledge and know-how transfer and cultural awareness initiatives for rural communities; rural population plans are among the main topics to address. To achieve it, technical, scientific and practitioner knowledge is needed, besides conductive policy environments.

Goal 3 has to do with food security, economic opportunities, goods and services for wider societies and Goal 6 with rural areas as flourishing sources of nature (PROSPEROUS and RESILIENT action areas).

The exercise highlighted the relevance, for the VCs' stakeholders, of the quantity and quality of the chestnut flour production. Increased and well-preserved biodiversity, genetic improvement and variety selection, PDO certification process and related valorisation can be obtained through the establishment of sustainability-oriented farming practices to tackle climate change challenges. Support from the research and technical stakeholders can be relevant in this sense.

Multifunctionality proved also relevant: it incentivises the revitalisation of abandoned chestnut groves and lands (ecosystem services) by also promoting the recovery of landscapes and the related cultural heritage preservation and valorisation. Moreover, multifunctionality reinforces the entrepreneurial capacity of local farmers by allowing them to widen their business horizons and bring innovations while increasing the number and quality of available services and productions at the local level, which can also be proposed to tourists. The integration of different economic activities, if carried out by different farmers, also reinforces local collaboration, trust and social cohesion (e.g.: integration of agropastoral activities in the chestnut groves; craftmanship, etc.). Finally, looking into ongoing market trends could favour economic prosperity (e.g.: gluten-free, organic).

Goals 4 and 5 (PROSPEROUS and STRONGER action areas) relate to dynamic communities focusing on well-being and inclusive communities. Multifunctionality is key in this sense. On the one hand, it increases the economic/entrepreneurial opportunities in the area, making it more attractive as it creates higher employability opportunities for locals—especially young and women, as the chestnut flour VC has been described as equally distributed in terms of gender—and newcomers, with some room for innovation.

Education and training are pivotal in this sense and have been highlighted during the exercise, also in connection with technological advancements, which is well aligned with Goals 7 and 8 (CONNECTED and STRONGER action areas). In this case, digital literacy and skills and access to emerging technologies are important to VC stakeholders to access new potential sales channels at the national and international level and for rural populations to acquire services and products not available locally.

In general, the presence of opportunities and services also attracts tourists. They are described by the foresight groups as people interested in connecting with nature (landscape), and with the local communities and their traditions and know-how. They are available to contribute to the well-being of the area, by also providing voluntary service during the stay and applying sustainable practices to reduce their impact.

The preferred scenarios provide an idea of rural populations able to keep existing in their places and made also of new flows of inhabitants, both temporary—like tourists—and new residents, newcomers or returning people, attracted by rurality as a sustainable lifestyle, also able to enrich the culture preserved and always re-enacted and renovated by locals with new insights and innovations. In this sense, Goal 8 refers to the presence of entrepreneurial, innovative, and skilled people and Goal 10 describes rural areas as places of diversity where people can express their talents, assets and potentials (PROSPEROUS and STRONGER action areas).

In this new atmosphere, schools and other public and cultural institutions can do much to create awareness for new citizens (children and young included) and foster intergenerational exchange (involving the elderly), through long-lasting but always renovated initiatives.

Nevertheless, referring to Goal 9 (STRONGER action area), where rural areas should be lively places equipped with efficient, accessible and affordable public and private services, the exercise did not particularly touch on solutions to overcome issues related to infrastructural limits that characterise the investigate mountain areas and that also increase the risk of outmigration and depopulation, such as the lack of essential services like viability, transportation, schools, healthcare facilities, social inclusion and cultural centres and initiatives. Participants only referred to the above-mentioned economic opportunities as boosters to the establishment of new services at the local level but did not identify specific approaches to achieve the related results (Fig. 11).

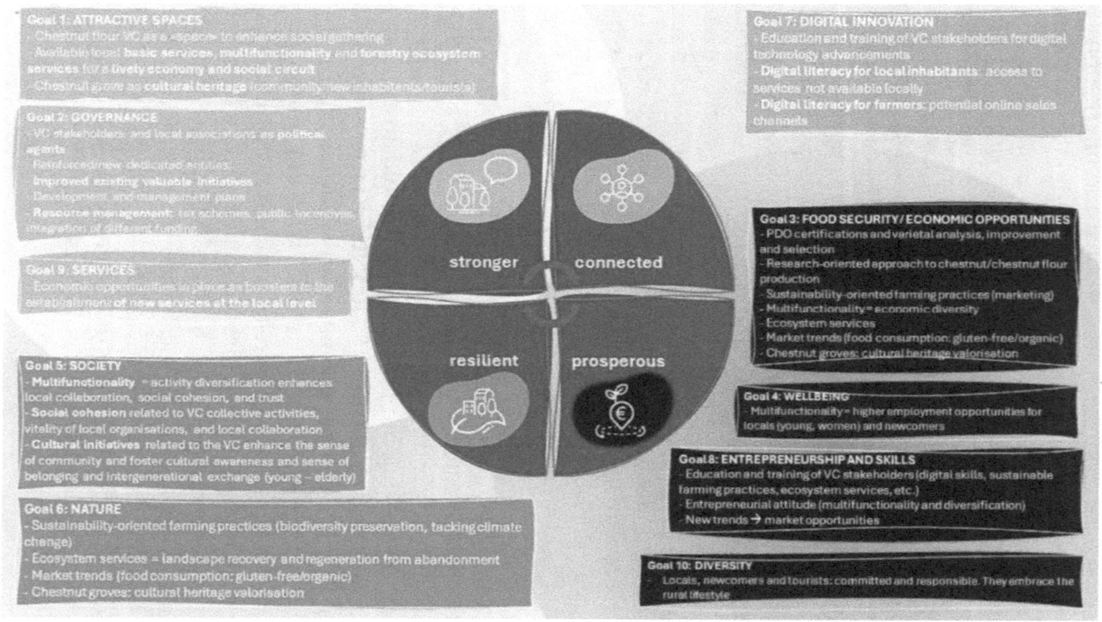

Fig. 11 The long-term vision for mountain areas: Northern Apennines and Corsica VCs' perspective (*Source* Authors' elaboration)

5 Conclusions

This chapter aimed at investigating challenges and potential actions to be implemented for the future of rural mountain areas according to the LTVRA goals and based on the results of a foresight exercise that took place in Northern Apennines and Corsica Mountain areas, with chestnut flour VC-related stakeholders. The outcomes collected from the three workshop discussions in both VCs represent valuable material for the development of the Northern Apennines and Corsica mountain areas and the related chestnut VCs and represent valuable support to regional and local decision-makers, in line with EU policies for rural areas. In terms of methodological approach, the integration of different typologies of scenarios enabled the achievement—throughout the different meetings of aligned, still multiple, visions about the most relevant issues and challenges facing the development of the study area. CVC foresight group worked in a more value-chain-oriented perspective, while the NAVC group took a wider perspective, by also considering aspects relating to the social life of rural populations. Nevertheless, several points of contact could be highlighted in the two cases, especially when it came to defining strategies and commitments to reach the set future objectives. The main point in the findings supported the need to reinforce the relationship among the inhabitants, VC members and policymakers of the mountain regions, giving the former political agency, a role as co-builders of their territories' future. The discussion related to the LTVRA supported a vision of rural areas retaining their inhabitants and offering them several opportunities to stay with enough space for newcomers to start living there with a sustainable approach, as well as tourists, described as temporary committed residents. Initiatives to boost cultural awareness and intergenerational exchange play a pivotal role in this sense. The more VC-related insights showed the relevant role of collaboration among stakeholders, training and education for farmers, also in terms of digital innovation and the implementation of actions, management and development plans, supported by policy interventions, reinforced and new dedicated bodies as coordinators and by public funding to apply sustainable farming practices that increase the quality and quantity of productions, by also recovering the landscapes with a renovated use of the lands. Multifunctionality is considered key in the foresight groups' perspectives. In general, the process of defining the action path and local strategy successfully stimulated reflections on the gap between local initiatives and broader regional policies. This alignment would ensure that local efforts were aligned with and complemented the overarching objectives and strategies of the wider area.

The study presents some limitations: the discussion did not deepen some relevant issues and challenges mostly related to essential services in rural areas. Moreover, the participatory approaches implemented involved a maximum of 15 stakeholders per workshop: this brought issues in terms of the representativeness of participants as their participation also depended on devotion and availability. Nevertheless, it has to be recognised that mountain communities, through these series of exercises, experienced a sense of recognition that had been lacking in the past. They felt acknowledged and valued for their unique perspectives and contributions. Moreover, especially in the NAVC foresight exercise, the collaboration between producers from Alta Versilia and Garfagnana facilitated the formation of networks aimed at sharing knowledge, pooling resources, and fostering collective efforts toward shared objectives. This interconnection enhanced their capacity to address challenges and seize opportunities together.

Future research can focus on improving the level of participation, by multiplying and diversifying the opportunities for exchange and discussion among stakeholders and can be run from a longitudinal perspective, by verifying whether, when a milestone is reached, the set goals have been achieved and if the most influential key variables and long-term forces identified are the ones actually influencing the realisation of the expected preferred scenarios and how.

References

Andreescu, L., Gheorghiu, R., Zulean, M., & Curaj, A. (2013). Understanding normative foresight outcomes: Scenario development and the 'veil of ignorance' effect. *Technological Forecasting and Social Change, 80*(4), 711–722.

Apicio, M. (2018). *Antica cucina romana. Testo latino a fronte*. Rusconi Libri.

Barjolle, D., Casabianca, F., Maglietti Smith, I., Piccin, L., Jaisli, I., Mora, O., & Schmitt, E. (2022). *D6. 1-guidelines for the foresight exercise*. EU Open ....

Bingley, K. (2014). *A review of strategic foresight in international development*. Institute of Development Studies (IDS).

Bock, A.-K., & Krzysztofowicz, M. (2021). *Scenarios for EU rural areas 2040.* Publications Office of the European Union. Joint Research Centre (JRC). https://doi.org/10.2760/29388

Brunori, G., Miller, D., Salle, E., & Chartier, O. (2020). *Overview of a sample of existing foresight and scenario studies carried out at EU and global levels.* SHERPA Project. Retrieved March 30, 2024, from https://rural-interfaces.eu/wp-content/uploads/2020/11/SHERPA-Overview-foresight-document_compressed.pdf

European Commission. (2024). *Report from the commission to the European Parliament, the Council, the European Economic and Social Committee and the Committee of the Regions. The long-term vision for the EU's rural areas: Key achievements and ways forward.* Retrieved March 30, 2024, from https://ec.europa.eu/commission/presscorner/detail/en/ip_24_1727 and https://eur-lex.europa.eu/legal-content/EN/TXT/PDF/?uri=CELEX:52024DC0450

Giambastiani, M., Maltoni, A., & Cia, M. (2004). *La vegetazione forestale delle colline e montagne lucchesi. Alberi monumentali ed elementi caratteristici.* Pegaso Edizioni.

Gibbs, G.R. (2018). *Analyzing qualitative data.* Sage.

Kwakkel, J. H., Auping, W. L., & Pruyt, E. (2013). Dynamic scenario discovery under deep uncertainty: The future of copper. *Technological Forecasting and Social Change, 80*(4), 789–800.

McGinnis, M. D., & Ostrom, E. (2014). Social-ecological system framework: Initial changes and continuing challenges. *Ecology and Society, 19*(2).

Moretti, M., Belliggiano, A., Grando, S., Felici, F., Scotti, I., Ievoli, C., Blackstock, K., Delgado-Serrano, M. M., & Brunori, G. (2023). Characterizing value chains' contribution to resilient and sustainable development in European mountain areas. *Journal of Rural Studies, 100*, 103022.

Nakicenovic, N., & Swart, R. (2000). *Emissions scenarios-special report of the Intergovernmental Panel on Climate Change.*

Navarro, J., Hayward, P., & Voros, J. (2008). How to solve a wicked problem? Furniture foresight case study. *Foresight, 10*(2), 11–29.

Önkal, D., Sayım, K. Z., & Gönül, M. S. (2013). Scenarios as channels of forecast advice. *Technological Forecasting and Social Change, 80*(4), 772–788.

Ostrom, E. (1990). *Governing the commons: The evolution of institutions for collective action.* Cambridge University Press.

Ostrom, E. (2009). A general framework for analyzing sustainability of social-ecological systems. *Science, 325*(5939), 419–422.

Perry, P. (1984). L'arbre à pain: Le châtaignier en Corse. *Annales du Midi, 96*(165), 71–84. https://annalesmidi.hypotheses.org/

Pomponi, F., & Arrighi, P. (1978). *Histoire de la Corse.* Presses Universitaires de France—PUF.

Reilly, M., & Willenbockel, D. (2010). Managing uncertainty: A review of food system scenario analysis and modelling. *Philosophical Transactions of the Royal Society B: Biological Sciences, 365*(1554), 3049–3063.

Rhydderch, A. (2017). *Scenario building: The 2 × 2 matrix*. Futuribles International.

Saldaña, J. (2021). *The coding manual for qualitative researchers*. Sage.

Schoemaker, P. J., Day, G. S., & Snyder, S. A. (2013). Integrating organizational networks, weak signals, strategic radars and scenario planning. *Technological Forecasting and Social Change, 80*(4), 815–824.

Störmer, E., Bontoux, L., Krzysztofowicz, M., Florescu, E., Bock, A.-K., & Scapolo, F. (2020). Foresight—Using science and evidence to anticipate and shape the future. In *Science for policy handbook* (pp. 128–142). Elsevier.

Wiebe, K., Zurek, M., Lord, S., Brzezina, N., Gabrielyan, G., Libertini, J., Loch, A., Thapa-Parajuli, R., Vervoort, J., & Westhoek, H. (2018). Scenario development and foresight analysis: Exploring options to inform choices. *Annual Review of Environment and Resources, 43*(1), 545–570.

Wuijts, S., De Vries, M., Zijlema, W., Hin, J., Elliott, L. R., Dirven-van Breemen, L., Scoccimarro, E., de Roda Husman, A. M., Külvik, M., & Frydas, I. S. (2022). The health potential of urban water: Future scenarios on local risks and opportunities. *Cities, 125*, 103639.

PART III

Sectoral Innovations and Transformative Approaches

CHAPTER 10

Towards a Participatory Approach of the Romanian Agri-Food Systems Governance Throughout a Multi-Actor Perspective

Monica Mihaela Tudor, Lucian Tanasă, Elisabeta Ștefania Roșu, Cristian Gheorghe Popescu, Claudiu Cătălin Munteanu, Lorena Florentina Chițea, Mihai Alexandru Chițea, and Ioan-Sebastian Brumă

1 Introduction

Empowering regional and local institutions and actors in the decision-making processes is essential to ensure that EU, national, regional, and local level policies are sufficiently cohesive to address specific rural challenges and meet the needs of rural inhabitants. Developing coherent rural policies requires Multi-Level Governance (MLG) structures (see Hooghe & Marks, 2001) that build on regional and local knowledge

M. M. Tudor (✉) · L. Tanasă · E. Ş. Roşu · C. G. Popescu · C. C. Munteanu · L. F. Chiţea · M. A. Chiţea · I.-S. Brumă
Institute of Agricultural Economics—Romanian Academy, Bucharest, Romania

D. Barjolle et al. (eds.), *Innovation and the Future of Rural Development in Europe*,
https://doi.org/10.1007/978-3-032-22570-2_10

while integrating this into policy-making. This requires holistic governance approaches to rural policy development based on open dialogue between institutions and stakeholders, and the inclusive participation of citizens, facilitated through the use of communication tools accessible for all range of rural stakeholders as not to exclude anybody for the debate.

The policy debate emphasises the need for a more integrated and holistic approach to rural policy development based on building stronger synergies between EU, national and regional/local level strategies. Slätmo (et al., 2021, D5.1) suggests that from a European perspective, place-based approaches to rural development are favoured because they aim to strengthen the resilience of rural areas to withstand global pressures. They do this by decreasing state dependency, and by increasing the economic competitiveness and innovativeness in rural areas (Wellbrock et al., 2013). Fragmented governance and limited coordination and collaboration between different types of actors have resulted in low policy coherence and limited participation of stakeholders and citizens in decision-making. More integrated rural strategies using multi-level collaborative governance and participatory approaches are needed. EU regional policy provides incentives for a more effective multi-level governance based on partnership and integrated place-based approaches within its structures, including the LEADER, CLLD and smart specialization programmes.

Miller et al. (2022) stress that the enhanced multi-level and territorial governance that empowers local actors and communities needs to be facilitated through flexible funding schemes relevant to the characteristics of different areas.

M. M. Tudor
Research Institute for Agricultural Economics and Rural Development, Bucharest, Romania

L. Tanasă · I.-S. Brumă
Gheorghe Zane Institute for Economic and Social Research, Romanian Academy, Iasi Branch, Iaşi, Romania

C. G. Popescu
National University of Science and Technology Politehnica, Bucharest, Romania

Piteşti University Centre, Piteşti, Romania

Through this chapter, the authors propose a critical approach to the participatory governance mechanisms that are used in drafting the policies that govern rural development in Romania and the agri-food system in particular, which is still perceived as the most important component of rural development. The chapter is based on the conclusions of discussions with the members of three multi-actor platforms within the SHERPA project in the period 2020–2023, including quadruple helix representatives; the discussions mainly focused on the assessment of regional and local agri-food systems, on how to increase their sustainability and resilience, with a particular emphasis in the last year of the dialogue on the governance of these systems, on the challenges, limitations and ways to improve the inclusive participation of actors from the agri-food chain in the decision-making process.

To complete the picture, the critical approach to the governance of the agri-food system is complemented by a brief presentation of outputs resulting from the implementation of the current governance mechanisms under the form of strategies and public policies aimed at agriculture, the other actors in the agri-food chain and the interrelationships between them.

2 Methodological Approach

Reaching sustainability goals in the agri-food system, as for the other anthropic systems, imply engagement of civil society, policy-makers and scientists in the joint development of strategic thinking and practical recommendations for a more effective participatory governance.

The main tools through which the knowledge and opinions of stakeholders were jointly harmonised for the purpose of developing recommendations for improving participatory governance on agri-food value chains in Romania are Multi-Actor Platforms (MAPs). Each MAP represents a local/regional or national network made by key stakeholders interested in the rural and agri-food topics such as local citizens and businesses (representatives from the civil society, NGOs, business and farmer organizations), researchers, and policy-makers. The MAPs activities were facilitated by neutral external support team consisting of a Facilitator and a Monitor in charge of running the MAPs and documenting the desk and context analysis and synthetising the discussion.

Three MAPs interactions with a total number of 32 members were run in 2022 and 2023 in Romania covering all variety of landscapes and historical and cultural paths describing local and regional agri-food systems (see Fig. 1).

For approaching the topic of participatory governance in the agri-food system, a **6-step Delphi method** was used, combining desk research, utilisation of quantitative data (e.g., geographic characteristics, economic structural indicators, socio-economic dynamics etc.), literature review on the topic and case-study areas with expert interviews and focus groups. These steps allowed the authors to collect data for different purposes, including national and regional policy and programmes focused on the agri-food value-chain topic, as well relevant publications and initiatives regarding the sustainability of value chains in Romanian context. The 6 steps are the following:

- Step 1: Desk research and context analysis regarding the state-of-play of regional agri-food value chains in the three case-study areas were conducted by the research team of the Institute of Agricultural Economics from the Romanian Academy (IAE-RA) in order

Fig. 1 Map of multi-actor platforms in Romania—territorial coverage

to shed light on the major characteristics of the regional agriculture, food industry, players of the local agri-food system and their interactions. These analyses served as ice breakers during the first round of focus group discussions with platform members regarding the sustainability of agri-food systems.

- Step 2: First round of focus groups with the regional group of stakeholders was focused on the topic of sustainability of the small-farm integration in the value chains of each case-study area and were conducted in the spring of 2022 separately on each of the three MAPs.
- Step 3: Focus-groups analysis for structuring the main challenges, opportunities and recommendations for a more sustainable integration of local farmers in the value chains was produced by the research team of IAE-RA based on desk research and inputs from focus groups for each of the three Romanian MAPs. The content of the resulting regional position papers were validated by consultation with the members of MAPs and could be consulted on SHERPA project website (https://rural-interfaces.eu/multi-actor-platforms/). Furthermore, these conclusions were disseminated to the representatives of the management authority for Romania's CAP National Strategic Plan 2023–2027 and served as a source of arguments for the points of view of MAP members during the public consultations for the elaboration of the NSP.
- Step 4: Desk research and context analysis on the policy context and governance processes on agri-food value chains was also performed by the research team of IAE-RA and shed light on the main national strategies and policy objectives that govern the agri-food system in order to feed the second round of focus group discussions with the Romanian MAPs members. A special attention was paid to the mechanisms through which public participation in public policy decisions is organised, as well as initiatives (where they exist) to increase the involvement of rural actors in the decision-making process.
- Step 5: Second round of focus groups on the key points of participatory governance of the agri-food value chain was performed in the spring of 2023 with the common participation of all three MAPs in common meetings.

- Step 6: Results validation consisted of a final round of focus groups with the MAPs members aimed to confirm the validity of conclusions formulated by the IAE-RA team of experts after analysing the information collected in the previous steps 4 and 5.

In the following subchapter, the conclusions of the Delphi exercises carried out with the participation of MAP members from Romania will be briefly presented regarding, in particular, their recommendations for improving the participatory governance of the agri-food system at the regional and national level.

3 Policy Context

Nowadays, there are numerous strategies in place regarding the long-term development prospects in Romania, in general, and in the rural area, in particular, developed by different reflection groups set up, mostly, at national level. In addition, there are also sectoral strategies targeting specific sectors or areas (agriculture, eco-tourism, the Danube area, etc.) as well as foresights of civic initiatives that address certain thematic and/or particular territory of Romania. The existing foresights place agriculture at the core of rural development. Thus, three strategies on the medium and long term, horizon 2030, covering the current time frame were launched immediately after 2010, with Romania's Government, the Ministry of Agriculture and Rural Development (MARD) and the Romanian Presidency being the three initiators.

In terms of general orientation, "*Romania's National Sustainable Development Strategy 2030*" adopted by Romania's Government in the year 2008 and revised in 2018, Horizon 2030 aims to get "*significantly close to the average performance of the EU Member States by that year in terms of sustainable development indicators*" (RG, 2018). In the same document, the targets set for the programming horizon directly addressing the rural area are, in most cases, formulated in general terms. The emphasis is laid on unlocking the agricultural potential and secondly, on the orientation towards a circular economy and sustainable exploitation of the other resources (landscape, local traditions). The public efforts to improve the rural living conditions are prioritarily directed to compact communities, included in the area of influence of the economic growth poles.

Among the objectives of the governmental strategy 2030, those addressing directly the rural area are the following:

- Doubling the share of agriculture in Romania's GDP, compared to 2018.
- Increasing the share of organic farming in total agricultural production.
- Maintaining and increasing the profitability of certain traditional occupations and methods for the valorisation of medicinal herbs and berries in the mountain area. Maintaining the local traditions by increasing the number of products with specific characteristics in terms of geographical origin.
- Connecting at least 90% of the population's households from towns, communes and compact villages to the drinking water and sewerage network.
- Development of a long-term competitive tourism, of agro-tourism, eco-tourism, rural, balneary and cultural tourism and improving Romania's image as a tourist destination.
- Development and implementation of a general spatial planning and land use programme in correlation with the sectoral strategies at national level, by applying the concept of polycentric and balanced spatial development, to support territorial cohesion.
- Strengthening efforts to protect and safeguard the cultural and natural heritage, the landscape elements in the urban and rural areas.
- Gradual shift to a new development model based on the rational and responsible use of resources, introducing elements of circular economy, elaboration of a roadmap (RG, 2018).

MARD, responsible for the management of agriculture and rural area in Romania, launched its own strategy under the slogan "*Smart capitalisation on Romania's agri-food potential. Horizon 2020–2030*" (MARD, 2015). MARD strategy focuses on the agri-food sector, with an adjacent approach to rural development from the perspective of improving the living conditions for the rural population.

MARD strategy vision for horizon 2020–2030 stipulates: "*Romania will have a sustainable and competitive agri-food sector, focused on the export of high value-added products, resilient to global challenges, which ensures well-being and living conditions for the population quite similar to those in the urban area*" (MARD, 2015).

Strategic objectives of the strategy include:

- Acceleration of structural transition to economically viable agriculture, in parallel with the implementation of environmentally friendly practices and gradual diminution of agricultural workforce.
- Increasing the coverage of food consumption needs from domestic production and regaining the status of net agri-food exporter, in line with the sectoral production potential and in response to the growing food demand worldwide.
- Limiting the carbon footprint of agriculture, promoting organic and climate change-resistant agriculture, adequate water management and encouraging renewable energy production.
- Improving living standards in rural areas, providing infrastructure and basic services comparable to those in urban areas, narrowing the rural income gaps between Romania and the EU average.
- Development of partnerships for education/consultancy, ICT, RDI and improvement of agricultural administration performance as a foundation for a competitive, knowledge-based agriculture (MARD, 2015).

These objectives are operationalised to a good extent, through the CAP National Strategic Plan 2023–2027 shorty described below.

The Presidential Commission for Public Policies for Agriculture Development launched the "*National strategic framework for sustainable development of the agri-food sector and rural area in the period 2014–2020-2030*" in the summer of 2013 (PCPPAD, 2013).

According to this position paper, the priority of agriculture and rural economy modernisation should be based on the vital economic and social functions of the agri-food system, through:

- Ensuring a balanced diet (hence food security implicitly) for the population, the necessary raw materials for non-agricultural activities and an active and profitable export of agri-food products.
- Ensuring a decent living standard for the farmer families.
- Environmental protection.

- Rural economy, in general, and agriculture in particular, represent a huge market for the upstream and downstream sectors, directly contributing to the development of non-agricultural branches, as well as of the sectors related to agriculture (and forestry).
- Enhancing the landscape capital of rural areas (PCPPAD, 2013).

Similar to approaches of previous strategic visions, agriculture remains the pivot around which the development prospects of rural areas are outlined, yet the members of the Presidential Commission emphasise the need"*to change the centre of gravity from the productivist aspect to the multifunctional aspect of agriculture*" (PCPPAD, 2013).

Among the sectoral strategies (nationwide), the most relevant for the rural area, given the abundance of protected areas, is the *"National strategy for ecotourism development in Romania—context, vision and objectives –2019–2029"*. Adopted by Romania's Government in the year 2019 (RG, 2019); this strategy sets out to promote eco-tourism, as a main form of tourism in the natural protected areas and adjacent areas with a relevant contribution to the economic development of these destinations and for the prosperity of the population in the communities at underdevelopment and social marginalization risk.

As it has been mentioned in the strategic approach, the vision of the Strategy for eco-tourism development is: "*affirmation of Romania's natural and cultural values, by creating and promoting a network of eco-tourism destinations with national and international notoriety, which will contribute to the improvement of the life of local communities and to the conservation of local natural and cultural resources*" (RG, 2019).

In the explanatory memorandum, the Government states that by adopting the vision and strategic objectives of ecotourism development in Romania, a first step has been made for the construction of green economy in the rural area, where natural protected areas also exist, which can become a catalyst for local development. Thus, the natural protected areas in particular, and nature conservation in general, can acquire an economic and social value at local and national level, by improving the degree of understanding and acceptance of this particular aspect of sustainable development.

The most important policy document governing the agri-food system, which also includes concrete measures and clearly defined funding sources to reach its objectives, is the National Strategic Plan (NSP) 2023–2027.

The NSP for Romania targets the development of a resilient, sustainable and competitive agricultural sector, focused on ensuring fair incomes for farmers, respecting the environmental commitments by remunerating farmers who contribute to environmental protection above the basic level requirements, development of deficient sectors and balanced socio-economic development of rural areas based on a SWOT analysis-substantiated strategy.

The NSP 2023–2027 aims to achieve the following objectives (MARD, 2022):

Promoting a smart, resilient and diversified agricultural sector that ensures food security, increases farm viability through the stabilisation of farmers' incomes and elimination of disparities between farms.

Under this objective, the NSP aims to consolidate the agricultural holdings to ensure an optimum level of viability and to revitalise the livestock farming sector through interventions focused on providing support to the crop and livestock sectors in areas with commercial deficit, with emphasis on the protein crop sector.

Strengthening market orientation and increasing the competitiveness of the agri-food sector through the intensification of cooperation, encouraging collective investments, farm modernisation and restructuring through investments to improve productivity simultaneously with the development and modernisation of food industry.

NSP 2023–2027 also aims to increase productivity, mainly for small and medium-sized farms, by supporting on-farm investments, mainly in the sectors that began to develop as a result of capital inflows from EAFRD (vegetable and fruit farming, bee-keeping, viticulture, animal husbandry), together with increased investments in precision farming and digitalisation-innovation.

Under this objective, reducing the competitiveness gaps is also targeted, in terms of agricultural raw materials and processed products, by: ii) stimulating cooperation and strengthening farmers' association that will improve farmers' position in the value chain, equilibrate the trade balance and farmers' vertical integration in the value chain (processing, distribution, marketing); ii) investments in conditioning/storage and processing units that will lead to the increase in the value added of Romanian agri-food products, contributing to self-sufficiency on the national market and equilibrating the trade balance.

Socio-economic development of rural areas by attracting and supporting young people and facilitating business development, promoting and increasing employment, social inclusion and local development in rural areas.

NSP supports generational renewal by providing direct payments to active young farmers, support for setting up of young farmers and consolidation of their farms. At the same time, it also aims at the creation and development of small-scale non-agricultural businesses, as an important source of employment and income diversification, leading to the increase of attractiveness of rural areas, reducing urban-rural disparities and migration to urban areas of young people in particular.

Among the foresights of civic initiatives we can mention as the most relevant "Balance Brings Beauty. Strategies for a Sustainable Southern Transylvania". This vision position paper was developed by a research team from Leuphana University Lüneburg (Germany) that conducted a detailed and inclusive exercise in 2019. The vision exercise involved many local actors representing economic, social and environmental interests. According to this vision, on the 30-year time horizon: *"policy focus on the environment, locals collaborate and are able to capitalize on high national and international demand for organic agricultural products. Sustainable use of resources co-exists with intensified land use via modern organic farming methods. Vibrant cultural tourism and eco-tourism stabilise people's incomes from the agricultural sector. Although few people are financially wealthy, economic and social inequalities are relatively low, and community spirit is high. Cultural and natural capital is valued and actively maintained"* (Fischer et al., 2019).

For the development of each of the strategies/programmes previously described, participatory mechanisms were used, through which, according to these documents, representatives of all stakeholders were called and involved in the political dialogue. However, it is worth noting that the strategic documents were, for the most part, synthesised at national level. The centralisation tendency at national level led, in most cases, to the circumvention of certain regional/local contexts and characteristics, which makes long-term strategies appear to be inadequate for certain specific territories or groups of less vocal actors and thus these see themselves as left behind.

4 Participatory governance in the Romanian Agri-food System

An Overview of Participatory governance in Romania

As a whole, the main challenge regarding the Romanian governance system is related to the low capacity of public authorities to incorporate a participatory approach in the planning process. *The State of Democracy in 2021* [in Romania], a report by the Coalition of NGOs for the Citizen, draws attention to the high degree of formalism in public consultation processes. Some of the problems signalled out in the report are:

Most local authorities do not respect the 30-working day deadline in which they are due to make draft normative acts publicly available. In the best cases, the draft is made public just 5 days before it is debated and voted on in local council meetings;

Most local public authorities do not keep a record of active organisations at the local level. Even in the cases when these organisations are known, there are no mechanisms in place for communicating with them and including them in the decision-making process;

Communication with citizens is more about solving up specific problems signalled out by citizens (responses to petitions). In general, there are no mechanisms for involving citizens in public decision-making, either referring to projects on the agenda of local councils or organising debates on topics of local interest (Coalition of NGOs for the Citizen, 2022).

The deficiencies in the functioning of participatory mechanisms contribute to the low motivation of people to get involved in governance and administration, as they feel marginalised in political, social and economic debates. Furthermore, the potential actors of the participatory process feel that they are not competent enough to act as an equivalent counterpart and a catalyst for change. The distance between citizens and public authorities is growing at ~~to~~ all levels, leading to a lack of confidence and public participation, mainly among the most disadvantaged groups, minority communities, women and children (Szalók et al., 2019).

A long term rural vision exercise conducted in 2020 in Transylvania (the western part of the country) reveals the weak points of participatory governance in the Romanian rural area. Thus, the 2020 analysis highlights that, in rural Romania, there is an acute lack of local leadership, and the public-private partnerships are dysfunctional (even formal in many cases). As a result, the development strategies are generic, without a clear vision on the valorisation of real potentialities of rural communities. The document draws attention to the main needs that, once satisfied, can make *local governance* functional: there is a need to develop the skills and capabilities of local actors (of employees in the public services in particular) to animate the territory and mobilise the community, so that all rural actors can be actively and effectively involved from the bottom up in the formulation of long-term strategies (Tudor & Brumă, 2020).

In the preparation process of the CAP National Strategic Plans 2023–2027, using the participatory approach was a mandatory requirement from the European Commission. Thus, it is intended to help the CAP managing authorities in the identification and assessment of stakeholders' perspectives and needs, which can be used to inform policy analyses and policy choices. Participatory tools are to be considered as being pivotal in ensuring the transparency, inclusivity, and legitimacy of CAP Strategic plans and in aligning the CAP with the needs and aspirations of those directly impacted by agricultural policies. Examples of such tools used in Romania: stakeholder consultations, focus and working expert groups, workshops, conferences, surveys, etc.

The evaluation of usefulness and effectiveness of participatory tools used in designing of NSP in Romania was performed during the autumn of 2023 throughout a focus group discussion with the NSP managing authorities (MARD) and research and farmers associations' representatives. According to the MARD staff, the most accurate view on the rural stakeholder needs is obtained by involving experts who have participated in the implementation and monitoring of the public programmes and/or have an overall vision of the field based on evidence from comprehensive analyses and studies, on one or several specific topics related to the EU targets. It seems that the main challenge in the participatory approach in Romania is *building consensus* between various and non-homogeneous groups of stakeholders in term of expertise and knowledge of European rigours and/or with farmers of various sizes. Stakeholders often lacked clarity on how their expressed needs influenced final decisions, which in turn led to dissatisfaction.

This challenge is partly derived from another weakness that hinders the participatory process—*fragmentation and lack of organisation of some categories of rural stakeholders*, namely small and medium-sized farmers from Romania. The low level of organisation in professional associations hindered their ability to provide streamlined inputs. Lack of organisation at the level of some rural stakeholders generated difficulties in the selection process of their representatives in public consultation process and resulted in a poor representation of these categories in developing the NSP and *unbalancing the power in the governance process*.

Another significant constraint for participatory governance used for designing NSP was related to the *time and skills constrains* for processing and analysing stakeholder input. Authorities often faced limitations in capacity and tools to effectively analyse and synthesise the input received, especially when adapting to online interactions. The shift to digital platforms during the COVID-19 pandemic further posed difficulties for stakeholders, such as farmers and other rural actors lacking the necessary digital skills to contribute meaningfully.

Reflections of the Multi-Actor Platforms Regarding the Participatory governance Process in the Agri-food System

Identified Strengths and Needs in the participatory Governance Process

From the perspective of the Romanian Multi-Actor Platforms participants, the **critical imperatives** concerning the formulation of policies encompass several key dimensions listed above. Foremost among these is the imperative to augment the representation of actors engaged in the participatory process. A prevailing sentiment among numerous local farmers and producers is powerlessness and marginalisation in national decision-making. This is due the fragmentation of representative organisations in terms of interests and opinions. The need to address this disparity is paramount to fostering a more inclusive and representative participatory landscape.

Another pressing concern is the necessity to rebalance power dynamics in the decision-making process between small local producers and bigger entities within the agri-food chain. The consensus among MAP members in Romania highlights the inadequate involvement and negotiating power of small local producer associations in public debates, events, and consultations. Consequently, an asymmetry emerges, tilting the scales in favour of large players in the agri-food chain.

Furthermore, there is a call to elevate the significance of local needs in the decision-making process at both national and European levels. Local authorities, territorial agricultural directorates, and Local Action Groups (LAGs) are often perceived merely as executors of political decisions, lacking the role of genuine dialogue partners or animators of the territory. The discrepancy between locally agreed-upon decisions and their consideration in the formulation of national and European plans and policies is also perceived as a major issue.

As a result, enhancing coordination and improving communication, both horizontally (among agri-food chain actors, producers, and local authorities) and vertically (between local, national, and European authorities), is deemed essential for increased policy and programme effectiveness. This necessitates improvements in staff skills at local and national levels, incorporating agricultural expertise, management, marketing, advisory, and communication skills to bolster the participatory process.

Moreover, there is a recognised need to address skill deficiencies among rural actors through dedicated programmes. These initiatives should empower them with the requisite capabilities for active participation in the governance process. Additionally, efforts should be directed towards promoting and facilitating access to public consultation processes for less vocal and technically adept rural actors. A reported lack of transparency in the organisation of public consultations underscores the importance of broadening access and ensuring inclusivity.

Finally, it is imperative to heighten awareness of the relevance of active participation in the decision-making process. The prevailing tendency of small local actors to adopt a reactive rather than proactive stance poses a risk of rendering the participatory process merely formal in nature. Urgent measures are required to instil a proactive approach among stakeholders and thereby fortify engagement of all actors in shaping policies and programmes.

Simultaneously, the participatory process in formulating policies and programmes at the Multi-Actor Platforms (MAPs) level in Romania is bolstered by **notable strengths**. A proactive stance is evident, particularly in fostering the involvement of young people in participatory governance. Additionally, there is a growing public awareness of the significance of local/regional short chains, education, and the cultivation of an agri-food culture, fostering an increased inclination to engage in participatory governance.

Further strengths lie in the presence of reliable local leaders, embodied by expert groups, universities, research centres, and NGOs. These entities serve as focal points for dialogue groups, aiding local authorities in facilitating public debates and substantiating decisions. The association of farmers and producers in "guilds" such as federations, confederations, traditional producer groups, and specialised farming associations enhances participation and involvement in participatory governance across horizontal and vertical dimensions.

Moreover, the existence of a regulatory framework mandating public consultations, coupled with allocated funding sources for diverse priorities and beneficiaries, acts as a catalyst for dialogue between authorities and potential beneficiaries within the participatory process. These strengths collectively contribute towards a more robust participatory governance structure at the MAPs level in Romania.

Initiatives Supporting Inclusive Participatory Approach of the Agri-Food System

Addressing issues listed before as limited capacity of public authorities to integrate a participatory approach into the planning process; lack of competences of small and unorganised (agri-food) actors in participating in negotiations as equal counterparts; power imbalance in term of knowledge and market share between small and big players in agri-food chains; reactive nature of citizen engagement etc. are essential to promote a more inclusive and effective participatory governance process in the agri-food system in Romania. In this context, it is important to highlight a range of initiatives and interventions that local actors have used to address this kind of challenges encountered by participatory process in Romania. Some of these examples are listed below and highlighting a bottom-up approach useful to be explored and used as support for developing inclusive governance process.

Agro-Transylvania Cluster (ATC) was established as a consultative body with the purpose of providing reflective support to the county council in the decision-making process concerning the requisite public measures aimed at enhancing the competitiveness of the agri-food sector in Cluj county. To fulfil this objective, in the autumn of 2013, ATC conducted an extensive assessment encompassing an analysis of available resources, as well as the discerned needs and expectations associated with the future of the agri-food sector in Cluj county. This analysis was conducted through the engagement of interviews with various stakeholders, including public officials, representatives from the business community, and county residents. The primary intent of the ATC study was to contribute to the facilitation of a constructive public discourse and to inform administrative decisions pertaining to the County Development Strategy, with specific emphasis on the agro-industrial component, covering the period 2014–2020.

The **Rural Development Research Platform (RDRP)** is a non-governmental organisation established in 2019, located in Iaşi county. RDRP's core objective is to foster the establishment of a functional local agri-food ecosystem. This is achieved by acting as a catalyst for the connection between local producers and consumers, facilitating the exchange of knowledge, and serving as a mediator to enhance interactions between various stakeholders within the local agri-food chain and public authorities. The initiatives undertaken by RDRP encompass the development of digital platforms such as "Gust de Iaşi" (Taste of Iaşi), which facilitates direct engagement between local producers and consumers in Iaşi city. Another significant initiative, "ECORURIS," is dedicated to promoting and endorsing environmentally sustainable practices within local agriculture, with a particular focus on enhancing the sustainability of local value chains. Moreover, RDRP plays a pivotal role in orchestrating dialogues between local authorities and farmers, processors or researchers. Furthermore, RDRP collaborates with Eco Ruralis to advocate for the interests of small-scale farmers and actively participates in the initiation and endorsement of open letters supporting agri-food short supply chains.

Eco Ruralis is an organisation founded in 2009, representing the interests and rights of peasants, as well as small-scale producers across all regions of Romania. It operates at national level and is boasting a membership exceeding 17,000 individuals. One of the pivotal methods by which Eco Ruralis actively participates in the participatory process is by endorsing open letters directed at government authorities and agencies responsible for the agri-food sector. Through these letters, they respond to existing decisions and put forth specific administrative solutions aimed at addressing ongoing issues concerning the sustainable integration of small-scale producers into agri-food supply chains. Notably, such letters have advocated for the maintenance of local agri-food markets during the COVID-19 pandemic, ultimately influencing the reconsideration of administrative decisions to close wet markets. Furthermore, Eco Ruralis plays a unifying role among similar organizations, by providing support for their participative governance advocacy efforts.

Food for Iaşi Living Lab (FILL) operates as an innovative collaborative hub in Iaşi city, aiming to connect various stakeholders within the urban food system to identify critical challenges and develop innovative solutions for sustainable local development. Participants in FILL include representatives from academia, businesses, consumers, civil society, and public administration. The primary beneficiaries of FILL initiatives are urban consumers and food producers. One notable outcome of FILL's participatory approach is the organisation of fairs, specifically "Iași in ecological, traditional, mountain, and artisan cuisine". These events are made possible through the collaboration of multiple entities, including the Iași Branch of the Romanian Academy, the Iași Municipality Town Hall, the Iași County Agricultural Directorate, Iași University of Life Sciences, and the Association of Local Producers "Produs în Iași" (Made in Iași).

Family Farm Association—Arges (FFA) represents a collective of small-scale, local producers based in Argeș county. The association is committed to advancing the "family farm" model and advocating for the interests of such farm structures. FFA has taken the initiative to engage in discussions with the Argeș Agricultural Directorate, with the aim of coordinating vocational training programmes designed for young farmers in Argeș county. These training courses cater to those actively engaged in EU-funded projects or individuals seeking support for agricultural and rural development initiatives, thereby fostering knowledge and skills essential for successful participation in such endeavours.

All five previously-described initiatives were mentioned by the members of Romanian MAPs during the various discussions on potential solutions and ideas for improving participatory mechanisms in the political and/or administrative decision-making process. MAP members highlighted the contribution that this kind of local initiatives can have in the establishment of think tank groups closer to the real needs of actors from marginalised groups / less involved in the debates (usually at national level) organised by the public authorities that invite to the dialogue table "the usual suspects", already known and used to such negotiations. Moreover, local participatory governance initiatives can significantly contribute to improving, besides the representativeness level of territories / small actors, their abilities to take an active part in the decision-making process by building the necessary capacities to participate in such a process.

Recommendations for Improving Participation in the Agri-food Governance in Romania

To ensure the efficacy of agri-food policies, active participation and engagement from a diverse range of stakeholders are essential. Further, we will explore a comprehensive set of recommendations for shaping future meaningful contribution of all interested parties in the governance of agri-food system in Romania as resulted from the focus groups discussions with MAPs members. These recommendations address various facets, including communication, organisational mechanisms, stakeholder involvement, knowledge sharing, and the promotion of inclusivity. By implementing these suggestions, Romania can foster a more effective and sustainable policy framework, one that is responsive to the specific needs and challenges of its agri-food system in particular and rural communities, in general terms.

The first major set of recommendations aims at **enhancing participatory mechanisms and communication**. To initiate and sustain an effective participatory process in rural policy formulation, public communication is paramount. Recommendations include clarifying the purpose of dialogue within the governance process and emphasising specific problems for which consensus is sought. Communication should be conducted in a language that is accessible to all stakeholders, avoiding jargon and complex terminology. Additionally, using communication channels and tools readily available to the target audience is necessary because transparent and accessible communication fosters trust and encourages broader participation (Wachinger et al., 2013). In these circumstances, the National Rural Development Network can play a significant role in enhancing the participatory process.

Recommendations include organising round tables, specialist workshops, and training courses for those interested in contributing to the decision-making process. Expanding the frequency and territorial coverage of these events ensures a wider range of voices to be integrated into the policy development process. Furthermore, the establishment of a national network for rural facilitators and consultants, who are specially trained and motivated to facilitate the participatory process, is a crucial recommendation. These facilitators can mediate horizontal and vertical communication, enhancing the quality and effectiveness of the participatory approach.

The second major set of recommendations aims at **strengthening facilitation and consultation between all stakeholders.** Technical assistance and specialised advising are recommended to develop professional training and information platforms in the field of agricultural production and agri-food marketing. Furthermore, rural actors should be supported in using digital tools to enhance their participation in digital platforms. Knowledge platforms can bring together multi-actor discussion groups and facilitate policy dialogue, enhancing the overall effectiveness of the participatory process. In addition, private agricultural chambers can be established, representing farmers' interests and providing specialised consultancy. These chambers would collaborate with agricultural chambers at county level and Local Action Groups (LAGs). Private agricultural chambers have the potential to play a significant facilitating role in the participatory governance process, ensuring that farmers' voices are integrated into policy development.

The third major set of recommendations aims at **creating a diverse and inclusive engagement process.** Reinforcing programmes that stimulate cooperation and association among local actors in the agri-food chain is important. Such programmes aim to increase rural actors' representation and their access to specialised knowledge and information. Cooperative efforts among local actors can enhance the development of more effective and responsive rural policies. Moreover, the mediatisation and dissemination of examples of good practice regarding collaboration and cooperation actions between multi-actors at local, regional, and European levels can boost up cooperation. These examples can inspire and serve as catalysts for active involvement and participation in the decision-making process. Sharing success stories promotes effective strategies and encourages broader participation in the governance process. Public events, such as fairs, exhibitions, and cultural gatherings, should be used as a means of communication and interaction within the participatory process. These events can also serve as a platform for identifying potential participants in public consultations.

To promote inclusivity and social equity, active involvement of vulnerable groups, particularly those at risk of poverty and social exclusion, is pressing. The creation of "social farms" can serve as a platform for the involvement of these groups in the political dialogue. Furthermore, social economy initiatives can provide opportunities for vulnerable individuals to actively participate in the decision-making process, contributing to their well-being and the overall development of rural areas.

The last set of recommendations is aimed at **youth involvement in the governance system.** To diffuse fresh perspectives and energy into the participatory process, stimulating the involvement of young people, especially farmers and small producers, is recommended. Young individuals can serve as change vectors, advocating for the participation of other stakeholders. Their active involvement can inject vitality into rural policy development. In this regard, the creation and implementation of educational modules for children and teenagers are also recommended. These modules are designed to increase their awareness of sustainable consumption, rural area development, and social economy. By stimulating the interest of the young generation in these important topics, we can foster an active involvement in the decision-making processes and ensure a sustainable future.

The recommendations outlined above collectively form a comprehensive approach to shaping the future of agri-food policies in Romania. These recommendations encompass enhancing communication, formalising mechanisms, involving a wide range of stakeholders, promoting knowledge sharing, and fostering inclusivity. By embracing these suggestions, Romania can develop a more effective and sustainable agri-food policy framework that is responsive to the specific needs of its rural communities, promotes social and economic development, and ensures a better quality of life for its citizens.

5 Conclusions

The main challenge regarding the participatory governance system in Romania is related to the low capacity of public authorities to incorporate a participatory approach in the process of developing public policies and communicate the benefits of cooperation and active involvement in the governance process. In essence, for an effective governance process, in Romania it is necessary to increase the degree of representativeness of actors involved in the participatory process, alongside with balancing the power between small local producers and the "big players" in the agri-food chain.

In order to capitalise on the desire of young people to be involved in the participatory governance process, as well as to encourage the involvement of less vocal actors, decision-makers could increase the weight given to local needs in the decision-making process. In this regard, the active involvement of young people (farmers) as well as vulnerable groups, through the development of the social economy, is important.

Likewise, the effectiveness of participatory governance can be improved in Romania by developing "networks of networks", which would bring together professional organisations from academia, consultancy, farmers and small producers. Thus, a national network can be created, in which rural facilitators and consultants that are specially trained will assist and mediate horizontal and vertical governance process. The creation of these "networks of networks" must be supported by programmes that stimulate association and cooperation between local actors in the agri-food chain. At the same time, the future involvement of young people in participatory governance can be encouraged through the development and implementation of educational modules aimed at increasing young people's awareness of sustainable consumption, the development of the rural environment and the social economy.

It is recommended to develop and implement inclusive mechanisms and tools that support the vertically participatory process and clearly communicate the benefits of participation. At the same time, supporting the decision-making process through relevant analysis of trends regarding the debate topics (at local, regional, national, EU and global level) and the public communication of these findings for the large public in an easy-to-digest manner, can significantly encourage participation and involvement.

Acknowledgements Authors acknowledge the members of Arges, Iasi and Transylvania Multi-actor Platforms that actively contributed to the discussions and other organisations, initiatives and projects that provide sources of data and information. SHERPA was funded from the European Union's Horizon 2020 Research and Innovation Programme under Grant Agreement No. 862448.

References

Coalition of NGOs for the citizen. (2022). *The state of democracy in 2021.* https://www.stareademocratiei.ro/2022/05/26/the-state-of-democracy-in-2021-a-report-of-the-coalition-of-ngos-for-the-citizen/

EU Commission. (2015). Local and regional partners contributing to Europe 2020, European Commission, Directorate-General for Regional and Urban Policy.

Faberi. (2018). Multi-level governance: linking up local, regional and national levels to deliver integrated sustainable energy action plans and projects, Odyssee-Mure Project Policy Brief.

Fischer, J., Horcea-Milcu, A.I., Lang, D.J., Thale-Bombien, L., Abson, D.J., Apetrei, C.I., Clarke, E., Derwort, P., Dorninger, C., Duse, I. A., Freeth, R., Jager, N. W., Klaniecki, K., Lam, D., Leventon, J. Newig, J., Peukert, D., Riechers, M., Schaal, T. (2019). *Balance Brings Beauty. Strategies for a Sustainable Southern Transylvania*. https://leveragepointsdotorg.files.wordpress.com/2019/03/balance-brings-beauty_en.pdf.

Hooghe, L. & Marks, G. (2001). Types of multi-level governance. European Integration online Papers (EIoP). *SSRN*, *5*(11), 1–24. https://ssrn.com/abstract=302786 or https://doi.org/10.2139/ssrn.302786

MADR. (2022). *National Strategic Plan CAP for Romania 2023–2027 (version 1.2—Nov. 2022)*, https://www.madr.ro/docs/dezvoltare-rurala/2022/PNS_2023-2027-versiunea_1.2–21.11.2022.pdf

Miller, D., Chartier, O., Salle, E., Zomer, B., Irvine, K., Schwarz, G. (2022). First set of recommendations for development of future rural policies, D7.3. *Sustainable Hub to Engage into Rural Policies with Actors (SHERPA)*.

Ministry of Agriculture and Rural Development (MARD). (2015). *Strategia pentru dezvoltarea sectorului agroalimentar pe termen mediu şi lung. Orizont 2020–2030* [Agri-food sector development strategy for medium and long term. Horizon 2020–2030]. https://madr.ro/docs/agricultura/strategia-agroalimentara-2020–2030.pdf

Presidential Commission for public policies for agriculture development (PCPPAD). (2013). *Cadrul naţional strategic pentru dezvoltarea durabilă a sectorului agroalimentar şi a spaţiului rural în perioada 2014–2020-2030* [National strategic framework for sustainable development of the agri-food sector and rural area in the period 2014–2020-2030]. https://acad.ro/forumuri/doc2013/d0701-02StrategieCadrulNationalRural.pdf

Romania's Government (RG). (2018). *Strategia naţională pentru dezvoltarea durabilă a României 2030* [Romania's National Sustainable Development Strategy 2030]. http://dezvoltaredurabila.gov.ro/web/wp-content/uploads/2018/12/Strategia-na%C8%9Bional%C4%83-pentru-dezvoltarea-durabil%C4%83-a-Rom%C3%A2niei-2030.pdf

Romania's Government (RG). (2019). *Strategia naţională de dezvoltare a ecoturismului în România—context, viziune şi obiective—2019–2029* [National strategy for eco-tourism development in Romania—context, vision and objectives—2019–2029]. https://agroromania.manager.ro/dbimg/files/strategia-ecoturism-2019–2019.pdf

Slätmo, E., Oliveira e Costa, S., Qvist Eliasen, S., Miller, D., Piter, L., Kull, M. and Potters, J. (2021). Methods for setting-up of MAPs, D5.1. *Sustainable Hub to Engage into Rural Policies with Actors (SHERPA)*.

Szalók, M., Cs, B., & Kozina, J. (Eds.). (2019). *Participatory urban agriculture governance plan for fighting social exclusion in the Danube region*. Central Transdanubian Regional Inno-vation Agency. https://www.interreg-danube.eu/uploads/media/approved_project_output/0001/29/7951bad5c888f772c6881fcf11713c3349b7d14b.pdf

Tudor, M.M., & Brumă, I. S. (2020). *Long term vision for rural areas: MAP position paper—rural Transylvania*. https://rural-interfaces.eu/wp-content/uploads/2021/02/MAP_Position-Paper_RO_LTVRA.pdf

Wachinger, G., Renn, O., Begg, C., & Kuhlicke, C. (2013). The risk perception paradox—Implications for governance and communication of natural hazards. *Risk Analysis, 33*(6), 1049–1065.

Wellbrock, W., Roep, D., Mahon, M., Kairyte, E., Nienaber, B., Domínguez García, M. D., Kriszan, M., & Farrell, M. (2013). Arranging public support to unfold collaborative modes of governance in rural areas. *Journal of Rural Studies, 32*, 420–429. https://doi.org/10.1016/j.jrurstud.2013.10.0

CHAPTER 11

Digitalisation as Key for Rural Development

Uri Marchaim and Idan Kopler

1 Introduction

We are in pursue for a successful digital future. Digitalisation has transformed societies and economies across the world for the past 20 years and continues to do so at an ever-faster speed (Vironen & Kah, 2019). In rural areas digitalisation presents both opportunities and challenges for regional development (Randall et al., 2018). When dealing with leveraging rural areas socio-economic status one should bear in mind the below mentioned bullet points reported in Eurostat's online publication *Urban–Rural Europe* (Eurostat, 2022):

- Between 2015–2020 negative crude rates of natural population change were reported in 355 out of 406 rural regions in Europe.

U. Marchaim · I. Kopler (✉)
European Wing Unit, MIGAL Galilee Research Institute, Kiryat Shmona, Israel
e-mail: idank@migal.org.il

U. Marchaim
e-mail: uri@migal.org.il

D. Barjolle et al. (eds.), *Innovation and the Future of Rural Development in Europe*,
https://doi.org/10.1007/978-3-032-22570-2_11

- Between 2015–2020 in these regions the number of youngsters fell at an average rate of -0.66% per year, the number of working-age people (20–64 years) fell at an average rate of -0.63% per year, while the number of older people (≥ 65 years) increased by an average rate of 1.80% per year.
- Between 2019 and 2050 twenty member states are projected to record declines in their overall rural populations, ranging from – 43.5% (Lithuania) to -0.6% (Austria).

In 2021, 25.2% of the European Union (EU) population lived in rural areas (Eurostat, 2022). The repercussions to rural areas demography, labour market and labour force, socio-economic status (i.e. risk of poverty and social exclusion), and overall trajectories, are broadly studied (Esparcia, 2014; Féret et al., 2020; SHERPA, 2020), including in this publication. Moreover, The COVID-19 pandemic proved the impactfulness of digitalization on the civilian society, highlighting with greater potency its innate independency on location and space that enabled people in rural and remote areas to reach out beyond their secluded territories. However, the pandemia also exposed the vulnerabilities, barriers and bottlenecks. As stated: "A new digital divide has also emerged, not only between well-connected urban areas and rural and remote territories, but also between those who can fully benefit from an enriched, accessible and secure digital space with a full range of services, and those who cannot" (Papazoglou et al., 2023).

In this chapter we will concisely delineate the main characteristics of Digitalization—a core component of the European twin transition. We will explain the essence of digitalization as a solution in the context of rural areas; we will dwell on relevant European policies, at the Union level, for the assimilation of digitalization in rural areas and we will try to clarify the challenges and barriers to success. We will conclude by presenting a case study for the implementation of digitalization in the rural area of the Galilee region in Israel as part of the case studies in the POLIRURAL project.

2 Digitalization—The Essence

Digital technologies include mobile internet, the internet of things (IoT), big data analytics and artificial intelligence (AI), 3-D printing, advanced robotics, next generation genomics, drones, online platforms and augmented reality (Brunori et al., 2023). One of the main differences among these technologies is that they vary in their degree of adoption at a scale necessary to have any meaningful impact on the way we live (Manyika et al., 2013). One of the more simplistic definitions to digitalisation is provided by Dufva and Dufva (2019): 'The act(s) of transforming various previously physical or analogue actions into digital data systems. This includes processes, interactions, and business models. Sabbagh et al. (2013) define digitalisation as 'the mass adoption of connected digital services by consumers, enterprises, and governments', stressing its large-scale adoption by different stakeholders. It positions digitalization as a catalyst for job creation and economic growth (Degryse, 2016). The European Commission (EC) (2015) echoes the transformative element of digitalization: 'Information and Communication Technologies (ICT) is no longer a specific sector but the foundation of all modern innovative economic systems. The Internet and digital technologies are transforming the lives we lead, the way we work—as individuals, in business, and in our communities'. Hence, digitalization is the large-scale adoption of new technologies into different parts of society generating a sequence of changes to existing facets of life (Randall et al., 2018). Given this, the transformative qualities of digital technologies are as equally, if not more, important as the novel aspects (Alm et al., 2016), and the transformation is contingent on the adoption of the technologies at a large-scale (Randall et al., 2018).

Digitalization is a tool for sustainable social, economic and environmental development (Randall et al., 2018). Digitalization is impacting the labour market, both through the automation of existing work functions and through the creation of new types of ICT of skills. e-Health—"the use of across the whole range of healthcare functions" (European Commission, 2004) benefit all parts of society by telemedicine and telecare, clinical information systems, e-prescribing, disease registries and other non-clinical systems, "Mobile" health (m-health), 'Personalised' health (p-health) and Big Data (Cowie et al., 2016). Digitalization enables fast expansion of business models that promote sustainable consumption through the "sharing" of goods and services through digital platforms (Alm et al., 2016). Digital business encompasses a range of processes and activities enabled by digital technologies that aim to integrate the digital and physical worlds (Gartner, 2021).

In the agricultural sector, the traditional role of agricultural machines has been transformed by the introduction of digitalization tools by which farmers can make tailor-made choices for executing the best intervention (e.g. with field sensors and applications providing advanced options). These new instruments provide the possibility to reduce the physical burden typically associated to farm labour and contribute at reducing the abandonment of agricultural activities and consequent depopulation of rural areas (Popescu et al., 2020). Digital technologies can significantly contribute to the achievement of the European Green Deal (European Commission, 2019) objectives in rural agricultural regions. The uptake of digital solutions and the use of data will help in the transition to a climate neutral, circular and more resilient economy. The substitution of business travel by videoconferencing reduces emissions while digital technologies allow greener processes in agriculture, energy, construction and building, industry, city planning and services, thus contributing to the overarching goal to reduce greenhouse gas emissions by at least 55% by 2030. According to a Deloitte report (Deloitte, 2021) by 2027 the digitalization transformation in Europe could boost the Digital Economy and Society Index (DESI) score to 90, which reflects a GDP increase per capita of 7.2% across the EU.

3 European Policies Facilitating the Digital Transformation in Rural Areas

Among the European Commission's six political priorities for 2019–2024 is a Europe fit for the digital age. It reflects yet another stage in the longstanding commitment of the EU policies towards digitalization in general and in rural areas in particular. These policies are disseminated via programs and communications, of which the main ones with references to rural areas are listed below in Table 1.

4 Digitalization in the EU Rural Context

Digitalization has a prominent role in the EU's Long-Term Vision for Rural Areas, affecting agriculture, forestry and the life of rural citizens. Small and rural communities face greater challenges than metropolitan areas in generating economic growth. Access to physical and industrial resources and distance from urban centres, are obstacles to rural communities (Liu, 2021; OECD, 2014). Furthermore, there are persistent disparities between urban and rural areas with respect to the availability of digital infrastructure and the adoption of digital technologies. Lynn

Table 1 A comprehensive list of European policies with references to the Digital Transformation in rural areas as disseminated via EU programs and communications

Program, Communication	*Main message*	*Objective*
Communication *Towards a European Gigabit Society* (European Commission, 2016b)	• **A vision for a European Gigabit society**. Availability and take-up of Very High-Capacity Networks (VHCN) enable the widespread use of products, services and applications	A downlink of at least 100 Mbps in all European households by 2025
European Union's Green Deal (European Commission, 2019)	• Rural areas are pivotal for achieving the goal of declaring Europe a neutral continent by 2050 • Digitalisation will have a major role in circular and bio-economy, the preservation of biodiversity and production of renewable energy for the implementation of EU policies	
Communication *Strategy for Shaping Europe's digital future* (European Commission, 2020a)	**Connectivity is the most fundamental building block of the digital transformation** that allows to develop and use digital solutions at scale	• A revision of the Broadband Cost Reduction Directive, an updated Action Plan on 5G and 6G, a new Radio Spectrum Policy Program (2021) • The Cohesion Policy legislation 2021–2027, the Technical Support Instrument, and the Digital Europe Programme form the financial pipelines for the investments necessary for the digital transition

(continued)

Table 1 (continued)

Program, Communication	*Main message*	*Objective*
Digital Education Action Plan (2021–2027) (European Commission, 2020b)	**Boosting digital literacy and competences at all levels of education** and, a reinforced Skills Agenda to strengthen digital skills throughout society	Action 4—"Connectivity and digital equipment for education and training", aim at supporting gigabit and 5G connectivity for smart communities and promoting 5G connectivity best practices in local communities and schools, alongside other education and training institutions
Cohesion Policy 2021–2027	• **The main EU's investment policy aimed at reducing regional disparities**. Particular attention is given to rural areas and regions hampered by natural or demographic impediments (Papazoglou et al., 2023) • Digitalization is a viable alternative for delivering cost-effective, remotely coordinated, public services in mountainous and sparsely populated European regions (Dubois & Sielker, 2022)	The European Regional Development Fund (ERDF) and the Cohesion Fund (CF) (European Parliament, 2021a) through Articles 3, 5, 10, exhibit intervention fields with a digital dimension (Papazoglou et al., 2023)
An exemplary EU-funded project improving lives in peripheral communities in context of digitalization is the EU ESIF and ERDF funded initiative (under the the Cohesion Policy legislation 2014–2020) to deliver internet access to some 5,000 villages in the Zagori region of northern Greece's Pindos Mountains that previously had either slow or non-existent web access		
Communication *2030 Digital Compass* (European Commission, 2021a)	**The digital divide causes a phenomenon that has been indicated as 'digital poverty'** (European Commission, 2021a), that needs to be eradicated	• Four guiding digital principles: (a) Access to high quality connectivity; (b) Access to sufficient digital skills; (c) Access to public services; (d) Access to fair and non-discriminatory online services • An emphasis is given to "Smart villages", i.e. communities in rural areas that serve as laboratories in which local people and policy-makers develop and test innovative solutions to improve their resilience

Program, Communication	*Main message*	*Objective*
An example of such a solution is enabling access to public services through a place-based digital platform for elderly people (MOBIL-AGE project)		
The Recovery and Resilience Facility (RRF) (European Parliament, 2021b)	• **The key instrument of NextGenerationEU**, the economic recovery package to support Member States impacted by the COVID-19 pandemic • All the Digital Decade cardinal points are expected to benefit from this funding (Papazoglou et al., 2023)	• The total digital expenditure amounts to €130 billion • The intervention field "1-051—Very High-Capacity broadband network (backbone/backhaul network)" is allocated 100% to the gigabit target. Circa €16 billion RRF reforms and investments have already been approved to deploy and upgrade digital connectivity networks in the next four years, especially in rural regions
Connecting Europe Facility (CEF Digital) financial instrument (European Commission, 2021b)	Directly managed by the Commission through its HADEA Agency	• The programme will grant €2 billion over 7 years for high-performance connectivity infrastructures in line with the 2030 digital connectivity targets • A third set of calls opened on October 2023 includes 5G coverage along transport Corridors (€100 million); 5G and Edge Cloud for Smart Communities (€51 million), both focusing on improving 5G connectivity also throughout rural communities

(continued)

Table 1 (continued)

Program, Communication	*Main message*	*Objective*
Communication on the Long-Term Vision for Rural Areas (LTVRA) up to 2040 (European Commission, 2021c)	'Rural Digital Futures'—a flagship initiative • More resilient rural areas that foster well-being, dealing with digital tools as valuable instruments for the preservation of natural resources, and the creation of areas resilient to climate change and potential economic crisis • Prosperous rural areas, stresses digital literacy as decisive for the diversification of economic activities	• An integrated set of actions (Brunori et al., 2022): **Digital connectivity:** closing the gap between rural and urban areas, enabling universal and affordable access to high-speed connectivity, mobilizing private-sector investments; **Digital technology:** digital innovation and new technologies contributing to the development of rural areas (AI, robotics, IOT solutions and Digital Innovation Hubs); **People:** boosting competencies related to the Digital Education Action Plan 2021–2027 objectives, promoting no-one-left-behind digital skills and entrepreneurship • Overall progress towards closing the digital gap will be measured through indicators—the Digital Rural Index • The Rural Pact and Rural Action Plan will summarize the actions identified
Europe's Digital Decade policy programme 2030 (European Parliament, 2022)	• **An executive and operational monitoring and cooperation mechanism** for achieving the goals and objectives outlined for Europe's digital transformation • The targeted key performance indicators (KPIs) are based on the pre-existing DESI aggregated data • It is fundamental to provide people living in villages, mountains and remote areas, adequate connectivity so no one is left behind and all can participate in the benefits of the digital society	• Gigabit connectivity for all and high-speed mobile coverage everywhere (at least 5G), to all EU citizens • Only with complete infrastructure coverage other KPIs regarding the digitalization of public services could be materialized

Program, Communication	*Main message*	*Objective*
The common agricultural policy: 2023–27 (European Commission, 2022)	Modernisation in agriculture and rural areas through knowledge exchange, innovation and digitalization is an explicit horizontal objective underpinning all CAP objectives	• Pillar II—digitalization in rural areas as the instrument to help foster knowledge and innovation • Member States should reach indicated targets: fostering and sharing of knowledge, innovation and digitization in agriculture and rural areas, and encouraging their uptake (Art. 5), enhance market orientation and increase competitiveness, including greater focus on research, technology and digitization (Art. 6 b), development and use of digital technologies in agriculture and rural areas (Art.102)
Communication establishing the Union-level projected trajectories for the digital targets (European Commission, 2023)	A refinement to the *Europe's Digital Decade* KPIs	• Gigabit connectivity—the percentage of households covered by VHCN. 5G coverage—the percentage of populated areas covered by at least one 5G network. Baseline values in rural areas: 45% (VHCN) and 81.2% (5G) • Fixed VHCN is expected to reach coverage of 94% of EU household through the deployment of optical fiber networks (FTTP)

et al. (2022) defined the urban–rural divide as 'an inequality between urban and rural areas with respect to the adoption and use of digital technologies, and the beneficial outcomes resulting from such adoption and use.

Digital technologies and innovations in rural areas may support quality of life, higher standard of transport and mobility solutions for citizens, better use of resources, reduce impact on the environment, and contribute to develop new opportunities for rural value chains, thereby supporting both inhabitants and businesses (European Commission, 2016a). Digitalisation can tackle the two trends that many regions are facing – shortage of jobs and sustainable business activity and the inadequate and declining services. However, 'this potential will only be fulfilled if rural communities are given the full benefits of digitization and connectivity' (European Commission, 2017). The European Network for Rural Development (ENRD) states three pillars in the rural digital divide, namely digital infrastructure, uptake of digital services, and digital literacy (Vironen & Kah, 2019).

Current Status of Digitalization in the Rural Areas of the EU

The number of households in rural areas of the EU that are connected to broadband internet by 2024 was 92%, reflecting an increase during the last decade, and a trend of narrowing the gap from cities, towns and suburbs to 2–4% (Eurostat, 2025). Still, 8.5% of households are not covered by any fixed network, and 32.5% are not served by any Next generation access (NGA) technology (Eurostat, 2022). The fourth and fifth generation technologies for broadband cellular networks (4G and 5G) are the prevailing technology for connecting to the internet across the EU, with 4G having 99.6% coverage (Eurostat, 2022). However, in 2021 the proportion of households connected to mobile broadband stagnated—in rural areas and in cities. Rural fixed VHCN coverage also improved from 29% in 2020 to 62% in 2021. A large gap between rural and national figures remains, demonstrating the regional disparities in digital opportunities (Eurostat, 2022). Moreover, EU regions that already had better digital infrastructure have increased internet speed more quickly in absolute terms (in microseconds). This suggests that digital infrastructure gaps between regions have been widening over time (Brunori et al., 2023).

By 2023 the share of people aged 16–74 years in the EU who accessed the internet on a daily basis was lowest in rural areas, although, this gap between people living in cities and people living in rural areas narrowed gradually between 2013 and 2023. Similarly, the share of individuals aged 16–74 years using all internet activities (telephone or video calls, sending/receiving e-mails, instant messaging, reading online news and internet banking and selling goods or services) was 10.7% in average lower in rural areas (Eurostat, 2024).

In 2023, the overall level of people with basic or above digital skills in the EU was lowest among adults who were living in rural areas (47.5% had basic or above basic digital skills). The gap in digital skills between urban-dwellers and residents in rural areas was 15.1% (Eurostat, 2024). In 2021, just 20% of the population aged 16–74 in rural areas of the EU reported above-basic overall digital skills, lower than the rate in cities, towns and suburbs (Eurostat, 2022). The lowest share of individuals (16–74 years) with above-basic digital skills were recorded in rural areas for all five areas covered by the composite indicator for individuals' level of internet skills, with the largest digital divide (16%) recorded for content creation skills (Eurostat, 2023).

The digital divide is still persistent with respect to the availability of digital infrastructure and the adoption of digital technologies. On the supply side, rural areas are lagging when it comes to the provision of NGA infrastructure. If the development of technology is designed without consideration for rural needs, the urban–rural digital divide is even further exacerbated. This has been identified in Switzerland where a negative spatial impact of digitalization was found to be larger in rural areas, thereby potentially increasing disparities (Willimann & Käppeli, 2017). On the demand side, a lack of skills and knowledge regarding digital technology in rural areas limits their possibilities for innovative service provision, business or customer use (ENRD, 2017). Therefore, rural and peripheral areas are continuously in a situation of catching up with urban areas, leading to digital exclusion, lagging rural development, or economic decline (Salemink et al., 2017).

Barriers and Opportunities to Successful Digital Transformation in Rural Regions

The main barriers for adoption of digital technologies in rural areas are socio-cultural, and particularly demographic and educational issues.

Connectivity is the most important technical barrier. Cost of technology adoption is the main economic barrier. Unclear data ownership is the main regulatory-institutional challenge (Ferrari et al., 2021).

Demographic issues related to socio-economic status, age, gender and health and sparse population are the main socio-cultural barriers. Technology requires skilled users that are less frequent among older people, as well as exchange of technological knowledge, and improving knowledge about how to develop and use digital services which is made difficult in a highly distributed and lower population densities context (Aguiar Borges et al., 2017). Elements of disadvantage are cross-cutting. For example, an elderly person living in a rural community may be subject to a "double digital divide" (Randall et al., 2018). Digital technologies can mitigate these negative outcomes of physical isolation, social isolation, and loneliness by connecting older adults to meaningful services and support provided they have access and the skills to use these technologies effectively (Francis et al., 2019). Rural communities also tend to rely on traditional values, and having negative sentiments towards novelty. These sentiments include distrust especially towards all those entities that are external to the rural environment, namely funders, regulators, and ICT suppliers (Ferrari et al., 2021).

Technological barriers mostly relate to connectivity, i.e., expensive and lengthy grid connections. Without internet connection, isolation is amplified as well as the possibility of using all those sensing technologies that rely on connectivity to properly function. Higher costs in some of the more peripheral rural areas due to longer distances and lower population densities can deter investment in new technologies (i.e. making it difficult for companies to achieve economies of scale or obtain a return on investment) (Vironen & Kah, 2019). Other relevant technical barriers are to the need to adapt technologies to ergonomic requirements of fields and forests (Ferrari et al., 2021).

Rural education attainment can significantly lag urban areas across education levels (Campbell, 2019; OECD, 2017). Rural communities often experience an emigration of skilled young individuals from rural to urban areas for tertiary education, many of which do not return due the greater employment opportunities and higher wages available in cities (Lynn et al., 2022). The situation of women with low levels of education is particularly adverse in rural areas (European Commission, 2008). Evidence from the FEMAGREE and SIMRA projects show how barriers to the empowerment of women in rural areas can be mitigated, or overcome, through social innovations such as on-farm provision of care for children and the elderly (Gramm et al., 2020; Marini Govigli et al., 2019).

Economic barriers are the costs of technology adoption, as well as scarce evidence of cost-effectiveness of certain solutions (Ferrari et al., 2021). Rural economies characterised by small players and atomized business structures, often cannot exploit the economies of scale favoured by the deployment of a technological infrastructure, i.e. the gig economy (Schwellnus et al., 2019), and the sharing economy (Laurenti et al., 2019). Nevertheless, these two economy forms, share the same benefits for rural communities in terms of access to income-earning opportunities and employment (Dreyer et al., 2017), in terms of environmental sustainability derived from resource use efficiency (Mi & Coffman, 2019), and in terms of commuting (Andersson et al., 2018). In that sense, the rapid transition of high-tech companies to working from home during the COVID-19 crisis and subsequently to a hybrid work model that combines work from home and the office, has opened new employment opportunities (Fig. 1).

Advanced Communication Infrastructures (Fibber Optics and 5G Generation) have a significant positive impact on economic development: GDP growth, new jobs and business productivity; they can significantly improve the digitisation capabilities of businesses, industry and public services, innovative technologies in the fields of agriculture and industry (Deloitte, 2022). It facilitates the rural digital hubs which have been proposed as a potential solution to improve broadband connectivity, improve overall digital literacy, attract new residents and visitors, and stimulate economic activity (ENRD, 2017). An example is the 'Mia

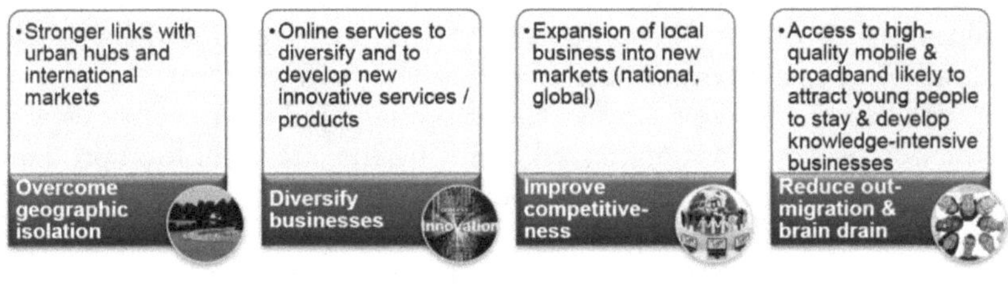

Fig. 1 Opportunities in rural and peripheral areas provided by digitalisation (*Source* Adapted from Nordregio (2017))

Engiadina' innovation centre in the Lower Engadine in Switzerland (Vironen & Kah, 2019). During the COVID-19 pandemic the hubs became a policy counter measure to support remote working backed by state and corporate support (Tomaz et al., 2021). For example, 380 remote working hubs were erected in Ireland by the Irish National Hub Network (Department of Rural & Community Development, 2021). However, the reliance on regional leadership and the essential funding from local and national authorities could be a shortcoming in some European regions.

Digitalization in Agriculture

Worldwide agriculture and the food system are currently undergoing rapid technological and economic changes driving the development and expansion of smart farming. From a technological point of view, there is a transition to precision-agriculture which combines innovative sensors and robotics. Digital technologies such as AI, robotics, blockchain, HPC, IoT and 5G have the potential to increase farm efficiency and improve production, and also to contribute to making farming systems more sustainable from an economic, social and environmental point of view. Examples abound at different stages of the agri-food value chain: remote satellite data and in-situ sensors improve the accuracy and reduce the cost of monitoring crop growth and quality of land or water and identify parameters such as surface conditions, fruit maturity, seed location etc.; and traceability technologies and digital logistics services offer the potential to streamline agri-food supply chains, while also providing trusted information for consumers. This technological development is expected to lower the risk in growing processes, thereby facilitating increased healthy agricultural produce, enable better decision making, and reshape the functioning of agri-food markets. People are freed from routine tasks by the application of smart farming technologies; they can carry out their work more efficiently and use resources in a more targeted fashion. In this way production processes are optimized, reducing the impact of food production on the environment and at the same time improving the quality of products. More sensor-controlled, automated processes are becoming available for optimizing production systems and for quality assurance. This contributes to an increase in competitiveness and to the sustainability of agriculture (OFCOM, 2020). It is estimated that the use of precision agriculture can improve the application of fertilizers and pesticides by about 21% to 25% (ecological importance), reduce the amount of water required for irrigation by about 25% (soygrowers.com, 2021), increase agricultural produce by up to 18% (USDA, 2019), and reduce manpower cost by 20% (Finco et al., 2021).

Research

A wide range of large-scale projects addressing digitalization in rural areas and smart solutions for agriculture have been implemented under the Horizon 2020 and Horizon Europe research programmes, including ScaleAgData, SmartAgriHubs, DEMETER, RUBIZMO, ATLAS, LANDSUPPORT, dRural, AURORAL, FUTUREFARM, SmartAKIS, and others. While many of these initiatives primarily emphasize technological innovation, the two selected projects were chosen to illustrate the social and policy dimensions of rural digitalization.

SHERPA (Sustainable Hub to Engage into Rural Policies with Actors) was a four-year project (2019–2023) (SHERPA, 2019) with 17 partners funded by the Horizon 2020 programme. It aimed to gather knowledge for the formulation of recommendations for future EU rural-areas-related policies, by creating a science-society-policy interface, which provides a hub for knowledge and policy. The key issues identified by the 20 regional and national SHERPA Multi-Actor Platforms (MAPs) were (Chartier et al., 2021): **Demographic change**—confirmed by most MAPs as a predominant challenge; **Climate change** and mainly extreme weather events that affect agriculture, forestry and fishing and may threaten entire sectors; Lack or poor quality of **infrastructure and basic services** such as healthcare, education, cultural activities, and entrepreneurial culture.

The H2020-funded project DESIRA (Digitisation: Economic and Social Impact in Rural Areas) (DESIRA, 2020) investigates the socio-economic impact of digitalisation in rural areas. Through a network of 20 rural Living Labs, the project assesses the socio-economic impacts of ICT-related innovation, aiming at improving the capacity of society to respond to the challenges and opportunities of digitalisation (Brunori et al., 2022). Some examples of the use cases implemented: Living Lab in the crofting communities on the West Coast of Western Scotland, the Living Lab in the Spanish region of Aragon, Living Lab in Cloughjordan Ecovillage in Ireland, Living Lab in the Rhineland-Palatinate region (Germany)—'Digital Villages'. Further details can be found at (https://agriculture.ec.europa.eu/factsheet-agriresearch-digital-trnsformation_en) and (https://sherpa-repository.eu/home).

5 Galilee, Israel Use-Case

Digitalization in Israel—in the Rural Context

In 2013, the Israeli government decided to establish the national enterprise "Digital Israel" aiming to transform Israeli society into a digital, innovative and technologically leading society, in which every citizen, business, local authority, and government body optimally utilizes the opportunities inherent in ICT. One of the overarching goals of the policy is to reduce the gaps that exist in society, with an emphasis on reducing the digital gap among the geographic and social periphery, the older population, and those with disabilities. In 2017, "The National Digital Program" report (Ministry for Social Equality, 2017) defined three main goals: reducing gaps, accelerated economic growth and friendly smart governance. Another goal formulated is support for the development of communication infrastructure in Israel, being an imperative condition for the existence of a prosperous digital society. Although the Ministry of Communication has set a goal to pro-actively encourage the roll-out of ultra-broadband internet infrastructure to all households in Israel, the gap between the Galilee and other regions of Israel persists. The pace at which advanced communications infrastructures are deployed via optic fibers was accelerated recently and reached 50% of the country's homes by the end of 2021, however the share of households located in the Galilee is negligible (Deloitte, 2022). The bottleneck lies in the fact that 46% of the households in the Galilee are defined as being located in incentive areas, areas in which the roll-out of the infrastructure is dependent on a future governmental mechanism financed through annual payments. These disparities between the periphery and central Israel stem in part from the low high-tech representation of certain societal sectors in these areas, and also due to disparities in the education system between parts of the country.

The Galilee Use Case

Background

The population in the Eastern-Galilee is 122,000 people (Fig. 2). The economic activity in the Galilee is mainly based on industry (79%), agriculture (18%) and tourism, incorporating both low-tech and high-tech industry. Agriculture is the main primary production in the Galilee, accounting for over 16% of the regional GDP. The Galilee is the main producer in Israel of agricultural products in the poultry and dairy industries; Most of the people employed in the agricultural sector and most of the agricultural farms in Israel are concentrated in the Galilee; Over 9.3% of the Galilean workforce is employed in the agriculture sector, compared to 2.1% in the rest of Israel; The average age of farmers is about 55 (Akirav et al., 2022).

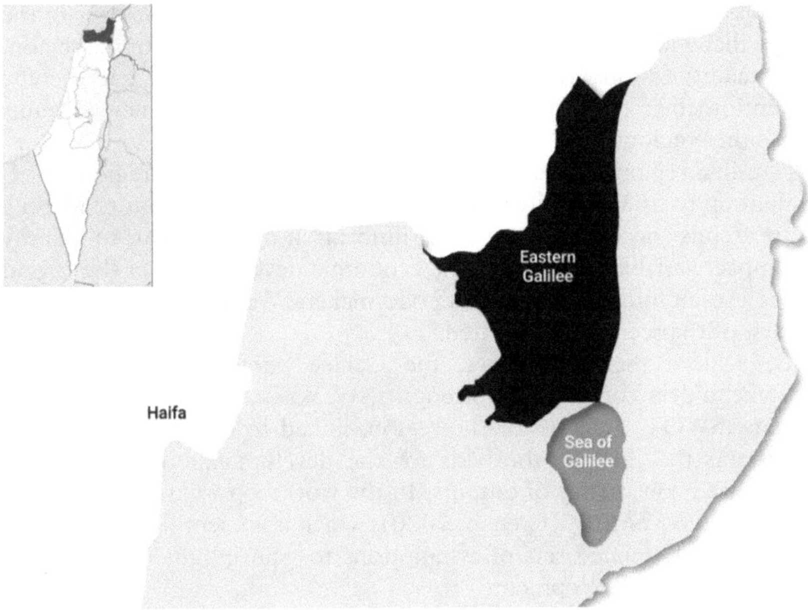

Fig. 2 The Eastern Galilee (blue), part of the Upper Galilee (red at the upper left map)

The Foresight Process

The governing disparities between the Galilee and the centre of Israel may deepen in the future given a business-as-usual scenario, subsequently imperil the sustainability and viability of the socio-economic ecosystem in the Galilee. It now becomes a regional priority to create the infrastructures which will enable new ventures and opportunities and mediate transformation more effectively. A well-planned foresight programme can delineate the transformative trajectories, but only if it clearly defines how policy aspirations can be converted into practical operational delivery. It is with this in mind that the Galilee Foresight programme has been designed as a step-by-step decision-making tool for practitioners.

The process of Foresight in the Galilee Pilot was developed in stages since February 2020, involving multi-actors from the region. A schematic description of the stages is shown in Fig. 3. The main premise and guideline were that youngsters are to be the key beneficiaries of this process. The mission is to lay the foundations for building a game changer in the region that will consequently increase the value and prestige of the region, thus making it more attractive to young people, both locals, and thereby preventing their emigration to other regions, and young new entrants from other regions.

Plausible regional scenarios that will harness the Galilee region development up to 2030 were developed. There was a requirement to identify future trends and drivers in regional innovation development, to identify key impact variables relating to the economic development of the region and as a result inform the regional policymakers. We also determined KPIs to each of the scenarios presented.

To achieve these outcomes, the Galilee pilot “leading team” of 21 stakeholders completed a Strengths, Weaknesses, Opportunities and Threats (SWOT) analysis for the region, linked to a series of economic subsystems that formed the basis for the development of the scenario and ensured consistency of outputs. In the workshop we used an adapted version of the *STEEPV* (Crehan, 2020), which is a scientific technique to construct well-defined sets of assumptions to gain insight into a system and its potential development.

Through this procedure, the “leading team” was guided towards a structured understanding of a system’s current state and its dynamics. It was performed by small groups with specialized expertise, dealing with different aspects of the system.

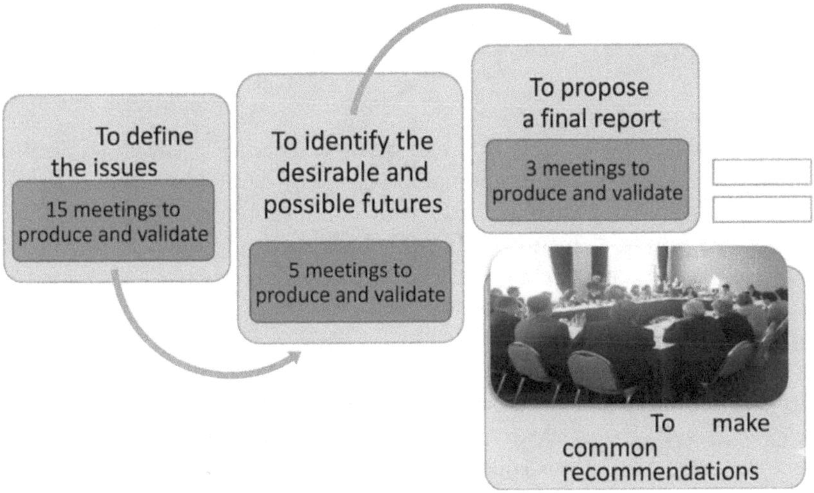

Fig. 3 A schematic description of the stages implemented in the process of Foresight in the Galilee Pilot

Each scenario was quantified in respect of its Plausibility, Desirability and Probability. For the most desirable scenario, we developed an Action Plan to get there (focusing on the key drivers). Interactive group sessions with a wide variety of people are central to storyline development, and the activities in Galilee were directed towards such involvement of stakeholders. The "Leading Team" identified a few key directions essential to the development of the Galilee, with emphasis on their impact on regional economic development and benefiting the community:

1. Establishment of The University of the Galilee.
2. Construction of connectivity infrastructure to bridge the digitalization divide in the Galilee.
3. Elongation of the train line to all parts of the Galilee.
4. Development of the tourism sector.

Bridge the digitalization divide was chosen by the "leading group" of 21 stakeholders as the governing scenario. It was approved by the Eastern Galilee Mayors and Chairpersons of the Regional Councils, as well as the Chairman and the CEO of the eastern Galilee Cluster of the 18 municipalities.

Key Performance Indicators
KPIs are measurable targets that can be monitored. For each main point (Table 2) we present the baseline and source of data. The choice of lead KPIs was based on existing KPIs which are monitored in the Galilee region and potential future KPIs for which methodologies would need to be developed, and relevant data need to be generated and extracted.

External Consultancy Report
To subject the foresight process and the selected scenario to an initial economic feasibility test, we approached the consulting company Deloitte. Its 40 pages report—"Policy Report—Communication Infrastructure Impact on the Galilee Economy" (Deloitte, 2022), postulates that investing in advanced communication infrastructure has the potential to boost the regional economy, strengthen the labor market and increase productivity. Below is an assessment of the potential impact of advanced communication infrastructures on the economy of the Galilee:

- An increase of up to 1.67% in GDP in the Galilee
- An increase of 3% to 16.5% in job creation, corresponding to up to 12,000 new positions in the Galilee at the upper range.
- An increase of $\sim$ 5% in business productivity in the Galilee.

As a final step, the work done was presented to the Minister of Communication. The meeting revolved around the Galilee pilot activities as part of the POLIRURAL project which deals with peripheral development. Under this framework the Deloitte report was submitted to the Minister. The delegate' aim was to provoke the Minister of Communication to lead a move at the government to turn the Eastern Galilee into a pilot project for upgrading the digitalization infrastructure in order to leverage the region's economy, establish start-up companies and bring young families to the Galilee.

Table 2 Key performance indicators (KPIs) for each cardinal point by 2030 and base line data (where available), divided to different dimensions of digitalization

Main point 1	*Secure and performant digital infrastructures*
Dimension	**2030 Galilee target vs baseline**
Connectivity	**All Galilee households** and industrial sites will be covered by optic fibers [2021 baseline: 14%]
Connectivity	**All Galilee households** and industrial sites will be covered by 5G cellular antennas [2021 baseline: 0%]
Cardinal point 2	Digital transformation of business
Adoption of digital technologies	**75% of Galilee enterprises** will take up: • Cloud computing services [2020 baseline: 26%] • Big data [2021 baseline: 14%] • AI [2021 baseline 25%]
Digital "late adopters"	**More than 90% of Galilee SMEs** reach at least a basic level of digital intensity (https://circabc.europa.eu/) [2021 baseline: 60.6%]
Connectivity	**More than 75% of agricultural fields in the Galilee** will be covered by 5G cellular antennas to facilitate precision agriculture [2021 baseline: 0%]
Innovative businesses/scale-ups	**Doubling the number of unicorns in the Galilee** [2021 baseline: 122]
Cardinal point 3	Digitalisation of public services
Government as a platform	• **100% online provision of key public services** available for Galilee citizens and businesses [2021 baseline: 75/100 (citizens), 84/100 (businesses)] • **100% of Galilee citizens have access to medical records (e-records)** [2021 baseline: N/A] • 80% of citizens will use a digital ID [2021 baseline: N/A]
Cardinal point 4	A digitally skilled population and highly skilled digital professionals
ICT specialists	**More women** using ICT for different purposes

6 Conclusions

The Galilee use case demonstrates how digitalisation can function both as a transformative instrument for peripheral regions, linking technological progress with social and territorial cohesion and a reflectance of structural disparities between central and peripheral territories. The process and outcomes of the Galilee foresight carry broader lessons that are relevant to the international community especially to regions in Europe and the Mediterranean that face similar structural, demographic, and spatial challenges.

Lessons Learned

Digitalisation as an equaliser for peripheral regions. The Galilee experience shows that targeted investment in digital infrastructure can offset the limitations of distance, low population density, and economic marginality. High-capacity connectivity—when aligned with education, entrepreneurship, and governance—serves as a catalyst for new forms of economic activity, social inclusion, and demographic renewal. For many rural regions worldwide, digitalisation offers a path to re-embed themselves in global innovation and knowledge networks.

From infrastructure to ecosystem thinking. The foresight process revealed that physical infrastructure alone is insufficient. Sustainable transformation depends on developing a regional digital ecosystem that interlinks education, research, governance, and entrepreneurship. In this sense, digitalisation becomes not merely a technological upgrade but a systemic enabler of innovation, encouraging cross-sector collaboration and strengthening regional resilience.

Participatory Foresight as a Governance Instrument. The multi-actor foresight methodology (STEEPV and SWOT) employed in the Galilee provided a structured mechanism for mobilising regional stakeholders, identifying shared priorities, and defining measurable Key Performance Indicators (KPIs). The exercise bridged local aspirations with national and international policy objectives, illustrating how participatory foresight can serve as a governance tool to operationalise the digital and green transitions at regional scale.

Digital inclusion as a lever for demographic and social resilience. Beyond its economic and technological implications, digitalisation emerged as a demographic stabiliser. By creating new professional opportunities and improving quality of life, digital transformation can mitigate out-migration of youth and attract skilled families to peripheral regions. The focus on inclusivity, particularly women's participation in ICT and digital entrepreneurship, is essential to ensure that the benefits of transformation are equitably distributed.

The role of multi-level governance and trust. The interaction between regional actors and national ministries underscored the importance of multi-level governance. Digitalisation initiatives require coordination between local clusters, regional authorities, and national policy bodies. Building mutual trust and shared accountability between these levels is as critical to success as the technological implementation itself.

Broader Implications and International Relevance

Digitalisation possess a dual function—as both a technological and social innovation—capable of addressing structural demographic and economic challenges common to many rural regions in Europe, the Mediterranean, and beyond. Digitalisation enables peripheral and rural areas to participate fully in the digital economy and the European Green Deal transition. It demonstrates the value of cross-sectoral coalitions, where academia, local authorities, and private industry collaborate to co-create digital strategies aligned with national and supranational policy goals. Linking digital and demographic policies can help address rural depopulation and foster balanced regional development.

Concluding Remarks

The Galilee use-case confirms that digitalisation can act as a transformative force that redefines the economic and social fabric of rural territories. Its success depends not only on technology, but on the capacity to mobilise actors, resources, and shared vision. The experience suggests that the path toward digital inclusion and territorial resilience must combine infrastructure investment with human capital, trust, and long-term governance. By articulating these lessons, the Galilee foresight contributes to the growing body of knowledge on rural digital futures and offers a concrete model for other peripheral regions seeking to bridge the digital divide while fostering sustainable, inclusive growth.

References

Aguiar Borges, L., Nilsson, K., Tunström, M., Tepecik Diş, A., Perjo, L., Berlina, A., e Costa, S.A., Fredricsson, C., Grunfelder, J., Johnsen, I., Kristensen, I., Randall, L., Smas, L. & Weber, R. (2017). White paper on Nordic sustainable cities.

Akirav, O., Noiman, A., Cohen, G., Barel-Shaked, S., Hershkovitz, A., Yehuda, L., Liberman, I., & Shami, L. (2022). *Galilee Index 2022.* The Galilee Research Institute, Western Galilee College. Retrieved November, 12,2023, from. https://www.wgalil.ac.il/10608-2/.

Alm, E., Colliander, N., Deforche, F., Lind, F., Stohne, V., & Sundström, S. (2016). *Digitizing Europe: Why Northern European frontrunners must drive digitization of the EU economy*. Boston Consulting Group.

Andersson, M., Lavesson, N., & Niedomysl, T. (2018). Rural to urban long-distance commuting in Sweden: Trends, characteristics and pathways. *Journal of Rural Studies, 59*, 67–77.

Brunori, G., Rolandi, S., & Arcuri, S. (2022). *Digitalisation of rural areas.* SHERPA Discussion Paper. https://doi.org/10.5281/zenodo.6421292

Brunori, G., Harasztosi, P., Merante, C., Rückert, D., & Weiss, C. (2023). *Digitalisation in Europe 2022–2023. Evidence from the EIB investment survey.* (p. 80). https://doi.org/10.2867/745542. https://www.eib.org/en/publications/20230112-digitalisation-in-europe-2022-2023

Campbell, C. (2019). *Those left behind—Gaps in college attainment by race and geography.* Center for American Progress. https://www.americanprogress.org/issues/education-postsecondary/reports/2019/06/27/471242/those-left-behind/

Chartier, O., Salle, E., Irvine, K., Kull, M., Miller, D., Nieto, E., Vestergård, L.O., Potters, J., Slätmo, E., Zomer, B., & Iadecola, F. (2021). *Long-term vision for rural areas: Contribution from SHERPA science-society-policy platforms*. SHERPA Position Paper. https://doi.org/10.5281/zenodo.4557440

Cowie, M. R., Bax, J., Bruining, N., Cleland, J. G., Koehler, F., Malik, M., Pinto, F., van der Velde, E., & Vardas, P. (2016). E-Health: A position statement of the European Society of Cardiology. *European Heart Journal, 37*(1), 63–66. https://doi.org/10.1093/eurheartj/ehv416

Crehan, P. (2020). *A STEEPV inventory of drivers of change*, European network for rural development. Belgium. Retrieved November 23, 2023, from https://policycommons.net/artifacts/1991030/a-steepv-inventory-of-drivers-of-change/2742795/CID:20.500.12592/tbrcws

Degryse, C. (2016). Digitalisation of the economy and its impact on labour markets. *ETUI research paper-working paper*.

Deloitte. (2021). *Digitalisation: An opportunity for Europe*. https://www.vodafone.com/Digitalisation-An-Opportunity-for-Europe.pdf

Deloitte. (2022). *Policy report—communication infrastructure impact on the Galilee economy.*

Department of Rural and Community Development. (2021). *Our rural future: Minister Humphreys announces €8.8 million in funding under the Connected Hubs Scheme.* https://www.gov.ie/en/press-release/a6253-our-rural-future-minister-humphreys-announces-88-million-in-funding-under-the-connected-hubs-scheme/

DESIRA EU Project. (2020). Available online https://desira2020.eu

Dreyer, B., Lüdeke-Freund, F., Hamann, R., & Faccer, K. (2017). Upsides and downsides of the sharing economy: Collaborative consumption business models' stakeholder value impacts and their relationship to context. *Technological Forecasting and Social Change, 125*, 87–104.

Dubois, A., & Sielker, F. (2022). Digitalization in sparsely populated areas: Between place-based practices and the smart region agenda. *Regional Studies, 56*(10), 1771–1782. https://doi.org/10.1080/00343404.2022.2035707

Dufva, T., & Dufva, M. (2019). Grasping the future of the digital society. *Futures, 107*, 17–28.

Esparcia, J. (2014). Innovation and networks in rural areas. An analysis from European innovative projects. *Journal of Rural Studies, 34*, 1–14. https://doi.org/10.1016/J.JRURSTUD.2013.12.004

European Commission. (2004). *e-Health—Making healthcare better for European citizens: An action plan for a European e-Health Area. COM (2004) 356 final.* European Commission.

European Commission. (2008). Poverty and Social Exclusion in Rural Areas. Available online: https://ec.europa.eu/social/BlobServlet?docId=2087&langId=en

European Commission. (2016a). *EU action for smart villages.* Retrieved October 28, 2023, from https://ec.europa.eu/agriculture/sites/agriculture/files/rural-development-2014-2020/looking-ahead/rur-dev-small-villages_en.pdf.

European Commission. (2016b). *Communication from the Commission to the European Parliament, the Council, the European Economic and Social Committee and the Committee of the Regions. Connectivity for a Competitive Digital Single Market—Towards a European Gigabit Society*, (COM/2016/0587 final). Retrieved October 31, 2023, from. https://eur-lex.europa.eu/legal-content/en/TXT/?uri=CELEX%3A52016DC0587.

European Commission. (2017). *Innovation and digitisation key for strong and sustainable rural areas.* Retrieved October 28, 2023, from https://ec.europa.eu/info/news/innovation-and-digitisation-key-strong-and-sustainable-rural-areas_en.

European Commission. (2019). *Communication from the Commission to the European Parliament, the Council, the European Economic and Social Committee and the Committee of the Regions. The European Green Deal*, (COM(2019) 640 final). Retrieved November 3, 2023, from https://eur-lex.europa.eu/legal-content/EN/TXT/?qid=1576150542719&uri=COM%3A2019%3A640%3AFIN.

European Commission. (2020a). *Shaping Europe's digital future.* Retrieved October 15, 2023, from https://commission.europa.eu/strategy-and-policy/priorities-2019-2024/europe-fit-digital-age_en

European Commission. (2020b). *Communication from the Commission to the European Parliament, the Council, the European Economic and Social Committee and The Committee of the Regions. Digital Education Action Plan 2021–2027 Resetting education and training for the digital age*, (COM/2020/624 final). Retrieved October 23, 2023, from https://eur-lex.europa.eu/legal-content/EN/TXT/?uri=CELEX%3A52020DC0624.

European Commission. (2021a). *Communication from the Commission to the European Parliament, the Council, the European Economic and Social Committee and The Committee of the Regions "2030 Digital Compass: The European way for the digital decade"*, (COM/2021/118 final). Retrieved October 12, 2023, from https://eur-lex.europa.eu/legal-content/en/TXT/?uri=CELEX:52021DC0118

European Commission. (2021b). *ANNEX to the Commission Implementing Decision on the financing of the Connecting Europe Facility—Digital sector and the adoption of themultiannual work programme for 2021–2025, (C(2021) 9463 final).* Retrieved October 25, 2023, from https://digital-strategy.ec.europa.eu/en/library/multiannual-work-programme-2021-2023-connecting-europe-facility-digital.

European Commission. (2021c). *Communication from the Commission to the European Parliament, the Council, the European Economic and Social Committee and The Committee of the Regions "A long-term Vision for the EU's Rural Areas—Towards stronger, connected, resilient and prosperous rural areas by 2040"*, (COM(2021) 345 final). Retrieved October 31, 2023, from https://eur-lex.europa.eu/legal-content/EN/TXT/PDF/?uri=CELEX:52021DC0345.

European Commission. (2022). *Common Agricultural Policy for 2023–2027. 28 CAP Strategic Plans at a Glance.* Retrieved November 13, 2023, from https://agriculture.ec.europa.eu/csp-at-a-glance-eu-countries_en.pdf.

European Commission. (2023). *Communication from the Commission "establishing Union-level projected trajectories for the digital targets"*, C(2023) 7500 final. Retrieved October 24, 2023, from https://eur-lex.europa.eu/CELEX:52023XC0929(03):EN:TXT.pdf.

European Network for Rural Development. (2017). *Revitalising rural areas through digitisation the experience of three rural digital hubs*. https://enrd.ec.europa.eu/sites/default/files/tg_rural-businesses_case-study_rural-digital-hub_0.pdf

European Parliament. (2021a). *Regulation (EU) 2021/241 of the European Parliament and of the Council of 24 June 2021 on the European Regional Development Fund and on the Cohesion Fund* (OJ L 231, 30.6.2021, p. 60). Retrieved October 25, 2023, from https://eur-lex.europa.eu/legal-content/EN/TXT/?uri=CELEX:32021R1058.

European Parliament. (2021b). *Regulation (EU) 2021/241 of the European Parliament and of the Council of 12 February 2021 establishing the Recovery and Resilience Facility* (OJ L 57, 18.2.2021, p. 17). Retrieved October 16, 2023, from https://eur-lex.europa.eu/legal-content/EN/TXT/?uri=CELEX%3A02021R0241-20230301.

European Parliament. (2022). *Decision (EU) 2022/2481 of the European Parliament and of the Council of 14 December 2022 establishing the Digital Decade Policy Programme 2030* (OJ L 323, 19.12.2022, pp. 4 26). Retrieved October 12, 2023, from http://data.europa.eu/eli/dec/2022/2481/oj.

Eurostat. (2022). *Urban-rural Europe—digital society*. Retrieved October 11, 2023, from https://ec.europa.eu/eurostat/statistics-explained/index.php?title=Urban-rural_Europe_-_digital_society#Households_connected_to_the_internet\.

Eurostat. (2023). *News Article—EU digital skills divide: Cities outpace rural areas*. Retrieved October 12, 2023, from https://ec.europa.eu/eurostat/en/web/products-eurostat-news/w/ddn-20230320-2\.

Eurostat. (2024). *Urban-rural Europe—digital society*. Retrieved October 23, 2023, from https://ec.europa.eu/eurostat/statistics-explained/index.php?title=Urban-rural_Europe_-_digital_society\.

Eurostat. (2025). *Towards digital decade targets for Europe*. Retrieved October 23, 2023, from https://ec.europa.eu/eurostat/statistics-explained/index.php?title=Towards_Digital_Decade_targets_for_Europe.

Federal Office of Communications OFCOM. (2020). *Digital Switzerland strategy*. Available online: https://www.bakom.admin.ch/bakom/en/homepage/digital-switzerland-and-internet/strategie-digitale-schweiz/digitale-schweiz.html

FEMAGREE EU Project. (2018). Available online: https://cordis.europa.eu/project/id/798421

Ferrari, A., Bacco, M., Gaber, K., Jedlitschka, A., Hess, S., Kaipainen, J., Koltsida, P., Toli, E., & Brunori, G. (2021). Drivers, barriers and impacts of digitalisation in rural areas from the viewpoint of experts.*Information and Software Technology*, *145*, 106816.

Féret, S., Berchoux, T., Requier, M., Abdelhakim, T., Slatmo, E., Chartier., O., Nieto, E., & Miller. D. R. (2020). *D3.2 framework providing definitions, review and operational typology of rural areas in Europe. Sustainable Hub to Engage into Rural Policies with Actors (SHERPA)*. Deliverable D3.2, Report to the European Commission, H2020 SHERPA, Grant Agreement No. 862448 (p. 73). https://rural-interfaces.eu/wp-content/uploads/2020/04/SHERPA_D3-2_Framework-rural-definition.pdf

Finco, A., Bucci, G., Belletti, M., & Bentivoglio, D. (2021). The economic results of investing in precision agriculture in durum wheat production: A case study in central Italy. *Agronomy, 11*(8), 1520.

Francis, J., Ball, C., Kadylak, T., & Cotten, S. R. (2019). Aging in the digital age: Conceptualizing technology adoption and digital inequalities. In *Ageing and digital technology* (pp. 35–49). Springer.

Gartner. (2021). Gartner glossary—Digital business. Available online: https://www.gartner.com/en/information-technology/glossary/digital-business

Gramm, V., Dalla Torre, C., & Membretti, A. (2020). Farms in progress-providing childcare services as a means of empowering women farmers in South Tyrol, Italy. *Sustainability, 12*(2), 467.

Laurenti, R., Singh, J., Cotrim, J. M., Toni, M., & Sinha, R. (2019). Characterizing the sharing economy state of the research: A systematic map. *Sustainability, 11*(20), 5729.

Liu, S. (2021). The urban–rural divide: The effects of the small business innovation research program in small and nonmetro counties. *Economic Development Quarterly*, 08912424211029709.

Lynn, T., Rosati, P., Conway, E., Curran, D., Fox, G., & O'Gorman, C. (2022). *Digital towns: Accelerating and measuring the digital transformation of rural societies and economies* (p. 213). Springer.

Manyika, J., Chui, M., Bughin, J., Dobbs, R., Bisson, P., & Marrs, A. (2013). *Disruptive technologies: Advances that will transform life, business, and the global economy* (Vol. 180, pp. 17–21). McKinsey Global Institute. Retrieved October 28, 2023, from https://www.mckinsey.com/business-functions/digital-mckinsey/our-insights/disruptive-technologies.

Marini Govigli, V., Górriz-Mifsud, E., Dalla Torre, C., Ravazzoli, E., Da Re, R., Pisani, E., et al. (2019). *Report on social innovation assessment in each selected case study. Deliverable 5.3—Social Innovation in Marginalised Rural Areas (SIMRA)*. Report to the European Commission (p. 34).

Mi, Z., & Coffman, D. M. (2019). The sharing economy promotes sustainable societies. *Nature Communications, 10*(1), 1–3.

Ministry for Social Equality. (2017). *The Digital Israel National Initiative: The National Digital Program of the Government of Israel*. Available online: https://www.gov.il/BlobFolder/news/digital_israel_national_plan/he/Digital_Israel.pdf

MOBIL-AGE EU Project. (2016). Available online: https://cordis.europa.eu/project/id/693319

OECD. (2014). *Innovation and modernizing the rural economy*. Available online: https://read.oecd-ilibrary.org/urban-rural-and-regional-development/innovation-and-modernising-the-rural-economy_9789264205390-en#page1

OECD. (2017). *Trends Shaping Education Spotlight 9*. Available online: https://www.oecd.org/education/ceri/spotlight9-CountryRoads.pdf

Papazoglou, M., Torrecillas Jodar, J., Cardona, M., Calza, E., Vazquez-Prada Baillet, M., Righi, R., Lopez Cobo, M.. & De Prato, G. (2023). *Mapping EU level funding instruments to Digital Decade targets*. Publications Office of the European Union. https://doi.org/10.2760/986930.JRC134647

Popescu, M. F., Chiripuci, B. C., Orîndaru, A., Constantin, M., & Scrieciu, A. (2020). Fostering sustainable development through shifting toward rural areas and digitalisation—The case of Romanian universities. *Sustainability, 12*(10), 4020. https://doi.org/10.3390/su12104020

Randall, L., Berlina, A., Teräs, J., & Rinne, T. (2018). *Digitalisation as a tool for sustainable Nordic regional development*. Discussion paper prepared for Nordic thematic group for innovative and resilient regions, January 2018.

Sabbagh, K., Friedrich, R., El-Darwiche, B., Singh, M., & Koster, A. (2013). Digitization for economic growth and job creation: Regional and industry perspectives. *The Global Information Technology Report, 2013*, 35–42.

Salemink, K., Strijker, D., & Bosworth, G. (2017). Rural development in the digital age: A systematic literature review on unequal ICT availability, adoption, and use in rural areas. *Journal of Rural Studies, 54*, 360–371.

Schwellnus, C., Geva, A., Pak, M., & Veiel, R. (2019). *Gig economy platforms: Boon or Bane? OECD*. Available online: https://www.oecd-ilibrary.org/docserver/fdb0570b-en.pdf?expires=1630150849&id=id&accname=guest&checksum=67D1394F5A1EBA29A1D760A09EB37D0F

SHERPA. (2020). SHERPA Discussion Paper. Long-term vision for rural areaS—Contribution from 20 science-society-policy platforms. Retrieved November 05, 2023, from https://rural-interfaces.eu/wp-content/uploads/2020/11/SHERPA_Discussion-Paper_Long-term-vision-rural-areas.pdf.

SHERPA EU Project. (2019). Retrieved November 05, 2023, from www.rural-interfaces.eu.

SIMRA EU Project. (2016). Available online: http://www.simra-h2020.eu/

soygrowers.com. (2021). The Environmental Benefits of Precision Agriculture in the United States, Association of Equipment Manufacturers, ASA, CropLife America, National Corn Growers Association. Available online: https://soygrowers.com/wpcontent/uploads/2021/02/Precision-Ag-Study.pdf

Tomaz, E., Moriset, B., & Teller, J. (2021). *Rural coworking spaces in the Covid-19 era. A window of opportunity?* Available online: https://halshs.archives-ouvertes.fr/halshs-03235464/document

USDA. (2019). *A case for rural broadband*. Available online: https://www.usda.gov/sites/default/files/documents/case-for-rural-broadband.pdf

Vironen, H., & Kah, S. (2019). *Meeting the challenges of digitalisation: Implications for Regional and rural development*. 111, European Policy Research Paper. University of Strathclyde Publishing.

Willimann, I., & Käppeli, S. (2017). Digitalisierung trifft Land härter als Stadt. *Die Volkswirtschaft-Plattform für Wirtschaftspolitik. Abgerufen von.* http://dievolkswirtschaft.ch/de/2017/04/willimann-06-2017/ImHerbst

CHAPTER 12

Exploring the Diffusion of Organic Agriculture in the Mountain Region of Grisons, Switzerland: A Social Network Analysis Approach

Emilia Schmitt, Carmen Forrer, Loredana Sorg, and Dominique Barjolle

1 Introduction

Over the last decades, organic farming has been on the rise everywhere, and to particularly high levels in Switzerland where organic agriculture has a long tradition. In the canton of Grisons, in the mountainous eastern

E. Schmitt (✉) · C. Forrer
ZHAW, Lausanne, Switzerland
e-mail: emilia.schmitt@uni.ch

C. Forrer
e-mail: carmen.forrer@zhaw.ch

L. Sorg
Biovision, Zürich, Switzerland
e-mail: l.sorg@biovision.ch; loredana.sorg@gmx.ch

D. Barjolle
ETH Zürich, Zürich, Switzerland

D. Barjolle et al. (eds.), *Innovation and the Future of Rural Development in Europe*,
https://doi.org/10.1007/978-3-032-22570-2_12

part of the country, the proportion of land under organic agriculture is especially high—at 66% in 2022, which make it the most organic region of Europe (Eurostat, 2019). It is often a mixture of different reasons and incentives (economic, social and environmental) that lead to the conversion of individual farms (Ferjani et al., 2010; Mann & Gairing, 2012). While studies have been carried out on the motives of individual farmers, the question of how the conversion to organic farming can be influenced at a regional and sectoral scale remains less explored. Studies on information exchanges among organic farmers are also rare, even though they have been found to differ from conventional information systems (Demiryurek, 2010). Vroege et al. (2020) have analysed how farmers' collaborations and competition with their neighbors influence diversification on farms and Skaalsveen et al. (2020) looked at how information exchange influenced the diffusion of no-till practices. Esparcia (2014) also summarized that besides factors such as geographical and environmental considerations, organisational structures, social capital, i.e. networks of actors both within the region and with the outside, is of great importance for the dynamics of a local food system. Beyond connecting with their neighbors and fellow farmers, producers learn about sustainable practices and are influenced by other actors like agricultural schools, extension services, state offices, market actors, etc. Such networks have been named "Learning and Innovation Network for Sustainable Agriculture" (LINSA) (Brunori et al., 2013) and one such network is present in Grisons.

LINSAs have been observed qualitatively and also through a quantitative method adapted to explore networks: Social Network Analysis (SNA). This method allows identifying central and peripheral actors from the perspective of the whole network, aka from those answering to a survey. It also allows investigating connections between actors, for example when exchanging information among each other and to assess the quality of the resulting web of connections. The patterns identified through SNA help understanding communication and collaboration systems, such as clusters and cliques appearing within a network. In our case, the network underlying organic agriculture in a specific region can be studied for understanding the LINSA's influence on the diffusion of organic agriculture. It is assumed that social interactions within LINSAs encourage

e-mail: barjolle@ethz.ch

synergies and motivation for the growth of organic agriculture. While these interactions are likely influential, we interpret them as part of a broader set of factors driving development. Traditional agriculture knowledge systems (AKS), are an inherent part of LINSAs and are seen as one element interacting with different formal and informal actors (Brunori et al., 2013). In the case of organic farming in the canton of Grisons, links to the AKS are of interest because they help understanding the role of established public and private education, extension services and research institutes. Through implementing their own projects, these actors often foster innovation in the respective region. Apart from the exchange of information, collaboration patterns are interesting to investigate as they indicate how information and innovation is incorporated into daily work life and thus how practices can be transmitted to and used by practitioners (Esparcia, 2014).

The present study shows and analyses the linkages between the development of the network over time and the increase of organic agriculture in the canton of Grisons. As stated in Galaskiewicz (2011) it is highly valuable to represent the evolution of a network over time in the context of a value chain. Lessons learnt from studying this LINSA could be valuable for comparison with other regions. This study responds to the need to understand what factors have contributed to the exceptionally fast and early diffusion of organic farming in the canton of Grisons and what role the LINSA has played in this respect. In order to design and then interpret the results of the SNA, personal time was invested in the region, expert interviews were conducted, and statistics and secondary literature such as protocols and newspaper reports were consulted during a timespan from 2011 until 2023. The results are most importantly based on two campaigns of SNA surveys conducted per post in 2012 and online in 2022. The resulting graphical representation of the network allows looking at interrelations visually while the quantitative analysis of actors' collaboration activities builds a sound basis for measuring social data.

The overall objective of this study is to describe the spreading of organic farming as an innovation process from the social network perspective and the following research questions are formulated:

- How can the development of organic agriculture in the canton of Grisons be explained by and through social networks dynamics?
- What enabling factors existed in terms of collaboration and interrelations between the relevant actors to foster organic agriculture?

- Can changes in the network over time be linked to developments in the organic sector?

2 Study Area

The Particularity of Organic Farming in Switzerland and in the Canton of Grisons

Organic agriculture in Switzerland started to develop as early as in the 1930s with trainings on bio-dynamic farming by Rudolf Steiner and knowledge exchange in the journal Demeter (Aeberhard & Rist, 2009). From then, pioneering farmers developed ecological cultivation practices and continued research. In the seventies, organic agriculture was still under scrutiny for scientific evidence and in 1974 the Research Institute for Organic Agriculture (FiBL) was founded on a private basis. In 1980, guidelines and a common label (the bud) were created, followed by the association of Swiss organic farmers in 1982, who started the certification of organic farms. Following those initiatives, official recognition emerged in the 1990s, along with market development by the two national retailing leaders (Aeberhard & Rist, 2009). The adoption rate of organic guidelines then increased constantly as farmers were incentivized by federal direct payments. In the past ten years (2012–2022), the total number of Swiss farms decreased by 15%, but the number of organic farms grew by 33%, reaching a proportion of 16% of all farms in the country in 2022 (Federal Statistical Office, 2023)Considering surface rates, 17,4% of the agricultural area in the country was under organic certification in 2021 (Willer et al., 2023). Nowadays, organic food products are integral to the Swiss market, and Switzerland maintains a leading global market share of 10.9%, including imports and exports, with the highest per-household spending on organic products worldwide (Willer et al., 2023).

When looking in more detail at which products and which regions contribute to the high share of organic production in Switzerland, it quickly appears that permanent grasslands, from which alpine cheese and meat are produced, take the lion's part with accounting for approximately 70% of the organically certified areas. Regarding regions, the mountainous canton of Grisons has been the leader with varying rates of organic farmers that passed the 50% mark in 2006, dipped just below in 2009 and finally grew again to reach 59% of farms in 2020 (Federal Statistical

Office, 2023). Although the proportions are impressive, the total number of farms has dramatically decreased in the canton (-15% in 10 years) while the number of organic farms remained constant (Federal Statistical Office, 2023). The most significant increase in the number of farms under organic production happened before the mid-2000s. Since then the numbers have varied in concordance with overall farming decline. Still, other regions in Switzerland have experienced a slower growth rate even though some of them are equally mountainous. Figures 1 and 2 below show the location of Grisons on the European map with organic shares in 2016 and Fig. 1b shows the evolution of area shares of organic agriculture in the canton since the official recognition of the term in 1990.

The map and statistics further show that the case of extensive grassland-production regions in the alpine areas is particular, with the second-highest rate of certified organic area at 52% for the region of Salzburg in Austria (Eurostat, 2019), making the whole alpine region an interesting case, particularly with the front-runner of the canton of Grisons.

3 Method

The methodology of SNA was applied as it defines steps to identify local actors and analyze their connections (information exchanges, collaboration and financial transfers). Particularly in the case of a network comprised by actors and institutions of various sectors and geographical regions, SNA offers useful formal tools and measurements (Ingold et al., 2010). The two most important elements used in SNA are the nodes, which represent the actors, and the ties, which are the connections between actors (Golbeck, 2015). We used several key measures to understand how actors are connected in the network. These typical network measures help us summarize who is most important, how tightly everyone is connected, and the overall shape of the network. For example, 'degree centrality' shows how many connections each actor has, while 'density' tells us how closely linked the group is overall. More details of the measures used are provided in Table 1.

These network measures were calculated based on indications collected from the actors themselves in surveys. The survey contains lists of the actors and respondents indicated the respective actors with whom they maintained relevant connections. The connections that were researched were information exchange (provided and/or received), collaboration

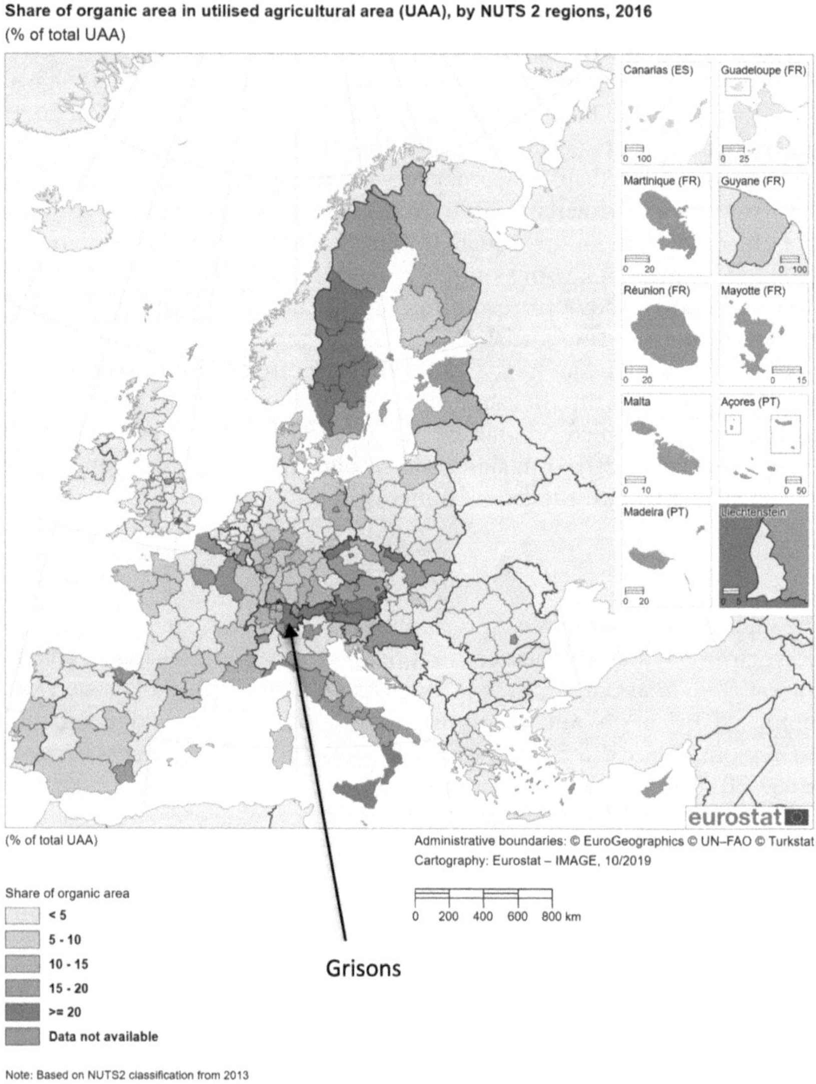

Fig. 1 The canton of Grisons on the European map by share of organic area in 2016 (Map by Eurostat, 2019)

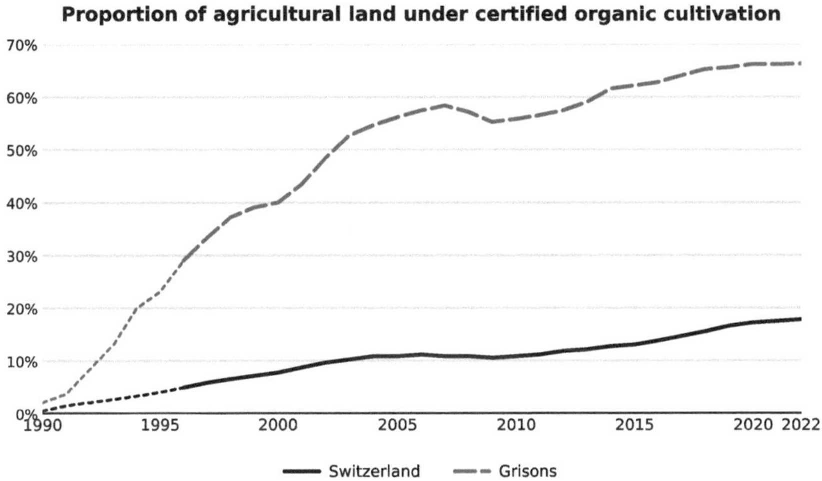

Fig. 2 Evolution of the share of agriculture area for certified organic agriculture in Grisons and Switzerland from 1990 to 2022. The data between 1991 and 1995 is not available and approximated from the data of 1991 and 1996 (source of data: (Federal Statistical Office, 2023))

(undirected) and financial flows (provided and/or received), for each time series, in addition to the perceived influence of each actor.

Interviews were conducted in preparation of the two surveys conducted (see below) in order to identify the survey samples and collect additional information. In 2012, seven interviews were conducted. In 2022, four new interviews were conducted. The results were calculated and modelized with UCINet software (Borgatti et al., 2002).

Time series

The work reported in this study has been carried out in two phases. The first phase of data collection took place in the year 2012 and the second in 2022. The SNA conducted in 2012 aimed at measuring and analysing the networks of previous times to understand their evolution. In 2022, the SNA was conducted again to observe the evolution that had occurred since 2012. This means that two surveys are analyzed jointly in this chapter. In both surveys, times series were defined to guide respondents on which timeframes to indicate their connections. The timeframes

Table 1 The calculations used for the networks with their meaning and use (Borgatti et al., 2002; Borgatti & Everett, 1999; Golbeck, 2015; Hanneman & Riddle, 2005; Marsden, 2005; Scott, 2004)

Measure	*Calculation*	*Meaning and interpretation*
Degree Centrality	The "degree" of each actor is simply the number of ties it has in the given network. It is calculated for each node in the network. The degree can be differentiated between in-degree and out-degree. The in-degree is based on all ties that come from other nodes to the specific node and the out-degree is the opposite	Degree Centrality shows the proportion of ties touching that node and thus the importance of an actor. In- and out-degrees only make sense for the type of ties that are directed, in our case for information and financial ties. Collaboration is considered undirected. In the network visualizations, the size of nodes is according to degree centrality
Average Degree	Average degree is the average of all the degree centralities of all actors in the network	The average degree indicates how many other actors each actor is on average linked to
Density	The density is the percentage of present ties compared to the total of potential ties if all nodes were connected. Density is thus calculated in percentage	A higher density means that more actors are in touch with each other, while a lower density means the network is more loosely connected. This helps spot how groups change over time or how different networks compare
Centralization	Centralization is a measure on the whole structure of how the network is centralized on one or more central points that have a very high degree while others score low (high centralization close to 1) or if all nodes have the same degree (low centralization close to 0)	Like density, Centralization is an index to compare networks and their evolution. It indicates if the network depends heavily on a few key actors at the center, or if relationships and information are more spread out among many participants. This gives insight into the balance of influence in the group

(continued)

Table 1 (continued)

Measure	*Calculation*	*Meaning and interpretation*
Clustering coefficient (transitivity)	This index measures the degree to which nodes in a network tend to "cluster" or form "cliques", e.g. the probability that when one node is connected to two nodes, that these two are also connected	A high coefficient (close to 1) shows that there are tightly-connected clusters in the network, forming localized connectivity. A lower coefficient (close to 0) shows a typology close to a random network
Average Distance	This number is the average number of ties necessary to reach all other nodes in the network	If the average distance is rather small, then there is efficient network communication and all nodes can be reached quickly. If the number is high then there might be bottlenecks in the networks or structures slowing down communication
Small Worldedness	This is a metric to quantify the "small-world" typology of a network using its clustering coefficient and average distance and comparing to those of a random network	A coefficient closer to 1 indicates high local clustering and a short average distance, a coefficient close to 0 indicates the opposite, e.g. a random or regular network. This coefficient is only calculated in undirected networks

were defined based on the indications collected during the preliminary interviews and according to important changes in the history of the sector such as policies.

The three time series investigated were:

- **1991–1995 (and before)**: The Swiss organic market is in its beginnings but growing steadily. The philosophy of organic farming is promoted in the canton of Grisons through information events for local farmers. From 1992 onwards, the canton of Grisons fosters conversion to organic farming with financial aid, and initiates first specialized training courses at the cantonal agricultural school. In 1994, the local association of organic farmers is created to represent local organic farmers' interests. This time serie ends with one of the big Swiss retailers taking on the promotion and sale of Grisons organic cheese. The rate of organic farms in the canton is at 12%.

- **1996–2009:** In this period, the demand for organic products keeps growing. The diffusion of organic agriculture continues and the share of organic farming in the canton of Grisons increases from 30% of the agricultural land in 1996 to 58% in 2007 (Federal Statistical Office, 2023). There are a few major changes in relevant institutions, e.g. with the combination of extension service and education in one center. A series of changes in the agricultural policy occur from 1996, when the constitution changes to recognize the multidimensional role of agriculture. Market-based support evolves into a conditional direct payment system (Metz et al., 2021). Over the years the subsidies moved from production outputs to area-based in an attempt to reduce overproduction and preserve the environment in the policy reform of 2007, which might have triggered a new growth in organic agriculture.
- **2010–2022**: the continued growth stagnates and is only relative in terms of number of farms. There is a supply surplus of organic cheese, meat and milk products. The growth of the organic market slows down. At the same time, several innovative small-scale projects are developing. The most significant changes that happen in the market are new discounters entering, new outlets and the multiplication of brands who may increase competition. The canton takes an important strategic decision to increase support for regional brands and products, focusing more on the localness and tradition than on the organic label. The agricultural policy experiences only one big reform in 2014 that pursues previous objectives into greening the production (Metz et al., 2021). The time serie ends with the global pandemic context and a new agricultural policy reform in 2022 that is experiencing major delays and difficulties in finding an agreement.

Sample

The seven preliminary face-to-face interviews with experts from the canton of Grisons allowed to identify the relevant actors of the network and the time series. Indeed, for respondents to select all actors they have had links with, the list of relevant actors needed to be identified beforehand, even if the option to add additional actors was still provided. While the diffusion of organic farming in the canton of Grisons was the primary study objective, the network analyzed based on the survey answers is not restricted to the study area itself. All actors playing a relevant role in the diffusion of organic farming in Grisons were included into the network, irrespective of whether their official location is national, regional or local. Furthermore, actors belonging to the organic sector as well as actors outside the organic sector (conventional agriculture, public institutions and market actors) were considered. This approach led to network boundaries best described as “the organic agro-food value chain in the canton of Grisons including its supportive structures”. It is also important to remind that individual organic farmers were not included in the survey. The list of actors is restricted to the LINSA supporting them. Some actors however also managed their own (organic) farm in addition to a representation, political or extension role. As Grisons is a well-deliminated region (administratively and culturally), all actors of the AKS and agro-food value chain could be included and no other pre-defined limits were needed.

To ensure validity and reliability, several pilot surveys were tested by people not belonging directly to the network sample. 68 actors were identified in 2012 and contacted via post. After conducting the SNA and interpreting the results, one validation interview with a central actor of the network was conducted. In 2022, five new interviews allowed to update the actors’ list. Difficulties emerged to make both lists correspond as a high numbers of institutions and small companies changed their names, closed or emerged. The 2022 qualitative interviews and ad-hoc research resulted in a new list of 92 actors that were asked to fill out the new survey online.

4 Results

Actors of the Grisons LINSA

The postal survey of 2012 reached a response rate of 57.4% (39 actors). In 2022, there were 68 new inputs (online), but only 42 that were fully filled. This equals a response rate of 74% and 46% respectively. The data from 2012 was then merged to complete missing information where adequate.

Qualitative information on these actors were collected and used as attributes to color the dots in the network graphs'. Attributes were mostly their role category and whether they are local or national actors. In all networks the proportion of local actors revolved around 67 to 70%. Because of the methodological framework of three time series and three types of connections, nine networks were plotted and analyzed. The first findings of this preliminary analysis are that the number of actors active in the network increased from around 63 actors in 1995 to 80 actors around 2010 and increased again slightly to around 90 in 2022. Considering the high dynamics in the existence and disappearance of organizations, only 39 (42%) remained exactly the same across the time series.

The Most Influential Actors

The first question in the survey asked which listed actors in the LINSA are particularly influential. The respondents consistently selected from 40 to 57 actors, increasing chronologically. By normalizing the mentions of influence in percentage of the answers to account for varying numbers of actors in the different time series, it appears that the highest mentions of influence occurred in the second time serie and were attributed to central actors also gathering high influence in other time series and high centralities in almost all networks. The list of actors who have reached the top quarter of influence (by sorting them in quartiles) is summarized for each time serie in table 2. These influences are only translating the perceptions of the respondents.

Networks' Indicators and Evolution

In parallel to the increase of the number of actors over time, networks' indicators indicate an increase of density and the average degree in all types of ties examined (information/collaboration/financial). The sub-chapters below describe detailed results within each type of ties.

Information Networks

Table 3 gives an overview of the network results of information exchange divided into the three time series. The network of information exchanges showed the highest numbers of ties across all time series as could be expected as these are the first types of exchanges and they are directed. When looking at the relative positions of actors in the networks, local organizations and individual personalities occupy influential and central

Table 2 Types of actors indicated as influential in the three time series

Number of actore per category in the top quartile (75%) of influence	*Before 1995*	*1996–2009*	*2010–2022*
Government offices	2	2	2
Research, education and consulting	3	3	5
Engineering and ecological offices, certification bodies	0	1	2
Associations, farmers' organisations, interest groups	2	1	4
Private companies, marketing, economy	1	1	4
Cheese dairies, alpine dairies, local product-oriented organisations	2	3	4
Individual actors and political figures	5	4	0

positions before 1995 and keep their central positions up to today. One of the central individuals was the consultant for organic farming at the local agricultural school and extension center and is seen as a pivotal agent in most networks in the two first time series. SNA metrics show that the average degrees were at 6,2 in the first time series and increased to 11,6. The centralization and density remained stable at around 0,6 and 0,1 respectively. The centralization peaked in the second time serie and then decreased again. The clustering coefficient and average distance between nodes both decreased slightly and were close to 0,4 and between 2,4 and 2 respectively.

Table 3 SNA indicators for information exchanges in the three time series

	Information Exchanges		
	Before 1995	*1996–2009*	*2010–2022*
Number of nodes	63	80	90
Number of ties	391	661	1042
Average Degree	6,21	8,26	11,58
Degree Centralization	0,58	0,65	0,60
Density	0,10	0,11	0,13
Clustering coefficient (transitivity)	0,41	0,36	0,34
Average Distance	2,38	2,19	2,03

Collaboration Networks

Table 4 shows the results of the calculated metrics for the collaboration networks. The results are very similar to the network of information exchanges and show the same trends. The average degree increased over the three time series and was the highest in the last time serie with 11,5. The centralization follows the same increase and decrease and the clustering and average distance the same decrease in the same ranges. The networks of collaboration are undirected and in this case the index of "small worldedness" could be calculated. It is first at 3 and decreases to 2,6 in the last time series.

To see the development of the collaboration between actors over the three time series, Fig. 3 shows its intensification from 1995 (3a) to the second time serie (3b) into the current time serie (3c). The collaboration increased and can be an indicator that the actors collaborate with a higher number and diversity of actors. Still, three local actors can be highlighted who have kept or intensified their central role over the years. In the last time serie, the density has varied the least but the central actors have slightly changed. The local education and extension center is still very central, but a few completely new organizations became central. Six actors in the top ten are small-teamed private value chain actors in the milk or cereal sector (blue squares in Fig. 3c), a certification office or civil society organization for farmers' representation. Other than them, local and national agricultural ministry offices and research institutions are very central. In the Fig. 3a–c it can be seen that local actors dominate the central positions (in blue).

Table 4 SNA indicators for collaboration in the three time series

	Collaboration		
	Before 1995	*1996–2009*	*2010–2022*
Number of nodes	64	80	91
Number of ties	279	460	521
Average Degree	4,40	5,80	11,50
Degree Centralization	0,55	0,68	0,62
Density	0,12	0,12	0,13
Clustering coefficient (transitivity)	0,36	0,35	0,32
Average Distance	2,26	2,10	2,01
Small Worldedness	3,1	2,9	2,6

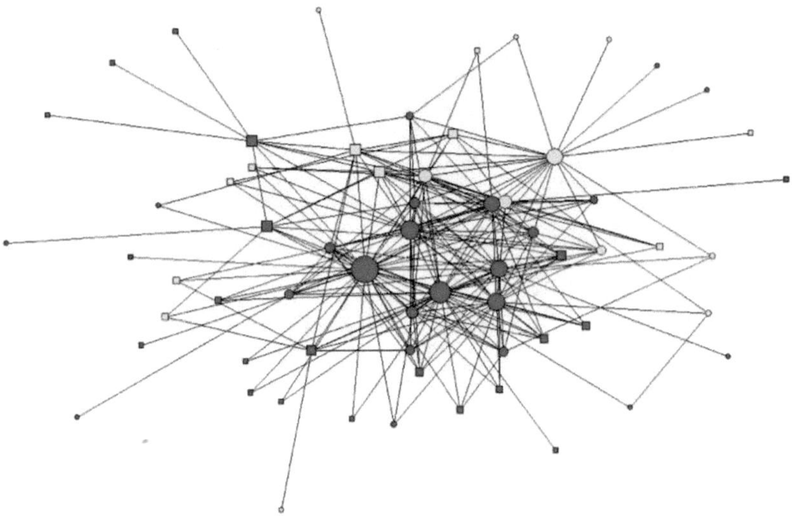

a 1990 – 1995

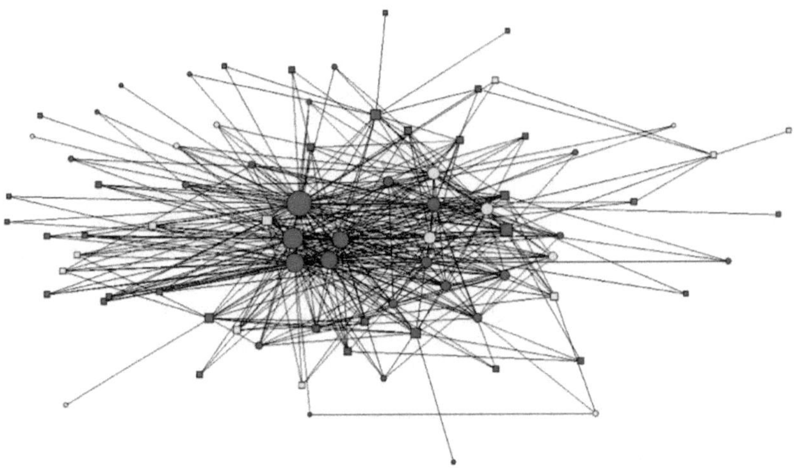

b 1996 - 2009

Fig. 3 Networks of collaboration in the respective time series (3a–3c). Colour legend: Blue for local actors; Yellow for non-local actors. Form: Circle for support actors (government, associations), Square for Value chain actors. Node size: according to degree centrality (size: 4–20)

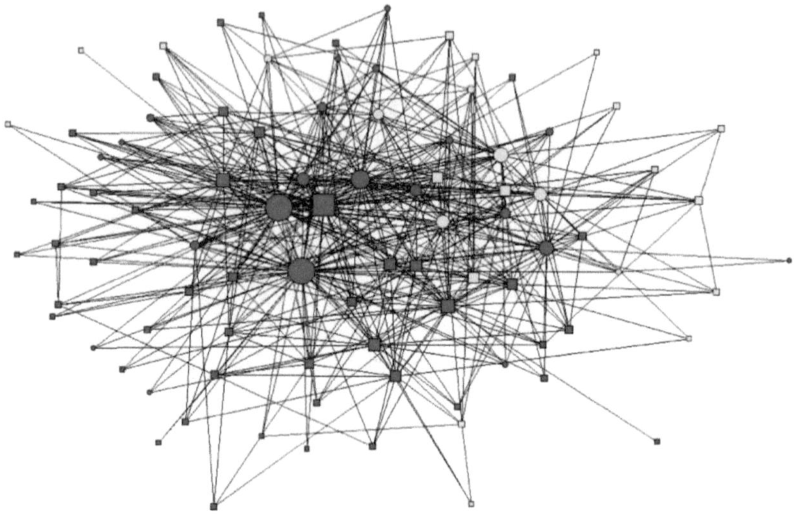

c 2010 – 2022

Fig. 3 (continued)

Financial Networks

The financial networks are smaller in number of actors and ties and in density. This is fairly common as not all actors are engaged in financial transactions and/or might not want to share that information. Nevertheless, these networks allow identifying the main donors and receivers. Table 5 shows the results of the network calculations for the financial transfers. The density has decreased from 6.5% to 4% but the average degree has increased from 1.75 to 2.3 from the first to the last time serie. The centralization has again peaked in the second time serie but overall remained low at around 0,3. The average distance has increased a lot from 1,9 to 3,76.

Concerning central actors, the one with the highest outdegree is a cantonal office which is supporting agricultural projects, from 9 in the first time serie, to 14 in the second and 16 in the third time serie respectively. Among the receivers of financial support are the education and extension center, the research institutes and several associations or projects developing and implementing organic agriculture. In the last

Table 5 SNA indicators for financial ties in the three time series

	Financial exchanges		
	Before 1995	*1996–2009*	*2010–2022*
Number of nodes	28	42	59
Number of ties	49	82	137
Average Degree	1,75	1,95	2,32
Degree Centralization	0,27	0,32	0,27
Density	0,07	0,05	0,04
Clustering coefficient (transitivity)	0,26	0,30	0,13
Average Distance	1,90	2,36	3,76

period, two private sector actors who are developing local value chains have the highest indegree with 11 and 10.

Additional Factors for the Diffusion of Organic Agriculture in Grisons

Additional qualitative information was retrieved from the expert interviews conducted in preparation of the surveys. When asked why the canton has a higher adoption rate than other mountainous regions, the experts repeatedly quoted three factors:

1. Adopting the organic standard did not represent a big change compared to former practices and farmers in the region are said to be open-minded and market-oriented
2. The extension service reacted quickly and offered tailored advice. The extension and mobilization were centralized by one contact person.
3. One large retailer ensured profitable sale channels for organic food, starting with cheese in the nineties, which created a virtuous economic synergy with the work of the cantonal extension officer

One interviewee also named the supportive direct payment system in Switzerland and additional financial support from the cantonal government. Successful lobbying from the national association of organic farmers was cited too, as were highly committed individuals and role-model farmers who effectively motivated other farmers to switch to organic production. In addition, the new organic cheese segment at the retailer created a chain reaction with cheese dairies fully converting. Therefore, farmers had to convert to organic milk production to continue delivering. The cheese dairies, which are actually farmers' cooperatives, were hereby crucial players. The conversion was more difficult in other sectors like cereal production, but there too, a local cooperative was created to find additional producers and organize a collective value chain from 1987 onward (Bardsley & Bardsley, 2014). The cooperative received essential financial support from a local foundation and the cantonal government.

Our surveys also included qualitative questions to learn about respondents' characteristics and opinions. In the first and the second survey, 43% and 65% of respondents, respectively, indicated working on their own or the family's farm, with almost 90% organically certified. This characterization of respondents in the LINSA shows that most of those who are professionally active in a LINSA organization or business come from the local organic sector. The majority converted to organic farming during the nineties. When asked what aspects the respondents associate with organic agriculture in 2022, the key words with most citations are: "sustainability" (n:33) and "conservation of nature, being close to nature" (n:33) followed by "diversity and biodiversity" (n:31), and then by "innovation" (n:17) and "new market potential" (n:16).

Regarding which kind of support would be beneficial for the organic sector, the first answer is that no additional support is needed (n:16). Then financial support (n:15), personal support (n:9) and finally technical support (n:7) is mentioned. The perception of the supportive role of the agricultural policy towards organic farming has been mainly positive (n:14) or partly positive and only partly negative (n:12). Remarkably, 22 actors (55%) in the online survey stated that the support for organic farming in the agricultural policy has improved over the last 20 years. A few specific examples have been named, like the area-based contributions or the implementation of direct payments for organic farming in the 90ies. A few actors named specifically the cantonal contributions in addition to the federal ones as a positive factor for organic farming. Furthermore, quite remarkably, over 50% of the 42 respondents said that the Covid-19 pandemic has strengthened the overall network.

5 Discussion

Important findings of the SNA have shown how a resilient network has grown and how it is configured after 30 years of existence. We have found a stable and steady growth of the network especially in the beginning. This shows some possible links with and influence on the parallel evolution of organic agriculture in the region, which we will discuss further in this chapter. The subsequent discussion elaborates on the research questions in light of other scientific studies and hypothesizes in terms of future trajectories for sustainable transformation in this and other regions.

Key Learnings from the Network Evolution 1990–2022

The upscaling of organic agriculture in Grisons is quite unique in its speed and consistency and can be explained by several factors and dynamics. The adoption model (Rogers, 1983)for example explains the diffusion of innovations through groups of innovators, succeeded by early adopters and a later majority. Padel(2001)adds that while the first group of pioneers is not risk-adverse, additional motivation for early and late adopters might be found in the influence of their organic neighbors or in market incentives. The development of a niche for organic products in the Swiss market during the nineties contributed to the growing adoption rate and we know from interviews and documents that pioneering farmers were very active in the regional and national politics at the time. Additionally, Isaac (2012) points out that the interactions of a variety of actors and the exchange of information within a network can substantially contribute to the adoption of innovative and sustainable practices. The SNA literature elaborates that not all types of network structures are equal in terms of resilience of the network itself and their ability to support a sustainable transformation of the local food system (Bruce et al., 2021; Luthe et al., 2012). The metrics and graphs depicting the LINSA of the canton of Grisons indicate that it fits with an archetype of the "small-world network" as described by Newman et al. (2011). Such networks have a high clustering coefficient, short average distances and a core of highly connected nodes. Our networks show these kinds of metrics and high "small-worldedness" indexes were found in the collaboration networks. Luthe et al. (2012) found similar metrics in a nearby region of Switzerland. At first glance such networks do not seem to be organized and actually combine randomness with some order, which is also remarkable in Grisons. Luthe et al. (2012) question such networks' abilities to enhance adaptation in the face of climate change especially because they can hide power imbalances. Still, such networks have been shown to be resilient and create transformation because they present local clustering and efficient global communication pathways (Brinkley, 2018; Dolfing Id et al., 2019). The characteristics of "small-worldedness" structure were most remarkable in the first time serie. With time, actors and ties increased and in the second time serie, the networks centralizations increased as did the centrality and influence of the core actors. The nodes' increase was the largest then and it is also typical that new entrants will first try to forge links with the most influential and central actors (Luthe et al., 2012), which might explain the higher centralization at that time. The network was then in a stage of consolidation. In the third phase, the nodes increased again but centralization decreased, indicating another kind of dynamics although shifts are subtle. The clustering coefficients decreased as did the small-worldedness but density increased very slightly. It could indicate a phase of more random or diverse growth of the network, as shown with the increase of a more diversified group of actors at the centre of the network.

The overall density is not particularly high, and very similar to what SNAs found in other LINSAs in Switzerland (Luthe et al., 2012) or across the world (Hinnou et al., 2022). The role of density in the scaling of innovations is disputed. Low density is either a limit to opportunities (Hinnou et al., 2022; Janssen et al., 2006)or a sign of efficiency in communication exchanges fostering innovation (Bruce et al., 2021). Bruce et al (2021) write that "too much density creates redundant communications and reduces the ability of people in the network to access outside sources of information and influence (Valente et al., 2007)". Furthermore, the access to external sources of information for early adopters is easier in less constricted networks (Valente et al., 2007). We interpret the lower density and higher small-worldedness structures observed in the earliest period as possible factors that supported the rapid adoption of organic agriculture in the region during the nineties; however, these trends likely interacted with other social, economic, and policy influences. The high centralization, while a risk for power imbalance(Luthe et al., 2012), was an asset as the vision for organic agriculture could be quickly spread from the core of the network and between clusters.

Importance of the Most Central Actors

In LINSAs the positions of different actors are of high importance for triggering innovation (Brunori et al., 2013). As outlined in the results, local actors in the canton of Grisons were crucial for stability due to their anchorage in the institutions and communities. External actors play rather marginal roles, except for the organic research institute, which was introduced to the network by regional actors. Such external actors provide an extra source of influence essential for early adaptors and for exposure to new information (Valente et al., 2007). They contribute to the "global connection" of the small-world type of networks. A dynamic and evolving LINSA is also dependent on new actors, who in our case were local private actors emerging over time and opening new knowledge topics and market spheres. This mixture of different actors could be especially conducive for innovative developments, while being strongly supported by the cantonal extension service and strong economic incentives. Esparcia (2014) found that one of the most important features of innovative projects is the closeness of actors and their interaction within a relatively robust and wide network. Moschitz et al. (2015)describe the process of co-evolution and shared reflection in the LINSA approach, where group learning and sharing are necessary. Both conditions are met in the Grisons' "small-world" type LINSA.

We see for example that information exchanges extend beyond organizations to innovative farms, exemplified by two notable cases in the SNA. The findings highlight the significance of robust information flow across the entire value chain—from innovative producers to marketing, labeling, and sales actors. Notably, processing actors, such as mills, appear less central in the networks, suggesting they may be perceived as more passive participants.

Economic actors (depicted as squares in Fig. 3a–c) are generally not prominently positioned in the SNA, particularly in the initial two time series. They are nevertheless acknowledged for the Swiss organic sector's growth (Mann & Gairing, 2012), enabling one of the most significant global increases in organic consumption and opening new organic sales channels in the region of Grisons. In the latest period, small-scale private actors, especially those involved in coordinating and certifying value chains in the region, have gained centrality, aligning with their role in facilitating coordination among producers and other value chain actors.

Even with diverse economic actors and numerous value chains developed in the region who played a pivotal role like the dairies, the pronounced influence of the local agricultural office in financial transfers underscores the significance of financial incentives from local governments, aligning with Home et al. (2019)'s assertion that financial aspects and subsidies play a crucial role in transitioning to organic farming. Additionally to providing this vital support, the local government holds a central position in the cooperation and information exchange networks. Esparcia (2014) similarly noted that most innovative projects in rural areas rely on external support. In Grisons, locally driven initiatives for organic certification and value chains receive backing from both local and national governments. In the cereal sector, when facing production challenges in 2005, a local foundation partnered with the local government to offer extra payments to farmers. It is likely that active individuals within a small-world network facilitate the establishment of such supportive partnerships, potentially a key factor in developing a resilient LINSA.

The LINSA approach described by Moschitz et al. (2015) emphasizes the importance of diverse and dynamic actors for successful networks. In the interviews conducted in the study at hand, this dynamic process and critical reflection by actors themselves was described. For example, two interviewees said that nowadays it is no longer the goal to increase the numbers of organic farms, but instead to increase the quality of the existing organic farms. Also, in the past years there has been more focus on organic wine production. This shows that local organizations continue to reflect their aims towards sustainable and innovative agriculture. This causes their strategy to shift from simply organic to (also) local products value addition.

Influence of the Network Configuration on Organic Development in Grisons

Summarizing key findings on the growth of organic farming in the region, most conversions occurred in the early nineties, reaching a peak in 2002 with 162 farms transitioning to organic farming (Federal Statistical Office, 2023). Subsequently, growth stagnated, albeit less dramatically than for non-organic ones. The total area under organic farming in the Grisons has continued to expand, and the number of processors adopting organic products or undergoing full conversion has been increasing steadily from 1990 to 2007 (Simon, 2009).

Our SNA reveals that the LINSA network grew faster in the nineties than from 2000 - 2010. Interestingly, the "small-world" structure was most pronounced in the initial period, becoming more centralized in the second. However, it would be a stretch to directly attribute a correlation with the slowdown in the transition to organic agriculture. It still raises questions about how the LINSA and growth rates of organic agriculture adapted to each other or whether both adapted to a more stable situation, potentially influenced by external factors like changes in policy and the market. Alternatively, the observed slowdown and stagnation could be due to reaching a threshold in the number of quickly convertible farms, with varying durations between early and late majority adopters (Padel, 2001). New conversions may now occur during farm successions or when additional sectors find better sales channel opportunities, as observed with dairies and cereals.

In the third time serie, the network decentralized, with a diverse group of small entrepreneurs gaining centrality. Although the number of organic farms stagnated, the organic agricultural area continued to grow, indicating that existing organic farms were managed profitable enough to acquire new farmland. Organic, in this context, no longer represents an innovation; rather, a new strategy emerged to promote local products under various denominations of origin and local brands. This shift aligns with changes in the network towards a more innovation-conducive form in the third time serie. Whether the changes in network structure caused the second innovation wave or vice versa remains uncertain.

Nevertheless, the changes in the network were subtle and it kept a small-world structure, or "network of networks" (Duit & Galaz, 2008) mostly organized within sectors (see for example the sub-network of cereals in Forrer et al (2024)) or municipalities (Luthe et al., 2012). This kind of network could be a representation of a long-lasting multilevel collaborative governance system that worked for a fit-to-challenge transformation of the local social-ecological system as theorized in Guerrero et al. (2015). So far, there is very few empirical evidence of such networks over longer time series and achieving such high levels of transformation. Even if the exact dynamics of bottom-up and top-down mechanisms remain largely unknown, the identification of parallels between the LINSA network and shifts in the agricultural value chain suggests that there is a potential for influence. It seems that the networks have integrated both approaches in a long-term multi-level collaboration that included the lobbying for and integration of political changes.

This can maybe explain why the online survey reveals a remarkably high positive perception of the agricultural policy, as most actors believe it has positively evolved in supporting organic farming. These results contrast with the national context where agricultural policy changes are often met with criticism and resistance (Metz et al., 2021). The 2014 reform, highlighted in the survey, introduced a new method in the direct payment system by replacing animal-dependent contributions with area-based contributions. An interviewee noted that this reform improved incentives for mountain crops cultivation, benefiting the struggling organic cereal sector. This positive perception aligns with the ongoing growth of areas under organic production and the revival of areas under organic cereal crop production after 2008. In contrast, areas under conventional mountain crop production stagnated, suggesting more favourable conditions for organic production (Federal Statistical Office, 2023). Metz et al. (2021) further confirm that the participatory design process of the 2014 agricultural policy fostered an acceptable consensus among different coalition groups at the national level, leading to a "greener" agricultural policy.

Reflexions for Future Trajectories

The future of organic farming in the canton of Grisons may undergo changes due to new guidelines for organic farming, specifically the requirement that 100% of organic feed for ruminants must originate from Switzerland according to the Swiss organic standard (Bio Suisse, 2022). This requirement could impact organic production, particularly if farmers allocate land for grass rather than crops or repurpose cereal for feed instead of food. Even more probably, some milk farmers will quite organic certification. Addressing this risk will be crucial in finding suitable solutions. The new guidelines align with regional and national strategies promoting local value chains and marketing for regional products. In one cantonal valley, a pioneering territorial strategy aims to establish a 100% local and organic food value chain system (Gros-Balthazard, 2022) but tensions exist at the intersection of sectors, value chains, territory, and governance levels, including language barriers. We suggest that the Small-world LINSA structure, with sub-clusters (high clustering coefficients) and connecting bridges (short average distances), supports the emergence and success of such initiatives like the one 100% local and organic valley. The "bridges", e.g. actors with high centralities, connecting clusters involve individuals who are central and trusted across clusters, acting as the "global connection" in the small-world network structure (Bruce et al., 2021).

To strengthen such "bridging" actors in other LINSAs, several factors regarding strengthening of the roles of the identified individuals could be considered and adapted. First their personal role as pioneers, with embedded positions in central organizations was already mentioned. Then many survey respondents with bridging roles have a family background in organic farming, suggesting that current LINSA participants may be the "children" of the first organic pioneers from the nineties. Interestingly, other bridging personalities are newcomers from outside the canton, contributing to the openness and diversity of the network. This is a characteristic rooted in the region's diverse language mix and high international connectivity as mentioned by one interviewee. These bridging actors collaborate closely with research partners, including both specialized local entities and international counterparts. The significant number of these bridging actors and their long-term institutional anchorage explain the high proportion of local actors in the collaboration networks depicted in Fig. 3a–c. Their proportion remains strickingly stable. Notably, there are no multinational companies identified in the LINSA (to the best of our knowledge), but rather a diverse array of small-scale food businesses.

Digitalization and developments in line with "smart agriculture" are also new trends that will need to be considered (Ehlers et al., 2021; Forney & Epiney, 2022)although our study does not seem to indicate drastic changes aligned with information technology in the region. However, information exchange density did increase in the last time serie, although not drastically. The effect of digitalization could impact the network by shifting the patterns of information exchange and help to reinforce the "global connection" part of the network, whereas the intra-cluster exchange could be weakening in proportion. There are very subtle signs of changes in this direction with the decrease of our clustering coefficient and average distance in the information networks.

The fact that over 50% of the respondents stated that the network was strengthened during the Covid-19 pandemic is remarkable, since both cooperation and information exchange seemed more difficult. The strengthened network during the Covid-19 pandemic can be understood as part of the overall economic growth in the organic sector, since demand for organic products increased during the pandemic (Willer et al., 2023). Furthermore, it shows that the network is indeed strong and resilient to overcome difficult times.

6 Conclusion

The study at hand shows the development of the Local Innovation Network for Sustainable Agriculture (LINSA) on organic farming in the mountainous canton of Grisons, Switzerland, between 1990 to 2022. Agriculture is an important and innovative sector in the canton of Grisons, where organic agriculture has grown to reach 66% of the agricultural land and where bottom-up initiatives for local value chains are spreading. The Social Network Analysis (SNA) we conducted greatly facilitated the understanding of the LINSA, although we met numerous limitations like the partial response rates to our surveys and the many changing actors between the different time series. We did find that a resilient, stable and growing LINSA is supporting the farmers and value chain actors in the region. While our SNA study does not establish direct causal relationships, it reveals parallel developments between the LINSA and the diffusion of organic agriculture and related innovations, suggesting that network dynamics may have supported these processes.

As an important finding, we highlight the increase in the number of actors as well as the number of ties from the 1990ies to 2022. These new actors were integrated in the network in a way to keep it resilient and strongly interconnected. We have identified a "small-world" type of structure that can be understood as a "network of networks" of locally interconnected clusters which are bridged and connected by highly central actors, often individuals. We confirm previous studies and theories on the value of such network structures to combine bottom-up participation with retaining a certain centralization for efficient diffusion of information, collaboration and implementation of a common vision. We explained how the LINSA's configuration over time is highly aligned to the diffusion of innovation and multi-level collaboration of actors, while a direct causation remains unclear. Multiple other factors have played conjointly for the diffusion of organic agriculture in the region.

From the two surveys combined with prior qualitative interviews and a post-analysis evaluation, conclusions on these other factors shed light on factors that could be supported intentionally in other regions and in the future. Policy support in the form of subsidies for farms and projects was an important accelerating factor but not the only one. The governmental office has been a central financial supporting actor of the network throughout and at the same time central in collaboration and information exchanges. The participation of local economic actors in the downstream value chain (processing and distribution) has been shown to have acted as a major catalyst for farm conversions and newer projects on organic and local food products. These actors do not show high centrality but could be efficiently linked to the rest of the LINSA thanks to the small-world structure. We further conclude that the inclusion of a high diversity of actors in the core and periphery of the network is conducive for innovation. Diversity was seen in the categories of institutions collaborating and exchanging information and also in the individuals within these institutions, often taking on the role of "bridges", with notably women and newcomers to the region and multiple languages being noticed.

The central importance of local actors in building, maintaining, and expanding a social network that is resilient in the long term was enhanced with stable structures such as governmental offices, the local extension service, agricultural school and farmers' associations and cooperatives. Even though individual personalities might have lost importance over the last decade, these institutions kept their high centrality and influence. Remarkably, the difficulty of interacting with all the actors involved in a growing network was overcome as shown in the increased density of information exchange and decreased average distance. Hence, effective measures, for example events including the whole network and sensitively using digital communication tools, could further support interactions between local actors in the future. This is especially important to preserve the small-world structure where local clusters are as important as the connection between them and with other sources of information. Furthermore, such a network can be a strong asset in dealing with future trends such as digitalization and climate change.

Finally, the study at hand shows that networks are important for successful scaling of innovations and sustainable transformation. The findings can support the design of food system transformation projects. Further comparisons with other networks and other regions would be greatly interesting for future research into the role of LINSAs. It is also important to consider that the LINSA in the Grisons constituted itself from the local associations and government structures without external interventions. So, although it might be tempting to replicate and adopt it in other contexts with the wish to increase adoption rates of organic agriculture, such a process might actually only work "organically" from the regions themselves.

Acknowledgements This research would never have been possible without the participation of local actors and insightful experts who answered our surveys and interviews. We wish to extend a special thanks to all of them who participated in insightful interviews and generously took the time to fill the surveys, providing invaluable perspectives and essential data to our analysis.

We express our sincere gratitude to ETH Zurich, the Research Institute of Organic Agriculture (FiBL) and the Zurich University of applied Sciences (ZHAW) for their invaluable support and resources. We would like also to acknowledge Christian Hirschi for his critical reflections and valuable inputs during the conception of the research design.

The research was funded by the European Commission under two research projects: The SOLINSA project under the 7th Research Framework Programme (Grant agreement number 266306) and the Project MOVING, which has received funding from the European Union's Horizon 2020 research and innovation programme under grant agreement Number 862739. This publication reflects only the authors' views. The European Commission is not responsible for any use that may be made of the information it contains.

References

Aeberhard, A., & Rist, S. (2009). Transdisciplinary co-production of knowledge in the development of organic agriculture in Switzerland. *Ecological Economics, 68*(4), 1171–1181. https://doi.org/10.1016/j.ecolecon.2008.08.008

Bardsley, D. K., & Bardsley, A. M. (2014). Organising for socio-ecological resilience: The roles of the mountain farmer cooperative genossenschaft gran alpin in graubünden, Switzerland. *Ecological Economics, 98*, 11–21. https://doi.org/10.1016/j.ecolecon.2013.12.004

Borgatti, S., Everett, M., & Freeman, L. (2002). *Ucinet for Windows: Software for social network analysis* (Version 6). Analytic Technologies.

Borgatti, S. P., & Everett, M. G. (1999). Models of core/periphery structures. *Social Networks, 21*(4), 375–395. https://doi.org/10.1016/S0378-8733(99)00019-2

Brinkley, C. (2018). The small world of the alternative food network. *Sustainability, 10*(8), 2921. https://doi.org/10.3390/SU10082921

Bruce, A., Jackson, C., & Lamprinopoulou, C. (2021). Social networks and farming resilience. *Outlook on Agriculture, 50*(2), 196–205. https://doi.org/10.1177/0030727020984812

Brunori, G., Barjolle, D., Dockes, A. C., Helmle, S., Ingram, J., Klerkx, L., Moschitz, H., Nemes, G., & Tisenkopfs, T. (2013). CAP reform and innovation: The role of learning and innovation networks. *EuroChoices, 12*(2), 27–33. https://doi.org/10.1111/1746-692X.12025

Demiryurek, K. (2010). Analysis of information systems and communication networks for organic and conventional hazelnut producers in the Samsun province of Turkey. *Agricultural Systems, 103*(7), 444–452. https://doi.org/10.1016/j.agsy.2010.04.002

Dolfing Id, A. G., Leuven, J. R. F. W., & Dermody, B. J. (2019). *The effects of network topology, climate variability and shocks on the evolution and resilience of a food trade network. PLoS ONE, 14*(3), e0213378. https://doi.org/10.1371/journal.pone.0213378

Duit, A., & Galaz, V. (2008). Governance and complexity—Emerging issues for governance theory. *Governance, 21*(3), 311–335. https://doi.org/10.1111/J.1468-0491.2008.00402.X

Ehlers, M.-H., Huber, R., & Finger, R. (2021). Agricultural policy in the era of digitalisation. *Food Policy, 100*, Article 102019. https://doi.org/10.1016/j.foodpol.2020.102019

Esparcia, J. (2014). Innovation and networks in rural areas. An analysis from European innovative projects. *Journal of Rural Studies, 34*, 1–14. https://doi.org/10.1016/J.JRURSTUD.2013.12.004

Eurostat. (2019, October 19). *Regional organic farming in the EU—Products Eurostat News*. https://ec.europa.eu/eurostat/web/products-eurostat-news/-/edn-20191016-1

Federal Statistical Office. (2023). *Employees, farmholdings, utilized agricultural area and livestock on level 1 of classification by canton*. https://www.bfs.admin.ch/bfs/en/home/statistics/agriculture-forestry/farming.assetdetail.24945307.html

Ferjani, A., Reissig, L., & Mann, S. (2010). Agriculture biologique en Suisse : Abandons et conversions. *Recherche Agronomique Suisse, 1*(4), 142–147.

Forney, J., & Epiney, L. (2022). Governing Farmers through data? Digitization and the Question of Autonomy in Agri-environmental governance. *Journal of Rural Studies, 95*, 173–182. https://doi.org/10.1016/j.jrurstud.2022.09.001

Forrer, C., Trueb, N., & Schmitt, E. (2024). *Innovative networks: A social network analysis of actors along a mountain cereal value chain in the Swiss Alps*. https://doi.org/10.2139/ssrn.4697424

Galaskiewicz, J. (2011). Studying supply chains from a social network perspective. *Journal of Supply Chain Management, 47*(1), 4–8. https://doi.org/10.1111/J.1745-493X.2010.03209.X

Golbeck, J. (2015). Chapter 21—Analyzing networks. In J. Golbeck (Ed.), *Introduction to social media investigation* (pp. 221–235). Syngress. https://doi.org/10.1016/B978-0-12-801656-5.00021-4

Gros-Balthazard, M. (2022). Emergence of Food Matters in Val Poschiavo (Switzerland) through the Definition of a Regional Transition Project. *Journal of Alpine Research*. https://doi.org/10.4000/RGA.10894

Guerrero, A. M., Bodin, Ö., Mcallister, R. R. J., Wilson, K. A., Guerrero, A. M., Bodin, Ö., Mcallister, R. R. J., & Wilson, K. A. (2015). Achieving social-ecological fit through bottom-up collaborative governance: An empirical investigation. *Ecology and Society, 20*(4), 41. https://doi.org/10.5751/ES-08035-200441

Hanneman, R., & Riddle, M. (2005). *Introduction to social network methods*. University of California. http://faculty.ucr.edu/~hanneman/

Hinnou, L. C., Sossou, R., Alidou, G. M., & Mongbo, R. L. (2022). Social network analysis of innovation platforms in the local rice value chains in Benin: Shield or showcase for endogenous innovation? *African Journal of Agricultural Research, 18*(8), 672–681. https://doi.org/10.5897/AJAR2022.16011

Home, R., Indermuehle, A., Tschanz, A., Ries, E., & Stolze, M. (2019). Factors in the decision by Swiss farmers to convert to organic farming. *Renewable Agriculture and Food Systems, 34*(6), 571–581. https://doi.org/10.1017/S1742170518000121

Ingold, K., Balsiger, J., & Hirschi, C. (2010). Climate change in mountain regions: How local communities adapt to extreme events. *Local Environment, 15*(7), 651–661. https://doi.org/10.1080/13549839.2010.498811

Isaac, M. E. (2012). Agricultural information exchange and organizational ties: The effect of network topology on managing agrodiversity. *Agricultural Systems, 109*, 9–15. https://doi.org/10.1016/j.agsy.2012.01.011

Janssen, M. A., Bodin, Ö., Anderies, J. M., Elmqvist, T., Ernstson, H., Mcallister, R. R. J., Olsson, P., & Ryan, P. (2006). Toward a network perspective of the study of resilience in social-ecological systems. *Ecology And Society*, *11*(1). https://www.ecologyandsociety.org/vol11/iss1/art15/

Luthe, T., Wyss, R., & Schuckert, M. (2012). Network governance and regional resilience to climate change: Empirical evidence from mountain tourism communities in the Swiss Gotthard region. *Regional Environmental Change, 12*(4), 839–854. https://doi.org/10.1007/s10113-012-0294-5

Mann, S., & Gairing, M. (2012). "Loyals" and "Optimizers": Shedding light on the decision for or against organic agriculture among Swiss farmers. *Journal of Agricultural and Environmental Ethics, 25*(3), 365–376. https://doi.org/10.1007/s10806-011-9309-3

Marsden, P. V. (2005). Network analysis. In K. Kempf-Leonard (Ed.), *Encyclopedia of social measurement* (pp. 819–825). Elsevier. https://doi.org/10.1016/B0-12-369398-5/00409-6

Metz, F., Lieberherr, E., Schmucki, A., & Huber, R. (2021). Policy change through negotiated agreements: The case of greening Swiss Agricultural Policy. *Policy Studies Journal, 49*(3), 731–756. https://doi.org/10.1111/psj.12417

Moschitz, H., Brunori, G., Roep, D., & Tisenkopfs, T. (2015). Learning and Innovation Networks for Sustainable Agriculture: Processes of co-evolution, joint reflection and facilitation. *Journal of Agricultural Education and Extension, 21*(1), 1–11. https://doi.org/10.1080/1389224X.2014.991111

Newman, M., Barabási, A.-L., & Watts, D. J. (2011). *The structure and dynamics of networks*. Princeton University Press. https://doi.org/10.1515/9781400841356

Padel, S. (2001). Conversion to organic farming: A typical example of the diffusion of an innovation? *Sociologia Ruralis, 41*(1), 40–61. https://doi.org/10.1111/1467-9523.00169

Rogers, E. M. (1983). *Diffusion of Innovations*. https://papers.ssrn.com/abstract=1496176

Scott, J. (2004). *Social network analysis: A handbook* (2nd ed.). Sage.

Simon, S. (2009). *Biolandbau in Graubünden-Einkommenseffekte und gesamtwirtschaftliche Bedeutung Organic farming, income effect, macroeconomic impact Einleitung und Zielsetzung* (10. Wissenschaftstagung Ökologischer Landbau, Ed.). http://orgprints.org/view/projects/int_conf_2009_wita.html

Skaalsveen, K., Ingram, J., & Urquhart, J. (2020). The role of farmers' social networks in the implementation of no-till farming practices. *Agricultural Systems, 181*, Article 102824. https://doi.org/10.1016/j.agsy.2020.102824

Valente, T. W., Chich, P. C., & Pentz, M. A. (2007). Community coalitions as a system: Effects of network change on adoption of evidence-based substance abuse prevention. *American Journal of Public Health, 97*(5), 880. https://doi.org/10.2105/AJPH.2005.063644

Vroege, W., Meraner, M., Polman, N., Storm, H., Heijman, W., & Finger, R. (2020). Beyond the single farm—A spatial econometric analysis of spill-overs in farm diversification in the Netherlands. *Land Use Policy, 99*, Article 105019. https://doi.org/10.1016/J.LANDUSEPOL.2020.105019

Willer, H., Schlatter, B., & Trávníček, J. (2023). *The world of organic agriculture: Statistics and emerging trends 2023*. https://doi.org/10.5281/zenodo.7572890

CHAPTER 13

Exploring Mountain Crops as an Alternative to Livestock Production in the Transformation of Swiss Mountain Agriculture

Isabel Jaisli, Fabienne Buchmann, Carmen Forrer, and Roman Grüter

1 Introduction

The Grison Alps—ranging from around 300 to over 4000 m above sea level—form the entire south-eastern part of the Swiss Alps and are characterized by high mountains, decentralized settlement, and extensive agriculture. With steep slopes, poor accessibility, and shorter growing seasons, farming in the Grison Alps is demanding. Nevertheless, agriculture has a long tradition in the region and plays a major role in forming

I. Jaisli (✉) · F. Buchmann · C. Forrer · R. Grüter
Institute of Natural Resource Sciences, Zürich University of Applied Sciences, Zürich, Switzerland
e-mail: isabel.jaisli@zhaw.ch

F. Buchmann
e-mail: fabienne.buchmann@zhaw.ch

C. Forrer
e-mail: carmen.forrer@hotmail.com

D. Barjolle et al. (eds.), *Innovation and the Future of Rural Development in Europe*,
https://doi.org/10.1007/978-3-032-22570-2_13

the typical Swiss landscape and is an essential basis for several mountain municipalities (Geiser et al., 2022a). Though, the form of farming in the region has changed over time. Once reliant on mountain arable farming for sustenance, the advent of new transportation routes led to its decline around 150 years ago (Schluchter, 2015). This gave rise to a shift towards livestock-dominated agriculture, and the encroachment of grassland, the "grasslandisation". Currently, agriculture in the Swiss Alps is primarily focused on cattle production for meat and milk and 90% of Swiss mountain farms do exclusively produce livestock on their land (BFS, 2023a). While this high specialization in grazing livestock makes use of the abundant grassland resources, it also makes farmers more vulnerable to milk and meat prices and livestock related subsidies (Bardsley & Bardsley, 2014). Agriculture in Switzerland, and to a higher extend in the mountains, is heavily reliant on direct government payments. Due to the harsher conditions, mountain farming seems to be only viable through these support measures (Flury et al., 2012). With less income from actual production, farming in the Swiss mountains is more extensive and has a higher proportion of organic farmers than in the rest of Switzerland (Ferjani & Flury, 2013). In the canton of Grisons for example, 60% of the farms produce organically, representing the highest proportion of organic farms in Switzerland (BFS, 2023b). While the support measures keep mountain farming alive, they also create a high degree of dependence on political decisions, which poses a risk to medium- and long-term planning.

With growing awareness of climate change and its causes, livestock keeping in general and especially ruminant production is increasingly being questioned, as signalled by the growing social trends towards veganism (Swissveg, 2022), animal rights movements, and climate change activism. This shift in public and political perception is part of a broader global debate on how to realign food systems with planetary boundaries and human health. The EAT-Lancet Commission on healthy, sustainable, and just food systems (Rockström et al., 2025; Willett et al., 2019) calls for profound transformations in both production and consumption patterns worldwide, including a substantial reduction of animal-based foods and an increased reliance on diverse plant sources. These global insights reinforce the urgency of exploring how mountain regions can

R. Grüter
e-mail: roman.grueter@zhaw.ch

contribute to a sustainable agricultural transition through diversified crop production.

Echoing these global recommendations at the national level, the guide "Pathways to Switzerland's Future of Food", published by the scientific panel Future of Food Switzerland (Fesenfeld et al., 2023) argues that a radical reduction of meat and milk consumption, by about 50% of current consumption, is needed for a sustainable Swiss food system. Such a reduction is likely to have massive consequences for agriculture, also for livestock dominated mountain farming. Although less radical, the "Climate Strategy Agriculture and Food" of the Federal Offices for Agriculture, for Food and Veterinary Sciences and for the Environment (BLW et al., 2023) also call for a change in diets to reduce greenhouse gas emissions from food. In terms of concrete implementation, both strategies emphasize the importance of increasing and supporting plant production for human consumption in Switzerland. With these changing consumer preferences and political trends, the Swiss livestock sector is expected to decline, with uncertain implications for mountain agriculture and the sectors dependent on it. The question is whether the desired shift towards increased plant production also offers opportunities for mountain regions and whether farmers are willing and able to adapt their production systems accordingly. Recent research by Salliou (2023) highlights that such transitions away from livestock farming involve not only economic and environmental considerations but also profound social and identity-related dimensions. Drawing on post-livestock farmers' experiences in Switzerland and the United States, the study shows that motivation, community support, and access to knowledge networks are critical factors for successful transformation. These insights underline that sustainable transitions in mountain agriculture will depend as much on the capacity of farmers to innovate and reorganize as on policy incentives or market demand.

Diversification has long been recognized as a key strategy for enhancing the resilience and sustainability of mountain farming systems around the world (Grilli et al., 2025; López-i-Gelats et al., 2011; Naudiyal et al., 2019; Nguyen & Hens, 2021; Stotten, 2021). However, much less attention has been given to diversification through the (re-)introduction of crop production into predominantly livestock-based systems—a development that has only recently begun to attract renewed interest as a niche activity to maintain traditions, diversify production portfolios, or enable product innovation. Several innovative farmers demonstrate that plant production is in fact feasible in mountain areas and could provide opportunities for the future. Gran Alpin, a cooperative for the production, processing and marketing of mountain cereals and products, provides a prime example of the diversification of traditional farming practices at high altitudes (Genossenschaft Gran Alpin, 2024). Its aim is to maintain the value chain of organic mountain cereals in the Grisons, after it had almost disappeared due to the lack of financial income opportunities from cereal farming in the region (Bardsley & Bardsley, 2014; Moschitz & Oehen, 2020).

The case of Gran Alpin in Grisons was selected as case study for EU-Horizon 2020 Project "Mountain Valorization through Interconnectedness and Green Growth" (MOVING) for the Swiss Alp region (Geiser et al., 2022a). The aim of this case study is specifically to explore the potential of crop production as a partial substitute for animal husbandry in mountain areas.

This article builds upon the result of the MOVING case study, including findings more specific to the case of mountain grains but also beyond to a more general view on mountain crop production. While the regional context mainly refers to the mountain zones of the canton of Grisons, its results are also applicable to other regions in the Alps and mountain regions beyond. Chapter two provides a general overview of the potential of crop production in Grison mountains from past to future. It also includes results from a feasibility study conducted as part of a regional development project in Safiental, Grisons, aiming to analyse the potential for diversification and innovation of plant production into the region (Grüter & Mathis, 2023). In chapter three the foresight study, conducted as part of the MOVING project, is presented, including different future scenarios and long-term visions for crop production in mountain agriculture and regional development. In the last chapter we will conclude with prospects for mountain crop production and policy recommendation to support regional development in the Swiss Alps.

2 Potential of Plant Production in the Grison Mountains

Past and Present of Plant Production in the Grison Mountains

Plant cultivation in mountainous regions faces particular challenges compared to the Swiss Central Plateau. The climatic conditions limit the growing season and require high frost tolerance of perennial crops. This limits the choice of suitable agricultural crops and varieties. Steep slopes, small-scale structures and limited accessibility make cultivation even more complicated. A look at the cultural history of mountain farming reveals that plant production used to be more important in the past and that some of the reasons mentioned above were partly responsible for its sharp decline over the last 150 years (Schilperoord & Heistinger, 2015). In fact, arable farming was practised up to high altitudes (up to 1800 m a.s.l.) in the canton of Grisons. Crops such as spring barley, flax or field beans grew on the highest fields (Schilperoord, 2020). At lower altitudes (below 1400 m a.s.l.), other crops such as spring wheat, buckwheat or hemp were also cultivated. In the nineteenth century, the development of transport routes, in particular the railway, led to a strong influx of grain from abroad. Where it was now cheaper to buy foreign grain than the produce of the local farmers, arable farming was abandoned (Schilperoord & Heistinger, 2015). After industrialisation, arable farming in the mountains was no longer competitive with farming in the foothills of the Alps and only livestock farming prevailed at higher altitudes. In the twentieth century, the reduction of spatial isolation led to a transition from self-sufficiency to a market economy. By the beginning of the twenty-first century, mountain farming in the canton of Grisons had declined further due to specialization in agriculture. It was until the 1980s that grain production was revitalised thanks to the establishment of the cooperative Gran Alpin and subsequently, production has recovered to some extent (see case study below).

With the success of pioneers, new initiatives arise. In 2018 the regional development project "Safiental" was initiated in the Canton of Grisons, aiming to support local value chains and to foster innovation in the agricultural sector. As part of the project, a feasibility analysis for the establishment of an innovation centre for mountain agriculture was conducted. To identify innovation opportunities in the region, the potential for diversification and innovation of plant production in mountain areas was analysed through literature search, analysis of statistical data and expert interviews (Grüter & Mathis, 2023). The study showed, that 70% of arable land in the canton of Grisons is used as temporary grassland. Within the arable land, there is therefore significant potential for expanding plant production. The results demonstrated the cultivation potential for a wide variety of arable and specialty crops in the area (Grüter & Mathis, 2023):

While grain production is established again in most larger valleys within the Grison mountain zone, a handful of pioneering farms are exploring alternatives by experimenting successfully with legumes, oilseeds and potatoes. In addition to growing traditional arable crops, specialty crops have also been cultivated in the region and hold potential for future production. In the past, high-stem fruit trees were planted in pastures at higher altitudes. While neighbouring alpine regions have already established successful models for vegetable and berry cultivation, such practices in Switzerland are still at an early stage. Although production remains limited, opportunities exist for expanding the cultivation of resilient berries such as currants, gooseberries, and blueberries. Vegetable production currently occurs on only a few small plots in the canton of Grisons, yet the development of storable, high-quality crops and local specialties—such as Swiss chard, a local cabbage variety used for *Capuns*—could substantially enrich and diversify future mountain farming systems. However, production remains constrained by small-scale structures, limited availability of locally adapted varieties, inadequate processing infrastructure, and the long supply chains typical of remote alpine farms. (Grüter & Mathis, 2023).

Case Study Gran Alpin—Success and Challenges

The value chain for grains of Gran Alpin in the mountain area of Grisons is an example of a traditional farming practice at high altitudes, mixed with innovative approaches. As part of the EU-Project MOVING, the mountain grain value chain was analysed in a participatory process through interviews, workshops and surveys with stakeholders of the value chain (Geiser et al., 2022a, 2022b; Schmitt & Geiser, 2022b). The findings revealed different success factors, but also identified challenges and threats for the future:

After the disappearance of mountain grains in the last century, it was thanks to the founding of the cooperative Gran Alpin, which unites mountain grain farmers and helps Grisons' grain stand out from the rest of the market, that grain production has been rediscovered (Schilperoord, 2014). Nowadays, about 120 organic farms of the cooperative Gran Alpin produce 600–700 tonnes of organic cereals (Genossenschaft Gran Alpin, 2024). The cooperative focuses on the local production and distribution of premium cereal products such as flour, pasta or beer. Through its organic certification, high quality and a wide diversity of grain varieties, the market demand for Gran Alpin currently exceeds production values, driven by the trend towards local, artisanal, and organic products. It is also claimed that the higher sun exposure, makes the grain more nutritious and sweeter (Geiser et al., 2022a).

Geiser et al. (2022b) identified a wide range of benefits associated with the value chain. With the high demand, premium prices can be achieved for the Gran Alpin products, providing valuable income opportunities for farmers, processors but also local retailers and gastronomy. By diversifying the landscape in this area alongside the predominant livestock farming, arable farming increases biodiversity and the resulting nature's contributions to people. Socio-culturally the revival of mountain grain production contributes towards the scenic beauty and uniqueness of this ancient cultural landscape. It contributes to the preservation of the Alpine habitat for the local population and visitors.

Major success factors identified include the cooperative's drive, partnerships with local processors and retailers, and premium pricing through organic and regional branding. To make mountain grain cultivation attractive to farmers, the cooperative pays a higher purchase price than other customers. The farmers also received additional financial support from the cantonal government for growing mountain cereal, in addition to the state direct payments (Forrer, 2022). Through the support of the cooperative in marketing the products, effort needed to increase or start grain production is reduced. It was, however, also shown that availability of locally adapted seeds and current support for livestock production in the region are the main factors holding back grain production on farms (Schmitt & Geiser, 2022a). Further challenges consist in the processing of the high variety of different types of grains with mostly small volumes and the remote location of the farms that lead to complicated logistics and long transport distances (Geiser et al., 2024). Moreover, the local infrastructure is insufficient, as proper machinery for small fields or more and smaller grain silos are needed. Also, there is a lack of qualified staff, especially in the processing stages, for example millers or brewers.

The participatory study also revealed a range of threats, that will challenge the future of mountain grain production (Schmitt & Geiser, 2022b). The stakeholders emphasized the importance of their ability to plan for the coming crop year. The increasing occurrence of extreme weather events like heavy rains and droughts, driven by climate change, will increasingly challenge arable farming, leading to yield loss but also impacting the quality of the product. The ongoing loss of grain varieties also threatens the viability of mountain farming. Due to the comparatively low economic importance, breeding effort for these specific needs is currently low. Under the mountain-specific conditions, and increasingly so, with climate-induced changes, future production highly depends on the availability of locally adapted grain varieties for mountain areas. At the same time, varieties need to meet the high-quality standards demanded by processors and consumers. Beside suitable varieties, also suitable machinery for small-scale structures is lacking. Technological innovation has been identified as a crucial factor, as various stakeholders have consistently highlighted the need for infrastructures and machinery adapted to the region's topography and small-scale nature, which contrasts with the prevailing trends in the technological development of large-scale machinery. Due to the high importance of the agricultural policies for Swiss agriculture, the future orientation of it will be key for the future viability of arable farming in the Alps. While the current Swiss agricultural policy promotes multifunctionality, which is generally beneficial for diversified crop production, certain incentives and subsidies contradict this principle. For instance, substantial funds are allocated to advertising for the Swiss meat industry or invested in animal housing infrastructure. Future changes in the policies might be beneficial or destructive for mountain grains. As already shown, the availability of skilled labour is already a limiting factor. With the ongoing emigration of young people from the rural area, this challenge will be increasingly relevant and threatens the possibility of local processing.

Following key recommendations for the Gran Alpin value chain were derived, for increasing resilience and prepare for future changes (Geiser et al., 2024):

- Increase collaboration with other value chains and actors in the region to leverage knowledge and resources, especially in areas such as logistics and infrastructure.

- Innovate in areas such as processing and storage to reduce costs, increase efficiency and improve product quality.
- Invest in training and capacity building for its stakeholders to improve their skills and knowledge in areas such as business management, marketing and quality control.

The case of Gran Alpin serves as lesson for crop cultivation in the alps, highlighting benefits and success factors, but also challenges and threats for the future.

3 Future of Crop Production in the Grison Mountains—A Foresight Study

Starting from the insights provided by the case study of Gran Alpin and other pioneers of mountain crop cultivation, a participatory foresight study was conducted as part of the MOVING project. The overall goal of the foresight exercises was to identify the socio-ecological drivers and game-changers that will shape the future of mountain value chains by 2050 and to provide visions of future trends and dynamics that permit identifying policy gaps and policy modernisation needs. For the foresight study in the Swiss Alps, the specific scope was defined as: "The future of crop production in the Grison mountain areas", with the aim of identifying the potential for change and what is needed to support farmers along the way.

Foresight Exercise—Methodology

For the foresight exercise, three workshops with stakeholders—the foresight group—were conducted between January and April 2023 (Jaisli et al., 2023). To ensure different perspectives in the workshops, participants from different sectors related to Grisons agriculture and value chains were invited. In total 11 stakeholders participated in the workshops including farmers, researchers, policy experts, regional product and tourism managers, as well as representatives from local authorities.

The overall approach for scenario building was based on the MOVING guidelines for the foresight exercise (Barjolle et al., 2022) and others (Glover & Sexton, 2015; Rhydderch, 2017). The foresight exercise followed a stepwise approach including three workshops with the foresight group as well as preparatory, and post-processing tasks by the research team (see Fig. 1).

As a first step the research team identified relevant megatrends by screening literature and statistical data and developed a first baseline scenario based on these trends and the current state of Grison mountain agriculture. During the **first workshop**, which was conducted online, the foresight group identified and discussed relevant drivers that will influence the future of plant production in the Grison mountains in the upcoming decades. Participants were requested to identify drivers from different categories, including social, technical, environmental, economic and political drivers. Following, the drivers were ranked based on their importance and uncertainty, to identify the uncertain driving forces. These "critical uncertainties" are drivers, which are both important for the focal question (plant production in Grison mountains) but do also have an uncertain outcome and are not predictable (Rhydderch, 2017). Finally, the group selected the most relevant "critical uncertainties".

For these selected drivers, two contrary expressions were formulated (e.g. electricity prices will increase versus decrease) to describe an axis. Combining two axes, a set of three four-cell matrices (2 × 2 matrix), each providing four distinct combinations of driver expressions, was build and then used to develop different scenarios. Prior to the second workshop the research team prepared a first draft of the scenarios, mainly describing the broader supra-regional developments to provide a context and starting point. The following questions were addressed for building these parent scenarios: How does society live? What does agriculture look like? How has the economy developed? What is the state of the environment?

In the **second workshop**, the three matrices and including scenarios were presented and discussed, before selecting one matrix to continue. For the further elaboration of the selected matrix, following questions were used:

- How has mountain farming developed?
- How are products processed and traded?
- Which elements in the scenario speak in favour of plant production in mountain regions?
- Which elements in the scenario speak against plant-based production in mountain regions?
- Who are the winners and losers in the scenario?

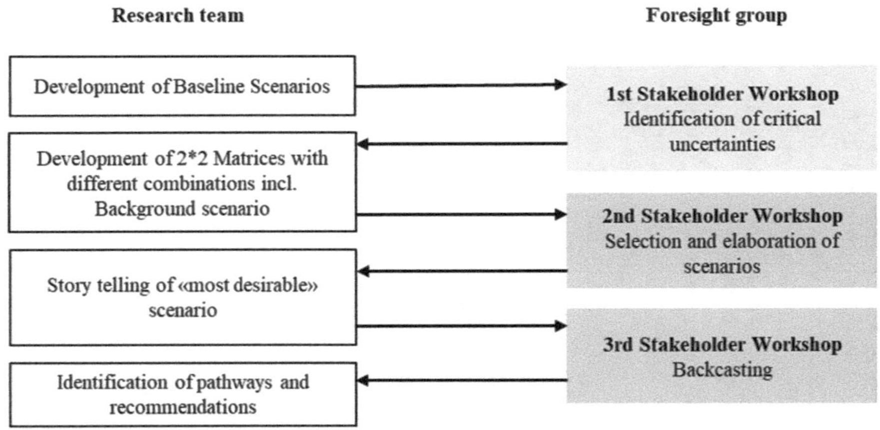

Fig. 1 Stepwise approach for the participatory foresight exercise "The future of crop production in the Grison mountain areas"

- What are the effects on the environment, society and the economy?

After sketching and discussing the four scenarios, each participant voted for the most desired scenario for the future of Grisons' mountain area.

In the **third workshop**, a backcasting exercise was conducted to design a pathway towards the selected, most desirable scenario, to identify constraint and framework conditions and to derive policy recommendations. In a first step, constraints, and hurdles for reaching the desired future were identified and discussed. For this task the participants were asked to take perspectives of different personas (farmer, processor, consumer, politician) and to answer from that perspective "What are the reasons for not having this scenario today?". To dig deeper into underlying causes, the 5 Whys technique was applied, where the question "Why?" is repeated several times to each answer (Serrat, 2009). From the root causes identified, the participants formulated framework conditions needed to overcome the obstructing causes. For imagining and describing a development path, the participants elaborated news articles from the year 2050, which described how the critical framework conditions were achieved and what milestones were needed, in a storytelling approach and from a future perspective.

All workshops were recorded and transcribed. A content analysis of the transcripts was carried out using a combination of inductive and deductive coding approaches, supported by MaxQDA software.

Results of the Foresight Study

Baseline Scenarios

As a starting point for developing future scenarios, the following megatrends in the region were identified:

- *Decreasing and aging society*: The lack of educational opportunities, job positions, and limited infrastructure's appeal to young individuals drive emigration among locals and exacerbate the shortage of skilled workers (BFS, 2020, 2022; Rat für Raumordnung, 2019).
- *Remote work*: Digitalization boosts mountain region appeal for remote work, especially during summer months (Rat für Raumordnung, 2019).

- *Agricultural centralisation*: While the number of farms and agricultural land is decreasing, the average size of a farm increases (BFS, 2021a). Diversification and own or joint local processing of some products counteracts centralization (BFS, 2021b).
- *Climate change*: Climate change is significantly impacting mountain farming, with reduced water availability, dry summers, and more frequent extreme weather events. Rising temperatures lead to decreased winter snowfall, contributing to the melting of glaciers, which are essential water sources for the region (Beniston, 2012; Vij et al., 2021). Warmer temperatures and less snow are extending the growing season at high altitudes and making more and more areas attractive for crop production (Erdin, 2023).

Starting from the identified megatrends, the following narrative baseline scenario for the future of the Grison mountains in the year 2050 was created:

> In 2050, a glimpse into the mountainous region of Grisons reveals significant transformations. The proportion of the 65+ generation is higher than in previous years, and this trend is on the rise. Notably, young people and working residents often leave the mountainous region, heading towards urban centres or even exiting the canton. However, departing locals are replaced by others seeking to realize their dream of mountain living, turning the region into a residential and recreational area with home offices for those who can afford it. Mountain farming has undergone a profound shift, marked by the extinction of smaller family farms and the emergence of a few large and modern agricultural enterprises that manage the available land. While navigating diverse challenges, farms sustain themselves through direct payments and diversification strategies such as agro-touristic offers. Challenges in mountain farming include the need to irrigate pastures and fields (when water permits) and protect agricultural land from extreme events, disrupting economic planning, especially in crop production due to climate-induced yield losses. Despite a decline in cattle numbers and increasing overgrowth of alpine areas, extensive dairy farming remains a standard on every farm. However, mountain farmers cannot capitalize on the growing poultry and pig numbers in the canton, as factory farming occurs in the valleys with the necessary infrastructure. The centralization of post-production steps in the value chain to large hubs further diminishes added value in the region, especially in certain product groups, driven by a shortage of skilled workers.

Drivers & Critical Uncertainties

During the first workshop the foresight group identified a wide range of drivers that will influence the future of crop production in Grison mountains, including social, technological, economic, environmental, and political drivers (Table 1).

Four drivers were selected as most critical uncertainties and for each two contrary expressions were formulated: (1) **Agricultural policies** in future could be oriented towards (a) maximization of production for achieving a high degree of self-supply in Switzerland or (b) be oriented towards resource conservation and biodiversity. (2) **Society** and its overarching values could develop (a) towards a focus on own interests (egoism) or (b) towards increasing responsibility for others. (3) **Climate change** could have a (a) net positive impact on plant production in the mountains due to longer growing seasons from increasing temperatures or a (b) net negative impact due to water scarcity and increasing extreme weather events. (4) Future **technologies** could either increasingly be supportive for (a) large scale structures, e.g. increasing size of land machines or (b) for small-scale structure, e.g. allowing for diversification through digitalization, drones, etc.

Table 1 Drivers for the future of crop production in mountain areas identified by the foresight group

Society	*Technology*	*Economy*	*Environment*	*Politics*
Future of work	Artificial intelligence	Economic development	Longer growing season	International relations (EU)
Basic income	Synthetic fuel	Availability of inputs	Extreme weather events	Civil unrest
Division of society	Energy	Tourism	Natural hazards	Agricultural policy
Security	Mobility	Gastronomy	Climate change	Direct payments
Pioneers	Digitalisation	Animal production	Wolf population	
Nutritional trends		Income/wealth		
Emigration of youth		Local infrastructure for processing		
Age structure				
Health				
Societal values				

Scenarios

Utilizing these drivers as axes, three matrices were formulated, with agricultural policy included in all three, as it was being identified as the most crucial uncertainty. The research team prepared the resulting matrices and initial scenario elements, outlining the general future state, as illustrated in Fig. 2.

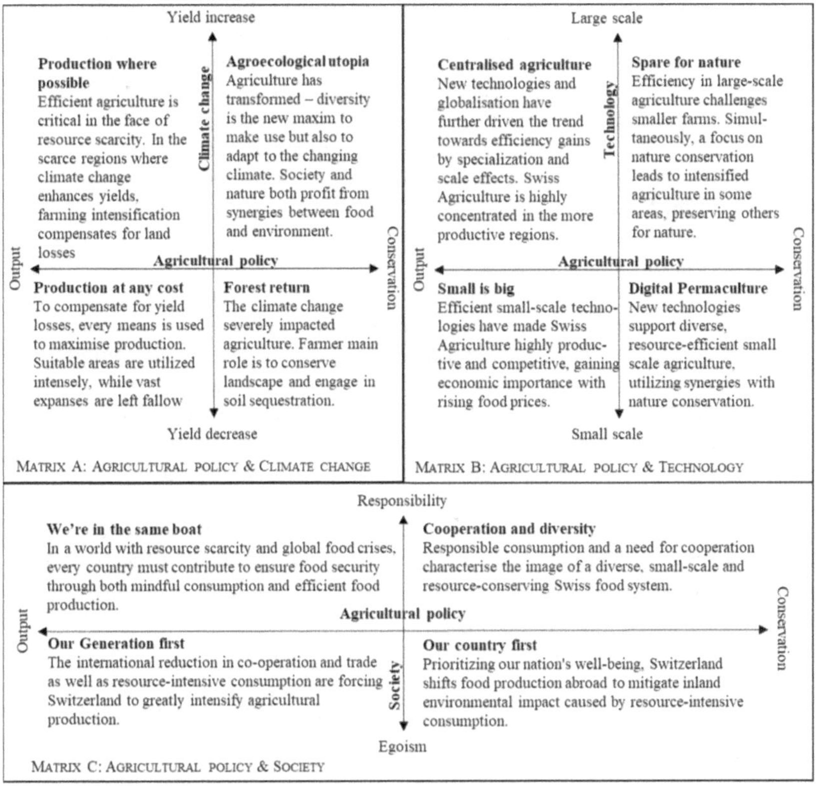

Fig. 2 Scenario matrices based on selected critical uncertainties in three combinations: agricultural policies either focusing on resource conservation or output maximization (Matrix A, B and C), Climate change either having a positive or negative net yield impact (Matrix A), Technologies rather supporting large-scale or small-scale structures (Matrix B) and Societal values developing towards increasing responsibility or egoism (Matrix C)

The foresight group selected Matrix C (Agricultural Policy & Society) and further explored on the four scenarios focusing on the role of crop production in Grison mountain areas:

Scenario 1: We are in the same boat (Output oriented agricultural policy and responsible society)

To respond to resource scarcities and global food crisis, Switzerland has reorientated agricultural policies towards increasing production yields in agriculture. This is mainly driven by social intentions so secure supply and affordable food prices, also for the poorer share of society. In the lowland production has been further intensified, with a clear focus on plant production for human consumption. Though total production has increased, the emphasis on agricultural intensification leads to deterioration of agrobiodiversity, soil health and its ecosystem services.
In the mountain areas extensive animal production makes use of the available grasslands. However, with decreasing direct payments for environmental services, mountain farming has become less viable and is declining. While total number of farms decrease, farm communities emerge, where collaboration among several farms is the norm. Amid climate change, a desire for cooler temperatures drives migration towards mountain areas. This trend also fuels the ongoing competition for land resources between agriculture and settlements. The influx of affluent yet conscientious residents has given rise to a demand for sustainable, vegan, and local products. This surge in demand presents opportunities for innovative local producers, who are capitalizing on new growing conditions for arable farming facilitated by rising temperatures. A small niche market of exclusive plant-based local products for the new local population arises.

Scenario 2: Our Generation First (Output oriented agricultural policy and egoistic society)

In a world driven by capitalism and individual profit-seeking, also agriculture in Switzerland has undergone a significant shift. The policy focus on output maximization led to a strong shift towards farm intensification, where high yields are possible. While smaller farms are not competitive, large scale industrial farms making use of the new available technologies dominate the picture of Swiss agriculture. This trend is also supported and driven by the demand that prioritizes cheap consumption over future considerations, neglecting animal welfare, natural resources, and environmental conservation. The intensive exploitation advances soil degradation and arable land is increasingly lost. Cost-saving measures in food production result in low-quality, inexpensive food.

With the cut of direct payments for environmental services, mountain farming is rapidly declining. The surviving mountain farms heavily rely on tourism. Climate change prompts a desire for cooler temperatures, leading people to migrate to mountain areas. With wealthy visitors, real estate investments and new residents, the competition for land in the valleys is increasing, leaving little space for arable farming. In contrast to the competition in the valley, land at higher altitudes is being abandoned and bush encroachment is on the rise. While livestock farming can partially survive, due to the rising demand for meat and milk products, crop production in the mountains is hardly viable and stays a minor niche linked to regional tourism.

Scenario 3: Our Country First (Conservation oriented agricultural policy and egoistic society)

In this future of Swiss agriculture, the landscape transforms into a showcase to attract tourists, with agrotourism becoming the predominant economic driver for farms. The focus shifts from extensive agricultural production to cultivating expensive niche products, while government decisions shape farming strategies and cultivation areas. The enduring presence of cows and Alpine pastures continues to play a pivotal role in the region's allure for tourists.

Socially, community bonds wane, giving way to individual priorities, yet a strong patriotic connection to Switzerland persists, fuelled by its picturesque landscapes and luxury products. A social disparity emerges, with some affording exclusive niche products, while others rely on more affordable imports.

Economically, the flourishing tourism sector, particularly agrotourism, serves as a showcase of the idyllic "Swiss paradise". The agricultural sector, crucial for landscape protection, receives substantial government subsidies, but a significant dependence on food imports arises due to a low self-sufficiency level.

Amid climate change and landscape alterations, effective measures boost biodiversity, and conservation takes precedence over extensive production. Rising temperatures create opportunities for expanding summer tourism, with alpine pastures contributing significantly.

Despite changes, bush encroachment remains confined to remote areas, allowing well-maintained alpine pastures to retain their allure.

The participants decided for the following Scenario 4 "Cooperation & Diversity" to be the most desirable. Some key elements of the scenario along the value chain are presented in Fig. 3.

Scenario 4: Cooperation and Diversity (Conservation oriented agricultural policy and responsible society)

The increased focus on resource conservation in agricultural policy, as well as the consumers valuation for sustainably and fairly produced food, has fostered a food system transformation, characterized by cooperation and diversity.
Despite the decreasing demand for meat and milk, mountain farming remained and even increased attractiveness and was able to profit from different developments: Environmental and animal

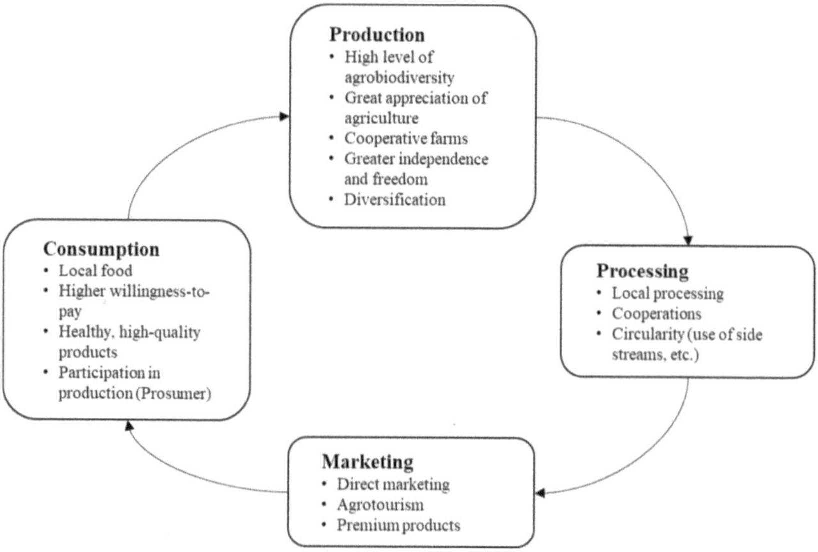

Fig. 3 Key elements of value chains in the desired scenario "Cooperation & Diversity"

rights considerations have led to an abandonment of industrial livestock production, limiting meat and milk production to the mountains, where abundant grassland resources allow for animal friendly husbandry. Additionally, also crop production has been brought back to the mountains, to meet the increasing demand for plant-based, local food. Plant production now embraces diversity with locally adapted varieties, and in steep areas, a harmonious blend of plants and animals is cultivated, including goats, sheep, or small cows. Through the higher willingness to pay and support environmentally friendly agriculture, a large number and diversity of farms contributes to the vitality of the Swiss agroecosystem. While farms are generally small-scale, community support and modern small-scale technology enable efficient and resource-conserving cultivation throughout the region.
Socially, a profound connection with fellow humans and nature prevails, fostering tight-knit communities. Society values and actively participates in agricultural production, promoting a sense of responsibility. This attractive way of living draws people to these communities, offering both on-site jobs and remote work opportunities, contributing to the overall happiness of farmers and residents.
Economically, collaboration, circular economy, and innovative thinking drive successful development. Societal responsibility translates into a willingness to pay a premium for food, increasing the value of agricultural goods. The local economy thrives, with a shift away from major retail companies towards local markets. Tourism, particularly agrotourism, flourishes as people seek to connect with and contribute to food production.
In response to climate change, effective measures increase biodiversity, and natural resources are managed responsibly through water systems, soil health initiatives, and renewable energies. Despite a decrease in Alpine pastures due to reduced animal farming, the landscape adapts positively with advanced bush encroachment control. This scenario paints a picture of a harmonious and sustainable coexistence between agriculture, society, and the environment.

The discussion showed that this scenario would be mainly beneficial for most stakeholders. In this scenario the agrifood sector boosts farmer incomes and caters to a growing consumer preference for quality food. This translates into more jobs and economic growth, enhancing the region's attractiveness. Sustainable farming practices benefit nature, promoting biodiversity and environmental value.

Consumers gain access to high-quality products, and small enterprises in the value chain thrive with the re-localization of the food system. However, low-income consumers may face challenges due to potential increases in food prices.

Constraints, Opportunities, and Strategies

Using the chosen scenario, Cooperation & Diversity, as a vision for the future, the foresight group identified constraints and frameworks for this scenario. **Constraints** were identified at different levels, often interdependent or linked to the same root causes. Agricultural policy was identified as one of the key constraints to transformation. Current support is heavily biased towards livestock production. The same orientation is reflected in agricultural education. Few incentives and trainings are currently provided for mountain crop production. In general, transitions at farm level face several constraints, as they require know-how, financial investments, and additional work. There is often a lack of framework conditions to support farmers to innovate. The limited duration of agricultural policy was seen as an obstacle to innovation, but also the very high dependence of farmers on the policy. Farmers tend to make decisions based on these regulations rather than on their own know-how, interests, or local conditions. Despite the high dependence on support measures, demand also plays an important role, especially for product innovations, which are often more expensive. Consumer habits, traditions, convenience, price, taste, marketing, lack of knowledge, but also lack of availability were seen as barriers to consumer demand and willingness to pay.

During the discussion, observations were shared that provide **opportunities** for transformation, including success stories of pioneers, changes in the support system, collaborations and research that foster innovation, but also the opportunity to build on local traditions.

Based on the constraints and opportunities, different strategies were discussed to support a transformation towards the desired scenario (Table 2). The main objectives of the identified **strategies** were to promote innovation, to support farmers to transform their farms and to manage demand. Changes in agricultural education are needed to provide farmers with innovation skills as well as the know-how needed for diversification and the establishment of new production systems. Similarly, agricultural policies need to be reoriented to allow for greater flexibility, ownership, innovation and openness to mountain crop production. Innovation centres, pioneers and research will also play an important role in this process. In addition to the supply side, adaptations on the demand side are also needed, e.g. incentives for local plant products through increased availability, marketing or pricing strategies. It was specifically mentioned that building on local traditions and identities will be an important strategy to guide future demand.

4 Discussion and Conclusion

Scientific expertise, but also societal and political developments direct towards a transformation of our food system, including a shift from livestock oriented production to plant-based focused agricultural systems in the future (Fesenfeld et al., 2023; Willett et al., 2019). With the current one-sided focus on meat and milk production, this trend could potentially threaten mountain farming. For the case of the Swiss Alps in the canton of Grisons, the potential of plant production to enrich or replace animal farming in the mountains was assessed, and possible trajectories developed.

As demonstrated by pioneers and already further established initiatives, such as Gran Alpin, plant production is viable in mountain regions of Switzerland, also reflecting a comeback of traditions that have been lost in the last 150 years. Supporting the diversification of agriculture with arable farming or specialty crops has proven to be beneficial in various respects. Schilperoord (2004) highlights the importance to conserve arable farming in the mountains as it contributes to the diversification of agricultural systems, the preservation of biodiversity, an attractive landscape, the conservation and generation of income opportunities and the fulfilment of the stakeholders involved, as well as having a socio-cultural significance for the region.

The case study of Gran Alpin and the foresight exercise have also shown that a further expansion of crop production in the mountain areas is desirable in the region. It was, however, stressed, that crops should enrich but not replace traditional livestock farming in the area. In fact, the same arguments that call for strengthening crop cultivation in the mountains also count as argument to keep grassland-based livestock farming alive. The availability of grassland allows for sustainable meat and milk production making use of areas otherwise not suitable for food production (Schader et al., 2015). Through grazing or mowing bush encroachment is prevented, protecting a highly valuable ecosystem and landscape for biodiversity and tourism. Also, animal husbandry has

Table 2 Constraints, opportunities, and strategies for a transformation of the Grisons agrifood system towards the desired scenario "Cooperation & Diversity"

Constraints	*Observed potentials/ opportunities*	*Strategies*
Land suitability for plant production is limited	• Climate change increases growing season	
Education focuses on livestock farming		• Strengthen crop-production in the education (specially for mountain crops) • Including "innovation" in the curricula
Agricultural policies oriented towards livestock/lack of support for mountain crop production	• Hemp receiving subsidies since recently • Cantonal subsidies where national support is missing	• Subsidizing mountain crop production • Supporting innovation and farm transformation
Barriers to changeover at farm level (investments, know-how)	• Arable farming has a long tradition in the region (e.g. hemp, mountain grain, flax) • Research initiates new projects • Pioneers • Youth	• Innovations centres to support mountain crop production (research, training, exchange) • Supporting pioneers • Reducing barriers for farm transformation • Providing support (e.g. machinery) for establishing new production endeavours • Increasing flexibility of support measures (supporting famers initiatives rather than directing production)

(continued)

Table 2 (continued)

Constraints	*Observed potentials/ opportunities*	*Strategies*
Demand for local plant products/willingness to pay for local (plant) products	• Innovative traditional meat products with local plant alternatives • Consumers demand for more plant-based products • Growing market for meat alternatives	• Building on food traditions/creating local plant-based products with local identity • Supporting local production and processing • Creating incentives for local products (e.g. gastronomy) • Marketing campaign for local plant-based products • Improve availability of products (gastronomy, local retail) • Incentivizing plant-based choices (pricing, nudging) • Meat-tax

a long tradition in the area, associated with a wide range of local practices, food specialties, and a regional identity. It was shown for different agricultural systems, that the integration of livestock and crop production allows for a wide range of synergies through increasing circularity in the system (Peyraud et al., 2014). In addition, on household and regional level, diversification has also a strong potential to increase resilience for natural drivers e.g. climate change, as well as changes in demand and political support (Grüneis et al., 2018; Whitaker, 2023). A vision for the future of Grison mountains therefore builds upon a more diversified system that integrates crop with livestock production on the one hand but also connects traditions with innovations along the whole value chain. The role of traditions as a chance for innovations was highlighted in our study. Gran Alpin, for example, can be seen as a successful example of retroinnovations, the purposeful revival of historical practices, by which traditional elements become drivers of innovations (Zagata et al., 2020). Other existing examples mentioned by the foresight group are innovative products that represent traditional regional specialties with alternative local ingredients (e.g. a vegan alternative imitating a traditional local dry meat specialty replacing meat with local beetroots). In general, building on traditions and locality, were seen as key opportunities for supporting innovations, such as new plant-based products in the local food system. Local gastronomy and tourism can hereby play an important role as sales channels. Collaborations along the whole value chain were one of the key aspects identified, to support innovations and secure a sustainable regional development, but also collaboration with research and extension services. In addition, the promotion of decentralized structures is seen as integral to the establishment of innovative sustainable local value chains.

The study revealed the benefits, potentials and needs for diversifying the predominant livestock farming in the mountains with crop production. To enable this desired transformation in the pursuit of sustainable development and the empowerment of mountainous regions, innovation emerges as a pivotal element. Especially on farm level, supporting and enabling innovations is urgently needed. This can only be achieved by reorienting agricultural policies and adaptations of the agricultural training. By intertwining innovation with education, these recommendations aim to create a dynamic environment where sustainable development becomes not only a goal but a tangible and enduring reality in mountainous areas.

Beyond the Swiss context, the experience from the Grison mountains highlights pathways that may inspire sustainable transitions in other mountain regions worldwide. Similar challenges—such as limited accessibility, structural constraints, and the need to balance tradition with innovation—are shared across mountain territories in Europe, Asia, and Latin America. The Grisons case illustrates how local cooperation, value-chain innovation, and the revival of traditional crops can contribute to globally relevant models of resilient and diversified mountain agriculture.

References

Bardsley, D. K., & Bardsley, A. M. (2014). Organising for socio-ecological resilience: The roles of the mountain farmer cooperative Genossenschaft Gran Alpin in Graubünden, Switzerland. *Ecological Economics, 98*, 11–21. https://doi.org/10.1016/j.ecolecon.2013.12.004

Barjolle, D., Casabianca, F., Maglietti Smith, I., Piccin, L., Jaisli, I., Mora, O., & Schmitt, E. (2022). *D6.1—Guidelines for the foresight exercise* (MOVING, p. 55) [Guidelines D6.1, unpublished]. Origin for Sustainability.

Beniston, M. (2012). Impacts of climatic change on water and associated economic activities in the Swiss Alps. *Journal of Hydrology, 412–413*, 291–296. https://doi.org/10.1016/j.jhydrol.2010.06.046

BLW, BLV, & BAFU. (2023). *Klimastrategie Landwirtschaft und Ernährung 2050. 1.Teil: Grundsätze, Ziele und Stossrichtungen*. Bundesamt für Landwirtschaft BLW, Bundesamt für Lebensmittelsicherheit und Veterinärwesen BLV, Bundesamt für Umwelt BAFU.

Bundesamt für Statistik—BFS. (2020). *Szenarien zur Bevölkerungsentwicklung der Schweiz und der Kantone 2020–2050*. Bundesamt für Statistik. Retrieved 3 June 2026, from https://www.bfs.admin.ch/bfs/de/home/statistiken/bevoelkerung/zukuenftige-entwicklung/kantonaleszenarien.assetdetail.14963221.html

Bundesamt für Statistik—BFS. (2021a). *Ausgewählte Indikatoren im regionalen Vergleich, 2021 (Kantone)*. Bundesamt für Statistik. Retrieved 3 June 2026, from https://www.bfs.admin.ch/asset/de/16484440

Bundesamt für Statistik—BFS. (2021b). *Landwirtschaftsbetriebe: Innerbetriebliche Diversifikation und Anteil am Gesamtumsatz nach Kanton*. Bundesamt für Statistik. Retrieved 3 June 2026, from https://www.bfs.admin.ch/asset/de/19644370

Bundesamt für Statistik—BFS. (2022). *Kantonale Disparitäten* (No. Demos 2/2022; BFS Aktuell). Bundesamt für Statistik.

Bundesamt für Statistik—BFS. (2023a). *Landwirtschaft und Ernährung. Taschenstatistik 2023* (p. 24). Bundesamt für Statistik.

Bundesamt für Statistik—BFS. (2023b). *Landwirtschaftliche Strukturerhebung für das Jahr 2022*. Bundesamt für Statistik.

Erdin, D. (2023). *Die Vegetationsperiode wird länger* (No. AGRISTAT 23-01). Retrieved 3 June 2026, fromhttps://www.sbv-usp.ch/fileadmin/sbvuspch/04_Medien/Agristat_aktuell/2023/Aktuell_AGRISTAT_2023-01.pdf

Ferjani, A., & Flury, C. (2013). Was wäre, wenn Bio flächendeckend wäre? *Die Grüne, 17*, 40–41.

Fesenfeld, L., Mann, S., Meier, M., Nemecek, T., Scharrer, B., Bornemann, B., Brombach, C., Beretta, C., Bürgi, E., Grabs, J., Ingold, K., Jeanneret, P., Kislig, S., Lieberherr, E., Müller, A., Pfister, S., Schader, C., Schönberg, S., Sonnevelt, M., ... Zähringer, J. (2023). *Wege in die Ernährungszukunft der Schweiz—Leitfaden zu den grössten Hebeln und politischen Pfaden für ein nachhaltiges Ernährungssystem*. SDSN Schweiz. https://doi.org/10.5281/ZENODO.7543576

Flury, C., Zimmermann, A., Mack, G., & Möhring, A. (2012). *Auswirkungen der Agrarpolitik 2014–2017 auf die Berglandwirtschaft* (Bericht Forschungsprogramm AgriMontana). Forschungsanstalt Agroscope Reckenholz-Tänikon ART.

Forrer, C. (2022, June 30). *Development of social networks in organic farming and mountain cereal cultivation in a Swiss Alpine region*. ZHAW—Zurich University of Applied Sciences.

Geiser, A., Forrer, C., & Lazzarini, G. (2024). *Scaling new heights: Strengthening the mountain cereal value chain with collaboration, innovation and education for greater resilience* (MOVING) [Practice Abstract]. ZHAW—Zurich University of Applied Sciences. Retrieved 3 June 2026, from https://www.moving-h2020.eu/wp-content/uploads/2023/08/20-MOVING_PA_Swiss-Alps.pdf

Geiser, A., Jaisli, I., & Schmitt, E. (2022a). *Swiss Alps: Mountain grain* (p. 6) [MOVING—Policy Brief]. ZHAW—Zurich University of Applied Sciences. Retrieved 3 June 2026, from https://www.moving-h2020.eu/wp-content/uploads/2022/02/20_Swiss_Alps_CH_Policy_Brief.pdf

Geiser, A., Schmitt, E., & Trüb, N. (2022b). *Extended value chain analysis for the Grisons mountain grain value chain in Switzerland* (MOVING) [Report Deliverable 4.2, unpublished]. ZHAW—Zurich University of Applied Sciences.

Genossenschaft Gran Alpin. (2024). *Gran Alpin*. Gran Alpin. Retrieved 3 June 2026, from https://www.granalpin.ch/ (Accessed 3 June 2026)

Glover, D., & Sexton, A. (2015). *Edible insects and the future of food: A foresight scenario exercise on entomophagy and global food security* (No. 149; p. 57). Institute of Development Studies. https://doi.org/10.1163/2210-7975_HRD-0148-2015066

Grilli, G., Pagliacci, F., & Gatto, P. (2025). Agricultural diversification at the margin. Strategies and determinants in Italian mountain and remote areas. *Agribusiness*. https://doi.org/10.1002/agr.22042

Grüneis, H., Penker, M., Höferl, K.-M., Schermer, M., & Scherhaufer, P. (2018). Why do we not pick the low-hanging fruit? Governing adaptation to climate change and resilience in Tyrolean mountain agriculture. *Land Use Policy, 79*, 386–396. https://doi.org/10.1016/j.landusepol.2018.08.025

Grüter, R., & Mathis, A. (2023). *Diversifizierung in der pflanzlichen Produktion im Berggebiet Graubündens. Studie im Rahmen der Abklärungen zum Innovationszentrum Berglandwirtschaft. Projekt zur regionalen Entwicklung Safiental*. Zurich University of Applied Sciences.

Jaisli, I., Forrer, C., & Lazzarini, G. (2023). *Participatory foresight exercise Swiss Alps* (MOVING) [Case Study Report, unpublished]. Zurich University of Applied Sciences.

López-i-Gelats, F., Milán, M. J., & Bartolomé, J. (2011). Is farming enough in mountain areas? Farm diversification in the Pyrenees. *Land Use Policy, 28*(4), 783–791. https://doi.org/10.1016/j.landusepol.2011.01.005

Moschitz, H., & Oehen, B. (2020). Creating value(s) by integrating local and extra-local resources in cereal production in the Swiss Alps. *The International Journal of Sociology of Agriculture and Food*, 48–68. https://doi.org/10.48416/IJSAF.V26I1.62

MOVING—Horizon 2020. (n.d.). MOVING. Retrieved 8 January 2024, from https://www.moving-h2020.eu/

Naudiyal, N., Arunachalam, K., & Kumar, U. (2019). The future of mountain agriculture amidst continual farm-exit, livelihood diversification and outmigration in the Central Himalayan villages. *Journal of Mountain Science, 16*(4), 755–768. https://doi.org/10.1007/s11629-018-5160-6

Nguyen, A. T., & Hens, L. (2021). Diversified responses to contemporary pressures on sloping agricultural land: Thai farmer's perception of mountainous landscapes in northern Vietnam. *Environment, Development and Sustainability, 23*(4), 5411–5429. https://doi.org/10.1007/s10668-020-00822-x

Peyraud, J.-L., Taboada, M., & Delaby, L. (2014). Integrated crop and livestock systems in Western Europe and South America: A review. *European Journal of Agronomy, 57*, 31–42. https://doi.org/10.1016/j.eja.2014.02.005

Rat für Raumordnung. (2019). *Megatrends und Raumentwicklung Schweiz*. Retrieved 3 June 2026, from https://www.are.admin.ch/dam/de/sd-web/L5D1UuOI7T4g/megatrends.pdf

Rhydderch, A. (2017). *Scenario building: The 2 × 2 matrix technique* (Prospective and Srategic Foresight Toolbox, p. 19). Futuribles International.

Rockström, J., Thilsted, S. H., Willett, W. C., Gordon, L. J., Herrero, M., Hicks, C. C., Mason-D'Croz, D., Rao, N., Springmann, M., Wright, E. C., Agustina, R., Bajaj, S., Bunge, A. C., Carducci, B., Conti, C., Covic, N., Fanzo, J., Forouhi, N. G., Gibson, M. F., ... DeClerck, F. (2025). The EAT–Lancet Commission on healthy, sustainable, and just food systems. *The Lancet, 406*(10512), 1625–1700. https://doi.org/10.1016/S0140-6736(25)01201-2

Salliou, N. (2023). Quitting livestock farming: Transfarmation pathways and factors of change from post-livestock farmers' accounts. *Frontiers in Sustainable Food Systems, 7*, 1122992. https://doi.org/10.3389/fsufs.2023.1122992

Schader, C., Muller, A., Scialabba, N.E.-H., Hecht, J., Isensee, A., Erb, K.-H., Smith, P., Makkar, H. P. S., Klocke, P., Leiber, F., Schwegler, P., Stolze, M., & Niggli, U. (2015). Impacts of feeding less food-competing feedstuffs to livestock on global food system sustainability. *Journal of the Royal Society Interface, 12*(113), 20150891. https://doi.org/10.1098/rsif.2015.0891

Schilperoord, P. (2004, January 9). Ackerbau gehört zur Berglandwirtschaft. *Bündner Bauer*.

Schilperoord, P. (2014). *Erfahrungen im Bergackerbau 2014*. Retrieved 3 June 2026, from http://www.berggetreide.ch/Erfahrungen_im_Bergackerbau.pdf

Schilperoord, P. (2020). *Kulturpflanzen in der Schweiz—Gerste, Kartoffel, Roggen, Ackerbohne, Erbse, Flachs, Weizen, Dinkel, Buchweizen, Hafer, Einkorn, Emmer, Rauweizen, Hirsen*. Verein für alpine Kulturpflanzen.

Schilperoord, P., & Heistinger, A. (2015). *Kulturpflanzen der Schweiz, Süd- und Nordtirol*. https://doi.org/10.13140/RG.2.1.4754.1844

Schluchter, A. (2015). Agrarzonen. In *Historisches Lexikon der Schweiz HLS*.

Schmitt, E., & Geiser, A. (2022a). *A future-oriented case of diversifying mountain farming through cooperative organic grain production* (MOVING) [Practice Abstract]. ZHAW—Zurich University of Applied Sciences. Retrieved 3 June 2026, from https://www.moving-h2020.eu/wp-content/uploads/2022/11/MOVING_PA_Swiss-Alps.pdf

Schmitt, E., & Geiser, A. (2022b). *MRL report for the Task 4.5 Switzerland—Grison Alps, mountain grain vulnerability, sustainability assessment and resilience appraisal* (MOVING) [Project deliverable Task 4.5, unpublished]. ZHAW—Zurich University of Applied Sciences.

Serrat, O. (2009). *The five whys technique*. Springer. https://doi.org/10.1007/978-981-10-0983-9_32

Stotten, R. (2021). The role of farm diversification and peasant habitus for farm resilience in mountain areas: The case of the Ötztal valley, Austria. *International Journal of Social Economics, 48*(7), 947–964. https://doi.org/10.1108/IJSE-12-2019-0756

Swissveg. (2022). *Anteil der Vegetarier und Veganer an der Gesamtbevölkerung in der Schweiz von 2015 bis 2022*. Statista. Retrieved 3 June 2026, fromhttps://de.statista.com/statistik/daten/studie/388189/umfrage/umfrage-in-der-schweiz-zu-vegetarischer-ernaehrung/

Vij, S., Biesbroek, R., Adler, C., & Muccione, V. (2021). Climate change adaptation in European mountain systems: A systematic mapping of academic research. *Mountain Research and Development, 41*(1). https://doi.org/10.1659/MRD-JOURNAL-D-20-00033.1

Whitaker, S. H. (2023). Analysing the impact of climate and social changes on small farms in the Italian Alps: The importance of the local scale. *Sociologia Ruralis, 63*(4), 795–822. https://doi.org/10.1111/soru.12453

Willett, W., Rockström, J., Loken, B., Springmann, M., Lang, T., Vermeulen, S., Garnett, T., Tilman, D., DeClerck, F., Wood, A., Jonell, M., Clark, M., Gordon, L. J., Fanzo, J., Hawkes, C., Zurayk, R., Rivera, J. A., De Vries, W., Majele Sibanda, L., ... Murray, C. J. L. (2019). Food in the Anthropocene: The EAT–Lancet Commission on healthy diets from sustainable food systems. *The Lancet, 393*(10170), 447–492. https://doi.org/10.1016/S0140-6736(18)31788-4

Zagata, L., Sutherland, L., Hrabák, J., & Lostak, M. (2020). Mobilising the past: Towards a conceptualisation of retro-innovation. *Sociologia Ruralis, 60*(3), 639–660. https://doi.org/10.1111/soru.12310

Index

D. Barjolle et al. (eds.), *Innovation and the Future of Rural Development in Europe*, https://doi.org/10.1007/978-3-032-22570-2

D

E

F

I

K

L

S

T

U

V

Zeitfracht Medien GmbH
Ferdinand-Jühlke-Straße 7
99095 Erfurt, Deutschland
produktsicherheit@kolibri360.de